CIVIL RACISM

CIVIL RACISM

The 1992 Los Angeles Rebellion and
the Crisis of Racial Burnout

LYNN MIE ITAGAKI

University of Minnesota Press
Minneapolis
London

The University of Minnesota Press gratefully acknowledges financial support for the publication of this book from the College of Arts and Sciences, the Department of English, and the Department of Women's, Gender, and Sexuality Studies at The Ohio State University.

Published by the University of Minnesota Press
111 Third Avenue South, Suite 290
Minneapolis, MN 55401-2520
http://www.upress.umn.edu

Library of Congress Cataloging-in-Publication Data
Names: Itagaki, Lynn Mie.
Title: Civil racism : The 1992 Los Angeles rebellion and the crisis of racial burnout / Lynn Mie Itagaki.
Description: Minneapolis : University of Minnesota Press, 2016. I Includes bibliographical references and index.
Identifiers: LCCN 2015022462
ISBN 978-0-8166-9920-9 (hc) I ISBN 978-0-8166-9921-6 (pb)
Subjects: LCSH: Los Angeles (Calif.)—Race relations—History—20th century. I Riots—California—Los Angeles—History—20th century. I Protest movements—California—Los Angeles—History—20th century. I African Americans—California—Los Angeles—Social conditions—20th century. I Minorities—California—Los Angeles—Social conditions—20th century. I Racism—California—Los Angeles—History—20th century. I Civil society—California—Los Angeles—History—20th century. I Courtesy—Social aspects—California—Los Angeles—History—20th century. I Burn out (Psychology)—Social aspects—California—Los Angeles—History—20th century.
Classification: LCC F869.L89 A2532 2016 I DDC 305.8009794/94—dc23
LC record available at http://lccn.loc.gov/2015022462

Printed in the United States of America on acid-free paper

The University of Minnesota is an equal-opportunity educator and employer.

23 22 21 20 19 18 17 16   10 9 8 7 6 5 4 3 2 1

To my son, Ziggy Fergus

CONTENTS

A NOTE ON TERMINOLOGY

I use the terms "Black" and "African American" interchangeably. I refer to Latina/o or Latinas/os and Chicana/o or Chicanas/os to explicitly include women within these groupings. I use Asian American unless the ethnicity is salient, e.g., Korean American.

All of these racial terms are inadequate and limiting. I use capitals for Black and White in order to emphasize the politicized construction of not only these racializations but also Asian/American and Latina/o as well. Part of my purpose is to examine the inherent instability within and provisional nature of each racial category, especially when examined alongside other racial categories.

I use the terms "interracial" and "cross-racial" interchangeably to signal connection or conflict among differently racialized individuals or groups. I use "multiracial" in both its meanings: mixed-race individuals and communities or those comprised of more than two differently racialized individuals or groups.

PREFACE

> In capitalist societies, education, whether secular or religious, the
> teaching of moral reflexes handed down from father to son, the
> exemplary integrity of workers decorated after fifty years of loyal
> and faithful service, the fostering of love for harmony and
> wisdom, those aesthetic forms of respect for the status quo, instill
> in the exploited a mood of submission and inhibition which
> considerably eases the task of the agents of law and order.
>
> —Frantz Fanon, *The Wretched of the Earth*

Protest disrupts the violence of the status quo.[1]

Recent protests and public reactions have shaken the status quo: the police killings of unarmed Black men, women, and children; the failure of grand juries to indict these officers; or jury verdicts that determine them innocent. The August 2014 police shooting of African American teenager Michael Brown rallied protests against racial profiling and police brutality for months in Ferguson, Missouri, and across the nation. Brown's death came just a year after a jury exonerated White Latino civilian George Zimmerman for his professed vigilantism in fatally shooting African American teenager Trayvon Martin in Sanford, Florida.[2] Responding to the global coverage of the circumstances of their deaths, the grand jury proceedings and trials, the protests in their communities and beyond, activists and bloggers connected these events to many other victims whose names never made national headlines, Black women and children who were the targets or collateral damage of police violence or the victims of "self-appointed law enforcers" and who received much less sustained media attention and public outrage (Savalli; White). Even fewer news articles connected these deaths to other police killings of and injuries to Asians, Latinas/os, immigrants, prisoners, the mentally disabled, the poor, and the home-less (Linshi; Jayadev; Coscarelli; Fitzpatrick).

Protest is thought to disrupt the peace and civility of the status quo. Mainstream policymakers, prominent civic leaders, and respected jour-nalists encourage those watching or viewing demonstrations, marches, sit-ins, or die-ins to cast protest as the gateway to destructive violence, whether from the indignant individual or the crowds that endanger the peace of mind and sometimes the bodily safety of bystanders. Their influential opinions deem threatening even peaceful or nonviolent pro-tests for the way they physically or sonically take up shared spaces or create a so-called climate of violence.[3] But detractors of protests often fail to acknowledge how peace and civility *require* force and violence.[4] And often, the peace and civility enjoyed by some rests on the force and violence directed at many more others, whether by heav-ily policing specific communities, imprisoning more people, or trans-ferring resources from the bottom to the top. In delegitimizing and vilifying protest, its critics cast this violence that upholds the status quo as just, fair, and democratic.

In this present moment, what exactly is this alleged status quo that protest disrupts? Some of the forces that have influenced contempo-rary forms of social inequality also shape the way we talk about it. Many indicators of racial discrimination still persist. Mainstream pun-dits touted the election of the first African American president of the United States as ushering in the postracial era: what many celebrated as a post-*racist* era, a society that had overcome its admittedly racist past but would now embrace its colorblind future (Haney López, 828–29). Those skeptical of this new nonracist, colorblind era identified the vast inequalities still facing communities of color and their dispropor-tionate vulnerabilities to economic downturns such as the catastrophic global financial crisis beginning at the end of 2007. African American households, for example, lost an average of 40 percent of their wealth in the Great Recession, or as another measure, their households went from holding ten cents for every dollar of wealth held by White house-holds in 2007 to six.[5] Government and private studies revealed that lenders were more likely to push borrowers of color and women into subprime mortgage loans, despite their eligibility for prime rates, who then became more likely to face devastating foreclosures and bankrupt-cies. After 9/11, U.S. foreign policy and military occupation abroad has had a profound impact on national racial politics. Polls show popular support for the racial and ethnic profiling of Muslims and people of Middle Eastern and South Asian descent. Prison guards found guilty of torturing prisoners at Abu Ghraib had worked in U.S. prisons with their largely African American and Latino populations before their deployment.[6] The drawdown of forces in Afghanistan and Iraq resulted in the surplus distribution of military equipment such as tanks, machine guns, and body armor to local police forces to use on their constituents, such as the protestors in Ferguson, Missouri, in the fall of 2014.[7] In 2013 the Supreme Court struck down the main provision of the 1965 Voting Rights Act meant to evaluate restrictions on minority voting, effectively suspending federal regulatory oversight over any violating district until Congress revised its formulas for those states under its jurisdiction. With each election cycle, new efforts to pass voter identification laws or curtail early voting opportunities have concerned voting rights advocates for their keeping disproportionate numbers of minorities and the poor away from the polls. Self-defense legislation such as the "Stand Your Ground" laws in many states came under national scrutiny for their racially biased outcomes in which White assailants were exonerated or never indicted for killing Black men, women, and children.

Meanwhile, scholars have opened up new ways of talking about race and racism through studies of unintentional behaviors. These studies explain nuanced analyses of racial and gender inequality by pointing to hidden forms of discriminatory behaviors in terms of implicit bias and microaggressions: how unconscious snap judgments result in unintentional bias and how these latent prejudices can result in vastly unequal outcomes.[8] Cognitive, economic, and legal studies examine anti-Black and anti-immigrant racial panics through enduring paradigms such as "racial paranoia," "reasonable racism," and taste-based and statistical discrimination.[9] Studies reveal how our actions and the stories we tell about ourselves to others, including researchers, might differ significantly from what we profess are our beliefs.[10] Despite a certainty that our behaviors stem from deeply held principles of equality and fairness, we inadvertently perpetuate unintentional harms and material inequalities. We can and do perform racist behaviors while espousing antiracist beliefs.

In light of such research, these racist attitudes and discriminatory behaviors reveal the limits of constitutional guarantees to free speech and assembly, protection from unwarranted search and seizure, and equal protection. The protests, the injustices they expose, and the wide-spread censure they face uncover which extrajudicial behaviors and outcomes are deemed legitimate, civil, and legal. Public opinion often assesses the guilt or innocence of the parties involved in terms of civility and incivility; those with uncivil behaviors seem guilty, but those with civil ones seem innocent. We thereby obscure the question of which innocent parties are injured unfairly by the presumed nonviolence of the status quo. Who benefits from the reliance on civility as the answer to social problems, and who is deemed undeserving of redress due to uncivil, "savage," and "barbarous" behavior? We assume that civil behaviors fairly benefit the deserving and disadvantage the undeserving. Such an assumption is tied to beliefs in a legal process that almost always punishes the guilty and helps the innocent rather than one that punishes the innocent or unlucky and exonerates the guilty.

State responses to the protestors and to the deaths of these African American men and women have evoked comparisons to past civil rights struggles. The recent sixtieth anniversary of Rosa Parks's challenge to segregation that triggered the Montgomery bus boycotts have prompted comparisons between this movement's actions that fought segregation and racial terror in the Jim Crow South and present-day protests against police brutality and racial profiling. Addressing the fall 2014 civil unrest in Ferguson while delivering a speech commemorating the anniversary of this landmark event in civil rights, Eric J. Holder Jr., the first African American attorney general, locates the roots of U.S. protest in the nonviolence and nonaggression promoted and practiced in the speeches and struggles of Martin Luther King Jr.: "Time and again, America's proud history has shown that the most successful and enduring movements for change are those that adhere to principles of non-aggression and nonviolence." But these civil rights protestors, while nonviolent, were frequently arrested for disorderly conduct and disturbing the peace after being subjected to often permanently disabling and deadly violence by White vigilante and police officer perpetrators who were not likewise detained or prosecuted. In the logic of the state, the nonaggressive protests of walking, singing, standing, or congregating incited violence. Nonviolent and nonaggressive resistance triggers state violence.

Moreover, Holder's emphasis on principles represents a slight omission: nonviolence was not just a principle but a strategy, and one among many. Nonviolence is remembered while the strategies of other

Black freedom struggles are deliberately forgotten. Moreover, arguably the "most successful and enduring movement for change" are the events that fomented the U.S. Constitution; the U.S. nation-state itself was forged out of the deadly violence and widespread destruction caused by the American Revolution. But the roots of protest on the American continent go back much further. Native American nations contested the European colonial project in their self-defense against invasion and their present-day struggles expose the genocidal and illegal land grab of the entire Americas. Since its inception, the U.S. democratic project has depended on the terrorism, genocide, incarceration, and exclusion of indigenous, enslaved, immigrant, and nonwhite peoples.

In the wake of the initial furor over Michael Brown's death, Holder put out guidelines for police departments nationwide in order to prevent racial profiling and deadly force. But other extrajudicial guidelines in the form of civic virtues come to the fore when the legal system fails or injustices have no legal remedies. After media coverage of the renewed protests and violence in Ferguson and New York City and around the world, in response to grand jury decisions not to indict the police officers involved in the deaths of Brown and Eric Garner, strangled to death in a police chokehold in July 2014, Holder launched a national initiative to repair the trust between community members and law enforcement. Similarly, rather than urging stiffer penalties for police officers' lethal force, local communities have been inspired to launch "civility projects" to encourage dialogue among community members. These actions are significant because trust is considered one of the foundational civic virtues undergirding society by forming strong bonds and facilitating goodwill among its members in private and public ways.

Civility is the way in which we should talk about important things; civility is also the way in which we do not talk about important things. Civility as a concept, political goal, and measure is also discursively constructed: what is one's civility is another's incivility. From the smallest rude remark to the institutionalized exclusion of groups, the flexibility of the term "civility" encompasses a tremendous range of customs, behaviors, practices, and traditions that are always contested.

These public protests captured in global news coverage recalled another civil unrest thousands of miles away and over two decades earlier. Indeed, news commentators and political observers talked about whether people might riot in protest of the Zimmerman trial, and journalists asked what the Ferguson police could learn from the past experiences of the Los Angeles Police Department. What spurred these comparisons was what has become popularly remembered as the 1992 Los Angeles riots. In April 1992, the acquittal and mistrial verdicts of the four police officers involved in the sustained beating and disabling of African American male motorist Rodney G. King on a highway just north of Los Angeles sparked one of the most deadly and destructive civil disturbances in U.S. history. The media and political firestorms in the aftermath of the recent fatal shootings, rulings, and verdicts; the involvement of the top levels of government—the White House, U.S. Attorney General, and federal and state troops; the number and scale of protests; the twenty-four-hour media coverage; and the casualties and property damage reminded many observers of this civil unrest in Los Angeles.

This book began with questions about why certain behaviors, when attached to people of color, are usually perceived as violent, illegal, irrational, and savage. Why are Black perspectives, bodies, and behaviors almost always deemed uncivil? Why are the cultural practices of citizens and immigrants of color, especially Asians and Latinas/os, considered perpetually foreign and un-American? Why are these same behaviors deemed civil when attached to Whites? Why is White violence against people of color overlooked and even encouraged? Whose perspectives are considered legitimate or *civil*? How does civility connect to the recognition of one's humanity?

My interest in the troubled connection between protest and democratic practice began with research on reconciliation and reparations movements in response to the historic World War II *Shoah,* the U.S. incarceration of West Coast Japanese Americans in concentration camps, and what was at the time unfolding events in South Africa and the Balkans in the 1990s. These global events similarly inspired civic organizations such as churches or volunteer groups to issue formal apologies and material reparations to people that their members had wronged in the past: for descendants of Asian settler colonists to Native Hawaiians, White civic groups that enforced Jim Crow segregation practices on their Black neighbors, and African American residents to Asian immigrant store owners in their neighborhoods.[11] I wanted to include a discussion of the 1992 Los Angeles rebellion with a chapter on the reconciliation efforts occurring largely through African American street gangs, immigrant rights organizations, and ethnic small business associations that remained far beyond the purview of the privately financed, yet state-sanctioned Rebuild L.A. and with little local and national coverage or corporate funding. My focus on this archive of personal memories, experiences, and bits of news coverage led me to think about how these people told their stories and crafted their narratives to effect political and social transformations. By the mid-1990s, novels, films, and plays appeared that talked about these often interpersonal and local efforts to strengthen community bonds through interracial dialogues. I began to examine how these writers, dramatists, and artists self-consciously experimented with their art and challenged their audiences' expectations in order to transform the way we think about racism, inequality, and injustice.

Far from taking a microscopic view, these pieces, texts, and cultural productions considered globalization, immigration, migration, and the postindustrial frameworks of race, gender, and class in the complex history of Los Angeles. In the 1980s and 1990s, the critique of White European heteropatriarchal supremacist culture met with backlash and accusations that such multicultural agendas would result in a balkanization and disintegration of U.S. democratic culture and society. Such demands for inclusion of racialized, gendered, queered, and global perspectives were felt to be contesting the tenets of "Western" civilization in questioning the notions of civic virtue and a common cultural foundation—what makes Americans *American*—an anxiety manifested in the aftermath of the breakup of the Soviet Union and the independence of the former Soviet republics, the ethnic conflict and mass killings in Bosnia Herzogovina, Rwanda, and Lebanon in the 1990s. International concerns shaped these national conversations about civic virtues, democratic participation, and social belonging. Scholars, pundits, and policymakers wrote about and admonished the U.S. public for their faltering civic virtues of trust, cooperation, mutual respect, individual responsibility, self-discipline, obedience, and patriotism. Often, debates over immigration and diversity questioned who might best practice such virtues and become full-fledged participants in civic and political life.

There are forms of state violence that are perceived as necessary and vital to the stability of any government: police enforcement, incarceration, sentencing, and punishment. This violence builds and maintains nations. Violence especially against people of color and the poor remains today a time-honored strategy of U.S. state-building. The violence of genocide, enslavement, forced removal, racial terror, policing, racialized imprisonment, wage theft, impoverishment, and lack of health care are all strategies of diversity management. U.S. cultural history memorializes this violence in cultural tropes that are considered quintessentially American: Indian killer, rogue cop, antihero, cowboy, outlaw, vigilante, soldier. U.S. popular culture has codified these White figures and their antagonists of color for global audiences: the western and war movies with Communist, Asian, Black, Latina/o, Muslim, and Native American enemies.

While this study focuses on the 1992 Los Angeles rebellion, it considers the wide-ranging ramifications of the "violent spring" in Southern California. Civil unrest and social upheaval, however brief or long-lasting, expose the forces that stabilize and destabilize the status quo. In the late 1980s and early 1990s, U.S. political elites were concerned about the continuing uncertainty of U.S. global dominance after the cold war. Looking at interracial violence in relation to civility transforms notions of justice and fairness and compels the reevaluation of the responsibilities of the individual and the state to protect rights and foster democracy. Examining perceptions of civility in relation to protest provides ways of thinking about U.S. society and tests the limits of inclusion and participation promised by the Constitution. Focusing on civility can change the ways we try to align our behaviors with our understanding of democratic practices. The way we promote civility reveals the way we think society and the state function best, how individuals and the state encourage us to shape our everyday interactions in ways that both facilitate and protest structures that protect and repress civil society.

INTRODUCTION

The 1992 Los Angeles Crisis

> The crisis consists precisely in the fact that the old is dying and
> the new cannot be born. In this interregnum, there arises a great
> diversity of morbid symptoms.
>
> —Antonio Gramsci, *The Prison Notebooks*

> Anger is loaded with information and energy.
>
> —Audre Lorde, "Uses of Anger"

"Can we all get along?" This plea, this question, has echoed across the decades. Its resonance, both simple and profound, ramifies far beyond the press conference held by Rodney King on the second day of what has become popularly known as the 1992 Los Angeles riots. Of course, King's words are an earnest plea for an end to the assaults, the fires, the looting. But there are other frequencies upon which his question registers. What kind of peace is possible? How can we get along when there is no justice for all? Or, how can we get along when there are perpetrators of violence—whether police or civilians—in our midst? King's question also asks us to consider what kind of society we hope to create. Do we desire a return to the status quo of how we might individually remember the past, perhaps with its imagined stability but related repression? Or do we imagine a future in which long-standing material inequalities and racial injustices are finally recognized and redressed? Will we go along to get along in order to have an uneasy peace or will there be new protests of further injustices that have again gone largely unrecognized and unredressed? King's now-famous question adds another anxiety about how we might survive what we have collectively witnessed and how might we, as a society, come to terms

with what has happened. How can we all get along after surviving the unprecedented magnitude of the violence and destruction?[1]

The 1992 Los Angeles civil unrest shocked audiences around the world. The multiracial violence and widespread devastation paralyzed Southern California for five long days. After the not-guilty verdicts and mistrial for the four police officers who had beaten African American motorist Rodney King were announced on Wednesday afternoon, April 29, 1992, more than fifty people were killed, thousands were injured, sixteen thousand were arrested, forty-five-hundred businesses were damaged or destroyed, and $1 billion in property was lost (Abelmann and Lie, 2; Chang and Diaz-Veizades, 9–10; E. H. Kim, 215; Zia, 171). The civil unrest in L.A. took a higher toll in human life and property than the Watts rebellion of 1965. More than a thousand were deported, most to Mexico;[2] tens of thousands were made homeless and jobless by the destruction. Despite continuing efforts at rebuilding, those parts of the city hardest hit by the violence remain scarred by piles of rubble and burned-out buildings that were never rebuilt. The residents who sustained the most devastating losses in lives, livelihood, and housing were disproportionately people of color, recent immigrants, and the poor.

Civil Racism scrutinizes the ways in which various publics have explained and remembered the 1992 Los Angeles "riots." The five days of violence that besieged one of the world's largest and wealthiest metropolitan areas profoundly challenged Americans' perception of the stability of U.S. society. These perceptions of what happened during those five days—what we said to each other and ourselves—reveal our expectations of how such twinned formations of civil society and the state, civility and democracy, should prevent such crises. The 1992 violence calls into question the responsibilities of individual citizens and those of the state in the maintenance of peace and order. The politics of race and gender shape the expectations for inclusion into the nation and the protections guaranteed by the state; one's racial and gender identities influence the scope of one's rights and claims on the state and the formal and informal penalties for violating norms. The reassessments prompted by the violence, I argue, must be interpreted through the intersection of two historical eras and their cultural politics: the post–civil rights and post–cold war eras. The representation of the 1992 Los Angeles "riots" brings together two deep-seated and interrelated political anxieties of these periods: first, the "culture wars" of the 1980s and 1990s over multiculturalism and diversity and, second, a renewed clamoring for civility in a changing hegemonic global order, respectively. Both anxieties circulate around what constitutes and sustains a robust national culture and the political communities that the crisis fundamentally troubles. *Civil Racism* considers how the events of the civil unrest itself and the material circumstances that provoked these anxieties are identified and alternately imagined in various cultural productions such as essays, novels, films, and plays. As Lisa Lowe argues, "Where the political terrain can neither resolve nor suppress inequality, it erupts in culture. Because culture is the contemporary repository of memory, of history, it is through culture, rather than government, that alternative forms of subjectivity, collectivity, and public life are imagined" (*Immigrant Acts,* (22). From a variety of disciplinary and interdisciplinary formations, I examine these "eruptions" in culture as they have emerged in the aftermath of the 1992 civil unrest in order to better understand the persistent racial inequalities that continue to be a defining characteristic of contemporary American life.

The unstable signifier of what is identified as the 1992 Los Angeles riots is no more apparent than in the naming of the violence itself. Often referred to as the Rodney King riots or the Rodney King rebellion, the violence has since become synonymous with the grainy video footage of King's beating that local and national networks broadcast nightly for over a year, the daily trial coverage of his police assailants on television and radio, and the days of continuous televised images of cars and buildings on fire and violence on the streets soon after the verdicts were announced.[3] These verdicts and the ensuing violence stunned a nation. The fifty-six baton blows and kicks in the eighty-one seconds of the videotape seemed for many to be clear evidence of excessive force, indisputable proof of police brutality that activists and residents of color claimed were all too common in their interactions with the Los Angeles Police Department. In between the images and reports of fires, assaults, and violence, news reporters tried to explain the unexpected acquittal and mistrial of King's assailants: the relocation of the trial to a predominantly White suburb an hour from Los Angeles proper with a large number of retired police officers, the absence of African Americans on the jury, jury members who planned to acquit the police officers early in the deliberations, and the sole Latina on the jury, who felt strongly pressured by the others to exonerate the defendants (Reinhold). One of the most startling revelations after the trial was that some on the jury believed that Rodney King's movements on the videotape were not pained responses to the baton blows and kicks to the abdomen but instead were continuing threats to the safety of the police officers.

Participants, survivors, scholars, policymakers, and pundits still struggle over the meaning and significance of this unprecedented civil unrest decades after the violence in Los Angeles. The various terms used to refer to the events of April 29 to May 2, 1992, identify distinct ideological viewpoints and political investments. Taking into account these debates, I use the term "crisis" to recognize the many conflicting and contradictory causes as well as the personal and collective reasons for the anger and violence.[4] Most obviously, the term alludes to the discourse of "urban crisis" in African American communities that has driven racial politics and public policy for much of the twentieth century and into the twenty-first.[5] Given the Greek definition of *krisis* to mean decision or judgment, the term is dependent "not [on] the quality of the object in question but the condition of a spectatorial mind" (Berlant, 760)—that is, the viewpoint of the observer.[6] Crisis makes claims on the state; it is a form of political communication within contentious politics, across and among the "central cleavages" in society (Jacobs, 9).[7] Crisis and critique are also etymologically linked in which "crisis is posited 'as' history itself" (Roitman, 7). I therefore self-reflexively use the term "crisis" to identify the violence for those five days beginning April 29, 1992, in order to encourage readers' own judgments, to uncover the facts, feelings, and opinions upon which they rely, and to examine the discourses that produced them.

The term "crisis" incorporates the many others used to identify the urban violence in Los Angeles and encompasses the range of conflicting viewpoints. Most prominently, citations in historical texts, mainstream media, and political discourse usually refer to these events as riot. A riot implies anarchic, disorderly, even random violence against persons and property, what then-President George H. W. Bush called the "brutality of the mob."[8] Others call the 1992 violence the "Rodney King riots," focusing on the central victim in the precipitating event.[9] Such a focus encourages the interpretations of film scholar Linda Williams, among others, who read the unrest in relation to the "long history of black/white antinomies reaching back to the late nineteenth-century institution of Jim Crow" (Williams, 357 n. 6). Although this historical connection foregrounds the police beating of King that triggered the protests after their acquittal and mistrial, this discourse of Black–White conflict fails to fully describe the demographics and visual images of Whites, African Americans, Latinas/os, and Asian Americans depicted as participants in the crisis in the news media.[10] This viewpoint elides recent immigrants, especially Asians and Latinas/os, because their histories of racial victimization and urban violence are less well known or acknowledged.[11] The term "uprisings" connotes an upsurge and coming into visibility, often used to identify decolonization movements during the cold war. "Rebellion," a counterbalance to the term "riots," indicates organized protest through violence and the possible initiation of new political movements by radicals and reactionaries.[12] In their book-length study of Korean Americans affected by the civil disturbances in Los Angeles, Nancy Abelmann and John Lie argue that the racially progressive or liberal use of rebellion or revolution identifies alliances with African Americans but ignores the racial targeting of other ethnic groups (8). Amid the widespread devastation that affected many multiracial communities in the area, looters and arsonists targeted Korean businesses, and Latinas/os constituted the majority populations in the most devastated areas. Some Korean Americans prefer *Sa-i-gu (p'oktong)* or the 4–2–9 (riot) in referring to the Los Angeles Crisis. Major events such as "significant uprisings, demonstrations, and political turns" in Korean history are referenced by the numerical date of the event, and this naming practice firmly places the L.A. violence in the context of Korean oppression and resistance against the Japanese colonial state and Korean authoritarian government, linking Korean Americans to a global Korean diaspora (Abelmann and Lie, ix).

Some activists and writers prefer terms they perceive to be more descriptively neutral.[13] While alternatives to riots such as events, civil unrest, and civil disturbance are more descriptive, these terms are not neutral or politically impartial. These terms still position their speakers amid the uneasy, shifting balance of power relations, political struggles, economic and racial priorities, and views expressed by different stakeholders. While civil unrest and civil disturbance do allude to negotiations and management of conflict within civil society, the term "crisis" incorporates this desire for neutrality and impartiality, which, in its refusal to mete out innocence or guilt, sympathy or condemnation, is a political judgment in and of itself.

The title of the book, *Civil Racism*, marks the triumph of a politics of civility at the expense of racial equality, as it has come to pervade the post–civil rights era. In the cultural and legal shift from the modern civil rights movement to the post–civil rights era, the goal of equality is portrayed as an ethical choice between the formal (legal) processes and empirical evaluations of the outcomes. Civil racism marks the ways in which racial discrimination has been allowed sanctuary in the private realms of individual, isolated behaviors. Discussions of remedies for racial discrimination are marked as impolite and uncivil. In recasting neoliberal civility as a form of civil racism, I make visible the structural racism of Whites' *and* nonwhites' active, even if unintentional, perpetuation of discrimination through everyday interactions with other individuals and the state. Civil racism often appears as a discourse of racial civility: what I define as the behaviors or practices expected of racialized subjects in order to assimilate into Whiteness or achieve the status and protections of U.S. citizenship. As such, the identification and analysis of civil racism provides an important corrective to the more dominant assessments of U.S. society as having a post-racist state despite intensely segregated and discriminatory conditions.[14]

As a main feature of civil racism, *racial burnout* refers to a contemporary political malaise affecting both the right and the left in regard to the apparent intractability of systemic racial inequalities. *Burnout* indexes a condition of generalized exhaustion and apathy that has come about, in part, as a result of the protracted inability and/or unwillingness of the U.S. nation-state to fundamentally alter conditions of racial injustice. The title evokes a growing "race fatigue" on the part of both conservatives and liberals and their general hostility and resentment toward the remnants of the Great Society's welfare state. In sum, *burnout* signals what sociologist Michael Omi has called the "relative exhaustion of the traditional civil rights paradigm" and the concomitant rise of a neoliberal state predicated on a wholesale disinvestment in public programs that primarily benefited women and minorities and increasing restrictions on, or even outright reversal of, governmental protections (163). The violence of 1992 that spread across urban centers from Los Angeles to Washington, D.C., was an explosive sign of structural trends that diminished the opportunities and quality of life for people of color under the hegemony of civility. These are the negative consequences of what I call *civil racism*, organized around the promotion of race neutrality, colorblindness, and equal treatment, as opposed to the pursuit of refining and developing means-tested strategies for equalizing outcomes.

In addition to analyzing the discriminatory hierarchies and implicit exclusions within civil discourse, *Civil Racism* contributes to the growing field of comparative racialization by further exploring how groups are racialized in relation to one another.[15] Analysis of the 1992 Los Angeles Crisis demands examinations of the conflicts and connections between and among the different racial groups. Comparative racialization plays an important role in civility by managing the claims on the state by differently racialized groups, recognizing one or some in order to disregard others. For example, the dominance of Black–White binaristic thinking about interracial relations in the United States and making the privileges of Whiteness invisible to the hypervisibility of other racial identities are two principal strategies deployed in what Omi and Winant identify as our racial hegemony. Just as Whiteness cannot exist without Blackness, I contend that the so-called distinguishing characteristics and features of both these racial identities cannot exist without the histories of Asian, Latina/o, and Native American identity formations. The pseudoscientific explanations of racist hierarchies depend on the stabilizing force of the comparative, contingent racialization of people. In relation to the core antagonisms of Black–Korean and Black–White racial relationships that animate the 1992 Crisis and its analyses, Claire Jean Kim's paradigm of racial triangulation most usefully organizes the logics of these uneven racial fields and the identification of racial hierarchies based on evaluations of civic virtue or foreignness. These comparisons emerge as "relative valorization"—the portrayal of Asian Americans as the model minority but African Americans as the underclass—and "civic ostracism," the societal rejection of Asian immigrant alien identities but incorporation of African Americans as American citizens (Kim, 107). Because both the alliances and the antagonisms between and among racial groups are significant in my analyses of interracial relations, intersectional approaches have clearly influenced theories and studies of these coalitions and conflicts. Leslie McCall defines intersectionality in terms of "the relationships among multiple dimensions and modalities of social relations and subject formations—as itself a central category of analysis" (1771). Intersectionality negotiates both multiple racial formations and also their interactions with such other formations as gender, class, sexuality, and citizenship status.

U.S. race relations comprise a matrix of these shifting "social relations and subject formations" (McCall, 1771), the complexities of which are made visible at the various intersections of these relations and formations. In her pathbreaking work *Black Feminist Thought,* Patricia Hill Collins defines a "matrix of domination . . . as an historically specific organization of power in which social groups are embedded and which they aim to influence" (228). As Kimberlé Crenshaw notes in her often-cited article on intersectionality and the law, commonalities that are points of political convergence and possibility emerge along each axis. McCall argues for more research on what she terms "intercategorical complexity" or that "scholars provisionally adopt existing analytical categories to document relationships of inequality among social groups and changing configurations of inequality along multiple and conflicting dimensions" (1773). Rejecting the "unitary" and "multiple" or additive approaches to research, Ange-Marie Hancock provides another aspect of analysis for what she calls the "intersectional approach"—that of examining the individual–institutional interaction. This additional lens is important in two ways: in describing the relationship between individuals and institutions and the "dynamic interaction between individual and institutional factors" (73). Not only are racialized individuals and groups triangulated and their identities contingent on each other, but they are also hierarchically arrayed in relation to the state.

Building on the paradigm of racial triangulation, the matrix of domination, and these working definitions of intersectionality, I posit that the various vertices or nodal points of intersection among racial groups can be imagined as a three-dimensional pyramid with its triangular faces. The racial pyramid usefully illustrates how relations are organized hierarchically and asymmetrically. For example, when viewed from one perspective, the three-dimensional pyramid that emerges from the racial binary of White–"Other"—usually manifested as White–Black—shows Whiteness at the apex and the various nonwhite racial groups as vertices of the base. However, unlike the original binary, the relations between and among the nonwhite racial groups and with Whiteness are more clearly disaggregated. In using this model, one could isolate Black–White or Black–Korean relations as many have in explanations for the 1992 Crisis, but the three-dimensional pyramid demands a more complex, multinodal contextualization and analysis of how these conflicts are mediated by other racial groups. This figuration also signals the multiracial archive of my study, the Asian American and Latina/o communities and histories that are often obscured by both Black–White and Black–Korean interracial conflicts. Pyramidization provides another way to imagine civil racism and racial burnout: the triangulation on the faces closest to the viewer obscures the furthest, hidden vertex, a racial erasure for one group that often may be ignored but is still a crucial, defining part of the figure.

In this book, the historical periodization of the post–civil rights and post–cold war eras importantly contextualize the political environments dependent on strategies of comparative racialization and civil racism. I begin with the post–civil rights era as a dominant, domestic frame of reference for understanding the Los Angeles Crisis. Historically, the era begins with two events—the 1968 assassination of Martin Luther King Jr. and Lyndon B. Johnson's signing of the Fair Housing Act—and encompasses such domestic and international structural forms as neoliberalism, post-Fordism, global capitalism, and deindustrialization. At the same time, the period includes significant and formidable counterhegemonic movements for such political transformations as Third World liberation, second- and third-wave feminism, and lesbian and gay rights. While these and other struggles for equality emerged and developed in the context of post–civil rights, equality increasingly came to be defined and assessed in the more narrow terms of the elimination of overt legal discrimination rather than in the more expansive terms of material and substantive parity.

The late 1960s marked a shift in activist agendas as national civil rights leaders and organizations were turning to address poverty across the nation and more forcefully champion substantive equality before the law. This emphasis in the movement's agenda came after the dismantling of legal barriers to voting, transportation, public accommodations, public schools, home ownership, and employment. Despite segregation's pernicious material effects, what emerged as far more difficult to address were the pervasive inequalities resulting from the long history of racial discrimination: disparities in income, property ownership, wealth, and quality of life differentials in infant mortality, health outcomes, and life expectancy. Such landmark protections as the Civil Rights Act of 1964, the Voting Rights Act of 1965, and the Fair Housing Act of 1968 prescribed specific types of remedies by advancing the rights of the citizen. The success of this legislation, however, requires vigilant, rigorous enforcement, such as the long-term monitoring of the voting process and school desegregation that occurred in the South until 2013. Since the 1970s it has been clear that these laws have little or no penalties for nonenforcement and that regulatory institutions can even obstruct them (Lipsitz, 148–49). These hard-won legislative and judicial remedies are hollow victories without continual enforcement.

While activists and researchers defined equality more expansively, conventional wisdom and public policy increasingly moved in the opposite direction: ending poverty and other material disadvantages should begin with the individual, not with the state. In fact, a growing number of liberals joined conservatives in thinking that positive state action to ameliorate poverty often had unintended negative consequences and that state action should be abandoned altogether or severely limited. The Nixon administration's "benign neglect" and the Carter administration's move toward deregulation did nothing to alleviate economic inequality. President Reagan delivered the government's official surrender in his last State of the Union address in 1988: "My friends, some years ago, the federal government declared war on poverty and poverty won." U.S. voters lacked the collective political will to challenge the equality gap and effectively opted to continue Reagan's policies into a third term by electing George H. W. Bush.[16] The Los Angeles Crisis hastened the end of the Bush-Reagan era by providing what appeared to be emphatic visual evidence that the sitting president was out of touch with the American people, who were suffering from a recession after the end of the Persian Gulf War and the cold war.

The work of achieving equal opportunities and outcomes rests on conflicting assessments of the civil rights movement.[17] Radical left critiques often insist that such a movement depends too heavily on the state for the protection of civil and human rights and guarantees of civil liberties. For libertarian and conservative critics, these state mandates intrusively limit the individual decisions and behaviors of private citizens by profoundly infringing upon their civil liberties. The direct causal harm of individual or private acts of discrimination, in the form of attitudes, behaviors, and speech, are difficult to assess and quantify, as is legislating the conditions under which the government intervenes.[18] Laws written in race-neutral language continue to have a disparate impact on specific racial groups—a form of indirect structural discrimination that would require more targeted remedies to achieve parity in outcomes without more radical institutional changes.

The Rehnquist and later the Roberts Courts were increasingly unwilling to uphold these remedies as constitutional. This question of the state's role in creating equal outcomes has a long history in the annals of U.S. democracy, dating back to the foundational debates over the U.S. Constitution, when some delegates, uneasy with the unprecedented political equality being proposed for all White men of property, were reassured that the existing *social* hierarchy would effectively counterbalance such equal *political* rights.[19] Such anxieties of radical equality across the social, political, and economic persist in the celebrated focus on civility over equality.

In order to more adequately address the structural factors that facilitated the particular form and singular achievements of the modern civil rights movement, any narrative of progress must be situated within a broader geopolitical context that includes the expansion of global capitalist markets and the realignments of hegemonic imperial power during and after the cold war. The post–civil rights era has been shaped by the dialectic between global dynamics and adjustments in national economic structures, as evidenced, for example, through domestic deindustrialization. Racial discrimination greatly magnified the impact of job losses and infrastructural decline that the relocating plants or vanishing industries had on communities of color throughout the nation.[20] The political turn toward increasing conservatism during the 1970s accompanied these shifts in production, giving rise to "supply-side economics," increasing racial and class disparities in incomes and wealth, the weakening of unions and loss of union jobs, neglect of the urban infrastructure, and disinvestment in social welfare. These global forces would dramatically shape the socioeconomic environment of Los Angeles in the late 1980s and early 1990s, especially in the communities hardest hit by the crisis. From 1982 to 1989, 131 plants in the L.A. area closed and moved to Mexico, putting 124,000 employees out of work (J. Johnson et al., 362). From the late 1970s to early 1980s, two hundred L.A.-based firms relocated (360).

The most severe job losses occurred near communities with primarily African American or Latina/o residents. The post–World War II boom economy that fueled the explosive growth of Southern California and attracted workers from all over the world would deflate with the shrinking of the military-industrial complex caused by the end of the cold war and immediately after the Persian Gulf War. By the time the 1991 recession made national news and concerned policymakers, areas such as South Central Los Angeles had already experienced two decades of disappearing jobs. In addition to unemployment rates that were persistently higher than national averages, over 40 percent of Black men and over 50 percent of Black women, ages 16 and over, were not in the workforce (Morrison and Lowry, 19). These numbers would reflect the socioeconomic composition of those arrested for looting—the most common offense during the crisis—in which two-thirds of the people convicted were unemployed and 11 percent were homeless (E. Smith, 6).

In the post–civil rights era, the economic and social barriers to equality still thwart parity in outcomes and are maintained through the persuasive argument that full, formal equality has already been achieved and its benefits bestowed—whether through the success of affirmative state actions or the decrease of formal and informal racial discrimination. Under these newly nondiscriminatory conditions, any differential outcomes are explained as due to inherited, likely insuperable, deficiencies in genes, intelligence, or culture. The post–civil rights era promotes two dominant justifications for the inequalities in the status quo: first, that people of color should *wait* for political, social, and economic equality since they have not yet *earned* their full citizenship rights; and second, that because the explicitly discriminatory laws of the Jim Crow era have been eliminated, these same communities should bear the responsibility for failing to benefit fully from the opportunities available to them since the 1960s. Both explanations rely on the belief that people of color are not yet ready for inclusion into the imagined community of the United States because of their alleged civic deficiencies: the purported backwardness and inadequacies of their culture, education, character, and mores that cause their failure to achieve parity in all kinds of social, political, and economic benchmarks.[21]

While these two justifications played out in the narratives condemning the crisis participants and their communities, the events of 1992 were also subject to comparisons with other international conflicts, thus dramatizing the United States' own susceptibility to social upheavals and collective political violence. The Los Angeles Crisis embarrassingly, and for some, distastefully, linked the United States to another nation's racial dictatorship, as the racial and color hierarchies were uneasily familiar to these other histories of racial segregation and terror, especially that of South African apartheid. This comparison of two nations' racial conflicts disturbed the views of many Americans who were loathe to admit that violence could still be committed by Whites in positions of authority against peaceable Blacks in the United States in the 1990s. They believed that the United States was both historically and philosophically distanced from anti-Black oppression and interracial conflict. Kimberlé Crenshaw and Gary Peller argue that many viewers perceived the police beating of King onscreen as emblematic of an "old-style, garden-variety racist power exemplified by the Bull Connor/Pretorialike images of heavily armed White security officers beating a defenseless Black man senseless" (58). This description links King's beating directly to a long, global history of institutionalized racial violence, encompassing not only segregation, lynching, and terror in the American past, but also the brutal racial oppression of South African apartheid. In contrast, the U.S. corporate mass media and government tended to posit South African apartheid and U.S. racial dynamics as polar opposites; as a racial dictatorship, South Africa was a foil for the U.S. racial democracy with its systemic inequalities. Audiences who were surprised that King's beating could occur in Los Angeles in the early 1990s or who interpreted the racial violence as an extranational event evidently held the conviction that this type of violence, sanctioned by the government and the criminal justice system through the police perpetrators, is an uncommon experience in the United States after the end of *de jure* segregation.

This comparison to South Africa was among the compelling discursive memes of national security and international conflicts. An op-ed published in the *Los Angeles Times* during the violence posited the crisis as "not simply a Los Angeles matter; it is an international incident" (quoted in Vargas, 219). The national news media also regularly alluded to the interethnic and religious tensions in the Middle East, international terrorism, and Muslim provocateurs in its coverage of the crisis (Davis, "Uprising," 147). In *Time* magazine, Richard Schickel argued that reporters depicted Los Angeles as "a mythical city, a sort of Beirut West, views of which would keep many viewers frozen in fear" (29). This kind of coverage effectively implied that the protestors and participants in the crisis were akin to homegrown terrorists and inside agitators common to the coverage of the upheavals in the Middle East.[22] Analogous to the national media portrayal of these Americans as agent provocateurs, the crisis participants were perceived as the enemy by federal troops. Combat maneuvers carried out in Los Angeles were part of a new type of tactical warfare emerging in the

1990s, which were then called military operations on urban terrain (MOUTs). These MOUTs were deployed in other U.S. interventions abroad, such as those in Bosnia and Somalia; in the L.A. violence, gang members were identified as the enemy combatants despite the low percentage of participants who were gang-affiliated and the lack of evidence of systematic or gang-related violent acts.[23] Whether the fear was caused by inner-city gang members or Rodney King's Black male body, such depictions allude to how nonwhite bodies have been perceived as foreign threats since the time of European invasion and imperialism, likening them to pestilence, savages, perils to European or Anglo-American civilization, or the enemy within.[24] In this conflation of domestic and international "racial paranoia," not only the fundamental Americanness of these nonwhite subjects is called into question, but also their allegiance to Whiteness. As victimized identity formations, Whiteness and Americanness frame violence against nonwhites and immigrants as preemptive and morally justified, since "about-to-be attacked" perpetrators could have been the intended targets and future victims of these marginalized people. Feeding xenophobic racism and inciting military invasions abroad to expand U.S. imperialism, these formations have also manifested themselves as patriotism in disciplining and excluding nonwhites and immigrants for their alleged anti-Americanism (Puar, 183–84).[25]

The discourse of civility is made more urgent by these comparisons, especially in the aftermath of the cold war and the geopolitical instability triggered by the fall of former Soviet Union and its nations.[26] By the 1990s, new social and political forces were at play, both domestically and internationally. After World War II, the "interest convergence" of cold war politics and the modern civil rights movement contributed to more democratic racial practices, as legal scholar Derrick Bell and historian Mary Dudziak have argued. After the fall of the Berlin Wall, the dissolution of the Soviet Union, and the breakup of Yugoslavia, international realignments shaped U.S. culture and politics in terms of these "cold war civil rights." Despite the much-touted triumph of capitalism, the political upheavals and civil wars that followed the collapse of the USSR instigated an anxious outpouring of U.S. research on civil society and its contribution to the durability and integrity of democratic states. Concerns about the "balkanization of America" variously attributed to increasing immigrant populations of racial minorities, affirmative action, multicultural education, and racial justice movements exemplify these multilayered fears of social instability while also revealing the unfounded belief that the United States was previously unified and homogeneous sometime in the past.[27] In this case, the master narrative of American progress fuels calls for civility, the exceptionalist bildungsroman of the maturing nation adopting increasingly robust notions of democracy and equality. By calling that dominant perception of the nation into question, the L.A. Crisis had a profound, though seldom acknowledged, influence on the way Americans thought of their country in the post–cold war and post–civil rights eras. The violence in Los Angeles punctured the illusion of American exceptionalism. Consequently, the 1992 Los Angeles Crisis provides competing perspectives from which to examine the complex relationship between equality and civility amid the deep anxieties emerging during the 1990s.

Civility has multiple definitions and a broad range of connotations that include civic virtue, citizenry, civil society, and civilization (see Sapiro). With its valorization of good manners and political communication, it is most popularly thought to encompass the rules and behaviors that constitute and strengthen civil society. Civility, thus, can be considered prepolitical as "an attitude of respect, even love, for our fellow citizens" (Carter, *Civility*, xii) that fosters democratic societies, or what might be called metapolitical—what Étienne Balibar designates as the "politics of politics, or a politics in the second degree, which aims at creating, recreating, and conserving the set of conditions within which politics as a collective participation in public affairs is possible, or is not made absolutely impossible" (15). Despite its broad definition, civility has a long tradition in liberal philosophy and is increasingly considered as important as other sociopolitical concepts such as equality and justice. Perhaps the term could stand to be disaggregated, much like equality has, into its *formal* and *substantive* manifestations: respectively, polite social behavior and "a sense of standing or membership in the political community with its attendant rights and responsibility" (Boyd, 864).[28] In either form, the concept implicitly relies on the abilities and behaviors of the abstract citizen, assumed to be roughly equal to other citizens in status within a political community and society in general.

Scholars subsequently emphasized the vital importance of a strong and active civil society in the consolidation and stability of democracy. Robert Putnam's 1995 popular essay, "Bowling Alone: America's

Declining Social Capital," and 2001 best-selling book, *Bowling Alone: The Collapse and Revival of American Community,* warned that civic culture in this country was declining at the very moment when newly democratic governments in Eastern Europe were looking to the United States as a model.[29] Heightened by the end of the cold war and the resulting increase in the failure of states, or "state death," these anxious calls for civility were ostensibly attempts to foster communication in the public sphere and, thus, strengthen the political communities that comprise democratic society. Such communication is, however, troubled by the specter of incivility that emphasizes the role of racism and the field of competing claims of racial injustice and economic inequality. From interpersonal relations to national dialogues, the stated goal of these debates was to foster more productive democratic deliberation through the mitigation of contentious disputes among political actors and communities. However, those at the forefront of the debates publicized and exaggerated the dire consequences and ostensible decline of civility in alarmist, even apocalyptic language: democracy would collapse without civility.[30]

The unresolved differences of civic values and virtues have been blamed for fracturing U.S. society, resulting in a so-called civility crisis.[31] Civil racism found mainstream, albeit coded, expression in the contentious "civility debates" of the mid-1990s. Instead of focusing on the more spectacular expressions of state and criminal violence, civility scholars condemned incidences of rude behavior. Such best-selling scholars and political advisers as P. M. Forni, Stephen L. Carter, and Kathleen Hall Jamieson delineated the benefits of civility in dialogue and behavior to deter social anomie, group conflicts, and criminality. As opposed to addressing growing wealth inequality, *de facto* segregation, wage stagnation, and the lingering effects of White supremacy, citizens were exhorted to listen to each other and promote interracial dialogues that did not require complex and contentious legislation. As the more academic and philosophical arm of the contentious culture wars of the 1980s and early 1990s, the civility debates were predicated on a putative national decline coupled with the erosion of "common values" presumed to bring together the diverse elements of U.S. society. In the mid-1990s, the civility debates reached their peak in public discourse with academics, politicians, journalists, government officials, bestselling authors, and pundits all contributing to the national discussion. There were much-discussed civility manuals, such as Carter's *Civility: Manners, Morals, and the Etiquette of Democracy,* and studies of

U.S. political culture, such as Jamieson's 1997 civility summit with U.S. Congressional Representatives and its resulting report, which had sought "a greater degree of civility, mutual respect and, when possible, bipartisanship among Members of the House of Representatives in order to foster an environment in which vigorous debate and mutual respect can coexist."[32] Think tanks and university institutes, such as the Johns Hopkins Civility Project and the University of Pennsylvania National Commission on Society, Culture, and Community, also weighed in to study and promote civic dialogues through programming and research.

In sum, the various proponents of civility extol the numerous positive benefits of civil behaviors. According to these scholars, civility primarily smooths social, economic, and political transactions and "eas[es] social conflicts and facilitat[es] social interactions in a complex and diverse market society" (Boyd, 863). Emphasizing the substantive definition of civility—one's standing and membership in a political community—Richard Boyd stresses that civility fosters the moral inclusiveness and equality that would then undergird a political inclusiveness (865). The smallest, everyday, civil behaviors promote feelings of belonging to a community of moral and political equals and cultivate an individual's investment in the collective well-being of and inclusiveness in that community. Most important, civility helps naturalize and legitimate legal and governmental jurisdictions and functions. The formation of the moral community or public helps individuals imagine what is right, just, and appropriate for the collective citizenry and then establish, with general agreement, the legal parameters of who belongs, who can vote, who can participate in civic discourse, and who remains on the margins or is excluded entirely. For proponents of civility such as Boyd, Carter, and Forni, one of the concept's primary benefits is its operation and solutions within mostly extralegal and nongovernmental spaces: "Civility discourages the use of legislation rather than conversation to settle disputes, except as a last, carefully considered resort" (Carter, *Civility*, 283). Functioning as a tacit social contract between those in the same political community, civility strengthens belonging by fostering political communication among its members in the public sphere. Civility is important, these scholars insist, because it is an indispensable precursor to democracy. But civility's liminal, extralegal advantages "at the interstices of public and private, social norms and moral laws, conservative nostalgia and democratic potentiality" (Boyd, 864) mean then that much of the dirty work of negative racist, sexist feelings—known to social scientists as rational and taste-based discriminations—can occur outside legal purviews and without state remedies.[33] Ostensibly neutral, statistical assessments of risk (rational discrimination) and personal preferences (taste-based discrimination) thus persist. This conceptualization, fixated on a process of development from civility to equality, unwittingly reveals how civil subjects can become excluded from equal status, standing, and outcomes when they fail to meet the tacit prerequisites for civic participation and inclusion. If civility as a precursor to equality is so crucial, then the period of waiting on the determination of civility or incivility itself can deny equal standing to certain individuals and groups. These scholars tout the benefits of civility without taking into account how differently positioned groups might be disparately assessed in relation to civility. While it may be vitally important to recognize that civility is used to assess whether individuals and groups *deserve* to be treated equally, the critical question remains: Should such a gatekeeping function continue to be promoted as an unqualified positive good?

In testing the limits of civility's merits, I posit that *incivility* reveals more about standards of civility. Indeed, civility scholars are much more definitive about behaviors that constitute incivility than those about civility itself.[34] Incivility is routinely defined as social behaviors that are rude, discourteous, impolite, insulting, lacking manners, or unfriendly.[35] It is useful to revisit how the curtailing of these incivilities built and sustains the modern state, as Norbert Elias has argued in his influential work *The Civilizing Process*. According to Elias, individuals were encouraged to suppress or discipline their violent bodily actions and feelings as the state was strengthened by its mandate to regulate and maintain such "pacified social spaces" that were largely purged of any uncivil behaviors (235). In his blunt paraphrase of Elias's main argument, John F. Kasson notes how

> intimate bodily activities—eating, coughing, spitting, nose blowing, scratching, farting, urinating, defecating, undressing, sleeping, copulating, inflicting pain on animals or other human beings—became governed by especially exacting standards and were assigned their special precincts, for the most part behind closed doors. . . . As a result, human affect and behavior were divided into aspects that might appropriately be displayed in public and others, especially sexuality, that had to be kept private and "secret." (11)[36]

Any perceived decay of manners thus reveals a society on the brink of savagery or chaos. For this distinction, Kasson utilizes the evocative metaphor of closed doors outside the purview of strangers, neighbors, and citizens at large. Thus, Kasson broadly defines incivility in terms of making public what should be private, or making conspicuous that which should be inconspicuous.

Proponents of civility appear to emphasize its positive outcomes rather than explore those that are more ambiguous and even contradictory.[37] While civility scholars do acknowledge that the worst of civility may be that, according to Edward Shils, "it serves as a device of hierarchy, difference and exclusion" (quoted in Boyd, 338–40), they generally gloss over the potential relationships between civility and inequality, incivility and equality: *polite* social behavior can mask deeply entrenched beliefs in and practices that promote the fundamental *inequality* of others, and *rude* social behavior can conceal deeply entrenched beliefs in and practices that promote the fundamental *equality* of others, respectively. Instead, incivility is simply presumed to indicate a return to the undesirable state of nature and to be avoided in all circumstances:

> Whether incivility takes the form of personal disrespect and low-level antisocial behaviour or rises to the extremes of rioting, looting and the wholesale destruction of personal property, the breakdown of civility bodes poorly for the constitution of society. . . . As Thomas Hobbes understood so well when he juxtaposed the condition of civil association to the vicissitudes of the state of nature, beyond certain limits incivility may nullify all the enjoyments of a humane and decent society. (Boyd, 874)[38]

This framework conceives of rioting, looting, and destruction of personal property as forms of antisocial behavior, rather than as political strategies that shape local and national politics or make claims on the state. Moreover, incivility allegedly undermines "a humane and decent society" that presumably existed before. Civility scholars tend to assume that civility and a civil society exist largely under the same conditions for each distinct political community within nation-states. They also rely on the assumption that these states cultivate, reward, and discipline the civil and uncivil behavior of the same bodies and spaces similarly and equally. But, as theorist Denise Ferreira da Silva points out, advocates of civility erase the violent origins of the state itself. The violence meted out by the state is overlooked because not only is it epiphenomenal to the appropriate processes of civility, but civility should also short-circuit such expressions.

Proponents of civility suggest few remedies for combating its perpetuation of the inequalities of the status quo, peace, law, and order. Ideally, civility *would* build moral relationships on feelings of respect and equality among people and likely achieves this much more often than not.[39] The truer test of civility, often overlooked, is how behaviors that promote it directly result in these laudable morals and feelings of mutual respect and equality. Historically, an "appreciation of human equality" (Boyd, 875) has been easily held by elites alongside the most heinous of racial injustices on the American continent: chattel slavery and the systematic genocide of indigenous peoples. Of course, recent proponents of civility may well argue that who is considered human has since expanded to its rightful membership of all human beings, pointedly including descendants of enslaved persons and indigenous peoples. There are two primary issues with this rebuttal. At its foundation, the *process* of beginning with civility and ending with equality can be manipulated to justify differential treatment and discrimination that have become the hallmark of post–civil rights justifications for racial inequalities. If "being civil is a way of generating moral respect and democratic equality" (ibid.), then determining a person's behavior to be uncivil can plausibly justify denying this person her moral respect and democratic equality. Less obviously, the devaluation of women and people of color marks certain bodies as intrinsically uncivil, much as determinations of their inferiority have marked them as inhuman and, thus, not worthy of "human equality" or legal protections.[40] While the disambiguation between levels of civility has its uses, minor individual acts of rudeness or microaggressions are, in essence, major group acts of repudiation; subjecting an individual to an incivility based on one's group identity, such as race, class, gender, or sexuality, indicates inequalities among these group identities.

Proving one's civility not only becomes a matter of proving one's equality but it also becomes a test of one's very humanity. If an individual doesn't behave well, then one doesn't deserve to be a member of a political community. One needs to earn one's membership in the political community if one is not perceived to be a part of it.[41] But this tacit requirement is precisely the problem: more powerful political communities will attempt to approximate the entirety of the democratic society.[42] Because not all bodies are considered equal, civil, or human, speakers are not heard with the same force or resonance. Moreover, those uncivil, "bad subjects" are blocked from accessing equal rights. Civility's benefits, in this sense, are precisely its failures. For example, if civility's primary function is to minimize conflict, then the presence of conflict signals the presence of incivility among the involved parties rather than the inability for civil behavior to resolve issues such as persistent structural discrimination. Furthermore, the unidirectional process from civility to equality means that political actors need to demonstrate that they are civil before they can be considered equal. There is a glaring failure to evaluate that equality might be more necessary for the kinds of civility crucial to a democracy.

The proponents of civility, thus, attach a precondition to the inalienable right of equality, one of the most cherished contemporary precepts of U.S. democracy. For these civility proponents, because all bodies can be civil, then all men are created equal.[43] While in the abstract ideal, all people might conceivably be created equal, not all bodies are *allowed* to be civil. However, just as all people are not treated equally, their racialized and gendered bodies are not universally perceived to be civil or capable of civil behavior. In fact, such determinations are contingent upon the type of body in question. Some bodies are perceived to be intrinsically civil despite their uncivil acts, and conversely, other bodies are perceived to be intrinsically uncivil despite their civil acts. Proponents of civility inadequately address how to overcome existing hierarchies between those who are considered "roughly equal" and those who are considered of inferior status even within democratic society, as manifested in their diminished claims to the rights and privileges of these other groups, their thwarted "right to have rights." In deploying the roughly equal abstract citizen, proponents of civility avoid and disavow the specific negotiations of power among individuals and groups who have different standings in relationship to each other. Furthermore, civility is inextricably tied to humanity, just as humanity is tied to civility: our ability to be civil proves our humanity just as our humanity proves our ability to be civil. However, the benchmarks for assessing civility are different for different bodies.[44] Perhaps most important, in their conflation of civility with equality or democracy (and insisting that a society cannot have one without the other), civility proponents must elide other uncivil avenues toward equality as well as the hidden inequalities of civility. For example, uncivil behavior may not necessarily lead to inequality but may actually lead to achieving substantive equality through protests and other civil disturbances, even violence. Incivility may be one of the only avenues available for recognition among individuals and groups accorded little access to the mechanisms of power. Civility proponents often deliberately elide and deride the actions of those who strategically deploy incivility and, thus, civility becomes a convenient way of masking attitudes and practices that might promote inequality while the codes of civil behavior and expression are rigorously followed.[45]

The most vocal advocates of civility, who Randall Kennedy has criticized as "the civilitarians" (84–90), espouse an unshakeable belief that the cultivation of civility invariably leads to the cultivation of democracy. In this line of reasoning, enhancements of civility automatically lead to enhancements of our democracy. Thus, civil behavior and actions are especially crucial, if not mandatory, to the maintenance, preservation, and promotion of democracy. But the main trouble with this unidirectional process from civility to democracy and equality is that proponents of this specific progression must ignore some other causalities: civility can foster substantive inequality, just as the fundamentally uncivil can foster substantive equality. There is a persistent refusal to acknowledge the role incivility might play in fostering a democratic society, if not in the violent origins of the U.S. nation-state recognized long ago by Thomas Jefferson, echoed in Henry David Thoreau's civil disobedience, and recurring in Martin Luther King Jr.'s speeches and writings.

Civility fosters the abstract citizen, much beloved by political philosophers and much criticized by feminist and antiracist scholars for its homogenizing and universalizing tendencies. The invocation of the abstract citizen tends to smooth out any difference from the traditional norm: White, male, property-owning, of European descent, able-bodied, adult, heterosexual, Christian. The civility debates become a useful strategy in avoiding difficult discussions of material redistribution as well as what have become the discomfiting racial ties of multiculturalism, even in its most anodyne forms. Civility has the benefits of being colorblind in its seeming race neutrality, while the uneven demands for certain kinds of civil behavior for racially marked bodies are predicated on fundamental hierarchies and inequalities. Fascinatingly, in proposing yet again the liberal autonomous subject unmarked by race and gender, discussions of civility emerge as a compelling way to talk *around* feminist and antiracist concerns with a determined and dedicated ignorance. With the abstract citizen and moral individual as its agents, civility manages strongly racialized and gendered antipathies and anxieties about the national community in resolutely race- and gender-neutral terms.

While civility has been taken up with extra fervor in the aftermath of the cold war, it has also been a marker of the break in attitudes that divide the modern civil rights movement from the post–civil rights era. Historian William Chafe usefully distinguishes between the legal, overt discrimination of the civil rights era and the extralegal, color-blind manifestations of the post–civil rights era:

> The civil rights laws enacted in 1964, 1965, and 1968 have ensured far wider legal protection of black citizens and have destroyed official sanction for most forms of racial discrimination. Yet the underlying goals of the sit-in demonstrators remain, in many ways, as far distant today as they were before the Woolworth's protests took place. Inequality and discrimination still suffuse our social and economic system, buttressed by the informal modes of social control even more powerful than the law. Although the means of keeping blacks in their place may now be implicit rather than explicit, they too often are just as effective as in the past. (Chafe vii–viii)

Chafe's identification of the shift from formal, legal inequality to informal, social difference is profound. The title of his landmark community history of Greensboro, North Carolina, *Civilities and Civil Rights* (1981), captures the interaction between these two terms by connecting the civil with the political, a long-standing division needing reconciliation within Marxist thought. Sociologist Michael Omi and political scientist Howard Winant argue that the state was transformed from a racial dictatorship into a racial hegemony that has been "achieved through consent rather than coercion" (67). Unequal relations that reaffirm subordination can be expressed in such positive ways as love, friendship, and affection (Jackman, 78),[46] far beyond the purview of the state, yet constitutive of its rights and privileges. Expanding on Chafe's distinctions in *Codes of Conduct: Race, Ethics and the Color of Our Character* (1995), literary critic Karla F. C. Holloway also identifies the continuation of racial subordination in covert forms in terms of how African Americans are kept "in their place" by informal social codes of behavior and conduct. This spatializing metaphor for civility describes not only how the subordinated experience de facto segregation but find their behavior more strictly regulated when they are perceived "out of place" (Cresswell, 334–36; Combs, 4–6) in multiracial or predominantly White environments. Civility is perfectly compatible with racism, sexism, queerphobia, ableism, and other oppressions.

In the post–civil rights era, polite and invisible forms of discrimination rely on the social and economic hierarchies that fundamentally structure civil society. Informal, legal discriminations, unregulated by state and individual actors, continue to perpetuate incivilities and inequalities. In analyzing the distinct discursive formations emerging in the post–civil rights era, Eduardo Bonilla-Silva affirms the prevalence of what he identifies as "color-blind racism," demonstrated through "the actual language used by whites to defend their racial views" (Bonilla-Silva, 12). This language, as political communication, approximates what I term racial civility. Bonilla-Silva usefully disaggregates "the frames" of the stories we tell ourselves and one another about race in the post–civil rights era: "All racialized societies produce dominant common stories that become part of the racial folklore and thus are shared, used, and believed by members of the dominant race" (70).[47] Identifying this shift from formal to informal discrimination, Lawrence Bobo, James Kleugel, and Ryan Smith detail the transition from Jim Crow racism to "laissez faire racism": "This new ideology concedes to African Americans basic citizenship rights; however, it takes as legitimate extant patterns of black-white socioeconomic inequality and residential segregation, viewing these conditions, as it does, not as the deliberate products of racial discrimination, but rather as outcomes of a free-market, race-neutral state apparatus and the freely taken actions of African Americans themselves" (38). Laissez faire racism as the result of "market and informal racial bias to re-create, and in some instances sharply worsen, structured racial inequality" (17) points to the impact of economic ideology on the maintenance of racism. Non-Marxist American traditions of economic thought since Tocqueville have abstracted civil society from market forces, in contrast to Hegelian and Marxist dialectical analyses of the relation between civil society and conditions of economic production. The possibility of autonomous, self-regulating markets inspired the theorization of the market as separate from the state. Analogously, the ideology of autonomous free markets shapes laissez-faire racism, as individuals are collectively organized within civil society, but their self-regulation— their civility—leads to the analysis of racial inequality as an externality or epiphenomenal effect.

As a dominant strategy of minimizing racism and discrimination, stories, narratives, and emotions "displace" legal injuries and material inequalities. This is not to say that language does not have material consequences in shaping cognition and naturalizing motivations or outcomes. Language can be radically individualized and trivialized as a vehicle of emotion. As Rebecca Wanzo (2010) argues, feelings can displace the material realities from which they originate: "'Hurt feelings'—a distinct but porous concept also linked to accusations of 'oversensitivity' and 'political correctness'—has played a prominent role in conversations about many racial conflicts in the 'post'–Civil Rights era. 'Hurt feelings' are integral to displacement projects, as stories that decry hurt feelings can serve to distract focus from the material realities to which 'hurt feelings' might be connected" (93). For Wanzo, the strategy of minimizing racism and discrimination in the post–civil rights era appears as displacement: the notion of "hurt feelings" renders "issues of racial conflict as failures of language, as opposed to failures of institutions and structures" (93), thus shifting attention from claims of injury to an existential register. I would go even further: outside intentional incivilities, racial conflict signals not only failures of language but also failures of communication, in which the aggrieved parties are accused of misunderstanding the racially benign, civil intentions of perpetrators or forced to disavow the magnitude of harm experienced. Most important, the hurt and harm that arise from private conversations and civic dialogues of citizens are out of the purview of the state and cast as beyond legal remedy.

As it marks this individualized, privatized shift in culture and politics, I argue that a discourse of civility characterizes the post–civil rights era in its justification of inaction toward racial injustices and reading intervention as incivility. This civility is often conceived of as the prepolitical and predemocratic, the realm of civil society as separate from the state and often even market forces. Politicians, pundits, and voters have engaged in public discourses about race that have significantly altered Americans' notions of good citizenship, community, and civil society. Recognizing racial difference activates allegations of both incivility and illegitimacy and racial considerations in government interventions are perceived as unfair, unconstitutional interferences into the life chances and individual decisions of all citizens. The struggle over remedies for historic racial inequality concerns the legitimacy of race and those affected by it. The alleged illegitimacy of race in civil discourse creates alternate *legitimate* discussions, largely abstract and rigorously expunged of any racial specificities.

Calling people and practices racist has primarily been considered impolite, divisive, and thus uncivil. After civil rights legislation attempted to change structural discrimination and alleviate material inequalities, a prominent argument developed that those inroads were no longer necessary, since overt discrimination was often not the lived experience of all racial groups, as perpetrators or victims. Civility, or perhaps the appearance of it, has thus historically been a useful guise for White supremacy among other forms of oppression. The existence and pervasiveness of racism and its material and psychic consequences have always been in the eye of the beholder, whether from the perspective of victims and their advocates, perpetrators, and institutional agents. Such a shift puts the responsibility on individuals for resolving conflicts, privately, outside the legal purview of the state. Moreover, discrimination becomes even more radically individual and private as a deeply personal affect. Indeed, Wanzo aptly identifies this era as primarily driven by affect, whereby material inequalities persist but political feelings and will have atrophied and the superficial remedy is to change how people feel.

In order to make the conditions that lead to "social movements, cycles of protest, and revolutions" (McAdam, Tarrow, and Tilly, 17) become meaningful and recognizable as forms of participation in the larger democratic society, political scientists such as Doug McAdam, Sydney Tarrow, and Charles Tilly have expanded the definition of democratic deliberation by positing the notion of "contentious politics": *"Contention* begins when people collectively make claims on other people, claims which if realized would affect those others' interests. Claims run from humble supplications to brutal attacks, passing through petitions, chanted demands, and revolutionary manifestos" (17; original emphasis). For McAdam, Tarrow, and Tilly, violent public protest and nonviolent actions are both crucial forms of political communication, however undesirable and alarming some may find either. Perceived as violating civil norms, interracial conflict is often devalued and rejected as a form of democratic deliberation. Proceeding from these dynamics of contention that revalue both protest and violence as significant forms of political communication, the thousands of incidents that comprised the 1992 state of emergency in Los Angeles and the narratives marshaled to define them as wanton, inexplicable violence reveal the negotiations of race in the contemporary era. The largely successful attempts to identify what was happening as evil, chaotic, criminal, and anti-American are no more evident in the prevalent use of "riots" to identify the crisis. How threatening the violence was to the status quo is signaled by the powerful institutions and narratives arrayed to invalidate the political and economic claims made by the participants, journalists, politicians, observers, and victims. Because nonwhite bodies were conspicuously involved and were not perceived as civil, any actions performed by such bodies cannot but be uncivil, any claims made cannot but be illegitimate. Hannah Arendt astutely claimed that human rights no longer guaranteed political rights in the face of imperialism and totalitarianism in the world, but in fact, one's political rights ensured one's human rights. By reading Arendt's claims in the U.S. context, I argue that one's civility, rather than one's civil rights, protects one's political identity, even one's humanity.

Civil Racism provides the often-neglected sociopolitical contexts of civility and civil racism that produce dominant readings of the Los Angeles Crisis; the ensuing chapters not only detail the fictional, filmic, and journalistic narratives of the crisis, but also delineate the ways in which artists and writers of color offer expanded notions of the civil through representations of the urban violence. *Civil Racism* brings together a range of texts from various media to explore the legacy of the 1992 Crisis in contemporary U.S. culture: plays, novels, visual art, photographs, and films by Asian Americans, African Americans, and Latinas/os. Examining the literature and art created in response to the crisis illuminates the aesthetics and politics of the post–civil rights era.

In the theoretical contexts of multiracial feminism and comparative racialization, the three-dimensional racial pyramid and its intersectional analytics manifest my approach to the texts and the organization of this book. In the first part, the perspectives of a single racial group anchor each of my readings in the first three chapters. However, as my analysis in each chapter makes clear, while one racial group's experiences may launch the inquiry and frame my discussion of the text in relation to the crisis and interracial violence, the intercategorical complexity of Asians, Blacks, Latinas/os, and Whites through the crisis and its aftermath produce racial differentiation that depends on the multiple racializations of these ostensibly distinct identity formations. In the second part, the artists themselves self-consciously perform the work and methodology of intersectionality in their innovative dramatic and novelistic structures. Their large casts of characters and multiple narratives encourage the reader to self-reflexively engage in dismantling and reconstructing identities; their works parallel the connection between character and narrative structure to the dynamic interaction between individuals and institutions.

In Part I, I analyze civil racism in its more specific manifestations: the promotion of racial civility in societal institutions such as the family, the school, and the neighborhood. Chapter 1, "Model Family Values and Sentimentalizing the Crisis," considers a major institution that has been deemed the foundation of and crucial to the transmission of civility: the family. The so-called decline of family values emerged as a dominant explanation for the 1992 Crisis; single-parent households, disrespectful children, and parental irresponsibility were blamed for the civil disorder. In contrast, mainstream media and conservative pundits celebrated the "traditional" Asian American family as the primary reason for Asian Americans' socioeconomic success. In the culture wars of the 1980s and the battle over family values in the 1990s, Asian Americans appeared to fulfill the central ideology of American culture: the American Dream in all its upwardly-mobile, neoliberal, and pro-family permutations. In analyzing two documentaries directed by Dai Sil Kim-Gibson, *Sa-I-Gu: From Korean Women's Perspectives* (1993) and *Wet Sand: Voices from L.A. Ten Years Later* (2003), I scrutinize the family narrative as it shapes constructions of Korean Americans and positions them relative to other racial groups. I place the vexed notion of family within the larger historical context of the 1992 presidential race and the nascent post–cold war era in which the Asian American family became the racialized repository for, and exemplar of, triumphalist American values. Finally, I argue that the sentimental basis of the documentary form—the sympathy evoked for the victims' narratives read as a political act—masks the form's potential for redrawing familial ties in more expansive, cross-racial, and relational networks of alliance that are necessary to develop a multiracial, comparative analysis of the 1992 L.A. Crisis and its aftermath.

In Chapter 2, I question the media and racial formations in the so-called civility crisis of the 1990s, which treated the 1992 violence as an exemplar of growing incivility in the United States. This chapter, "In/Civility, with Colorblindness and Equal Treatment for All," considers civil racism in terms of proscriptions of civility in our schools and political discourse. I examine Paul Beatty's 1996 satiric novel *The White Boy Shuffle*, which follows the picaresque, coming-of-age journey of Gunnar Kaufman, an internationally famous poet, nationally recruited college basketball player, and immensely popular Black leader, who preaches mass suicide for African Americans as the greatest protest in history against racial inequality. While civility has been traditionally defined as the civic virtues, community-building, and deliberative practices of good citizens, the novel exposes how discourses of civility—redefined as politeness and respect for authority—increasingly stand for the strengthening of the racially repressive status quo. Beatty's work identifies the emergence of civil racism in the U.S. public educational system through the absorption of civility into the ideal of meritocracy: those deemed meritorious are those with the most civic virtue. Civility operates in a similar logic to merit, in which some people are considered meritorious despite their unmeritorious acts. The novel registers the transformation of struggles for equality during the modern civil rights movement into struggles over civility in the post–civil rights era.

Chapter 3, "The Territorialization of Civility, the Spatialization of Revenge," examines the spatialization of civility in the segregated neighborhoods of Los Angeles. In his novel *The Tattooed Soldier* (1998), Guatemalan American journalist and novelist Héctor Tobar refers to the 1992 Crisis as "days of revenge," a controversial naming of the violence. His novel explores how punishment, and its hidden motive of vengeance, shapes racial civility by organizing memories and resentments into actionable claims and injuries. Tobar negotiates the complex histories of different Spanish-speaking populations in Los Angeles and challenges the perceived homogeneity of the Latina/o community by documenting the invisible population of homeless Latina/o immigrants and their gendered, racial, and class perspectives on the 1992 Crisis. In analyzing Tobar's fiction, essays, and journalism, I discuss the relationship between place and belonging, articulated most prominently in humanist geography. People of color are continually perceived as being out of place and not belonging to mainstream society or the U.S. nation-state. Latinas/os, stereotyped as illegal aliens, criminals, and indigents, have a uniquely troubled relationship to place. Racial civility in this case perpetuates the criminalization of immigrants and their positioning in opposition to the citizenry, naturalizing their exclusion and expulsion from the American imagined community.

In Part II, I look at two texts that adopt a multiracial perspective and contest manifestations of civil racism in their appropriations of media styles and forms in order to articulate coalitional notions of identity. Chapter 4, "At the End of Tragedy," addresses the ways in which critics and journalists dramatize the violent events, losses, and traumas as tragedies and how this tragic mode shapes the political discourse in the aftermath of the crisis. Amid the tense atmosphere of fear and mistrust that prevailed after the crisis, African American actor and playwright Anna Deavere Smith interviewed hundreds of people about their responses to the violence. Developing these conversations into more than twenty monologues to create her widely celebrated play, *Twilight: Los Angeles, 1992,* Smith incorporated a wide spectrum of participants and their often-conflicting perspectives on the crisis. I examine Smith's unique artistic methodology of interviewing people about their reactions to the 1992 violence, and performing excerpts from their conversations onstage, sometimes in front of the very people who had been interviewed. I argue that, reading *Twilight* through what I call a "tragic framework," Smith models a relationality in her ethical commitment to transracial dialogue—a paradigm of interracial relations after the crisis.[48] While Smith's plays incorporate a wide-ranging array of perspectives and people, this dramatic methodology is not just superficially inclusive but also transformative in how her performances critically expose audience assumptions of the production and impact of the news media and public opinion in relation to such polarizing issues raised by the Los Angeles Crisis: interracial violence, civic participation, and democratic principles. In doing so, Smith deploys the range of recent feminist methodologies in the documentary dramas she has lately called "testimony theatre": standpoint epistemology, intersectionality, hybridity, world-traveling, and differential consciousness. Antiracist feminists have identified this interracial tragedy as both the failure of and the need for intersectional alliances and multiracial feminism; Smith's artistic methodology and performance art are, I contend, the theatricalization and innovation of feminist practices of relation.

Chapter 5, "The Media Spectacle of Racial Disaster," addresses the specific role the media plays in constructing race and determining the parameters of "civil" racial discourse. While scholars analyze dominant media depictions in terms of content, images, and narratives, most do not discuss the form or the technology of the media that drives the dissemination of news and information or how live broadcasts shape viewers' experiences. Media conventions and technological innovations shape the very terrain upon which audiences comprehend issues of race and racism. Karen Tei Yamashita's groundbreaking novel, *Tropic of Orange* (1997), uses seven protagonists and their innovative appropriation of media forms, styles, and genres to critique the media's construction of race. With characters who have various levels of access to mainstream media and serve as alternative sources of information, the novel focuses on acts of resistance by the politically disadvantaged—undocumented immigrants, the unemployed, the homeless. *Tropic of Orange* is a parable of the everyday acts of the oppressed, illegal, invisible, forgotten, and powerless that nonetheless influence and shape the world. Contesting the racist practices of racial civility, Yamashita depicts the imaginative and often subtle ways in which the less powerful resist the demands of the more powerful. In the novel, resistance is largely expressed in terms of media consumption. The characters do not passively accept media representations; rather, they appropriate and modify media styles and logics around technologies of the live in their unusual lives and unique worldviews.

Examining the causes of the L.A. Crisis exposes the material inequalities faced historically and in the present day. These spectacular displays of the force and violence underlying civility and peace must be explained away in order to justify these persistent, unequal conditions. Although viewers respond with senses of outrage, violation, and betrayal, these reactions are directed to myriad and conflicting frustrations: police brutality or lack of policing, more social welfare or less, more political power or less to people of color. These acts of violence reveal different mind-sets that expose the differential access and opportunity within such commonly accepted narratives as the American dream, its meritocracy, and "liberty and justice for all." In the epilogue, "Lives That Matter," I consider how what I call the counterdiscourse of civility operates in struggles against civil racism in relation to the terms set forth in the book. The founders created the #BlackLivesMatter Movement in response to the police and vigilante killings of Black men, women, and children. In response to the appropriation and distortion of their goals for #BlackLivesMatter, the founders interrogate the *family of feeling, biologization of civility,* and *racial equilibrium* that have been used to manage racist hierarchies and interracial conflicts, and evaluate how *performances of proximity* and *transracial coalitions* might function.

The ethics of comparative racialization also organizes these works.[49] In the case of Korean Americans who lost too much in the crisis, one of the most compelling frameworks available to racialized subjects is that these deserving people with demonstrated civic virtues and family values should have been protected by the state. The documentary films *Sa-I-Gu* and *Wet Sand* move from ethical demands of care and protections from the state for model minority subjects. However, to expect care and consideration from the state, to assimilate into its racist, sexist, exploitive structures, is to uphold and reinstantiate the state's authority and superordinate power. *The White Boy Shuffle*, through its badman antihero, posits that the only ethical position is to resist assimilation into any politics at all, even one that the hero personally endorses. In chapter 3, Tobar fictionalizes the alienation felt by undocumented immigrants of color, expelled and criminalized because of their unofficial status, that justice is extralegal for surplus populations and also never fully realizable given the extraterritorial crimes of the U.S. nation, in this case supporting the dictatorship and prolonging the civil war in Guatemala. The second half of the book evaluates the transracial possibilities of these assertions and opportunities. Smith's interviews and performances of her interview subjects in *Twilight* raise questions of ethical practices and interpersonal relations: Smith qualifies her poststructuralist acting methodology of walking in "the speech of another" (*Fires*, xxvii) by insisting and performing the radical inassimilability of this Other, this ethical difference and contiguity. In *Tropic of Orange*, Yamashita exhorts readers to scrutinize the methods of these cross-racial intimacies and relationalities and how they affect the transformative potential of a counterdiscourse of civility.

The critiques in *Civil Racism* developed from reading radical discourses about race and subordination in which scholars turned to art and literature not only to frame their studies, but also to identify the persistent dreams that collectively imagine new practices of equality, justice, and freedom. I was struck, for example, by political scientists, who, in analyzing the 1989 Tiananmen Square protests, posited the insufficient development of the institutions of civil society—including poetry journals alongside small businesses and "think tanks"—as contributing to Chinese activists' failure to achieve democratic reforms. These public spheres and political communities in which civilities and democratic practices are negotiated stand at the very intersection of art and politics. As Lisa Lowe and David Lloyd argue in their introduction to *The Politics of Culture in the Shadow of Capital*, "'culture' obtains a 'political' force when a cultural formation comes into contradiction with economic or political logics that try to refunction it for exploitation or domination. . . . The politics of culture exists as the very survival of alternative practices to those of globalized capital, the very survival of alternatives to the incessant violence of the new transnational order with its reconstituted patriarchies and racisms" (1, 26). The institutions and organizations built around an art and literature that revives and renews civil society develops out of the "arts of resistance" to domination that James C. Scott has outlined in "the development of dissident sub-cultures": "millennial religions, slave 'hush-arbors,' folk religion, myths of social banditry and class heroes, world-upside-down imagery, myths of the 'good' king" (198). In a little-acknowledged passage in Omi and Winant's influential treatise on racial formations, they cite the boundless creativity of peoples persisting under the most oppressive of circumstances: the "music, religion, African traditions and family ties" that constituted a "free" Black identity, Native American religious ceremonies, and *corridos* (Omi and Winant, 80). Cultural historian Robin D. G. Kelley's remarkable work *Freedom Dreams* identifies "the alternative visions and dreams that inspire new generations to continue to struggle for change" (ix), using the artistry and politics of such influential musicians as Thelonious Monk and George Clinton. Kelley argues for evaluating radical movements in terms of the "desires, hopes, and intentions of the people who fought for change," focusing on the "merits or power of the visions themselves" rather than assessing their success in reaching their goals (ix).

Literature and the arts sustain oppositional thought through the darkest, most repressive moments of the post–civil rights era. Each of the writers and artists included in this study seeks to create or rehabilitate political communities, to articulate a conception of civil society and state that is more receptive to the realization of equality and justice. These "alternative visions and dreams" are intended to inspire future generations to new forms of struggle. In their innovative appropriations and parodies of legal and media narratives from the entire range of the political spectrum—whether radical or reactionary, liberal or conservative—these writers, playwrights, and filmmakers challenge popular representations of the unprecedented interracial violence in their attempts to imagine new ways of achieving a more just world built from the ashes of Los Angeles.

Part I: Racial Civility

1 MODEL FAMILY VALUES AND SENTIMENTALIZING THE CRISIS

IN LOVING MEMORY
EDWARD SONG LEE
WE GRIEVE TOGETHER AS
ONE FAMILY FOR THE
LOSS OF OUR BRAVE SON

—*Sa-I-Gu*

THE 1993 DOCUMENTARY FILM *Sa-I-Gu: From Korean Women's Perspectives* tells of a mother's love for and loss of her son, one family's horrible tragedy. In centering this archetype of maternal love, Dai Sil Kim-Gibson, writer, director, and coproducer of *Sa-I-Gu*, emphasizes the universality of one mother's grief beyond the particularities of race, ethnicity, and circumstance, beyond Jung Hui Lee's experiences as a Korean immigrant woman living, working, and raising a family in the Los Angeles area, and even beyond *sa-i-gu* itself—the 1992 Los Angeles Crisis.[1] Of the 4,500 businesses damaged or destroyed and $1 billion in property lost, half were owned and operated by one ethnic minority, Korean Americans, who, at the time, comprised barely 0.8 percent of the population in L.A. County and merely 24,000 people in the densely populated Koreatown in Los Angeles (Abelmann and Lie, 11).[2] Documenting reactions merely weeks after the violence, *Sa-I-Gu* interviews Korean immigrant women who painfully recount the loss of their life savings, livelihoods, and loved ones during the 1992 L.A. Crisis.

   Sa-I-Gu perpetuates this sentimentality around what I term "model family values" as it explores the familial bonds between mother and son against the larger backdrop of interracial relations and violence in Los Angeles. Though Kim-Gibson focuses somewhat less on the Korean American family in her 2004 documentary *Wet Sand: Voices from L.A. Ten Years Later,* she again turns to the Lee family's loss of their oldest son in this later film's opening sequence as a frame for understanding the pain of the riots. Edward "Eddie" Lee's death and the family and community that grieve him anchor both of Kim-Gibson's documentaries on the L.A. Crisis. While recording the anger against the police and the local, state, and federal institutions that failed to protect the lives and property of Korean immigrants and their families, *Sa-I-Gu* juxtaposes the familial bond between parent and child and the relationship between the state and its subjects. Though the symbolic counterparts of parent and state both are expected to protect child and subject, in *Sa-I-Gu,* the failure of both are conflated in Lee's death and the tremendous losses experienced by the Korean American community, as one young man's death represents the injuries sustained by an entire ethnic group. Min Song argues that these women were "not cared for" in terms of the "physical security usually expected from a benevolent state" and "as if what they had suffered and were suffering did not register as anything that deserved to be mourned" by the U.S. nation (134). Kim-Gibson contrasts Lee's overwhelming grief and guilt for her son's death to the state's perceived abandonment, what Lee refers to as the "sacrifice" of Korean American small business owners and their property in South Central L.A. and Koreatown in order to prioritize police and National Guard protection of Whiter, richer, and more politically powerful enclaves such as Beverly Hills and the Bunker Hill financial district of downtown L.A. Elaine H. Kim, one of the producers of *Sa-I-Gu,* asserts that many Korean immigrants firmly believed in a U.S. "democratic system that protects its people from violence"—marking the ostensible difference between the United States and South Korea for them—but this conviction was betrayed by the state's response to the L.A. Crisis: "The familiar concept of privilege for the rich and powerful would have been easy for the Korean immigrant to grasp if only those exhortations about democracy and equality had not obfuscated the picture" (Elaine H. Kim, 219).[3]

The magnitude of the L.A. Crisis, and arguably the violence itself, was caused by the state's failure to protect its subjects, thus modifying the social contract between them, and this chapter evaluates the attempts to exhort national audiences to both empathy and action through asserting what I identify as a *multiracial family of feeling*. This chapter adds to the considerable scholarship on the L.A. Crisis and the relationships between African Americans and Korean Americans during and after the crisis by exploring how a neoliberal, heterosexual, nationalist, and racialized family-values model can magnify the problems caused by the state's inaction. I begin by highlighting the role of the family in the racial triangulation that dominated and fueled hostilities in the death of Latasha Harlins and the trial of Soon Ja Du, a Korean immigrant woman who fatally shot Harlins in late March 1991, and which made the nightly news and national headlines alongside the footage of Rodney King's beating. I then assess the efforts of *Sa-I-Gu* and *Wet Sand* to overcome Black–Korean racial divisions through the construction of a shared, multiracial, filial connection among U.S. citizen-viewers, and suggest alternative means of building solidarity around Black and Asian losses.

Sa-I-Gu: From Korean Women's Perspectives clearly counters the reductive characterization of Du and of all Koreans in the limited terms of the Americanness, virtue, and humanity of the Korean American family. The film deploys the notion of family in ways that subordinate gender to race and class. Although research on women of color and their families expose the subordination of gender to other identity formations, *Sa-I-Gu* is unusual for its interracial vision, however brief, that rewrites and expands the film and exposes its audience's inability to imagine such interracial affective ties. I argue that the sentimental basis of the documentary form—the sympathy evoked for the victims' narratives and read as a political act—and the construction of "the family of feeling" are vexed strategies for redrawing familial ties into more expansive cross-racial alliances crucial to a multiracial analysis of the 1992 L.A. Crisis and its aftermath.

Model Family Values

Decades before Rodney King was pulled over by LAPD officers in 1991, Korean Americans became a nationally recognized racial and ethnic minority as media and government attention focused on conflicts between Korean storeowners and Black customers in urban centers. These conflicts were depicted in widely discussed films such as Spike Lee's *Do the Right Thing* (1989) and Albert and Allen Hughes's *Menace II Society* (1993), and songs such as "Black Korea" by rap artist Ice Cube. By April 29, 1992, the "Black-Korean conflict" had become "part of American urban mythology" (Claire Jean Kim, *Bitter Fruit*, 1). From 1990 to 1991, just two years before the L.A. Crisis, a coalition of African American, Haitian, and Caribbean activists held the longest-running boycott and picket line against a Korean-owned store in the Flatbush section of Brooklyn. Other protests, boycotts, and conflicts in New York City, Chicago, and Los Angeles had made local and national news since the 1970s. The most infamous of these events was the March 16, 1991, shooting death of a Black teenage girl, Latasha Harlins, by Korean storeowner Soon Ja Du in South Central Los Angeles. Media and pundits used Harlins's death to exemplify the Black–Korean conflict that plagued inner cities across the United States, and Du's trial seven months later and the White trial judge's reduction of Du's sentence to time already served, community service, probation, restitution, and a suspended sentence—an unusually light punishment for the charge of voluntary manslaughter—sparked national outcry and protests. Scholars have performed valuable intersectional analyses of this legal case, the most explosive one to lead up to the trial of Rodney King's police assailants.[4] Showing how race, class, gender, and sexuality all matter, these scholars have usefully identified the family dynamics of both Harlins and Du. Building on these analyses, the discourse of the family, I argue, *makes* these complex identity formations visible, thus motivating the controversial sentencing.

Using *The People v. Soon Ja Du,* I discuss how the different permutations of good insider/bad outsider (Black/Asian) and good outsider/bad insider (Asian/Black) obscures White privilege by pitting the two racialized groups against each other.[5] This dynamic also importantly modifies the discourse of family; parent-child relationships are gendered and racialized by the state in order to justify certain kinds of material redistribution and criminal justice. For instance, because Judge Joyce Karlin refused to believe Latasha Harlins was a worthy citizen and dutiful daughter, instead believing her to be a masculinized criminal who "used her fists as weapons" (quoted in Gotanda, 248), the judge was able to construct Du as a victim, an honorable and self-sacrificing mother, a hardworking Asian woman who would not have killed Harlins unless provoked and who would not be a future threat to society. Du, in Karlin's reasoning, thereby deserved a lesser, suspended sentence with no immediate jail time. The judge predicated protection and redress through the law—the benefits of good citizenship—on performance of family duties. The performance of appropriate gender roles in the family merits legal protection. This model minority family narrative shapes constructions of Asian Americans and positions these groups as superior and inferior to other racial groups. A controversial figure, Soon Ja Du was complexly constructed by her defense lawyers, the presiding judge, and the media. I examine how she is rendered invisible by these state narratives except in terms of her family, terms that contravene both the American myth of individualism as well as more radical feminist notions of a collective or networked identity.

Despite their local and national notoriety in mainstream media and political discourses, Korean Americans and other Asian Americans were rarely, if at all, represented on camera to comment on these events, nor were their perspectives and personal histories in the communities aired, except in ethnic, often Asian-language news media outlets such as the Los Angeles–based bilingual newspaper *Korea Times* and Radio Korea.[6] *Sa-I-Gu's* director and producer, Kim-Gibson, and the other producers, Christine Choy and Elaine Kim, envisioned the film as a media document that would humanize and represent Korean immigrants who had been dehumanized and silenced by the pervasive media stereotyping in news coverage of the L.A. Crisis. In one of the individual interviews with the three producers that prefaces the documentary, Kim identifies three gendered and racialized representations that emerged again and again in the 1992 media coverage: (1) a Korean storeowner shooting a young Black girl in the back of the head and killing her; (2) Korean male merchants with shotguns perched on the roofs of their businesses, "caring about property, not human life"; and (3) Korean female storeowners who cried, anguished, in front of burned-out buildings but were, in Kim's words, "hysterical" and "inarticulate," their emotions and words often untranslated in news reportage (Kim-Gibson, *Sa-I-Gu*).[7]

From the footage and images on the nightly news, Soon Ja Du emerges as a provocative amalgam of these negative stereotypes of Korean immigrants: the heartless capitalist, gun-toting vigilante, and incomprehensible victim. In many of the later images and much of the broadcast footage of the trial in November 1991, Du is a silent figure and passive participant. National mainstream coverage of the tragedy primarily showed an edited version of the security tape, the few seconds in which Harlins turns to walk toward the door and Du fires the gun, killing Harlins. The edited footage excluded their earlier argument and physical struggle that began when Du grabbed at Harlins's backpack and then pulled on her jacket. During the trial, Du would explain that she thought Harlins was shoplifting by putting other items in her backpack besides the bottle of orange juice.[8] But this footage, at either length, would prove to elicit deeply conflicting interpretations. Journalist Helen Zia writes of two federal mediators, one Korean American, one African American, having opposite assessments of the same tape: "'I watched the video and saw a frightened Korean American woman whose gun went off accidentally. My black colleague watched and said, 'That settles that. She shot the girl in cold blood'" (quoted in Zia, 176).[9]

The first images of Du after being arrested showed that her face was visibly bruised from four punches Harlins had landed before the shooting. That Du's defense would successfully portray Du as the victim, despite her role in both escalating the violence and in Harlins's death, evidences the powerful intersection of race and gender and the material effects of their interlocking oppressions. Brenda Stevenson argues that Du's defense attorney, Charles Lloyd, a prominent Black lawyer, transformed Harlins, a junior-high honor student with no gang affiliations, into a shoplifter at best, a violent "gangbanger" at worst. Not only did Du's defense play on Whites' historic fears of the Black criminal, but her attorney and the judge also masculinized Harlins by identifying her as the dominant aggressor: "She punched awfully hard, possibly as tough as any guy at the same age" (quoted in Stevenson, "Latasha Harlins," 168). Building on this gendered reading of Harlins's strength, Stevenson explains how racial groups are gendered through their perceived active or passive characteristics: Asian Americans, read as model minorities and victims, are feminized in relation to how African Americans, read in terms of "brute force, violence and aggression," are masculinized (Stevenson, 169). In this case, Asian Americans such as Du, her husband, and son are the innocently passive, feminized victims to African Americans such as Harlins who are the criminally active, masculinized perpetrators. Such gendered transgressions are racially marked as criminal and such racial coding is marked with gender instability: Harlins didn't know her *place* as a young Black woman within these class, gender, and racial hierarchies.

Harlins's place in this hierarchy of race and gender is crucial to the outcome of the trial. In what she terms a "case study of multicultural female violence on the urban frontier," Stevenson makes visible the gendering of race in the trial and its aftermath. In a close reading of trial judge Joyce Karlin's sentencing colloquy of Du—her explanation for Du's unusually light sentence—Neil Gotanda identifies the "racial stratification" that positions the three women differently in relation to the law and the state, a complex hierarchy of relationships among the White judge, Korean immigrant defendant, and Black victim. Although Harlins's death would appear to make her the victim and Du the perpetrator, Karlin's sentencing colloquy demonstrates that legal categories are fluid and even interchangeable. Karlin reads Du as the victim and sentences her accordingly, arguing that since Du does not pose a danger to society now, she is not a criminal, because Harlins forced Du to become one: "She led a crime-free life until Latasha Harlins walked into her store and there is no reason to believe that this is the beginning of a life of crime for Mrs. Du" (quoted in Gotanda, 250).[10] Despite the arguments of the district attorney, Karlin's colloquy repeatedly refers to the "terror" and "fear" Du experienced, but not the similar emotions Harlins might have faced: "The district attorney would have this court ignore the very real terror experienced by the Du family before the shooting, and the fear Mrs. Du experienced as she worked by herself the day of the shooting. But there are things I cannot ignore. I cannot ignore the reason Mrs. Du was working at the store that day. She went to work that Saturday to save her son from having to work" (quoted in Gotanda, 248). Karlin endorses the Dus as decent, hardworking people, and she perceives Soon Ja Du as a self-sacrificing mother who worked in unsafe conditions in order to protect her son from such an environment.

As Stevenson and Gotanda both note, Karlin valorizes the Asian American family through her sympathy for Du and vilification of Harlins. As a good parent who works hard for her family despite adversity and fear, Du is contrasted to Harlins, who is characterized as the belligerent, criminally inclined youth, and this negative portrayal implicates the family who raised Harlins as also guilty of wrongdoing.[11] Karlin's sentencing colloquy indirectly reveals her perceptions of Asian American and Black families: unlike Du's admirable reasons for working in the store that day, Harlins's remarkably stable family life, despite the early death of her mother and desertion by her father, made no difference in the outcome of the trial or its subsequent appeal.[12] Despite Harlins's earlier academic achievement, active church membership, and work at a local youth center, Harlins's implied, unproven connection to gangs—a criminal "family" that replaces legitimate ones—trumped her positive role in her family and community.[13]

The family is a crucial foundational unit to educational and economic systems. Expected to nurture future generations, the family fosters and reinforces pro-social behaviors and civic virtues that will sustain the state in perpetuity.[14] Discourses of good parents and good children abound in cultural narratives that manifest expectations and assumptions about who creates good and bad families and which families create good and bad civil subjects of parents and children. Competing public discourses of family and its gender roles are used to mete out racial rewards and punishments—inclusion and exclusion from state protections, respectively. For both the political right and left, the family is an inordinately rich and complex "interpretive framework," as noted by Patricia Hill Collins, precisely because the "power of this traditional family ideal lies in its dual function as an ideological construction and as a fundamental principle of social organization" (Collins, "It's All in the Family," 63).[15] As an example of this dual function, during the cold war, the nuclear, heteropatriarchal, largely Protestant family became an expedient, if reductive and inaccurate, means for explaining the difference between a capitalist state and a communist one in accessible, affective terms for the U.S. public (May, 9). This political paradigm still holds sway. In the post–civil rights era of increasing privatization and structural discrimination, the family in its multiple manifestations is forced to replace the government as an individual's social safety net as best it can; therefore, families from the poor and working class, increasingly Black and Brown, are deemed pathologically, even criminally, inferior for failing to provide adequate care for and supervision of their family members, for not "responsibly" shouldering such duties formerly shared with or provided by state institutions and public programs—all this while U.S. workers were also facing declines in real wages and salaries since the 1970s. In the aftermath of the L.A. Crisis, as in the wake of urban rebellions of the 1960s, social conservatives and liberals cited the breakdown of the Black family in the inner city as the factor that unleashed the violence and destruction.[16] The dysfunctional Black family had been a well-rehearsed reason given for lower Black educational achievement and upward mobility since sociologist and Assistant Secretary of Labor Daniel Patrick Moynihan's 1965 study, *The Negro Family: The Case for National Action,* more commonly known as the Moynihan Report, the policy standard that holds Black mothers and single-female-headed households responsible for generations of maladjusted children. Moreover, it would be upon the capitalist foundation of Christian, heteronormative, two-parent households that the "clash of civilizations" in the post–cold war era would be waged and ostensibly won (Huntington).[17] Thus, in the broader context of the late twentieth century and in the specific case of the Los Angeles Crisis, the deceptively simple concept of the family does a tremendous amount of complex political work.

These discourses around family have had a disproportionate impact on nonwhite minorities and public policies intended to redress structural and historical discrimination. One such discourse of family stems from the "model minority thesis" that has been applied to Asian Americans as an explanation for their higher household incomes, educational achievements, and rates of social and residential "integration" than those of Blacks and Latinas/os. Mainstream media and conservative pundits have grounded the model minority thesis in the ostensible superiority of the Asian American family, the values it upholds and instills in the next generation, viewed as the primary reason for Asian Americans' socioeconomic successes. In the culture wars of the 1980s and the battle over family values in the 1990s, Asian Americans appeared to fulfill the central ideology of U.S. national life and culture: the American Dream in all its upwardly mobile, neoliberal, and pro-family permutations.

This focus on the Black–Korean conflict elides its mediation by the criminal justice system: Karlin's own intervention as an agent of the state and her very real exercise of power by deeming one group superior and another inferior. In the case of *The People v. Soon Ja Du,* Karlin's implicit use of the model minority myth that mitigates Du's behavior and crime denies Harlins's family what they see as justice and adequate redress for the tragic death of a family member. This invisible exercise of power pits less powerful groups against each other. The model minority discourse of Asian American success justifies neoliberal state policies and capitalist exploitation by setting Asian Americans against other people of color.[18] Just three months after Harlins's death, one writer for the conservative journal *National Review* expounds how Asian Americans, "The Silent Minority" with their varied histories of immigration and core values, are an untapped, promising demographic for the Republican Party and its conservative political agenda: entrepreneurs, anticommunists, pro-defense, and most important "almost all of them boast strong families, a not uncoincidental *[sic]* factor in their economic success" (McGurn, 19). Asian Americans, as a racial minority, and their ostensible social and economic success in the United States have become the standards by which other racial groups' claims of disenfranchisement and discrimination have been invalidated (19).[19] The hard work involved in their relative academic achievement, above-average family income, and strong patriotism makes Asian Americans desirable and compelling examples of the American Dream sans big government: their success despite their ostensible rejection of public policies that are geared toward developing a well-funded and comprehensive social safety net (20).

In this complex interracial negotiation, there are multiple value systems that operate along axes of race, class, gender, and sexuality. Claire Jean Kim posits the concept of racial triangulation that usefully disaggregates the complex workings of race, class, and citizenship among Asians, Blacks, and Whites (Kim, "The Racial Triangulation"). Kim identifies ways in which Asians and Blacks are placed in contention with one another in terms of "relative valorization" and "civic ostracism." The former operates in terms of superior and inferior categorizations—the good and bad minorities—based on the perception of morals, values, or behaviors more closely aligned with ostensibly White ones.[20] Thus, Asian Americans, perceived to be the model minority, will be positioned above African Americans. However, in terms of civic ostracism, Blacks will be placed above Asian Americans along the axis of insider/outsider. Asian Americans, imagined as perpetual foreigners, inassimilable aliens, or eternal sojourners, lack historic inclusion in the U.S. national imaginary in the way African Americans have already been incorporated.

Further complicated by the structural power and privilege of Whiteness, an analysis of racial triangulation first and foremost makes Whiteness visible as nonwhites are favored or repudiated. A minority group's perceived proximity to Whiteness in relation to another group shows the ways in which perceptions of superiority and inferiority of one's

race, gender, class, and/or sexuality might lead to derision or conde-
scension in the criminal justice system and in redistributive public
policy. Kim's conceptualization of interracial relations is important
in the triangulation of Du, Harlins, and Karlin. Clearly, in this case,
Karlin found relative valorization most persuasive. Du, with her good
immigrant, or family, values, is valorized relatively to Harlins, and, as
Stevenson has argued, Karlin was able to identify with Du more so
than with Harlins (Stevenson, "Latasha Harlins," 169).

It is important to mention another, more infamous context that
heavily influenced the public perception of Harlins's death. Harlins's
death was compared to Rodney King's beating; Harlins was fatally
shot just thirteen days after King was beaten on March 3, 1991. While
King's beating by the LAPD was videotaped by George Holliday, a
resident of a nearby apartment building, Harlins's death was caught
on a grainy black-and-white security camera from the Du's liquor
store. Local and national media networks played the footage of King
and Harlins together in news cycles for weeks following the incidents
and in coverage of the trials themselves, sustaining the public outcry
against the LAPD for the officers' excessive force in apprehending
King and against the Korean American community for Du's shooting
of Harlins. In the juxtaposition of the two videotapes in media broadcasts, Korean Americans are, like the police officers, the perpetrators
of anti-Black violence, and later, such violence appears sanctioned by
the state in terms of Du's reduced and suspended sentence. But con-
flating the LAPD with Korean storeowners masks the power the police
wield as an enforcement and regulatory function of the state. Because
both victims were African American—although their assailants were
Whites and a Korean, police officers and a storeowner, respectively—
the circumstances of the violence against Harlins and King, as well as
their criminalization, signaled to the U.S. public a kind of collusion
between Whites and Asians, against Blacks. In explaining this interracial formation, cultural critic David Palumbo-Liu posits the concept
"racial ventriloquism," in which Korean Americans function as White
surrogates: "Korean-Americans were represented as the frontline forces
of the white bourgeoisie. Not only were they successful even under
the most oppressive circumstances, they were not afraid to arm themselves against blacks and Latinos to protect what is not only their
territory, but also the buffer-zone between the core of a multiethnic

ghetto, and white middle-class America" (Palumbo-Liu, 371). For Asian Americans to be successful despite such difficulty, Palumbo-Liu argues that White supremacy established through U.S. capitalism can now appear race-neutral, what I would call a "racial laundering" of social and capitalist hierarchies—the process by which unequal outcomes become deracialized and promoted as the result of colorblind practices: "It involves a racially different group, and therefore vindicates the 'neutrality' of American capitalism. The supremacy, the ultimate 'soundness,' of the capitalist economics that have disproportionately favored whites over racial and ethnic minorities now seems colorblind because 'yellows' have found it to work in their favor, too" (375). Korean Americans, and Asian Americans by extension, are posited as the front guard of racial and class warfare in the service of White supremacy.

In the context of historic Black–White struggles and the more recent Black–Korean conflicts, the juxtaposition of Harlins and King simplified the unevenness of racial classifications in the merging of Korean Americans with the criminal justice system: lumping a racial minority, predominantly immigrant, with the institutional power of the police and the courts, long the preserve of White dominance. Asian Americans would appear to benefit through a form of "honorary Whiteness," a proximity to power as a favored racial minority (375). For Danny Park, a community activist for the Korean Immigrant Workers Advocates, who was interviewed in *Wet Sand,* placing the two events and victims "side-by-side" in the media gave the impression that the "Korean community [was] part of the problem." And despite the tenor of most mainstream media coverage, not all Korean Americans approved of Du's "tragic act" (Zia, 179); some Korean storeowners criticized her actions and deplored the sentence, but this debate within the Korean American community went largely unnoticed by other racial groups, even other Asian Americans.

An interpretation of Du's trial also shows a further analytic dimension of racial triangulation that extends Kim's own framework, that of good or bad citizenship, an assessment of racialized subjects not just as moral creatures but also as civic agents. In addition to light-skin privilege, Karlin was able to identify with Du because of gender and class sympathies. Thus, the relative valorization of Kim's racial formulation is actually dependent on gender and class distinctions: namely, Du and Karlin shared similar notions of "appropriate gender behavior for females" (Stevenson, 169) and the same upwardly mobile, middle-class aspirations from which Harlins was excluded during the trial. Du's defense and Karlin's colloquy devalued Harlins for what they argue was her masculinized, criminal, and lower-class behavior. Harlins's criminalization as a Black teenager in South Central Los Angeles and her devaluation as victim because of the light sentence Du received also speak to a different kind of civic ostracism that Blacks face as criminals instead of citizens; in other words, the insider/outsider, citizen/immigrant, or American/foreigner classifications that disadvantage Asian Americans operate alongside the dichotomy of citizen/criminal that is leveraged against African Americans. The citizen/criminal binary merge the superior/inferior and insider/outsider model of racial triangulation: criminals are outside good society, generally imprisoned and physically quarantined, in contrast to citizens who constitute good society and move freely within it. While race appears to be the most crucial classification in the triangulation observed in this case—a microcosm of U.S. interracial relations—race becomes visible through the aggregate discourses of gender, class, and citizenship, just as these discourses obfuscate race itself.

I return to the originary interpretation of the family that was crucial to Karlin's colloquy. Such provocative discourses of gendered citizenship and racial triangulation are only visible through the institution of the heteropatriarchal family, and most important, as the prepolitical, private cornerstone of civil society. In Karlin's colloquy, the judge provocatively repeats her inability "to ignore" certain circumstances of the case: "I cannot ignore the reason Mrs. Du was working at the store that day. She went to work that Saturday to save her son from having to work" (quoted in Gotanda, 249). Karlin conspicuously and performatively rewrites Du back into the narrative of U.S. economy and society, rescuing Du's character and intentions from erasure by the prosecutor, the media, and Harlins's family and supporters. But Karlin recuperates Du back into the dominant state narrative that maintains family as the primal source of civility and the cornerstone of U.S. capitalism as expressed through the figure of the small business entrepreneur whose work supports a family unit. Soon Ja Du is not only, in these terms, a conduit of capitalism, the petit bourgeoisie, but also a pillar of civil society and model of civic virtue. Karlin proposes a contradiction: Du is a good mother *and* her crime is genderless. Du is interchangeable with any member of her family who regularly worked in the store because the person fatally shooting Harlins just *happened* to be Du, not her son or her husband, who would have been more likely to be working behind the counter that day. Because anyone in Du's family could have conceivably acted in a similar deadly way to the putative threat Harlins represented, a reasonable person could therefore be inferred to act in this manner according to Karlin's logic. Harlins, cast as a (gender) transgressive criminal, recedes as a victim against Karlin's reframing of Du's genderless *and* gendered claims of self-defense and the protection of her family's private property. And, as critical race scholar Jody Armour posits, Karlin upholds Du's implicit claims of "negrophobia," in which reasonable racism is, once again, a legitimate legal defense for the exclusion, intimidation, disabling, or killing of African Americans—although now on both explicit and disavowed gendered terms.

In a meritocracy adjudicated by the criminal justice system, good behavior should be rewarded: in this case, Du's altruistic maternal impulses that saved her son not only from the dangers of working in the store but, by extension, also from standing trial as the possible defendant in Harlins's murder.[21] There are two things to be learned from this logic: (1) that altruistic motherhood is meritorious, and (2) this interchangeability of mother and son reinforces family relations as more important than the specific individuals involved in them. Moreover, the safety and security of the family business, the Empire Liquor store, is an extension of the safety and security of the family—the protection of the store is the defense of the family itself. Du, described as the small, slight wife and mother who would not usually be working in the store, *is* the private property that is being defended through Karlin's discourse of the family. The very body and person of Soon Ja Du is overdetermined in explosively competing discourses of capitalism, family values, and traditional liberal constructions of the family. Therefore, Karlin can believe that she is protecting the racially laundered family and not just White interests. By bringing the son into the space of the store, Karlin remade a public sphere into an extension of the family.

What emerges as model family values for Asian Americans is also the celebration of the unchecked exploitation of men, women, and children's labor within the family unit. While self-discipline and hard work support educational achievements and upward mobility, these values also develop better laborers who might be more willing to tolerate difficult working conditions for perhaps less pay. Later in this chapter,

I discuss the intense sentimentality that regards the family as the intentional privatized production of a capitalist unit. The perception that Asian Americans produce idealized families is such a powerful claim that even domestic violence is overlooked. A police officer at the scene after Harlins's death testifies that Harlins's punches rather than Billy Du's slapping his wife repeatedly caused the bruises on Soon Ja Du's face. Du's assault continues for such a prolonged period that the officer explains how he finally steps in to stop this violence and why he initially failed to intervene: they were "at first not so hard, gradually to very hard slaps until I had to stop him . . . because of the force he was using" (Ford). The documented domestic violence reveals the Dus as a less than model family, but Soon Ja Du's various sacrifices—working in place of her son, surviving her husband's abuse, protecting the family business—reestablishes these model family values. Erin Khuê Ninh memorably conceives of the Asian American family as a unit of U.S. capitalistic production that is especially renowned as a "cottage industry" that produces "good, capitalist subjects": model minority progeny who will become professionals such as doctors and lawyers. In this logic, Du, as well as other Asian American mothers, is valued for her ability to (re)produce good Asian American subjects in which gender is stripped from this means of production and simultaneously revalued as evidence of good motherhood (vii).

The Family of Feeling and the U.S. Nation

The family is tied to assessments of not only one's social value and legal identity but also one's basic humanity. To be a good family member is to be a good citizen, or a deserving member of the U.S. body politic, and a valued part of the U.S. nation. If only good family members and citizens can be imagined and pitied as victims who deserve justice and redress, then establishing this condition becomes an effective strategy toward attaining the full rewards of citizenship—the franchise as well as social and economic equality and protection of opportunities. Given such powerful discourses of family that construct the individual's worth and sympathy as a victim, I posit the multiracial "family of feeling," which is generated through a documentary film such as *Sa-I-Gu*. The "family of feeling" relies on a sentimental logic that, in amplifying affective ties and relationships, binds citizens to one another and to abstract institutions such as the nation. I examine

Sa-I-Gu's reliance on its audience's sympathetic feelings—that is, on sentimentality's objectives of individual self-refinement and affective realignment—to bind the film's Korean American subjects, their families, and losses to non-Korean viewers so that they can imagine the nation as an extended family of feeling. I evaluate *Sa-I-Gu*'s sentimental strategy and its efficacy in fostering interracial coalitions and transforming political institutions.

Sentimentality is a broad cultural expression spanning centuries, national traditions, and media forms. In American literature, it is often perceived to be an expression of "women's culture" in response to forces of industrialization and urbanization, a socialization of proper behaviors and emotions, and a literary tradition "whose chief characteristic is that it is written by, for, and about women" (Tompkins, 269). Another critic describes "the culture of sentiment" as "the tension between the pleasure of sympathy and the power of sympathy—between relations of sympathy and relations of power" (Samuels, 8). These relations of sympathy and power are most closely tied to oppressed groups: people with disabilities, the poor, women, and racial minorities. Another characteristic of sentimentality focuses on human suffering and the compassionate feelings in response that should foment intervention and amelioration of the conditions that cause this suffering. Sentimental discourse focuses on victims, whether maligned or forgotten.

In the discourse of sentimentality, the first step to a better world is cultivating a refined character that is based on compassion and sympathy. The response sentimentality provokes is at the level of private feeling, perhaps shared by an "intimate public" conditioned to recognize, laud, and emulate such affective responses. Sentimentality "represented a genuine political tool for writers otherwise disenfranchised" (quoted in Nelson). However, Lauren Berlant argues that sentimentality changes the terms of effective citizenship into ones that highlight appropriate behaviors and feelings instead of political agency: "In the United States a particular form of liberal sentimentality that promotes individual acts of identification based on collective group memberships has been conventionally deployed to bind persons to the nation through a universalist rhetoric not of citizenship per se but of the capacity for suffering and trauma at the citizen's core" (Berlant, 636). Thus, the nation is built on individual responses to other people's suffering; individuals feel affective ties to the nation through their compassionate behavior toward others.

The sentimental is not only the province of women artists and literary critics to construct the victimized and appropriate sympathetic responses to these circumstances. For example, commentators and scholars, in reference to the L.A. Crisis, engaged in a provocative form of sentimental shorthand with gendered dimensions. To illustrate in compassionate terms a desperate and impoverished population, progressive critics frequently used the image of mothers who stole baby diapers and formula rather than car stereos and television sets, implying that these women were unable to provide the most basic necessities for their families and who thus might understandably capitalize on these illegal opportunities as a means of survival. Images of mothers, young children, and families countered the more popular images of young men who were identified as looters, arsonists, "thugs," "hooligans," and "gangbangers."

For Korean Americans, the dire stakes of their collective dehumanization were quite similar, given the invisibility of their community and history in the United States and their hypervisibility in mainstream media discourse as cold-blooded, racist vigilantes. In the media coverage of the L.A. Crisis, as of Du's trial, the perspectives of Korean Americans and Asian Americans were again astonishingly absent.[22] One of the most revealing absences was in the front-page piechart of a *Los Angeles Times* survey conducted with more than one thousand L.A. residents about the 1992 Crisis that included only "Whites, Blacks, Hispanics and Others." Helen Zia quoted Shelby Coffey, then-editor of the *Los Angeles Times*, who claimed that "Asians were not statistically significant enough to include," despite the fact that both Blacks and Asian Americans each "made up 11 percent of the Los Angeles population" (Zia, 183). Uncovering an inconsistent methodology in this major newspaper's front-page survey, Zia shows how a sizable minority population becomes insignificant and overlooked: that Asian Americans were not *thought*, rather than proven in fact, to be a "significant enough" demographic in a city that has boasted the second largest concentration of Asian Americans in the United States for decades. The lack of media access and representation differentially experienced by Korean Americans is one that Kim-Gibson and the other producers of *Sa-I-Gu* attempted to rectify with the production and dissemination of the documentary.

Sa-I-Gu importantly focuses on the hard work and daily sacrifice of these immigrant women. Abandoned by the state, their neighborhoods, their community, the film makes its most memorable interview subjects visible through the discourse of family: as exceptional wives and mothers. Their children reinforce such images of good, meritorious families. One storeowner's son, a member of the National Guard, asserts his parents' personal and professional self-sacrifice on behalf of their children: "She came to America for her children, for me, Ken and Liz. . . . They gave up absolutely everything. In Korea, my mom never worked; she had maids and my father was the boss. They literally gave up everything, just for us" (Kim-Gibson, *Sa-I-Gu*). The interview is concluded with footage of the adult children seated on one side of the kitchen table and the parents' standing behind them, reemphasizing these parents as the nurturers and protectors of their children. Although the family is likely arranged around the kitchen table for the practical reason of fitting all five members onscreen, the family is posed as if for a family portrait. Close-up shots amplify the parents' reactions to their children's comments and allow the audience to witness and commemorate the close-knit relationships among them. In a later interview, footage of another woman, Jung Hui Lee, alternates between her individual interview and a succession of family photographs at various stages of her son Eddie's childhood, while the audio of her interview continues as a voice-over narration. Lee tells of how she and her husband raised their two children without any help, not even babysitters, arranging their day and night work schedules so that one parent was always home. The visual and verbal account of Lee's death disrupts these images of a happy, well-cared-for childhood, a carefully nurtured family.

Lee's death frames both of Kim-Gibson's documentaries on the L.A. Crisis—*Sa-I-Gu* and *Wet Sand*, her solo directorial effort—even though the latter film interviews people of different races, ages, and viewpoints.[23] Both films include Lee's retelling her experience of acknowledging the fact of her son's death and of losing all hope that he might still be alive. The visual narrative of this segment cuts between stationary camera footage of her interview and shaky hand-held camera footage of burning buildings and violence in the streets. Speaking in Korean with English subtitles at the bottom of the screen, Jung Hui Lee reveals her initial confusion over verifying her son's death: when she is called to identify her son in the morgue, she clings to the hope that Lee is still alive because, in the *Korea Times*, the black-and-white photograph of the young man fatally shot shows him wearing a T-shirt that is black. But her son, she remembers, left the house wearing a *white* T-shirt, hoping to help defend Korean American storeowners from looters and arsonists. Because Lee couldn't possibly have changed shirts, his mother tells of this false hope in voice-over narration, and as she speaks in Korean, the camera rotates around a black-and-white image with the English subtitles appearing at the bottom of the screen. After the frame's rotation stops, the image is colorized; dark red blood stains the victim's white T-shirt, blackening it. Lee explains how, in the color photograph in the *LA Times* that day, her son's white shirt was clearly red with blood, but in the *Korea Times'* black-and-white image, it was black.

This sequence of Jung Hui Lee's dawning acknowledgment of her son's death is one of the most complexly narrated and riveting segments of the film and appears in both *Sa-I-Gu* and *Wet Sand*. Translating Lee's powerful emotions into film imagery and cinematic effects, Kim-Gibson uses multiple auditory and visual documentary techniques in order to recount Lee's tragic story. Kim-Gibson first intercuts Lee's interview with scenes of the violence and devastation that have come to characterize the L.A Crisis: burning buildings, people running, and the debris in the streets. Her modulated, subdued speaking voice is heard while English subtitles are superimposed against the bottom of static images or on moving shots across different parts of the photographs for emphasis. Most notably, to contrast Lee's hopes with her eventual tragic realization, Kim-Gibson emphasizes different parts of the two versions of the photograph. Originally, the image shown is the grainy, black-and-white newspaper-quality photograph of a young man lying in the street, with a black shirt, gray jeans, and white sneakers; in the background of the image, other wounded young men are propped against a glass storefront with police officers leaning over them. The camera is so close to the photo that the textured grain of the newsprint is visible and obscures the image itself at first. The next newspaper photograph, this one in color, is shown in sections. First, the camera angle is tilted on the background scene, focusing on one of the injured young men leaning against a window, and then the camera slowly rotates clockwise away from the image to reveal the Black police officer interviewing him. The next shot is the foreground of the photo, of Lee, lying on the ground. The tilted and rotating shots convey Jung Hui Lee's initial disbelief and disorientation in trying to confirm her son's possible death; the extreme close-up of the paper texture implies how minutely, yet confusedly, the image is scanned for meaning over time. The next cut shows Eddie Lee's body in an image that widens to fill the screen, alluding to the mother's gradual recognition of her son's death in filmic terms.

The film deploys the sentimental tradition in its focus on a child's tragic death, a mother's grief and love, and the audience's sympathetic feelings for those suffering the loss. Eddie Lee's death activates one of the most compelling tropes of sentimental discourse: the death or sacrifice of a child. Remarkably, Jung Hui Lee states that it wasn't just one person who shot her son, and she refers to his death as a sacrifice. This understanding of her son's death, so weighted with sacred meanings, connects to another aspect of sentimental politics in which "the child's suffering body [operates] as an agent of moral reform" (Tompkins, 273).[24] While Tompkins is referring specifically to Little Eva's tragic death in *Uncle Tom's Cabin*, the significance of a child's death is crucial to the moral ramifications of the novel: "Death is the equivalent not of defeat but of victory; it brings an access of power, not a loss of it; it is not only the crowning achievement of life, it is life. . . . When the spiritual power of death is combined with the natural sanctity of childhood, the child becomes an angel endowed with salvific force" (273). Lee's death is clearly "endowed with salvific force" through its moral and political significance in the film and the Korean American community.

Memorializing Lee's death is one of the primary reasons for the unprecedented thousands who gathered along the route of his funeral procession and at his memorial service. One of those Asian American participants held a sign with the block letters in the epigraph above: "WE GRIEVE TOGETHER / AS ONE FAMILY." An expression of Korean American ethnic solidarity, the words echo scholars and activists who felt a distinctly Korean *American* identity emerging during and after the 1992 violence.[25] This family that collectively mourns Lee's death thus symbolizes the strengthened ties among the Korean American community in the face of this tragedy: "The reporter John H. Lee used the Korean word *chŏng*—'it's one part love, equal parts affinity, empathy, obligation, entanglement, bondage and blood'—to describe how he felt as a Korean American during the riots" (quoted in Abelmann and Lie, 39).

But I would argue for an additional possibility: that the bold assertion of "ONE FAMILY" on the sign deliberately exceeds the limits of affective ties that are naturalized for the monoethnic, monoracial family and keep apart ethnic and racial groups. The rally was intended for a national, mainstream, and English-speaking audience, not just for coverage by local Korean and Asian American media. This hand-lettered sign was likewise meant to be viewed by a wider public that could bear witness to a U.S. nation conceived in terms of family affiliation and coalesced around the loss of a son. The filmmakers themselves clearly intended to encourage a more inclusive nation, carefully reimagined through the interracial family. In the closing moments of *Sa-I-Gu,* for instance, the film is dedicated to "Edward Song Lee and the fifty-three sons and daughters" who died in the violence. In this poignant dedication, we are importantly reminded that more families—Asian, Black, Latina/o, and White—have suffered tragedy through the loss of a child, parent, sibling, and relative in the urban conflagration of 1992. Following the associative logic of the documentary in the filmmakers' expansion of the central mother-child dynamic, the film's dedication is to the survivors, not only the parents and families who are mourning their loved ones but also a multiracial community and nation that must survive this cataclysm and can begin by mourning the loss of these sons and daughters as their own.

Sentimental logic ties one mother's grief to a nation of mothers, a family of feeling writ large. The tradition of documentary film is particularly well suited to sentimental strategies. Critics of the documentary film genre such as Brian Winston have traced the evolution of the form and its employment of technological advances to achieve audience empathy: from highlighting "heroic actors" to solidifying a "tradition of the victim" (35). The documentary film intends for the audience, once aware of a victimized individual or group and their circumstances, to feel more sympathy toward the victims and perhaps be galvanized to act on the documentary subjects' behalf or for their benefit: "Until recently, most victims have passively allowed themselves to be transformed into aesthetic creations, news items, and objects of our pity and concern. Society condones this action because it is assumed that the act of filming will do some good—cause something to be done about the problems" (Ruby, 52). Winston's primary criticisms of documentary for its political failures, its substitution of "empathy for analysis," and its privileging of "effect over cause" (41) are evocative of common critiques of sentimentality as a political tool.

The director and producers of *Sa-I-Gu* use both historical traditions of documentary film—the tradition of the victim and also the tradition of heroic actors. Their subjects are extraordinary women who, just a few weeks after the L.A. Crisis, are trying to hold their lives and families together after such devastating losses that few have ever had to face. With Jung Hui Lee's story prominently placed at the beginning, middle, and end of the documentary, her son's death powerfully frames the overarching narrative of the film, and Lee's interview serves as the structure that connects the vignettes of the other women who were interviewed. Not only do *Sa-I-Gu*'s filmmakers hope to make us, the audience, aware of these women's stories, but they also posit Lee's death as an important prism through which we organize our understanding of the L.A. Crisis, our sympathy for the victims, and our political prerogatives after watching the film.

Kim-Gibson has faced criticism for this selectivity. In a letter to literary critic Min Song, she tells of how, at one screening of *Sa-I-Gu,* an African American man in the audience angrily asked why the film focuses exclusively on one teenager's death when so many young Black men die each day (Song, 246 n. 15). His question is provocative on a number of levels. In a forty-minute film that focuses on Korean American immigrant women's experiences, there are elisions in terms of gender, race, and class. Most obviously in terms of gender, the documentary explicitly centers immigrant women. In terms of race, the film looks at Korean Americans affected by the violence and not other minority and Asian small business owners who were similarly hit by losses and in other parts of Los Angeles: for example, Cambodian-owned stores that were burned in Long Beach (Zia, 191). In contrast, other Asian ethnic business owners had not explicitly been targeted as Korean Americans had been, nor did any other ethnic or racial group suffer as many damages as Korean Americans. In terms of class status, the film primarily interviews (former) storeowners but does not include the perspectives of nonfamily employees who would presumably also have lost their main sources of income. This absence exposes a class bias toward those with enough capital to have developed or purchased such businesses over other Korean Americans in wage labor.

But documentaries are necessarily subject to such exclusionary claims by the selection of their interview subjects. Kim-Gibson responds to such critiques in her 2004 directorial return to the subject of the 1992 Crisis, *Wet Sand,* which includes interviews with Black and Latino business owners whose stores were looted and vandalized and a Latino employee of a Korean storeowner. However, the question of privileging one death over many others appears to be more about interracial competition in a world of finite resources; in this case, the resources are not economic but constituted in terms of recognition and compassion. Song analyzes the background assumptions of the man's question: "There is a limited supply of grief and an abundance of losses, and a viewer of this film cannot be expected to run through this supply for only one death when so many others remain unrecorded, unacknowledged, lost in the shrugs of too much indifference" (Song, 164). The man's anger and question stem from issues of racial equivalence and representational parity, and this audience member asks, why is the one death of a Korean American so significant that it is worth our time and attention that the multiple deaths of African American young men fail to receive? The question is framed in sentimental terms: these invisible young men are victimized by overriding and outsized concerns for other young men such as Edward Lee. In his brief expression of indignation, this man alludes to the complexity of a racial triangulation in terms of those victims who are most worthy of our concern, sympathy, and redress, but in the different context of the media: effective access and accurate representation. According to racial triangulation, Korean Americans, in their exclusion from the U.S. body politic, may enjoy relative valorization as the audience member posits, but a range of Korean American perspectives was far from well represented in the media. Korean Americans can thereby be more easily used as scapegoats in the racial hierarchy of media representation; there are few positive representations to counter such negative ones. Given this absence, many Korean Americans were frustrated with how little was known of the regular violence they faced at work. Nancy Abelmann and John Lie interviewed one Korean self-identified housewife and former store manager: "They [the mainstream media] depict us like crazy people holding guns, but they have no idea how many Koreans died doing business—people struggling to make it, people who had finally made it, students from Korea about to return, young people, old people" (quoted in Abelmann and Lie, 40). For example, in the year after Harlins was killed, Zia writes of "48 murders and 2,500 robberies [that] were reported in L.A.'s Koreatown, and the number of hate crimes against Korean Americans topped all other anti-Asian incidents"—these are rates of one murder and fifty robberies almost weekly in just a five-square-mile area (Zia, 178).

But in the highest levels of government, Korean Americans received public acknowledgment and support, while other minorities were criticized for their perceived roles in the violence (Nopper). Most prominently, President George H. W. Bush declared his sympathy for Korean Americans and their massive losses in the L.A. Crisis; however, such official acknowledgment came alongside blistering attacks on Blacks and Latinas/os for their alleged propensities to riot, loot, and destroy—the "brutality of the mob." David Palumbo-Liu considers the implications of this sentiment framed in terms of dehumanizing other racial groups, Latinas/os and Blacks: "Thus, we have the Asian-American as white surrogate in the battle of capitalism against chaos, and Latinos as deportable surrogates for a black population that cannot be 'legally' disenfranchised because of their birthright" (369 n. 8). While Korean Americans were symbolically embraced by prominent politicians as the deserving minority or "white surrogates," there were frustratingly few policy implementations to reflect such rhetorical inclusion and even governmental roadblocks to reestablishing businesses and rebuilding neighborhoods hardest hit by the violence—merely half those businesses destroyed in the L.A. Crisis were ever rebuilt in the years after the violence. Politicians' sympathy for Korean Americans paralleled the documentary's limitations of more sentimental feeling than material changes.

In the face of inadequate policy responses and ambivalent, neglectful media coverage, there is the undeniable, yet understandable, particularity of the filmmakers' decision to focus solely on Korean immigrant women. The imaginary of America's landscape has failed to include Blacks and Koreans as bodies worth collectively mourning (Song, 163–64). In response to what Kim-Gibson describes as the fierce anger provoked by the prominence of Lee's death in the film, Min Song asks, "What would it take to think of Edward Lee's death as representing these other deaths? Is there any way to imagine Lee as symbolic of the many losses that fail to register in public as a loss worth grieving over" (164)? But the question that remains unasked and unanswered is: Why have the daily deaths of other (Black) teenagers failed to represent Lee's? His death, symbolizing the losses sustained by the Korean American community, is the driving force of this film precisely because media coverage of the dozens of deaths, thousands of casualties, and thousands of businesses destroyed failed to represent Korean American experiences during *sa-i-gu*.[26]

I believe that there is a way to see these deaths as analogous to each other, rather than in competition: to point toward the injustices in the deaths of Blacks while pointing toward the injustices in the deaths of Korean Americans. In light of the earlier examination of the way racial triangulation negotiates the benefits and restrictions on citizenship and protections claimed by people of color, critic and poet Elizabeth Alexander identifies Blacks as having "always existed in a counter-citizen relationship to the law" because the "American way with regard to the actual lived experience of African Americans has been to write a counternarrative which erased bodily information as we knew it and substituted a countertext which in many cases has become a version of national memory" (Alexander, 80). Alexander asserts that such a counternarrative and countertext has, for example, justified the geno-cidal intent and human rights violations of slavery and lynching. As countercitizens despite their formal legal citizenship, African Ameri-cans have also had to bear the erasure not only from the protection of the law, but also the erasure of their "bodily" knowledge and "actual lived experience" from "national memory." As the inspiration for her essay, Alexander takes a provocative question from a multimedia in-stallation that includes the sections of a reproduced photograph of a Black man before his lynching that appeared in *Life* magazine and the artist, Pat Ward Williams, has the following question scrawled around the four photographs: "Can you be BLACK and look at this without fear?" Alexander posits the Black body, historically tortured, disabled, annihilated, and silenced, as the center that brings together the imag-ined community of Blacks: "What do black people say to each other to describe their relationship to their racial group, when that relation-ship is crucially forged by incidents of physical and psychic violence which boil down to the 'fact' of abject blackness? Put another way, how does an incident like King's beating consolidate group affiliations by making blackness an unavoidable, irreducible sign which despite its abjection leaves creative space for group self-definition and self-knowledge" (77–78)? Alexander ruminates on what to call the imag-ined community of Blackness forged by a history of hate crimes and state-sanctioned terror. The criminal justice system and its agents—judges, lawyers, juries, and police—reclassified both King's beating and Harlins's death as crimes warranting little punishment, victims seen with few claims to justice and redress. In the first state criminal trial, Rodney King's assailants were found not guilty on all but one count, and that count was declared a mistrial—a legal absolution of the seri-ous injuries the police officers inflicted on King.

However, Edward Lee's death, too, like most of the crisis-related deaths, was never prosecuted as a homicide; no one was identified as responsible for his death, one among many other murders without legal redress. Moreover, in the years leading to the 1992 Crisis and in its aftermath, Korean Americans had to face the almost complete mainstream media blackout of their perspectives. In their own counter-citizenship status as recent immigrants, their "lived experience" was denied by "national memory." Using Alexander's provocative question and thinking analogously, what kind of "creative space for group self-definition and self-knowledge" can be created for Korean Americans? Using Williams's question at the very center of her art and thinking analogously, in watching the scenes of violence and the images of Lee's death in *Sa-I-Gu,* can you be KOREAN and look at this without fear?[27] I think it crucial to emphasize the analogous relation between the anti-Black, state-sanctioned atrocities and anti-Asian violence throughout U.S. history. The diasporic history of the Korean people's brutal and systemic oppression as colonial subjects in the Japanese empire, the Korean War, and the violent lineage of historical events that gives rise to the nomenclature of *sa-i-gu* itself could possibly forge these commonalities, but this discussion is largely absent from the documentary. Representing such a historical legacy of repeated colonial violence and its implications, of U.S. aggression in Korea and its later cultural imperialism, might occlude an understanding of the Korean immigrant women's narratives as important *American* stories.[28]

This chapter criticizes the depiction of the Korean/Asian American woman in both the trial and in the documentary; however, my critique must acknowledge a pragmatic politics. Women *and* men without heteronormative, nuclear families stand in lesser, even invalidated, relations to the state. Therefore, it is understandable, even preferred, for cultural workers such as *Sa-I-Gu's* filmmakers to assert their primary interview subjects as contextualized by their families.[29] The filmmakers partially employ this strategy to contend with the invisibility of the Korean American community and its complexity. I am critical of this strategy but not the reasons for its deployment: more just representations of Korean/Asian Americans. This chapter identifies the filmmakers' constrained representations and meanings, especially when their artistic production and political communication is overdetermined by the experiences of other Asian ethnic and racial groups. Korean Americans, and, by extension, Asian Americans, are politically legible in familial terms; they have more legitimate claims for protection and justice as members of their good, meritorious families rather than as individual citizens before the law and in public opinion. These limited means of representing complex humanity reveal our impoverished cultural symbolism: that our common ground of representation is capitalism, exploitation, and our increasing reliance on the family to hold everything together. But this development is symptomatic of the well-worn grooves of our symbolic matrices of representation.

Thus far, I have focused on two women, Soon Ja Du and Jung Hui Lee, who were portrayed as mothers trying to care for and protect their sons. This comparison highlights one prominent way of reading this chapter and the primary responses and representations of the families deeply affected by urban violence and the L.A. Crisis. We can easily see the parallels between Du and Lee since they are both Korean, relatively recent immigrants, women, and mothers. We can easily compare the sons as fallen or imperiled protectors of their families and communities: Joseph Du taught his mother how to recognize gang members and planned to testify against robbery suspects in a local gang; Edward Lee left home to protect Korean-owned stores from looters and arsonists during the 1992 violence. Both sons are imbued with filial and civic purpose to restrain a community in upheaval, trying to protect the American dreams of their families and other Korean Americans.

Sa-I-Gu's sentimental strategies reentrench the Americanness of these women's struggles as their hard work, their model families, their love for their children are swept up in verbal and visual proofs of their allegiance to the American dream that is purged of its Korean and Black dimensions. For example, it is less obvious, harder, to link the two slain victims, Latasha Harlins and Edward Lee, to see the deaths of these two teenagers as parallel losses. Yet both were killed because of tragic misunderstandings: Du believed Harlins was a shoplifter; Lee was likely thought a looter. Both are mourned by their families, who feel that there has been no justice for their deaths. *Sa-I-Gu* begins this relational work in its attempts to highlight Lee as one of the many sons and daughters who died. He is remembered as "our brave son" who is grieved by "one family"—us, the film's audience. In recognizing these many sons and daughters, film audiences are defined as the mothers, fathers, or surrogate parents, members of one family of feeling, one nation, that come together over such tragedies. *Sa-I-Gu* aims for this connection that traverses ethnic and racial divides. But we have not done the work that would make such analogies among the victims of the 1992 Los Angeles Crisis automatic. Nor have we done the political work that would make a woman's familial role irrelevant to her individual civic merit. For these affective and political analogies to hold, the outcry over injustices against Korean Americans must refer to injustices against Blacks; the struggles against the erasure of Black lived experiences must point toward those against the erasure of Korean American ones. Though Kim-Gibson's subsequent documentary on the 1992 Crisis, *Wet Sand*, attempts to draw these cross-racial connections, its continued focus on the American family as the center of viewers' sentimentality inhibits the full potential of understanding across difference. In *Sa-I-Gu,* as in the decades since the L.A. Crisis, these analogies have been unevenly manifested, if at all.

2 IN/CIVILITY, WITH COLORBLINDNESS AND EQUAL TREATMENT FOR ALL

> If the rich and powerful were encouraged by the general culture
> to believe that they fully deserved all they had, how arrogant they
> could become, and, if they were convinced it was all for the
> common good, how ruthless in pursuing their own advantage.
> Power corrupts, and therefore one of the secrets of a good society
> is that power should always be open to criticism. A good society
> should provide sinew for revolt as well as for power.
>
> —Michael Young, *The Rise of the Meritocracy*

> There's a thin line between to laugh with and to laugh at.
>
> —Richard Pryor

GUNNAR KAUFMAN—an internationally famous poet, nationally recruited college basketball player, and wildly popular African American
leader—wins worldwide notoriety for preaching the mass suicide of
African Americans. Gunnar promises this will be the greatest protest
in history against racial inequality, a preemptive strike against "the
slow deaths of toxic addiction and the American work ethic" (Beatty,
2). Translating the revolutionary suicide of Black Panther cofounder
Huey P. Newton and the cult charisma of Jim Jones for a new generation, Gunnar is the young, magnetic "badman" of the best-selling 1997
satire *The White Boy Shuffle* who clashes with the ever-shifting rules
of social decorum and success in school, on the basketball court, and
in everyday interactions.[1] Given standards that shift higher, move
lower, or change arbitrarily to justify the exclusion and censure of
people of color, Gunnar calls into question just what kind of equality
is possible "in a society that applies principles without principle" (225);

that professes to uphold ideals of individual merit, colorblindness, and race neutrality; and whose elites violate these principles with impunity, turning a blind eye and indifferent spirit to systemic inequities and racial subordination.

In *The White Boy Shuffle,* African American poet and novelist Paul Beatty identifies the failed promise of the American shibboleths of democracy and equality by ridiculing new cultural justifications for inequalities. The wide-ranging satire of *The White Boy Shuffle* alludes to iconic events and long-standing debates over equal citizenship in U.S. history: the Constitutional Convention, Reconstruction, the legacy of slavery and lynching, the modern civil rights movement, Black nationalism, affirmative action, and the growing wealth gap, to name just a few constellations of Beatty's extensive references. The terms of engagement are not equal treatment or equal outcomes, but assessments of *civility*: politeness, deference, or just going along to get along. In the final lines of the novel's preface, Gunnar describes his first-person narrative as "the battlefield remains of a frightened deserter in the eternal war for civility" (2). Signifying on both the Civil War and the modern civil rights movement, Gunnar conspicuously does not refer to an "eternal war" for equality, freedom, or justice—the classic ideals of U.S. liberation movements since the American Revolution. Instead, Beatty reclassifies the contemporary manifestations of these epic struggles into more mundane scuffles over civility, exposing a dilution and misdirection of previous egalitarian agendas in mainstream political discourse. It is an odd, yet revealing, reinterpretation of the expanding (and contracting) democratic project that has characterized U.S. political participation since the early nineteenth century.[2] What legal scholar Patricia Williams has called the "alchemy of race and rights" is instead, in *The White Boy Shuffle,* the transmutation of civility into equality: the bait-and-switch of paternalism for parity and subordination for fairness. While civility's historical meanings have encompassed concepts as broad as citizenship and civilization, expansive definitions of civic virtue narrow to evaluations of individual politeness and good manners in common parlance; and, in the "broken windows" theory of behavior that trivial violations escalate if they are not immediately and perhaps overzealously addressed, to be impolite is believed to challenge the very weft of civilization.[3]

The smallest uncivil act is perceived as a gateway to more heinous crimes in dominant theories of urban law and order since the Reagan era. The 1992 Los Angeles Crisis crystallizes the tension between order and unrest, security and fear—anxieties of civil society that permeate *The White Boy Shuffle*. I argue that the novel negotiates these fundamental tensions of civility and incivility in order to point to the discourses of civil racism that undermine equality. The urban violence of the L.A. Crisis, occurring precisely in the middle of the novel, is a provocative lens through which these issues are explosively imagined. Beatty dramatizes the uneasy relationship between civility and racism through the iconic events that have come to signify the L.A. Crisis: the assault of a White truck driver, the mass looting of local stores, the arson of a Korean-owned store, and a near-fatal police beating. These events reveal how, under a state of emergency, small acts of defiance or even everyday practices can become magnified into the criminally suspect and corporally punishable. Gunnar's experiences bring to light the inadequacy of education with its misleading lessons of civic responsibility and virtue, multicultural credos and colorblind principles that ill-equip younger generations to understand and address the causes of social conflict and violence over racial difference. Beatty reflects this social disorder and its remedies in the novel's satiric exaggeration in language and structure: the incivility in the narrative strategy of the novel mirrors the incivility in society, as manifested in the L.A. Crisis and its aftermath.

While the civility debates of the 1990s have largely subsided from the political mainstream, the "civility crisis" spawned by these national conversations continues to frame political discourses that define citizenship, community, and national belonging. One manifestation of these purported crises of civility has been the privileging of meritocracy over equality, which has created an imagined community of the deserving, civil few.[4] In the logic of meritocracy, those with the most merit, or the most civility, should garner more advantages and privileges, having earned the right to keep these material benefits and pass them to their heirs. This proverbial sleight of hand grafts meritocracy onto democracy and tilts the level playing field that is presumably the metaphoric foundation of egalitarian societies. The intersection of civility and meritocracy perpetuates legacies of disenfranchisement and exploitation, now masked by ostensible standards of parity and fairness. In identifying these externalities, Beatty exposes how the socioeconomic hierarchies of the meritorious increasingly rationalize the invalidation of racial remedies such as affirmative action and civil rights legislation.

Such stratification has the net effect of defending the increasing consolidation of success and wealth for established elites. While fairness is now posited in meritocratic terms—those with the most merit, deserve the most resources—Gunnar finds that the reversal of such cause and effect holds truer: that those who already possess the most resources are perceived to have the most merit and should be entitled to more. This tautology justifies the concentration of resources for a tiny minority, an effect that characterizes the globalization of capital, the privatization of risk, and the deregulation of markets since the 1970s. This closed loop of distribution leads to exclusionary and discriminatory outcomes in which merit determines those who can be deemed a citizen of the imagined community of the deserving. This calculus of equal treatment and meritocratic doctrine invariably produces outcomes deeply unequal and unfair to populations historically already derogated as unworthy and meritless: nonwhite, female, queer, and noncitizen. Citizenship is placed in the economy of merit rather than one of equality.

In the fine line between the civil and uncivil, Gunnar's sharp eye and sharper wit shape the novel's first-person satire. *The White Boy Shuffle* most often criticizes imbalances: how the reaction of the state is outsized in relation to the action, the punishment never fits the crime, and representation distorts the object represented. Beatty deploys his satire through humor as an "art of resistance"—one that simultaneously upholds and undermines the very system of domination his readers are to laugh with or laugh at, a contradiction often made visible by his exaggerated storytelling.[5] Beatty uses humor primarily to highlight his larger satire and to challenge perceived notions and common knowledge. Gunnar benefits from the myriad functions of humor: smoothing the rough edges of social interaction, making negative criticism entertaining, and pushing the limits of the appropriate, polite, and proper. As satire facilitates a "change in perception" of the world (Knight, 3), Beatty draws on the dual functions of satire's common features—the double-voicedness of irony and parody—to point out the inconsistencies between what Gunnar is told and what he experiences, between what Beatty depicts and what the reader perceives. Humor is Gunnar's strategy of survival in White-dominated spaces, insofar as he assimilates into White social groups as the "funny, cool black guy" (27). This assimilation exposes the double standards that he encounters. Although the American dream promises unlimited opportunities and respectful, equal treatment regardless of color, creed, or class, Gunnar witnesses the repeated failure of those equally and even more talented than he. Gunnar makes the necessary compromises of his individuality and integrity for these opportunities and equal treatment, but even then, his success is appropriated or downplayed by the gatekeeping elites: teachers, bureaucrats, admissions officers, police. Criticizing aspects of the civility debate and its assimilation of equality that constitute the novel's political agenda, Beatty's satirical strategy exposes the contradictions and weaknesses of the various ideological and political positions Gunnar encounters.

The White Boy Shuffle identifies the ways in which the terms of civility restrict both conservative and liberal proposals to rectify racial injustices; both are premised on a refusal to acknowledge the complexity of race and racism beyond the simplistic, homogenizing view that results from the filter of civility. As a satirical bildungsroman of Gunnar's education through White and Black spaces, civility smoothes over the multiple discriminations that can implicitly motivate multiculturalism and even generates its own inequalities. Beatty's protagonist directly confronts the unstable logic and internal contradictions of a meritocracy built on professions of a colorblind ideology. Beatty ridicules the context-specific and highly individualized assessments of civility that prevent people such as Gunnar from fully participating or experiencing unqualified inclusion in civil society. Marginalized or invisible populations are not imagined as a significant part of the United States: as media viewers, consumer markets, political constituencies, and beneficiaries or casualties of public policies. While Gunnar is the trickster, badman figure, heroic in his antiheroism, Beatty also portrays him as the con man conned, the unwitting dupe who is buffeted by society's mores and finds himself tilting at the windmills of equality and justice. Finally, Beatty laughs last, for the ultimate joke— the expectation of logic and consistency, of coherent politics, of realist certainty—is on his readers.

About Humor

While the dominant cultural representations about the civil rights era might invoke responses of sincerity, seriousness, and tragedy, in *The White Boy Shuffle,* the representations of the post–civil rights era provoke irony, amusement, and parody. Gunnar's misadventures on the battlefields of civility are both terribly funny and deeply troubling for what the novel's "slash-and-burn finale" of mass suicide and potential nuclear annihilation reveals about U.S. politics and society and its epic swindle of equality for civility. Beatty's satire of the contemporary African American experience in Los Angeles is one of a number of other satires, largely television and film comedies that parody the 1992 Crisis and the sociocultural conditions of the neighborhoods most affected by the "urban crisis": in film, *Fear of a Black Hat* (1994), *Don't Be a Menace to South Central While Drinking Your Juice in the Hood* (1996), and *L.A. Riot Spectacular* (2005); in television, episodes of the sketch comedy *In Living Color* and the situational comedies *A Different World* and *The Fresh Prince of Bel Air*. While all are notable for their satiric elements and larger social commentary, Beatty's novel is remarkable for its complex, wide-ranging critique of African American and American traditions in literature and visual culture and its intervention into the central political debates that have haunted the U.S. liberal democratic state since its founding. Because Beatty's satire is so intricately allusive and Gunnar so entertainingly self-deprecating, *The White Boy Shuffle* thwarts possible expectations of mimetic realism through its distortion and hyperbole. Beatty frustrates an easily understood and transparently constructed realist world in ways both trivial and crucial to the novel. For example, he renames Gunnar's public schools in honor of miscegenation and a leading brand of kosher foods—Mestizo Mulatto Mongrel Elementary and Manischewitz Junior High, respectively—and Gunnar farcically rises overnight from complete political obscurity to the most prominent contemporary leader of his late twentieth-century generation by advocating mass suicide.

The White Boy Shuffle inaugurates Beatty's widely praised fictional contributions to the satirical tradition in African American literature. The range of Beatty's works address what literary critic Darryl Dickson-Carr has identified as a major cultural strategy that takes up present political issues: "As the past glories of black culture and political work continue to fade and/or fall into decay in the post-Civil Rights era, some African American authors have increasingly turned to satire to pursue seemingly contradictory goals: a call for a return to intellectual, social, and political strategies that succeeded for African Americans in the past and a push for solutions that will jettison the baggage of those ideologies that have lost their efficacy or popular appeal"

(202). Beatty begins his distinguished career in poetry and humor, winning the first Nuyorican Café poetry slam, which resulted in the publication of his first collection of poetry, *Big Bank Take Little Bank* (1991), followed by his second collection, *Joker, Joker, Deuce* (1994). Beginning with *The White Boy Shuffle*, Beatty deploys his characteristic style of ironic narration and dizzying encyclopedic allusions in order to satirize contemporary Black culture and politics and renarrate African Americans' misunderstood or ignored significance in U.S. history. *Tuff* (2000) examines the rise of a petty criminal to local politician in Harlem. *Slumberland* (2008) considers the influence of African American culture, especially jazz, in Europe. *The Sellout* (2015) explores the contemporary understanding of slavery and segregation through their present-day reestablishment in one town in California. Deeply invested in the comic and satirical traditions in African American literature, Beatty edited the anthology *Hokum: An Anthology of African-American Humor* (2008), which included an eclectic range of humorous perspectives and practitioners from Zora Neale Hurston and Malcolm X to Ishmael Reed and Suzan-Lori Parks.

Indeed, Beatty's strategy of over-the-top satire is often misconstrued or ignored altogether. Fellow Black satirist Ishmael Reed has notably criticized Beatty's work for lacking a coherent and consistent political vision (I. Reed). In a *New York Times* book review, Richard Bernstein opines, *The White Boy Shuffle* is "aimed almost as much at black self-delusion and revolutionary pretension as at the surrounding racism of white society. . . . Whenever 'The White Boy Shuffle' seems about to adopt a position, Mr. Beatty pulls it into parody" (Bernstein). In addition, Bernstein argues that Beatty's political vision is too ambiguous in "pulling" its punches. Bernstein and Reed both compliment and criticize Beatty's self-reflexive strategy. However, Beatty's political commitments appear ambiguous in the novel because he aims his mocking, irreverent tone at various ideological camps, attacking and ridiculing all of the inconsistencies Gunnar encounters on whichever side of the political spectrum he encounters them. Despite these prominent reviewers' criticisms, Beatty sets the terms of his engagement not on equality, the ostensibly expected political position of any Black leader; the terrain of Gunnar's struggle is civility and merit. Here the reader finds an anchor to Beatty's seemingly unmoored politics and is introduced to the most conspicuous form of the novel's incivility, its satiric style.

Bernstein's criticism revealingly veers onto the terrain of authenticity debates that have plagued writers of color and evaluations of their work. In these debates over realism, critics judge the aesthetics of creative work by how closely its textual and visual representations correspond to its critics' and readers' beliefs about the experiences of racial minorities, in this case a young Black man's childhood and early adulthood in Los Angeles. The ending, in which Gunnar begins to advocate mass suicide, parodies both international civil rights leaders and the genocidal heart of global racism. However, while Beatty's insights are "full of the precision that the prism of mockery can provide," Bernstein finds fault with the ending of the novel in revealing, unwittingly contradictory ways:

> In its back stretches the novel becomes less scalpel-like and more fun house mirror, losing its edge as its distortions veer further from reality. Mr. Beatty's verbal inventiveness rarely flags, but his satire slips over the border into a kind of nihilistic slapstick. Or to put this another way, when Mr. Beatty draws on his actual experience growing up sharp-eyed and black in Los Angeles, his novel reaches its heights. When he attempts a kind of inner-city magical realism, the less successful product falls somewhere in that vague zone between the Swiftian absurd and kvetchy political posturing. (Bernstein)

Bernstein's critique of the novel continues several long-standing debates in the arts about the relationship between aesthetics and politics for artists and writers of color. On one hand, Bernstein himself acknowledges the novel's protagonist as "what has become the sociological cliché" of the "young black male," the target population of scholars and policymakers of the law-and-order and racially liberal camps throughout the 1980s and 1990s. On the other hand, Bernstein seems unaware that he has demanded his own version of this cliché in his backhanded praise of the novel: when "Beatty draws on his actual experience," he is more successful than in his conclusion of "inner-city magical realism," which Bernstein dismisses as "political posturing." This series of claims is remarkably unsubstantiated for a review that conceivably could have contained a biographical sketch of the author and could have validated, or countered, Bernstein's speculations that Beatty's life was the inspiration for the novel.

Contemporary readers and literary critics are not the only ones who suffer from this limited sense of artistic representation; their taste and expectations have been cultivated by decades, if not centuries, of distortions in art and scholarship. Cultural critic Henry Louis Gates Jr. has most famously identified this creative bind in his study *Figures in Black:*

> Black writers themselves seem to have conceived their task to be the cre-
> ation of an art that reports and directly reflects brute, irreducible, and inef-
> fable "black reality," a reality that in fact was often merely the formulaic
> fictions spawned by social scientists whose work intended to reveal a black
> America dehumanized by slavery, segregation, and racial discrimination, in
> a one-to-one relationship of art to life. . . . Art, therefore, was argued implic-
> itly and explicitly to be essentially referential. This theory assumed, first of
> all, that there existed a common, phenomenal world, which could be reli-
> ably described by the methods of empirical historiography or else by those
> of empirical social science." (Gates, 45, quoted in Warren, 84)

Gates's criticism is twofold: first, these inaccurate "formulaic fictions" of "black reality" have narrowed the scope of art; and second, restrictive notions of artistic merit have fostered limited perspectives of Black America. Through influence on public policy and national politics, the invisible hand of these researchers' opinions and prejudices about the lived experience of African Americans is the standard to which artists and writers are measured. Recent scholars have identified the influence of sociology not only on cultural texts but also on policy decisions, congressional debates, and presidential actions.[6] Thus, the realism of literature depends upon a sociologically constructed reality.

This question of authenticity or mimetic representation leads to the most important tool of satire—parody. Bernstein is operating within the somewhat circumscribed expectations of parody: for parody to work, the imitation requires an original that the reader can recognize. The logic of parody is analogous to the desire for verisimilitude in literary representation; African American fiction should be about a "black reality," empirically proven and experientially based. Given such a dependence on these all-too-subjective notions of a Black reality, the question arises whether the parody can exist when the more accurate original is unrecognizable, ignored, or idiosyncratic. What if the critic's or the reader's conceptions of Black experience are different from the author's? And what if the original itself is a distortion, a fiction? Beatty provides a parody of a parody: parody can disrupt the expectation of mimetic referentiality in its palimpsestic duality of both the imitation and its original—also an imitation. Bernstein's imagery of the "fun house mirror" of endlessly reflected and refracted images—

meant to criticize Beatty's crafting of the novel—can, on second glance, be interpreted against the grain as a welcome metaphor, a useful strategy of disruption since the image is already distorted. Beatty's strategy of parody of a parody exposes the ostensible original as a parodic distortion itself. Aesthetics and ideology intersect and the primary assessment of artistic merit is dependent on readers' and reviewers' determinations of what the *real* experiences of a young African American narrator could be.

Other forces have an impact on the artistic representation of Black life at the end of the twentieth century. Embracing his "bourgie, black boy" identity ("New Black Aesthetic," 235), writer and critic Trey Ellis posits the "New Black Aesthetic," or NBA, as a "synthesis" of the New Negro Renaissance and Black Arts Movement: "In the Twenties blacks wanted to be considered as good as dominant culture. In the Sixties we wanted no part of dominant culture at all. Today the NBA wants to dominate it. We feel 'separate but better'" (Ellis, "Response to NBA Critiques," 250). Through this aesthetic, Ellis directly counters the alleged inauthenticity of NBA filmmakers, writers, and producers such as George Wolfe, Lisa Jones, Greg Tate, Robert Townsend, and Russell Simmons. These individuals are "cultural mulattos" because they are "educated by a multi-racial mix of cultures, can also navigate easily in the white world," and "no longer need to deny or suppress any part of our complicated and sometimes contradictory cultural baggage to please either white people or black" ("The New Black Aesthetic," 235). Echoing the research studies that cite the growth of the Black middle class and the splintering class interests within a postsegregation racial politics, Ellis alludes to the material conditions that have created a substantial "minority's minority mushrooming with the current black bourgeoisie boom" (234). Inherent in Ellis's appropriation of Addison Gayle's 1972 *Black Aesthetic* and Larry Neal's 1968 essay on the Black Arts Movement is the NBA's patchwork inheritance, a postmodern pastiche of a "few Seventies pioneers that shamelessly borrows and reassembles across both race and class lines" (234).[7] However, even Ellis's argument and opening operates in the logic of authenticity: we should accept these voices as valid because there is evidence of their socioeconomic existence; the syncretic circuits of their hybrid cultural influences are traceable.

The White Boy Shuffle engages with the NBA, embracing the hybrid racial and class experiences of a kid like Gunnar. Although Beatty is less definitive in the political leanings of both his fiction and essays than is Ellis in his manifesto, the pattern of Gunnar's frustrations is distinct—the expectations of others thwart his own personal aspirations and expressions. One primary frustration that organizes the text is a preoccupation with suffering as proof of one's equal citizenship and humanity.[8] A ramification of these authenticity debates is that claims of injury can be used to construct a deserving identity, a meritorious individual, in contrast to those who are deemed undeserving and unmeritorious. One popular reading of the post–civil rights era asserts that the racial remedy of affirmative action "injures" the Black subject as its preferences create a stigma of inferiority; Beatty joins in these debates by playing with the idea of affirmative action as stigma and the injury itself. The figure of the tragic mulatta/o, for instance, once the standard bearer in American culture for the injustices of slavery, racial terror, segregation, second-class citizenship, rape, and violence, is now the tragicomic "affirmative action baby" of Black success in White spaces and who Beatty parodies as feeling so fatally damaged by these experiences that s/he wants to kill himself/herself.[9] *The White Boy Shuffle* considers whether proof of suffering or legal injury guarantees acceptance as a citizen. Echoing philosopher Hannah Arendt, Gunnar finds the answer is always no, because to ask the question is to already determine that the subject was not deserving of citizenship or equality in the first place, a condition antithetical to the promise of inalienable rights. Gunnar challenges philosopher Yukio Mishima's philosophy of suffering by juxtaposing a collective form of spiritual purification and communion with the horror of the Holocaust, the Middle Passage, and the Bengal tiger's mass killing:

> Mishima goes on to say that "only bodies placed under the same circumstance can experience a common suffering. . . . Through the suffering of the group the body can reach the height of existence that the individual can never attain." I agree, but this "height of existence" trip doesn't have much value on the open market. I think that 6 million gassed Jews, 15 million dead Africans, their lungs filled with saltwater, 436 Champawat Indians eaten by a single tiger in 1907, might agree with me. And not everyone experiences pain and suffering in the same way. I can see some masochistic slave fucking up on purpose just for a few precious licks of rawhide. (Beatty, 191–92)

With the timing and rhythm of a comedic punchline, Gunnar breaks up his solemn polemic on mass atrocity with the absurd image of a slave's enjoyment from being whipped. First and foremost rejecting the contempt and pity of his readers, Gunnar partially rejects the aesthetics and spirituality of suffering in his characteristic style of hypotactic argumentation: each successive thought undermines its predecessor, each claim is dismantled by qualifiers and exceptions. Gunnar then proceeds to undermine his own counterargument with its exception: the individual's distinct reaction to and desire for pain—perhaps it is a form of pleasure, a corollary to Mishima's philosophy. The process through which this idea unfolds exemplifies the contradictory nature of Gunnar's thinking, which creates the unstable ground of his assertions. It also adds to the complexity of his engagement with ideas and exemplifies Gunnar's consistent challenges to any claims to universality, even his own.

For a novel that is replete with allusions from popular to highbrow culture—from classical philosophy to children's startling insights—and for which readers could benefit from a compendium of the more obscure allusions, much like those in the works of James Joyce, Thomas Pynchon, and David Foster Wallace, the novel's jokes about suffering, whether individually or collectively felt, are not merely cheap laughs. Rather, these repeated barbs form a pattern throughout the wide-ranging scope of the novel, and Beatty's criticism of discourses of injury and suffering extends to his later writings. In his preface to *Hokum: An Anthology of African-American Humor* (2006), Beatty's mockery of *I Know Why the Caged Bird Sings* by Maya Angelou, one of the most venerated and widely read texts by an African American author, establishes how suffering and injury should be read in his novel. In an essay published in the *New York Times Book Review*, Beatty tells of his first encounter with African American literature in his signature hyperbolic style:

> I suppressed my craving for a Taco Bell Bellbeefer (remember those?) because I feared the restaurant wouldn't serve me. My eyes started to water and the words to "Roll, Jordan, Roll," a Negro spiritual I'd never heard before, rumbled out of my mouth in a sonorous baritone. I didn't know I could sing. I tossed the book into the kitchen trash. I already knew why the caged bird sang—my family was impoverished every other week while waiting for my mother's paydays—but after three pages of that book, I knew why they put a mirror in the parakeet's cage: so he could wallow in his own misery. ("Black Humor")

In a conspicuous repetition of the verb "know" in this passage, Beatty mocks the anachronistic logic of state institutions such as the public school system that requires students to read about past histories of injury and oppression but that strenuously ignores contemporary inequities such as their hardships faced while growing up within such financially constrained families. Beatty swipes at Jim Crow segregation, African American folklore, and protest culture by imagining himself being refused service at a fast-food restaurant and reacting by spontaneously singing spirituals, experiences that allegedly connect readers to the hardships of slavery and segregation, as well as those of Black freedom struggles to dismantle these institutions. Beatty's younger self, puppetlike, enacts these iconic experiences of African American history. In keeping with his previous fictional style and substance, I read Beatty's self-consciously overwrought reactions as a parody of both the type of text by African American writers and the kind of representation of Blackness that are popular with nonblack audiences and that fulfill expectations of African American art and expression. In line with his earlier critiques, Beatty also criticizes how these cultural explanations and representations detract from basic questions of inequality by focusing on the welling up of his involuntary emotions, rather than on material want. Beatty pokes fun at the seriousness of civil rights, asserting the farce of the post–civil rights era by ridiculing society's intransigent commitment to inequality and the racism masked as civility deployed in the name of equality. Alleging that the "defining characteristic of the African-American writer is sobriety" ("Black Humor"), he clearly seeks to challenge such a prescription and a mien.

In *The White Boy Shuffle,* Beatty appears to be both mimicking and repudiating the genre of the Black bildungsroman in African American literature. In this novel of development, Beatty's mockery and imitation serve important functions in revealing the expectations and reading practices of this form. As the protagonists of the bildungsroman learn how to assimilate into society, they are both heroes and victims; they challenge the parameters of the social contract they encounter and negotiate, but they are also buffeted by its contradictions and subject to its injustices. For the African American protagonist, such heroism and victimization often met with responses of contempt and pity, what W. E. B. Du Bois identified in *The Souls of Black Folk* (1903) as the two primary clusters of attitudes about African Americans. For Du Bois and later scholars, such as historian Daryl Michael Scott, contempt and pity are two sides of the same coin; both are powerful feelings that nonetheless continue to disqualify their objects as equals and deserving individuals. Scott argues that policymakers and politicians used theories of psychological damage in "making and justifying social policy" throughout the modern civil rights movement (D. M. Scott, xviii), resulting in such landmarks as the 1954 *Brown v. Board of Education* Supreme Court decision and the 1964 Civil Rights Act and 1968 Fair Housing Act. Scott argues that the strategy of damage and pathology has not only failed to eradicate "biological and cultural notions of black inferiority" but may have actually "worsened the plight of black people" because racial conservatives have used this imagery and theory to "justif[y] neglect and draconian policies" and racial liberals have "made the black community wary of self-examination and self-criticism" (ibid.). Given these externalities, Scott concludes that "experts who study social groups, particularly those who engage in policy debates, should place the inner lives of people off limits" (xix).

In his narrative choices, Beatty appears to support Scott's critique of this exploitive use of the "inner lives of people." This claim might appear to be odd, even contradictory, given that the novel's first-person point of view would necessarily explore the narrator's "inner life." Gunnar reveals his parents' domestic violence and their eventual divorce, his own sexual abuse by his father and two older neighborhood girls, his near-fatal beating by his father during the L.A. Crisis, the death of a member of his gang, and the suicide of his best friend. While most of these events are narrated with Gunnar's sarcastic wit and contempt for overblown emotion, the narrative reveals very little of Gunnar's emotional responses except an ironic detachment that facilitates the satire. Given Gunnar's contrarian narration and Beatty's critique of African American literature, I suggest that Gunnar's inner life, the psychological landscape that has become fodder for public policy, is surprisingly "off-limits." Despite the reader's expectation of an emotional and psychological intimacy that a first-person narrative usually provides, I contend that the critical dissatisfaction, articulated by Bernstein, with the distortions produced by "inner-city magical realism" at the end of the novel is because Beatty offers very little exploration on the lasting effect of these particular experiences on Gunnar's emotional life, despite an entire novel spent focused on Gunnar's observations and experiences. Beatty is more concerned about the effects of dehumanization through contempt and pity than he is with establishing the universal humanity of African Americans via nonblack audiences' affective identification with suffering Black protagonists. In largely repudiating both sociological and psychological realism, Beatty repudiates the idea of damage and its affective politics through his somewhat flat characterization of Gunnar.

These narratorial elisions make possible various conflicting readings of Beatty's characterization. First and foremost, these traumatic experiences are unspeakable.[10] Their horrors leave little possibility for humor or irony and manifest an emotional numbness achieved through crucial elisions in the narrative. Second, these significant events in Gunnar's life might further reinscribe the sociological cliché of the dysfunctional African American family and its cycle of damaged progeny. These are the types of abuses that could be and have been deemed as pathological to impoverished and criminalized peoples, the claims of sociological and anthropological studies of deviancy that persist to this day. Last, Gunnar is the so-called supernegro who extraordinarily rises above such injuries and against all odds. Gunnar's ability to survive such personal traumas could cast him in a heroic light, worthy of the reader's approval as well as pity that such an innocent, young protagonist must suffer so much at the hands of family members and neighbors.

Beatty's satiric strategy of exaggeration makes visible his readers' implicit demand for realist representation while also exposing the distortion that is inherent in this desired representation. Paradoxically, the hyperbole of satire emerges as a mimetic representation and the exaggerated turns out to be the unexaggerated reality. It is ironically the appropriate style for Gunnar's hyperbolic existence, in which Gunnar's actions result in overreactions and disproportionate responses. Gunnar's formative childhood encounter regarding "negrophobia" and "reasonable racism" occurs during the 1992 Los Angeles Crisis.[11] In repeating the logic of outsized reactions, Black kids such as Gunnar and his best friend Nick Scoby reduce a White man to incoherence by their mere presence. After hearing the not-guilty verdict in the police beating of Rodney King, Gunnar sees a Wonder Bread truck careen dangerously through his neighborhood and then tip over. The shaken White driver emerges and is suddenly frightened by two skinny thirteen-year-olds: "I'd never seen anyone afraid of me. I wondered what my face looked like. Were my nostrils flaring, my eyes pulsing red? I was about to shout 'Ooga-booga' and give the guy a heart attack" (132). Gunnar and Nick beat him with bags of bread, and the driver's negrophobia reduces him to more psychological distress than physical injury. Just before the L.A. Crisis, Gunnar narrates the arrival of a production team for a rap music video that depicts his neighborhood as an urban jungle, replete with the White director's colonialist fantasies straight out of Edward Rice Burroughs's *Tarzan* series. Thus, Gunnar is forced to confront the figure of the savage African, a stereotype that emerged in justifications for antebellum slavery, the invasion and colonization of Africa, and a figure popular in late twentieth-century media representations of the gangsta rapper or Black thug. For capitalism and imperialism, White desires position these figures counter to citizenship in terms of their alleged criminality and savagery.

During the 1992 Crisis, Gunnar confronts a White man's fear of the savagery he believes Gunnar can unleash in a moment Fanonian in its intensity. Instead of the French girl who questions her mother about seeing Frantz Fanon, a Black Algerian, on the train, Beatty inserts a confrontation with an adult White truck driver who is paralyzed by negrophobia with the irrational fear of Gunnar's potential Black savagery. The driver, however, appears to suffer more from the perceived, rather than actual, physical threat of these two young Black teenagers in the novel. The driver is clearly afraid of potential racial retribution: "Bug-eyed with fear, he babbled something about having 'never done nothing to nobody'" (132). In the face of this man's overwhelming terror, Gunnar is stunned to realize how much White fear constructs his Blackness.

Nick and Gunnar's Wonder Bread attack on the White delivery truck driver obviously parodies the attack on Reginald Denny, the most widely known victim of the violence and one of the earliest crisis-related beatings caught by news cameras. A White man, Denny was stopped near the intersection of Florence and Normandie avenues, the epicenter of the most severe destruction in South Central Los Angeles during the 1992 Crisis, when he was pulled from his big rig and beaten by at least four African American men. Although hundreds of other White, Latina/o, Asian, and African American men and women were beaten or injured, the mainstream media directed national attention to Denny's beating. As the visual and racial complement to King's beating, Denny's beating exemplified Black-on-White violence, a reversal of the White-on-Black beating of Rodney King. In the next chapter, I pursue a more thorough analysis of theoretical ramifications of this purported manifestation of racial revenge; here, I consider the allegorical dimensions of Beatty's parodic fictionalization of Denny's attack.

Gunnar and his best friend pummel a White truck driver with "doughy pillows" of Wonder Bread, believing that this beating merely terrorizes the man rather than physically injuring him. In this complexly allegorical moment, two Black kids beat a White man with loaves of white bread. As slang for humdrum (White) middle-class, white-collar lives, values, and aspirations, Wonder Bread is a symbol not only of the boys' own but also the other man's oppression—the "white bread" standard to which neither individual nor group, Blacks and working-class Whites, will ever fully attain. However, the historical conflation of race with class, with what legal scholar Cheryl I. Harris has termed "whiteness as property," signifies that Whiteness is something one has, not earns, and what historian George Lipsitz has called a "possessive investment in whiteness" can only have value in relation to the devaluation of Blackness. Furthermore, Gunnar leads us to believe that the truck driver passes out more from fear of their Blackness than any actual physical threat they pose, and Beatty has framed the attack in such a way that the man is terrorized by his deeper fear of racial retaliation. In the odd scene of assaulting the man with Wonder Bread, Gunnar and Nick appropriate and deploy the tools of racial oppression that the truck driver and other working-class Whites enable for the maintenance and spread of Whiteness. In this instance, racial antagonisms trump possible interracial class sympathies; the truck driver may have previously benefited from his racial Whiteness, but at this moment he is poised to bear the brunt of the blame for such racial exploitation.[12]

This parody of Denny's beating and the "five-fingered discounts" (123) at the local stereo store is undercut by the severity of Officer Kaufman's brutal beating of his son into unconsciousness on the first day of the violence, punishment for Gunnar's theft of a package of air fresheners. Gunnar's experience of the 1992 events is reversed: Gunnar's final memory of the violence is not as participant or witness, but actually as victim of a Rodney King–like beating by his father, a Black LAPD officer. This beating is masked by Gunnar's silence, his father's badge, and the larger surrounding chaos of the violence. In fact, in a novel characterized by its incessant parody of all political opinions and agendas, the father's psychological, physical, and sexual assaults on his son are some of the only actions of the novel that are acknowledged only briefly with Gunnar's characteristic witty flippancy. The 1992 L.A. Crisis introduces a punishment that far outstrips Gunnar's crime and exposes the hyperbole of racist reason and civility.

The Biologization of Civility

The novel's interrogation of civility is framed by Gunnar's vastly different educational experiences as he moves among various neighborhoods in Los Angeles and Boston. Education, often considered the crucial leveler of difference, instead reinforces and exacerbates inequalities through the promotion of U.S. society as first and foremost a meritocracy. In this idealized system, the government is run, society structured, and resources allocated by those with the most talent and ability and their corresponding benefits of wealth and social status. Meritocracy fits well with the American dream of upward mobility for those who work hard, persevere, and innovate. However, meritocracy in the service of civility becomes a technology of inequality in its distribution of the most resources to the most talented elite. Meritocratic discourse drives civil racism, which creates and sustains a transitive equivalency among equality, civility, and meritocracy. This interchangeability implies that equality is not an inherent right but rather something earned through civic virtue, narrowly redefined as merit and economic success. Such a redefinition dominated the racial discourses of the post–civil rights era as a way to preserve an informal socioeconomic hierarchy that could no longer officially exist in government and law. It emerged, among various forms, under the banner of the "civility crisis," engineered by the "civilitarians" or "virtuecrats"—the cultural workers and policymakers such as historian Gertrude Himmelfarb, former Secretary of Education William Bennett, and political adviser Ben J. Wattenberg who largely influenced the purported resolution of this "crisis" through educational prerogatives and societal norms.

In contrast, Beatty's novel highlights the perspective of the targets of such civility education. Gunnar is a young urban Black man who is statistically the usual suspect for behavioral correction and discipline by the criminal justice system, as well as the target audience for lessons in civil and meritocratic conduct. In response to this hyperscrutiny, Gunnar transgresses social conventions, alternately flouting and exploiting rules in order to expose their uneven applications, arbitrary punishments, and haphazard rewards for people of color. Gunnar's deliberately outrageous behavior, intentionally "uncivil" in his advocacy of mass suicide, defies the interrelated and interlocking definitions of civility in terms of politeness and the cohesiveness of the citizenry itself.[13] As a basketball player who performs a blackface minstrel routine in which he burns his uniform before his last high school game, a poet who strips off all his clothes in public to protest his college classmates' fawning adoration, a community organizer who chops part of his own finger off to prove his commitment to mass suicide for his worldwide audience, Gunnar is a master of the shocking, the offensive, the uncivil.

Set in the late 1970s and continuing into the mid-1990s, the novel's post–civil rights landscape is a dizzying array of absurdities, contradictions, and paradoxes that are most acutely felt in the disparities between Gunnar's formal education and his experiences outside the classroom. In the post–civil rights era, equality is primarily defined as equal treatment, that is, treating everyone, even those differently situated, as the same.[14] Equal treatment is most often expressed in terms of colorblindness and race neutrality that, alongside multiculturalism and diversity, are made into putatively benign forms of assimilation and inclusion.[15] In the classroom and on the basketball court, Gunnar's teachers explain multiculturalism and colorblindness in ways that exalt the myth of America as a classless, race-neutral society, with endless abundance and upward mobility for all. However, Gunnar's educational experiences repeatedly contradict this heady mythos, because he is so often arbitrarily singled out or excluded, receiving unmerited derision or even praise that belie the lessons on colorblind treatment and equal opportunities.

Through this bildungsroman, Beatty assesses the conflicting values and virtues that Gunnar's family, friends, teachers, and the media teach him. Moving away from his predominantly White, wealthy suburb by the beach to the more multiracial, more struggling neighborhood of Hillside during his middle school years, Gunnar likens his new community, walled off from the wealthier enclave at the top of the hill, to the barbarians at the gate of civilization, the "hordes of impoverished American Mongols" at the foot of a "great wall" (45). To emphasize Hillside's perceived disconnection from the benefits and norms of civility, the educational curricula deemed fitting for these children are

PBS documentaries titled "Our Youth at Risk" and the monthly school assemblies, which are "hour-long deprogramming sessions [that] were supposed to liberate us from a cult of self-destructiveness and brainwash us into joining the sect of benevolent middle-class American normalcy" (112). Children, especially young boys like Gunnar, must be "deprogrammed"—saved from themselves and from their morally permissive families so that they might achieve upward mobility, or, at the very least, the appropriate malleability in the "smelting factory of young widgethood" (59). The lives of these children are managed by the Foucauldian disciplinary society: through family, school, factory, and prison.

Explaining intergenerational poverty through the poor's culture of failure and immorality, racial conservatives such as Vice President Dan Quayle argue that "a welfare ethos . . . impedes individual efforts to move ahead in society, and hampers their ability to take advantage of the opportunities America offers" (Quayle). These words were part of a well-known speech delivered by then Vice President Dan Quayle soon after the L.A. Crisis and during the 1992 presidential campaign. In the speech popularly dubbed the "Murphy Brown" speech for Candice Bergen's sitcom character's single motherhood, Quayle linked intergenerational poverty to a pervasive depravity that caused the 1992 Los Angeles Crisis: "I believe the lawless social anarchy which we saw is directly related to the breakdown of family structure. *[sic]* personal responsibility and social order in too many areas of our society" (Quayle). Both sides of the political aisle, in their emphasis on personal responsibility, echoed often-repeated political dicta on precarious families, social mores, and communities that had received the force of truth in public policy as a "culture of poverty" by the early 1990s. Intergenerational poverty resulted not from structural barriers to economic mobility but from a lack of character.[16] Poverty was not simply one's lack of money and a lived experience of deprivation and want but signaled a failure of individual will, evidenced by moral deviancy, shiftlessness, and criminality.

The post–civil rights era shows a marked shift from definitions of race in terms of biological determinism to ostensibly race-neutral concepts of "the underclass" and "the culture of poverty" in what sociologist Eduardo Bonilla-Silva has termed the "biologization of culture" (139). One of the dominant frames of colorblind racism of the post–civil rights era, this biologization of culture is repeatedly manifested in Bonilla-Silva's interviews with White subjects, who attributed to African Americans a lack of "the proper values" that was the cause for their disproportionate poverty. In this logic, instead of parents transmitting lesser genes to their offspring, parents are now passing on cultures of poverty and failure. Vilified as deserving failures within the meritocracy, their generational poverty of resources allegedly indicates their generational poverty of values. This causation and its connotations look very similar to conservative responses to civil rights and egalitarian movements: the inheritability of undesirable traits, contamination by physical proximity, and the fundamental *civility* of waiting one's turn, given the inevitable forward progress of equality and the fairness of others.[17]

Beatty has an unusual take on this implicit claim about an intergenerational culture of poverty. Far from the heroic ancestors of W. E. B. Du Bois's *The Souls of Black Folk* (1903) or Alex Haley's best-selling *Roots* (1976), Gunnar's antecedents are an immoral, yet very successful, bunch of sellouts and confidence men. The entire first chapter of the narrative details Gunnar's genealogy through "a set of weak-kneed DNA to shuffle in the footsteps of a long cowardly queue of coons, Uncle Toms, and faithful boogedy-boogedy retainers" (5). His mother, an orphan, so relishes the Kaufman family's assimilationist, antiheroic background that she has adopted her ex-husband's infamous forebears with pride.[18] His male ancestors reenact and promote the most demeaning stereotypes of African Americans for personal gain. Beatty parodies not only the racist belief in Black irrationality and excessive emotion but also anti-Black nostalgia for antebellum life in the family story that tells of one ancestor, Sven, reenslaving himself because he is so moved by the beauty of slave work: "The rise-and-fall rhythm of the hoes and pickaxes and the austere urgency of the work songs gave him an idea for a 'groundbreaking' dance opera. A renegade piece that intertwined the stoic movement of forced labor with the casual assuredness of aristocratic lyric" (13). In another one, Wolfgang, a janitor for a Chicago radio station, helps Freeman F. Gosden and Charles J. Correll develop their sketch comedy material for the hugely successful radio and television show *Amos & Andy*, which was heavily protested by the NAACP for disseminating demeaning depictions of African Americans in the big city. With such conspicuously Greek, Germanic, and Swedish names as Euripides, Wolfgang, Sven, Rolfe and Gunnar Kaufman, Beatty is not only alluding to the shared culture, heritage, and destiny of Black and White but also the absurdity of an affinity for White culture through an abasement of Blackness.

By exposing the successes of these ancestors as the result of immoral and unethical behavior, Beatty questions just what kind of role models and values Gunnar is taught to emulate. For example, Gunnar tells the much-loved story of Euripides, an eighteenth-century ancestor, who buys his freedom with the fees he charges Whites to rub his head for luck. One of Gunnar's few narrated memories of spending time with his father that does not concern sexual and physical abuse details how Rolfe laughs the loudest at the anti-Black jokes told by other police officers and makes Gunnar follow suit. In order to survive and prosper under slavery and Jim Crow terror, his ancestors get ahead with toadying and selfish behavior, and these achievements can be interpreted as meritorious because of their positive, even enviable outcomes of individual success.

In the logic of the meritocracy, in which you are what your ancestors were, Gunnar should be the apotheosis of assimilationist dreams, the quintessence of the unobjectionable Black image in the White mind. His last name means "merchant" in German and Gunnar peddles a number of contradictory political agendas and ideological critiques. Although Gunnar's last name also refers to Beat poet Bob Kaufman, known for his improvisation and oral poetry, his first name alludes to Gunnar Myrdal, the Nobel Prize–winning scholar famous for his 1944 study *An American Dilemma: The Negro Problem and Modern Democracy,* which helped establish the terms of Black success as White assimilation and Black poverty as the failure to assimilate into White heteropatriarchal norms of family, more forcefully expounded in Daniel Patrick Moynihan's 1965 report "The Negro Family: The Case for National Action."[19] In Gunnar's stories, he is quick to point out the dishonesty and exploitation of oneself and others in achieving success. In this vein, *The White Boy Shuffle* is a morality tale, in which Gunnar exposes the unsavory side of a meritocratic myth of upward mobility. Upward mobility, Gunnar points out, is not about deserving or earning equality through virtuous effort, but rather seems to require a heavy dose of good fortune and luck. Beatty offers possible readings of Gunnar's incredible fortune in having enjoyed success *despite* having such embarrassing cowards and sycophants as ancestors. Or, if heroism is defined in trickster-like survival or innovative self-exploitation, as is the case of Euripides Kaufman, Gunnar is successful *because of* his ancestral ingenuity. Or even another: given Gunnar's espousal of everyone else's mass suicide, Gunnar is an even more embarrassing coward and yes-man than his ancestors—encouraging others to commit suicide in a pact he has no intention of keeping. Beatty implies that Gunnar conducts his message of bad-faith advocacy much in the spirit of his aforementioned ancestor Euripides, whose reckless heckling of British troops exposes his best friend, Crispus Attucks, to their retaliatory gunfire. Attucks's death becomes one of the famed first casualties of the American Revolution. In both situations, someone dies, the Kaufman lives. But if heroism is defined by tricksterism and self-exploitation, these varying interpretations merely highlight the shifting frames of reference and the contingencies of success.

Given this complexity, merit is in the eye of the beholder, and what Gunnar finds is that the most pervasive definitions of merit are reserved for the already powerful. *The White Boy Shuffle* upends the logic of meritocracy: those like Gunnar, who bear diminished life chances and opportunities even with individual merit, personal success, and successful ancestors. A meritocratic society is not a democratic one. In theory and practice, a meritocracy deploys antidemocratic features of other forms of government that have been traditionally reviled, such as those in which the concentration of power is established by birth or wealth. Meritocracy's seductive yet false promise of fairness led to sociologist Michael Young's satiric warnings of the dystopic effects in the exchange of democracy and equality for merit in his book *The Rise of the Meritocracy* (1958), which coined the term itself.[20] Young identifies the phenomenon of what I call "the biologization of merit," a meritocracy that will be inherited and even more unshakeable because of the belief that merit has been earned through fair competition.[21]

Economist Amartya Sen notes that one of the benefits of privileging merit is that it can function as an incentive for increasing the good in society, in whatever terms "the good" might be construed (Sen, 8). Yet, too often, merit is mistakenly attributed to people, not their actions, in contradistinction to what this instrumental use of merit as incentive would suggest (ibid.). In other words, because merit identifies who they are rather than what they do, some *people* are accorded more merit than others rather than some *actions* being accorded more merit than others. Thus, for groups that fail to meet norms, standards of behavior, and quality of life, this conflation can easily serve as the genetic and biological bases for differential treatment and access to resources. Despite the difficulty in conclusively correlating success with meritorious behavior, merit is often defined as "intelligence-plus-effort" (7, quoting *Fontana Dictionary of Modern Thought,* 521). However, if intelligence and genetic inheritance are so crucial to economic success, as one marker of merit, then the bell-curve "distribution of intelligence" should closely mirror the "distributions of income and wealth" (McNamee and Miller, 13). But these correlations do not exist in the one-to-one correspondence necessary for such prescriptions.

Thus far, I have traced the ways in which race, culture, and merit have come to be viewed as biologically determined. In the context of the debates over the civility crisis in terms of social capital, I identify the emergence of the biologization of civility: how the "have nots" lack the civic virtues that build a democracy and thus deserve to be amputated from it. According to this logic, if the state cannot exclude these people from democratic participation, the state or civil society can significantly disadvantage them from participating fully in the benefits and privileges that such a democratic society might offer through citizenship. These citizenship hierarchies produce the biologization of civility alongside the biologization of culture and of merit. The biologization of civility is so dominant a frame because it is couched in terms of merit. The insidious logic of the meritocracy posits that first, *people* are meritorious rather than their actions, and second, people are retroactively meritorious since civic virtues can only be adduced through meritorious and successful behaviors. Therefore, only meritorious people can perform, enact, and embody meritorious and successful behaviors and only past generations of this elite can reproduce themselves.

Contemporary civil rights jurisprudence exhibits this logic. Legal critic Kenji Yoshino posits that the new battle for civil rights is on the terrain of behaviors. This range of behaviors includes those that foster one's assimilation into one's neighborhood, school, social group, and workplace, but are also those that are necessary to succeed, keep one's job, stay out of jail, or survive an encounter with the police. Certain forms of assimilation, which Yoshino calls "covering," function as bias and discrimination when competing claims are ignored or invalidated: "Covering demands are the modern form of that subordination: racial minorities must 'act white' because of white supremacy, women must hide parenting responsibilities at work because of patriarchy, gays must hide displays of same-sex affection because of heteronormativity"

(177). Since these behaviors are seen as mutable, in that people can choose to perform them or not, they are not protected under existing civil rights statutes, unlike immutable characteristics in the historical markers of identity difference: the color of one's skin and the shape and size of one's eyes, head, nose, and body. Yoshino argues that there must be a compelling reason to discriminate against certain behaviors instead of bias, because all too often, social demands for "normal" behavior never face the same standard for compelling reasons that nonnormative behaviors must meet and their discriminatory outcomes persist.

Exclusion from meritocratic civility is most often justified in various ways: through cultures of criminality and deviancy, the uncivil's inability to work with one another and for others, failure to assimilate into the mainstream economy because of rule-breaking or lack of discipline, and last, an incapability of working effectively with economic and political elites. As the inherited punishment for the undeserving, this socioeconomic predestination leads to stasis or downward mobility, an ostensibly just outcome. The biologization of civility refers to social expectations to foster and sustain an adequately meritorious community as if such merit were a genetic ability. Such assumptions are made visible primarily through racial groupings that thwart an individual's claims on the state for citizenship, for humanity.

Merit Rules and Multidiscrimination, or Equality without Equality

U.S. social stratification is widely perceived as a meritocracy that is synonymous with democracy, a connection that I have argued is an awkward misalliance. This contradiction has been handily resolved by the ideals and practices of equal opportunity (for racial centrists and liberals) and equal treatment (for racial conservatives) rather than by more equalized outcomes (for racial radicals). In this section I explore colorblindness and multiculturalism, Gunnar's childhood targets of satire and parody. The irony is, of course, that the more multiracial Gunnar's neighborhood is, the less his neighbors talk about multiculturalism and colorblindness.

In her famous essay "On Race and Voice: Challenges for Liberal Education in the 1990s," feminist scholar Chandra Talpade Mohanty urges her readers not only to acknowledge the historical and political specificity of difference, but also to recognize difference as a "conflict, struggle," or "disruption" (181)—actions that are often perceived as inherently uncivil. Mohanty questions whether her readers will continue to grapple with the concept of race and struggle over the function and significance of these differences in everyday interactions, or whether readers will stand aside to facilitate the substitution of one group's experience for another—a "harmonious, empty pluralism" in which all differences are sanitized, made "benign" (ibid.), and rendered meaningless. Mohanty's call for struggle attacks the influential neoconservative approaches that try to manage racial difference through pluralism, colorblindness, and multiculturalism. These approaches tend to oversimplify and elide racial conflicts and injuries in the United States while appearing to advocate racial diversity and inclusion. I extend Mohanty's analysis to identify how difference that cannot be sanitized in this way can be delegitimized as uncivil, and often inhuman.

Narrated in the parodic style of the novel, Gunnar relates his own experiences with misguided strategies to achieve racial diversity in the U.S. educational system. For Gunnar, racial diversity on campus entails coercive assimilation into Whiteness. From attending the improbably named Mestizo Mulatto Mongrel Elementary in a southern California beach community to Boston University, Gunnar endures the negative effects of integration experienced through bussing inner-city children to Whiter, wealthier suburbs and recruiting for elite basketball camps, high school, and college admissions. At each new school, Gunnar notices people's contradictory reactions to his highly visible status as a top basketball player, college student, and published poet. He implicitly criticizes the prevailing political and judicial interpretations of Equal Protection jurisprudence that advance racial diversity in sports arenas, college campuses, and media venues in theory but further debilitate racial minorities in practice. Beatty's continual depiction of how students of color are forced into subordinate roles subject to the evaluations and expectations of their White peers. In one instance, Gunnar is shocked by the racist reception his high school poetry receives— poems published as a collection without his knowledge or consent. The students and even his professor fawn over Gunnar's impoverished friends and family and confess their appreciation of Black artistic expression. Far from parity or even praise, these interracial relations expose the illusion of pluralism that obscures new forms of inequity such as nominal integration via tokenism and post–affirmative action racial stigmatization. Gunnar identifies the contradiction and the per-petuation of disadvantages faced by students of color in terms of new manifestations of old stereotypes: the lazy, deceitful slave of the ante-bellum era develops into the undeserving, substandard beneficiary of affirmative action; the vaudeville performer is now the celebrated poet and star athlete who must appease and entertain his White authority figures and peers in the classroom and on the courts.

Beatty criticizes the practices of colorblindness and its popular deployment as a metaphor, "the level playing field," or the basketball court in the novel. For Gunnar, it serves not only as an obvious meta-phor for life's struggles, failures, and triumphs, but also a justification for the unequal distribution of resources. In the novel's epilogue and at the fullest height of his international fame, Gunnar expresses bit-terness toward the diminished opportunities available for those like himself and the futility of further struggles: "Black America has relin-quished its needs in a world where expectations are illusion, has re-fused to develop ideals and mores in a society that applies principle without principle" (225). This principle that Gunnar contends society applies indiscriminately and unethically is equality without equality. By transmuting democratic equality into a meritocratic civility, Gunnar alludes to specific racial injustices long unresolved in U.S. history, in which state institutions targeted African American men and women for harassment, violence, and discrimination.[22] Equality persists as a par-amount American value despite these events, but Gunnar exposes how the principle of equality is applied "without principle"—inequitably—in the past and during the novel's contemporary moment of the mid-1990s. To translate from one satirist to another, Beatty to George Orwell, some animals are indeed more equal than others.

Gunnar's classroom experiences in elementary school exemplify this equality without equality. Throughout *The White Boy Shuffle*, Gun-nar's most immediate environments are the public school and univer-sity, and the novel traces Gunnar's education from third grade to his first year in college. Education is expected to inculcate the tenets of citizenship and the ideals of a nation-state in each new generation. Equal access in admissions policies to educational opportunities has emerged as the leading test case for evaluating the principle of "equality before the law." Given this background and Gunnar's perpetual encoun-ters with formal and informal, explicit and implicit, classroom and com-munity lessons in pluralism, multiculturalism, sexism, colorblindness, and racism on the playground, it is important to analyze Gunnar's interpretation of this principle of equality as it applies to his educational experiences.

Rather than multiculturalism as an equal appreciation for all cultures and their differences, Gunnar finds that what I term *multidiscrimination* is more accurately multiculturalism's primary methodology and outcome. Gunnar's formal and informal education incorporates ostensibly competing conceptions of difference: one that tries to erase the importance of identity differences in material inequalities and another that finds humor in offensive stereotypes. In elementary school, for example, Gunnar notices the disparity in the lessons taught in the classroom and those learned on the playground, and for him and the other children the lessons of the latter are much more memorable. He distinguishes between classroom multiculturalism, "which reduced race, sexual orientation, and gender to inconsequence," and schoolyard multiculturalism, "where the kids who knew the most Polack, queer, and farmer's daughter's jokes ruled" (28). Both versions of multiculturalism are actually discriminatory rather than equality-producing.[23] In the refusal to see material differentiation, proponents of colorblind multiculturalism reduce these identity categories to inconsequence, minimize their importance, and refuse to counter inequalities—all forms of multidiscrimination. Students like Gunnar are much too smart to be hoodwinked by multiculturalism's erasure and question among themselves: If differences are as easily ignored as the teachers say, then why do they exist in the first place, and why are the teachers so enthusiastic to teach that these differences do not exist? Classroom multidiscrimination smooths out differences to "inconsequence," but this educational strategy fails to address the differences that the children can identify in entertaining yet derogatory ways. These jokes are immensely memorable for the children, and what is learned in the classroom hardly counteracts the offensively compelling playground humor. Because race has been placed off-limits by well-intentioned teachers who are less savvy than their students, the children reinstantiate racial prejudice and other forms of subordination such as sexism, homophobia, classism, and ethnocentrism with no adequate counterdiscourse.

Beatty exposes the incivility and civility that dually function in these parables of multidiscrimination. While these jokes are uncivil through their raunchy and discriminatory punchlines, the children bond socially over this shared humor. This classroom multiculturalism and its discriminatory practices are linked to colorblindness in complementary ways, though colorblindness, in its emphasis on individual merit and racial neutrality, might at first appear to stand in direct opposition to multiculturalism and its explicit focus on cultural groupings and pluralist cultures. However, multiculturalism emphasizes cultural, not racial, diversity. Just as definitions of diversity in education have depended less on the recognition of racial differences, multiculturalist practices oversimplify racial identities into just one of the many U.S. cultures celebrated at Gunnar's school. Moreover, multiculturalism enables calls for colorblindness in that one's cultural identity displaces or subsumes one's racial identity. The elementary school teacher Gunnar singles out for an extended critique in *The White Boy Shuffle* elides contemporary manifestations of racial discrimination and the lingering material effects caused by skin colors that have been accorded differential treatment in the past. These interlocking oppressions are neither directly addressed nor countered in his teacher's attempts to present race as obsolete and invisible.

Gunnar learns the lesson of multidiscrimination as a form of assimilation to civil racism: going along to get along in order to feign belonging inside and outside the classroom. His teacher repeatedly points to what Gunnar calls the "multiculturalism propaganda" above the blackboard: "Eracism—the sun doesn't care what color you are" (29).[24] During these kinds of lessons, Gunnar notices that his teacher particularly directs his and two other students' attention to the classroom slogan. It would seem that Gunnar's teacher especially wants to imbue these nonwhite children with self-worth and the belief that their racial identities can and will be ignored in determining their individual merit. His teacher thus encourages her three students of color to believe that they will be treated with indifference to their racial identities, rather than addressing the attitudes of other students and their parents who may perceive these students of color as different and act accordingly. Although expressing a shorthand version of colorblindness, the personification of the sun fails to equip the children to recognize and fight discrimination inside and outside the classroom.

Offering another lesson about the ease with which students can adopt colorblindness, the teacher conspicuously wears a logo on her T-shirt with a list of colors representing the different races recognized in legal and popular terms throughout U.S. history—black, white, red, yellow, and brown. Each of these words is crossed out except the final word, "Human" (28). This tired truism of all humans belonging to the same species attempts to refute a history of racist science that tried to prove nonwhites were a subhuman species. This list also functions as an equation that offers the illusory finiteness and reductive precision of mathematical processes such as addition and subtraction, that racial identification can be subtracted from one's daily practices just as it was once added; his teacher's shirt can symbolically cross out the "colors" associated with racial groups and leave "Human" as the equation's only difference that matters.[25] The utopian appeal of her universal human- ist beliefs ignores the historic question that has functioned to exclude some groups: Who will be allowed to occupy the category of "human"? Within the logic of scientific racism, non-Europeans and nonwhites have been evolutionarily differentiated from *humans,* a determination that made them vulnerable to genocide, forced removal, and concen- tration camps, practices that did indeed attempt to cross out and erase racial groups.

Beatty notes the relationship between the refusal to recognize racial difference and the refusal to include people of color and their experi- ences. Gunnar again encounters the contradiction between the physi- ological and ideological reactions to color differences when he is given a test for visual colorblindness during a routine physical at school. The doctor unsatisfactorily addresses Gunnar's insight that colorblindness is physically impossible, even for those who have this type of visual impairment.

> "Our teacher says we're supposed to be colorblind. That's hard to do if you can see color, isn't it?" . . .
> "So just pretend that you don't see color. Don't say things like 'Black people are lecherous, violent, natural-born criminals.'"
> "But I'm black."
> "Oh, I hadn't noticed." (31–32)

Gunnar's interaction with the doctor reads much like the transcript for a comedy routine. Whites such as Gunnar's teacher and the doctor can insist they choose not to see racial difference based on skin color, but these differences persist for those who do not make this choice. Just as the doctor's advice is highly contradictory, his other colorblind prac- tices are littered with inherent deceptions. In the doctor's explanation of colorblindness, he advises Gunnar to "pretend that you don't see color" (32). Colorblindness, therefore, is something one merely *pretends* to have as if it were a fraud. The doctor's reply encourages Gunnar to deny what he sees; by extension, Gunnar should pretend that he does not see race, and, it is implied, its material manifestations. The doctor hardly seems aware of the contradictions between what he says and what he does. When Gunnar jokes to dispel his uneasiness when the doctor checks Gunnar's groin for a hernia, the doctor responds by calling Gunnar "one of those funny cool black guys" (31)—obviously contradicting his earlier remark that he did not notice Gunnar was Black. Clearly, the doctor has already characterized Gunnar stereotypically as "one of" a larger generality, but this contradiction between what he says and does stands uncontested. Of course, being a "funny cool black guy" contrasts with the stereotype of "lecherous, violent, natural-born criminals" (ibid.) that rolls so easily and unselfconsciously off the doctor's tongue. Rather than reading Gunnar's Blackness as a threat, the doctor casts Gunnar as a harmless, funny, and cool Black child seeking to entertain and thus be accepted by his predominantly White audiences: this doctor, the teacher, and other students. This is a very different stereotype than the one that scared the Wonder Bread truck driver during the L.A. Crisis, instead one through which Gunnar earns acceptance and qualified inclusion by being entertaining.

In *Seeing a Color-Blind Future,* Patricia Williams tells a similar story of her own son who is diagnosed with visual colorblindness, but who in fact has been innocently trying to practice what his teachers are preaching by refusing to see the color of anything like the grass or the sky (Williams, 3). Here civility is defined as conflict avoidance rather than resolution. Because of the teachers' irresponsible discussions of racial identity and politics as merely colors, her young child is diagnosed with a visual disability. Williams uncovers the reasons behind such misleading lessons: there has been interracial conflict in the classroom between White and Black students. The teachers' misguided solution was to insist that children not see color and thus not see race in order to avoid conflict. Ironically, Williams's son has absorbed these teachings diligently, as a good student would, but he is punished for learning his lessons too well—his teachers identify his "disability," but it is one that they themselves have created through their negligence.

These examples demonstrate the hubris of claiming a race-neutral and colorblind outlook. Confused between not being a racist and antiracist practices by well-meaning but irresponsible adult authority figures, Gunnar becomes responsible for his own education, especially in identifying the contradictions between what adults say and do, between colorblind ideology and its discriminatory practices. In their ostensibly progressive agenda of multiracial harmony, the multiculturalist, colorblind teachings ultimately fail to prepare students to recognize the discrimination they suffer and indeed perpetrate. In the teachers' restricted focus on race, they ignore the lived reality of racism rather than provide the students tools with which to combat it. Well-intentioned misinformation leaves these students unprepared for interactions with those who were taught different lessons of racial inferiority and biological determinism and negotiations with longstanding institutions premised on such inequalities during the era of formal exclusion and racial terror. Philosopher Cornel West argues that in much political rhetoric, whether liberal or conservative, nonblacks try to shift the burden of racial equality onto African Americans, who are forced "to do all the 'cultural' and 'moral' work necessary for healthy race relations" (6). At Mestizo Mulatto Mongrel Elementary School, Gunnar realizes that these multiculturalist, colorblind teachings are inadequate, false, and misleading and that he must figure out racial relations and appropriate interracial practices for himself. Given this mis-education, Gunnar recognizes what his teacher cannot.

Colorblind multiculturalism derives from the historical conception of racial identity as biological, genetic, and inheritable. In the middle of a lesson on racial color-blindness, the teacher tells the parable of inexplicably warring herds of white and black elephants that, even more inexplicably, go into the hills one day and return generations later, suddenly "a harmonious and homogeneous herd of gray elephants" (32). The story implies that the violence was caused by different skin colors and ends when there is just one. Since gray is indeed the color of elephants today, the story also resonates in terms of the fabular, happening a long time ago. Such harmony and homogeneity in his teacher's story blatantly allegorizes the Black–White racial conflict in U.S. history as past and resolved, while proffering generations of interracial heterosex and the resulting offspring as proof of such resolution and reconciliation.[26] The teacher implies that the idea of racial antagonism is a thing of the past. Due to increasing numbers of interracial relationships and the growing numbers of mixed-race children in the United States, pundits, journalists, and scholars often project the "face" of the future American people as an amalgamation of these different skin colors. Like the warring elephants, different skin colors will no longer produce conflict because there will someday be only one, according to the parable of the elephants. The symbolism of these lessons is given even more power by the improbable, ironic names of Gunnar's school and his teacher. At Mestizo Mulatto Mongrel Elementary School, the school appears to recognize race-mixing and interracial hybridity in its very name as does Gunnar's teacher, Ms. Cegeny. Her name obviously puns on the term "miscegenation," the nineteenth- and early twentieth-century euphemism for heterosexual White and nonwhite relations—predominantly Black–White—that could result in the biracial children variously identified in the school's name. The pejorative terms for multiracial identities, "mulatto" and "mongrel," resuscitate a racist hierarchy that has been used to distinguish mixed racial heritage from pure White or European "blood" or ancestry. From Gunnar's perspective, the classroom and faculty demographics hardly reflect the race-mixing in the school's name.[27] The utopian visions of a multiracial future promote the inevitable eventuality of racial harmony advanced through sexual reproduction—the gray elephants from their White and Black ancestors.

Gunnar, however, is wise to such morphologic sleight of hand: changing the object of inquiry does not change the structures or patterns of inquiry itself, the way we look at race and why it has been deployed for centuries continues to frame mixed-race identities. Gunnar counters Ms. Cegeny's evolutionary fable and, by extension, *Time* magazine's liberal interracial fantasy with the scientific fact of spontaneous genetic variation: "Just like some human babies are born with tails or scales, some unfortunate baby elephants are going to be genetic flashbacks and come out albino white and summer's nap black. Then the whole monochrome utopia is going to be all messed up" (33). Though a third-grader, Gunnar understands that circumstances may change, but ideology persists. Gunnar also contests the easy, harmonious models of interracial relationships posited by his teacher and his doctor. Gunnar realizes that despite being taught this fictitious outcome of one skin color and thus one race, reactions to difference will persist. Gunnar intrinsically understands the futility of his teacher's wish for this "monochrome utopia"—one future race with a homogeneous phenotypic expression achieved after years of interracial reproduction.

As the *Time* magazine cover photo's tanner version of White implies the lightening of dark skin through interracial heterosex, Gunnar begins to realize that "human" signifies another version of pluralistic, multicultural Whiteness that fundamentally excludes people of color, especially African Americans. Implicit in the analogy to the future monochrome utopia of gray elephants, people who have darker skin would have not yet been lightened through years of interracial sexual reproduction. Perceived as evidence of a lack of genetic and cultural assimilation—a lack of racial enlightenment in both senses of the word—these racial minorities are, then, symbolically not yet as evolved as those Whiter and lighter on this utopian family tree, a further rationale for assumptions of their inadequacy. In her teachings, Ms. Cegeny furthers this lack of political coevalness by implying that it is Gunnar and the other students of color who need the colorblindness training most of all. Their experiences of discrimination are obstacles to her colorblind utopia and belie the success of her universal humanist project to see only "human." As West has observed, it is for minorities to turn a blind eye to their disparate and disparaging treatment. This new social contract and terms of civility—citizenship itself—are predicated on the racial blinding and silencing of the most vulnerable.

Civility without Civility

As the most striking sites of Gunnar's education of inequality and incivility, the school playground and the basketball court are perhaps the two most important spaces for providing a critique of democratic egalitarianism. The basketball court, an extension of the school playground, is an extended metaphor for the intersection of the methodology of satire, the demands of civility, and the multidiscrimination in commitments to equal consideration. Beatty explores this dynamic through the basketball court: the ostensibly "level playing field" that organizes most of Gunnar's adolescent and young adult experiences during the 1980s and 1990s.[28] A streetball and pickup-game player since junior high, Gunnar's remarkable basketball abilities enhance his educational opportunities from high school to college and thrust him into the national spotlight. Far from the level playing field as the stage for recognizing individual merit and equal treatment symbolized by good sportsmanship and league regulations, however, Gunnar documents the peculiar reactions to the game and its players that expose other influential factors apart from the playing field itself: before and after regulation play, off the court, and outside the sports arena. Gunnar discovers that these unregulated and unrefereed aspects of the game such as harassment create a playing field that is not level or fair at all, paralleling the novel's broader critique of colorblindness and the failure of equal treatment to promote racial equality. Gunnar's and his best friend Nick Scoby's receptions on and off the court indicate the larger fallacy of legal determinations of individual merit.

Gunnar uses the basketball court as a stage to mount his biting critique of the system of racial discrimination and privilege that has brought him to the court. Uninterested in the fans and playing to the crowds, Gunnar's appearance during college basketball games garners him boos and trash thrown from even the home crowd. But while Gunnar finds such attention amusing, even invigorating, his best friend, Nick Scoby, is deeply shaken by the hostility his own play garners. Even more remarkable than his athletic ability is Nick's inability to fail: incredibly, he has never missed a basket in his life. However, the college media and fans, rather than celebrating Nick as an indisputable asset to the team, instead feel that he is somehow exploiting an unfair advantage. His incredible talent and perfect scoring statistics foment racial antagonism. During the game, Gunnar notes the different etiquette for Nick: "Usually when you dive into the crowd for a loose ball, the fans try to catch you, help break your fall. When Nick goes headlong in the stands, the reporters scatter, picking up their coffee cups and laptops and letting Scoby crash into the table. They don't even help the nigger to his feet" (193). This continuing discrimination and hostility hounds Nick until he unexpectedly commits suicide in college.

As the subject of countless scientific studies on and theoretical hypotheses about his scoring abilities, Nick is troubled by the hostility his skill foments. Gunnar, meanwhile, is indignant over the scrutiny his friend faces: "Nick's thrown every theory, every formula, every philosophical dogma out of whack: he's like a living disclaimer. 'I am perfection; everything else is bullshit. Your life is meaningless.' . . . They would be a lot better off if they simply called Scoby a god and left it at that, but no way they'll proclaim a skinny black man God" (192). From the fans' perspective, since a Black man cannot be perfect, he must be cheating. The fans and the media develop their own form of entertainment in attempting to rattle Nick from his focus: "Scoby's introduction is communal catharsis. Within moments the court is covered with bananas, coconuts, nooses, headless dolls, and shit. I'm into it, but Scoby gets shook" (193). Unlike Gunnar, Nick does not deliberately antagonize the crowd, but rather, Nick's shooting perfection riles even his home audiences in a way that Gunnar never can. Certain historically popular images of Blackness shadow Gunnar's educational experiences. Gunnar continually wonders what he, a Black man, can do in a society that has already prescribed inflexible roles for African Americans as criminals or token minorities—whether objects of contempt or pity, either are fodder for American political and economic rhetoric. Gunnar continually battles these stereotypes that label African Americans as impoverished, ignorant, criminal, or amoral. Even seemingly positive stereotypes such as the poet, athlete, political leader, or media celebrity ultimately reinforce stereotypical assumptions about African Americans. Thus, Gunnar faces a stigma for succeeding when most African Americans are expected to fail. Attempting to thwart these connotations, Gunnar identifies and condemns the ways he is exploited by individuals and institutions—his teachers, coaches, recruiters, schools, collegiate sports—and exposes the contradictions between their seemingly progressive attitudes toward racial equality and the unequal treatment he endures.

But Gunnar finds that one must play outside the rules because most things are determined off the field of play. Life plays out on unregulated fields of play that are far from level. In Beatty's play with language and Gunnar's wisecracking irreverence, the exaggerated, hyperbole-driven narrative is crucial in discerning the political commitments of the novel. Beatty parodies the colorblind approach that has been advocated and established via affirmative action programs to effect fairness and equal opportunity. In our media-saturated existence, Gunnar feels his only opportunity to reach his audience is to shock his readers and listeners into activism by claiming the futility of any struggle and thus advocating the mass suicide of his followers. In his increasingly outrageous yet infinitely media-savvy behavior over the course of the novel, Gunnar adopts the role of the heroic badman with relish, believing this strategy to be the most effective in exposing the deep-seated inequality and self-destruction at the core of contemporary assertions of colorblind equality and cultural pluralism by both conservatives and liberals. The chilling answer to pernicious racial discrimination, for Gunnar and, it seems, for the entire Black population in America, is suicide. In what he considers the final glaring proof of the untenable present of this post–civil rights era, Gunnar believes his only choice is to die—a blatant rejection of ineffective attempts to achieve racial equality.

In characteristic style, Beatty both embraces a so-called Black reality culled from well-intentioned policymakers and scholars and Ellis's "cultural mulattoes" with their familiarity and successful negotiations of Whiteness and Blackness. At the same time, he criticizes both of these paradigms, which promote their own versions of authentic representation, shaming readers, authors, and critics alike. Beatty springs a richly deserved trap for unwary readers, perhaps too smug or passive in their perceptions of Blackness and of race. Bernstein's metaphor of "a fun house mirror" is apt, but not in the way that he intended—that the distortions detract from the "truth" of the figure before the mirrors and that the "figure in black" was already a figment of someone's imagination. Instead, Beatty casts our gaze to the distortions of distortions of distortions that have cultivated his readers' racist desire for more distortions. Allegiances to style, form, and characterization are constantly drawn and redrawn so that there is no stable ground from which to build static notions of African American experiences. The exhaustion of the reader leads to the exhaustion of the paradigm.

3 THE TERRITORIALIZATION OF CIVILITY, THE SPATIALIZATION OF REVENGE

> Diasporas always leave a trail of collective memory about another place and time and create new maps of desire and of attachment.
>
> —Arjun Appadurai and Carol Breckenridge,
> "On Moving Targets"

> One chooses dialectic when one has no other means. . . . Is dialectic only a form of *revenge* in Socrates?
>
> —Wendy Brown, *States of Injury*

THIS CHAPTER TAKES UP one of the most prevalent, yet opaque, readings of the 1992 Los Angeles Crisis—that these acts of violence were motivated by revenge. I return to two events that galvanized the city: the beating of Rodney King and the subsequent acquittals and mistrial of the police defendants; and the case of Latasha Harlins, a teenage girl fatally shot by a Korean immigrant storeowner, Soon Ja Du, who received a suspended sentence and $500 fine. Framed as revenge, iconic events during the L.A. Crisis, such as White truck driver Reginald Denny's beating by Black men and the disproportionate property losses sustained by Korean storeowners, are given meaning as payback. Citing the graffiti "For Rodney" and "For Latasha" spray painted on buildings and advertisements around town, critics and interviewees on the nightly news explained that "rioters" were exacting vengeance for King and Harlins or others disabled or killed by police and routinely treated disrespectfully by non-Black storeowners. Bearing the scars of his attack, King represented the many unidentified and unredressed victims of police brutality in Black neighborhoods. In the grainy security camera footage replayed nightly on the evening news, Harlins's death represented the uneasy race, class, and gendered tensions among inner-city merchants and customers, especially between Korean immigrants and Black residents. Together, the trials of King's and Harlins's assailants would come to represent a justice system that upheld the racialized privileges of presumptive innocence and good intentions of Whites and Asians while devaluing Black lives. These high-profile trials and their unexpected sentences and verdicts thus accorded African American victims' lives little value and remained private grievances that would remain publicly unaddressed until the crisis and beyond.

The emphases on the Black–White and Black–Korean conflicts also erased Latinas/os within the racial pyramidization of Los Angeles. In California, as in the rest of the United States, Latinas/os have also experienced police brutality and surveillance for decades; a criminal justice system accords their lives, losses, and suffering little value by reflexively associating Latinas/os with illegal immigration, criminality, and unfair labor competition. During the L.A. Crisis, Latinas/os comprised half of those arrested, most of those made homeless by the fires, and some of the wounded or dead; in its immediate aftermath, the Immigration and Naturalization Service deported hundreds. The deportation of more than a thousand undocumented immigrants is revenge for their collective participation in the looting and mayhem, expelled from the United States in a way that citizen Black agitators could not be (Palumbo-Liu, 371). The national and international media made Reginald Denny a household name and the symbolic victim of Black rage and Black–White hostilities, while largely obscuring the more than thirty other victims who had been attacked and beaten at the corner of Florence and Normandie avenues that same afternoon. One was Fidel Lopez, a Guatemalan immigrant and father of three: unknown assailants hit him over the head with a car stereo, the resulting injuries required 250 stitches, and his attack caused permanent hearing loss, difficulty speaking, and debilitating dizzy spells (Gross). Compounding the theft of his construction materials and tools during the L.A. Crisis, these disabilities would prevent him from working steadily and his family would eventually lose their home. Like Denny, Lopez could not identify his alleged assailants at the trial. He and his family would speak to a *Los Angeles Times* reporter of his attack "without bitterness" and Lopez himself would say that he approved lesser charges and sentences because he believed it would keep the peace: "If they sent those guys to jail, those people would be mad and do it all over again" (Gross). The cycle of violence and revenge ends, the news article implies, through the resigned understanding of Lopez and his family, who forego justice in the name of peace.

Such private and public negotiations of crime and punishment, acceptance and vengeance, shaped the U.S. electorate's persistent debates over entitlement programs or the social safety net, and appeared in heavily racialized and gendered policies. The 1992 presidential election year heightened the discourse of revenge that filtered into mainstream politics. Racial conservatives and liberals in the national media both agreed on characterizing the arson, looting, and assaults during the L.A. Crisis as retributive violence, but they disagreed on the causes. From the racially conservative perspective, such responses evidenced the character and nature of the participants and, by extension, their racialized communities and neighborhoods, which perpetuated cycles of poverty and criminality. From a more racially liberal perspective, this violence was a kind of vigilantism on the part of African Americans and Latinas/os who had been treated unjustly by neighborhood merchants (Korean) and the police (Whites). The reasons given for these disastrous circumstances fell into competing policy camps: the state had done too much or not enough. These ideological and political debates over big government and personal responsibility framed discussions of the crisis and its causes, resulting in bivalent readings of the "riots" and violence and divergent policy proposals. For racial conservatives, an overly generous welfare state supported and rewarded "riot" participants—and their bad behavior. For racial liberals, the participants had legitimate grievances, but the violence stemmed from a misdirected anger that harmed innocent victims and disrupted proper, legal channels. Both mainstream policy assessments interpreted the violence as payback, whether for misguided entitlement programs or existing inequalities. Furthermore, both promoted the reading of the participants as acting criminally and immorally, whether due to their allegedly damaged psyches, pathological family structures, or cultures of poverty. These readings echo each other in their anxiety about, if not outright condemnation of, the instability and human suffering caused by the urban upheavals.

These divergent readings, yet shared premises, perpetuated racialized narratives of revenge. The discourse of revenge both organizes memories and resentments into actionable claims and injuries and recasts public priorities as natural and just. These tales of revenge, I argue, redefine the relationship between state and civil society. This chapter analyzes how revenge shapes civil society through discourses of justice and punishment and explores its ramifications on communities of color throughout the L.A. Crisis. Since revenge is generally negatively regarded as a criminally extralegal and uncivilized justice system, those who commit acts of revenge or acts perceived as revenge are criminals (working against the state) and primitives (working against "the civilizing process") with an intrinsic propensity for vengeance. Thus, such relationships define individuals and groups tautologically: criminals who break the law for revenge are savages; savages who enact vengeance are criminals. This association with deviance and savagery transmutes revenge into an innate *racial* characteristic. In this way states rigorously preserve their capacity to evaluate justice and adjudicate punishment in order to make a reading of state violence as state revenge unthinkable and masks state vengeance as just punishment.

"Vengeful" alludes to the negative characteristics and racial behaviors of people of color. While chapters 1 and 2 discuss civil racism in terms of the family and education, this chapter examines how punishment, or state action that defines the legal boundaries of civil society, codes race as revenge, and is mapped onto the people and neighborhoods of Los Angeles in what I call the territorialization of incivility. In the same circular logic that blurs the lines between cause and effect, civility is primarily determined to belong to who is perceived to deserve and not deserve punishment. And such punishment is not only assessed over criminal acts or legal violations but also emerges in cultural politics over the transgression of tacit codes of civility.[1] In the 1998 novel *The Tattooed Soldier,* Héctor Tobar crafts a morality tale of vengeance through the twinning of Antonio Bernal, a political exile from Guatemala and former student activist fleeing the assassinations of his wife and infant son, and Guillermo Longoria, the son of a poor K'iche' Mayan farming family who had been conscripted into the Guatemalan military and later, as a leader of a paramilitary death squad, murdered Antonio's family in addition to hundreds of other political dissidents and civilians in the final, bloodiest years of the country's three-decade civil war. Antonio's and Guillermo's intertwined narratives circle around the memory of this war and the narrative of Elena, Antonio's wife. Both men immigrate to the Pico-Union district of Los

Angeles, one of the putative epicenters of the L.A. Crisis, and confront their joined pasts against the backdrop of the *quemazones,* or the "great burnings," Tobar's name for the crisis. Tobar situates the interpersonal tale of revenge within the larger contexts of the 1992 violence as well as the long-standing racial and class inequalities in Los Angeles and the United States. I show how Tobar places the smaller tale of a personal vendetta within a far-reaching geopolitical logic of racist governmentality extended through cold war imperialism. By shifting between the United States and Guatemala through the figure of the homeless immigrant body, Tobar identifies the strategy of mapping incivility onto nonwhite, noncitizen bodies and the places they inhabit by marking them as deserving state vengeance in the form of punishment both inside and outside the United States.

Revenge propels the narrative in which Antonio happens to recognize Guillermo, the man who killed his wife, in a Los Angeles park. Antonio plots to kill him, and the novel ends with Antonio's fatal shooting of Guillermo on the first day of the crisis and his abandoning Guillermo's corpse in a sewer tunnel; Guillermo's death will likely be counted as one of the fatalities of the 1992 violence.[2] Tobar complexly layers the novel with narrative shifts between the dual protagonists, their lives in Los Angeles, and flashbacks to their pasts in Guatemala. The novel uses these two narratives to map the unofficial, delegitimated spaces of homeless people and undocumented immigrants in the United States. Influenced by the Los Angeles School of Urbanism that emerged in the 1980s and most famously represented in the works of Mike Davis and Edward Soja, Tobar maps the tenuous positionalities of noncitizens who are especially vulnerable to the violence and surveillance of the state and exclusion from the body politic. Through extended flashbacks of life in Guatemala and the United States, Tobar juxtaposes state-sanctioned genocide with the violence and destruction of the 1992 Crisis. The novel interweaves themes of retribution on the local and global scale, linking class conflicts and surplus peoples created in the United States to the genocidal repression and the *desaparecidos,* the disappeared, in Central America that were fostered by U.S. interventionist foreign policy. Tobar's juxtapositions—of protagonist and antagonist, Antonio/Elena and Guillermo, Guatemala and the United States, people and the state—expose the inner workings of U.S. imperialisms and global capitalism both within and without the nation-state.

In my analyses of Tobar's works, I discuss the relationship between place and belonging, developed most prominently in humanist geography, to reveal how language constitutes the built environment and constructs ways of knowing and patterns of thinking. Continually perceived as being out-of-place (Cresswell), people of color are both physically and imaginatively expelled from civil society or the U.S. nation-state. Latinas/os, maligned as illegal aliens, born criminals, and indigent parasites, experience a particularly forceful and often violent exclusion from the U.S. national imaginary. Civil racism against Latinas/os perpetuates the belief that immigrants are criminals since the category of "immigrant" is placed in opposition to that of "citizen," just as law-breaking criminals are posited against law-abiding citizens and spatially, as well as morally, relocated outside civil society.[3] In evaluating the layers of Tobar's fictional narrative, I trace the genealogy of violence and revenge in terms of race and gender in law, politics, and culture: through larger historical formations that call for retrenchment, are masked by nostalgia, and are manifested in backlash politics, spurred by revanchism and "reclaiming" America. These movements in law and politics have shaped civil society through proscriptions on violence and revenge, reserving punishment as the sole province of the state. Civil unrest is categorically vilified rather than interpreted as a vital form of communication and a manifestation of contentious politics; acts of violence are refused definition as acts that make legitimate claims on the state and its citizens. But revenge, like the policies it motivates, is attached to bodies, communities, and neighborhoods; spatializing revenge and territorializing incivility excludes these people and these localities from belonging to the U.S. nation-state.

The Revenge Plot

Tobar repeatedly returns to these issues in his reporting for the *Los Angeles Times,* his fiction, and his memoirs. Working for the paper his father once delivered, he began his early career moving up the ranks of the *LA Times* news staff, eventually becoming bureau chief in Mexico City and Buenos Aires. He shares a Pulitzer Prize awarded to the newspaper staff for coverage of the 1992 Crisis. Soon after receiving his MFA from the University of California, Irvine, Tobar published his first novel, *The Tattooed Soldier,* which became an *LA Times* bestseller and a finalist for the PEN Center/USA West prize, one of the few works of fiction by a Guatemalan American writer published by a major press. While a foreign correspondent, Tobar published *Translation Nation: Defining a New American Identity in the Spanish-Speaking United States* (2005), his collection of personal essays incorporating his experiences reporting on Latinas/os across the United States. His second novel, *Barbarian Nurseries* (2011), is set in the early 2000s after the dot-com bust and satirizes the awkward interactions between the very rich and very poor, recent immigrants and second-generation citizens, older and newer Chicana/o and Central American mixed-status, multiracial neighborhoods in Los Angeles and its suburbs. In *Deep Down Dark: The Untold Stories of 33 Men Buried in a Chilean Mine, and the Miracle That Set Them Free* (2014), Tobar's critically acclaimed nonfiction narrates the horrifying ordeal and later lives of the thirty-three Chilean miners trapped for sixty-nine days in a collapsed mine shaft. In his fiction and nonfiction, Tobar explores how crisis situations affect people's perspectives and relationships, revealing the complexities of their character and the vagaries of the human condition. In all of Tobar's fiction, nonfiction, and journalism, he represents the impact of U.S. foreign policy on Latin America and the Latina/o experience in the United States.

Tobar structures his first novel, *The Tattooed Soldier,* around a series of binarisms—forgetting and remembering, present and past, the United States and Guatemala, peace and war, life and death—but allows these binarisms and the borders that separate them to blur through the intersecting narratives of the two protagonists, Antonio Bernal and Guillermo Longoria. Such blurring is not evenly experienced, nor is it a pro-social or positive condition.[4] The demand for assimilation and U.S. nationalism is couched in the following terms: in order to take part in America's peace and prosperity, immigrants must forget their pasts of suffering and trauma and overlook how social stability and wealth in the United States depends on the continued violence in their countries of origin. This privileging also imbues the United States with forward-looking, life-fulfilling connotations against Guatemala's backward-looking, life-negating ones—persistent legacies of U.S. and European imperialisms that have continued to hierarchize the Global North over the Global South. These divergent connotations reaffirm both the successful tales of immigration and assimilation into the United States mainstream and the accessibility of this dream. Connected to the specific conditions of the 1992 Crisis, other binarisms emerge around division and inequality: us and them, citizens and immigrants, legal and illegal, nonviolent and violent, the United States and Latin America.

Antonio's memory moves between the United States and Guatemala. This juxtaposition of memories and experiences comprises Tobar's comparative strategy of the novel. Rather than privilege the U.S. sides of the binarism, Tobar establishes the contiguity of the juxtaposed concepts, putting ostensibly dissimilar things into metonymic relation. Tobar uses flashbacks initiated by similar objects, emotions, and circumstances to trigger Antonio's reminiscences of Guatemala and the murders of his wife and infant son. These moments function like narrative trapdoors through which Antonio suddenly falls, rabbit holes to a whole other world in his mind and memory. The third-person limited omniscient narrator describes the moment that Antonio encounters his family's assassin in terms of descent and fall: "A box at Antonio's feet as he waited for the bus. Antonio falling, spiraling with his box, falling for many years, landing in Los Angeles. . . . Antonio spun in the flux between decades and countries, time and space distorted. He was in a park in Guatemala, a park in Los Angeles. The present, the past, somewhere in between" (79). No longer just mirroring Alice's fall into Wonderland, Antonio has fallen into knowledge, expelled from the comforting, familiar Eden of his regret and self-recriminations and into the sin of his vengeance as he plots and carries out the murder of Guillermo. As in Walter Benjamin's "Theses on History," in which the image of falling engages the notion of depth and linearity often associated with forward-moving time and history, the parataxis of the phrase noting the park in Guatemala and the one in Los Angeles conflates the two temporal moments synchronically and juxtaposes two geographically distinct life experiences: Antonio's earlier life in Guatemala and his current life in the United States.

Given U.S. intervention in Central America, these temporal and physical spaces should not seem disconnected, but their perceived discontinuities manifest the forgetting that has forged a post–cold war U.S. national identity. "The present, the past, some*where* in between" (79; emphasis added) represents more than just Antonio's mental confusion. His disability symbolizes the perpetual liminality of Latina/o immigrants: thought to be neither White nor Black, neither quite American nor quite citizen, despite their potential legal claims to all of these identities. For nonwhite immigrants, racial identity will always signal incomplete claims to American identity and belonging. Until this meeting that is cataclysmic for Antonio and puzzling for Guillermo, Tobar has trained the reader to expect, and even welcome, these synchronic moments as revelations of character and plot motivations. As the narrative moves between Antonio's and Guillermo's third-person perspectives, the temporality shifts between the novel's present time of April 1992 and the narrators' pasts in Guatemala. In the first of three sections, Tobar reinforces their paired destinies by referring to the characters as Antonio and Longoria, one character's first name and the other's last name, respectively.[5] Despite their opposition as protagonist and antagonist, Antonio and Guillermo represent different symptoms of the same economic and political conflicts caused by globalization and neoliberal imperialism. Guillermo, the antagonist, has a personal history of trauma, and the deliberate forgetting of his first name alludes to both his initiation into the military and an obliteration of his individual identity. Guillermo is the name of the K'iche' Mayan teenager, forcibly conscripted into military service, an impressionable young man whose fierce ambition, unquestioning obedience, and brutal efficiency in torturing and killing fellow Guatemalans enables his survival and advancement. Tobar uses Guillermo's last name in order to distance the reader from the sergeant and his crimes against humanity both in psychological and moral terms. Through such narrative strategies, Tobar activates significant binary oppositions between citizen and immigrant, American and Latina/o, and haves and have-nots.

The fates of these men intersect through the remarkable life and brutal death of a woman, Antonio's wife, Elena. While the titles of the three parts of the novel—"Antonio and the Sergeant," "Antonio and Elena," and "Antonio and Guillermo"—clearly identify Antonio as the main protagonist, Guillermo's third-person limited omniscient perspective interrupts Antonio's dominant voice in Antonio's narration of his immigrant life in Los Angeles. Elena's narrative, told from the beginning of their relationship at a university in Guatemala to her political murder a few years later, interrupts Antonio and Guillermo's narrative struggle. Although the novel's present takes place just days before the Los Angeles Crisis, the second part of the book is set almost a decade earlier and concludes with Elena's assassination, which forces Antonio to flee Guatemala and begin his long journey to the United States.

Tobar narrates the second part of the novel, "Antonio and Elena," almost exclusively from Elena's point of view, beginning with their courtship and ending with Antonio's flight from Guatemala. Antonio and Elena first meet at a university in Guatemala City while she is a student activist involved in protests against state oppression. She mentors Antonio's growing interest in dissident historical and political narratives regarding the June 1954 military overthrow of the democratically elected president Jacobo Árbenz Guzmán; the displacement and exploitation of rural peoples, especially the indigenous Mayans in the *altiplano* or the mountainous highlands; and the appropriation of land by U.S. transnational companies such as United Fruit. After several student leaders, close friends, and former lovers are disappeared, Antonio and Elena, newly married and expecting a child, flee to the *altiplano*. Elena and their son are killed two years later, in 1985, the historic election year of the first civilian president. Although a constitution was drafted the year before, critics note that the Guatemalan government codified democratic features of governance alongside the institutionalization of extralegal forces such as the paramilitary death squads, one of which, led by Guillermo Longoria, murders Antonio's young family. Antonio, the actual target of the assassination, flees again, this time emigrating through Mexico to the United States. The novel takes place approximately seven years later, on the eve of the 1992 L.A. Crisis, when Antonio, now about thirty, has worked a variety of low-wage, unskilled and skilled jobs as an undocumented immigrant.[6]

Tobar uses Elena's perspective to confirm and challenge the omniscient narration occurring primarily through Antonio's and Guillermo's perspectives in the first and last parts of the novel. Elena's narration is uninterrupted by the other narrators' points of view until the final scene of her and her son's murder, in which Antonio, coming home from work, recounts the horror of discovering their dead bodies gruesomely arranged on their front steps. Antonio takes over as the narrator after Elena's death in order to describe Antonio's narrow escape from the assassination and his identification of his family's murderer from a bus window by his jaguar tattoo that will crucially motivate the plot and orchestrate Guillermo's murder. Indeed, unlike the narratives that tell the plot from Antonio's or Guillermo's perspectives and loop back to previous memories, Elena's narrative is noticeably more chronologically linear with only a few brief anecdotes about her childhood and life as an undergraduate.

The character of Elena connects the novel's plot to the broader social and historical context of the Guatemalan civil wars. Antonio's memories and her narrative suture their experiences in Guatemala with his life in the United States. As the plot and structural axis upon which this novel turns, Elena's life as a student activist and her death at the hands of Guillermo's death squad necessitate not only a gendered reading of her life and death but also her symbolic representation of the role of women in activism throughout the civil war and its aftermath. Although human rights organizations have kept military and governmental abuses in Guatemala on watch lists for decades, U.S. and global audiences are perhaps most familiar with Rigoberta Menchú, activist, politician, and a 1992 Nobel Peace Prize recipient. Menchú published her controversial, best-selling autobiography, *I, Rigoberta Menchú: An Indian Woman in Guatemala,* in 1983, exposing the Guatemalan government's scorched-earth policies that resulted in the genocide of tens of thousands of indigenous Mayans, including some of her family members. The 1986 critically acclaimed fictional film *El Norte,* directed by Gregory Nava, depicts the eradication of an entire village and the disappearance of the adults, which propels two young K'iche' Mayan siblings to flee Guatemala and cross the U.S.–Mexico border at great personal cost.

International and Guatemalan human rights organizations have pressured the government for truth commissions since the 1980s. Despite three appointees seen as sympathetic to the political right in power, one of the earliest efforts initiated by the Guatemalan government dissolved itself, stating they could not locate any of the victims. A few years later another inquiry into unlawful detentions through the Supreme Court ended despite thousands of petitions (R. Wilson, 19). The 1994 Oslo Accord created the Commission for Historical Clarification (CEH), charged "to clarify with objectivity, equity and impartiality, the human rights violations and acts of violence connected with the armed confrontation that caused suffering among the Guatemalan people."[7] Human rights organizations have continually feared that the Guatemalan government will protect military and state officials involved in the two hundred thousand deaths, thirty-eight thousand disappeared, and even more survivors of torture over thirty-six years of civil war; many of those unofficially accused hold high-ranking positions in both of these most powerful institutions.[8] The CEH included newly declassified CIA documents and recorded seventy-two hundred interviews with eleven thousand people.[9] Also influential and with investigations predating the CEH, Bishop Juan Gerardi Conedera and eight hundred volunteers compiled the 1998 four-volume study, *The Official Report of the Human Rights Office, Archdiocese of Guatemala Proyecto Interdioceseno de Memoria Historia* (REMHI), which named one thousand perpetrators, documented fifty-five thousand human rights violations, and found the Guatemalan military responsible for 85 percent of the violations in contrast to the guerrilla army's 9 percent. REMHI's efforts were notable for its far-reaching scope through the network of Catholic churches in the more rural areas and how it established local offices with a bilingual staff in Spanish and Mayan languages.[10]

The following year the condensed one-volume English-language version was published as *Guatemala: Never Again!* (1999). The English version includes a chapter devoted to the particular forms of torture, terror, and suffering inflicted on women. The report details the conspicuous, often sexualized, display of women's mutilated bodies and the use of sexual violence as a method of torture, coercion, and murder (73–80). Former soldiers admit to also using children to manipulate their parents. The report further notes that the surviving women must bear the responsibility for continuing the family and the community; it positions women at the center of human rights activism demanding justice for the disappeared and punishment for the torturers and murderers (83–85).

I dwell on Elena's importance to the novel not only as a narrative bridge and background to Antonio's and Guillermo's lives in Guatemala and the United States, but also as her experiences and Antonio's memories juxtapose the past of 1980s Guatemala and the contemporary moment of 1992 Los Angeles. With memories of Elena as a constant reminder of Guatemala for Antonio, Tobar deploys conventional tropes of affective politics that tie women symbolically to the nation. Antonio longs for his wife's confident radical mentorship as he tries to connect the theories of revolution that he had learned from Elena and her radical activism in Guatemala with the urban unrest in Los Angeles, believing that she would "have loved to see the throngs of nannies taking over the streets of an American city, like the garbage workers they had joined in Guatemala all those years ago" (*The Tattooed Soldier,* 306). In the concluding lines of the novel, Antonio still longs for her definitive moral and political interpretation of his murderous act:

"If she were alive, Elena would put her arms around him and whisper all the answers in his ear" (307). After the chaos and violence of the city, Tobar implies that the audience, like Antonio, is also waiting to learn the significance of the Los Angeles Crisis both within and beyond the United States.

Within the value system of the novel, Antonio's nonnormative mental state indicates his humanity, whereas Guillermo's lack of remorse, his perfunctory ability to kill, and the satisfaction he derives from assassination as a job well done evidences his inhumanity. Antonio has a deeply rooted guilt for what he sees as a lack of courage to kill his wife's and son's murderer, to avenge them, even though to have done so would likely have meant his own death, since he was the death squad's intended target. Guillermo, in contrast, feels no regret for the people he killed, despite having acted under threat of his own life. As sociologist Leigh Payne has posited regarding perpetrator narratives and the appropriate displays of affect that she refers to as "confessional performances," there are popular beliefs of the abnormal psychology and immorality of perpetrators: "Public attention may result from fictional and news accounts that depict perpetrators as extraordinarily evil, sadistic, and psychopathic. By contrast, most academic studies consider perpetrators of authoritarian violence normal" (Payne, 16). In a sense, this recent turn in the scholarship away from the rhetoric of perpetrators as evil monsters and inhuman villains reveals a more troubling human propensity for continually perpetrating the most heinous of crimes. Recent human rights studies identify most perpetrators as "violence workers," disciplined by institutional circumstances and agendas rather than individual morality and principles.[11]

Tobar's use of the backdrop of the L.A. Crisis and U.S. cold war interventions in Guatemala resonates precisely because Tobar allows for multiple, conflicting readings of the morality of Antonio's crime and Guillermo's culpability. Some of Antonio's friends and Antonio himself perceive his tracking down and murdering Guillermo as retributive justice and fitting punishment for a torturer and murderer of hundreds. It may appear even more justified especially given that so few of the highest-ranking officers who gave the orders for torture and mass killings have ever been indicted, tried, or sentenced. Even the highest-profile indictment and conviction of former general and ex-President José Efraín Ríos Montt was overturned on appeal just ten days after the 2013 verdict and he was declared mentally unfit to stand trial two years later. Guillermo's own situation reveals the difficulty in prosecuting war crimes. As a loyal soldier and government employee who strongly believes in the integrity of his commanding officers and the justness of his actions, his culpability becomes less definitive in his service to the nation: the expectation that a rank-and-file soldier would defy his commanding officers during combat or that a diligent government employee would contravene his responsibilities.

Although Tobar makes possible a sympathetic reading of Guillermo—his impoverished childhood, forced conscription into and service in the Guatemalan military—the novel juxtaposes Guillermo's success and untroubled conscience with Antonio's symptoms that could be ascribed to Post-Traumatic Stress Disorder, whether originating from memories of the horribly mutilated and tortured corpses of his and Elena's friends that pushed them to flee Guatemala City, the brutal deaths of his wife and son, or the difficult journey of his undocumented migration into the United States. Seeing the vestiges of a razed city neighborhood prompts Antonio's disconnection from the present: "He had forgotten something, and this had triggered another one of his famous depressions. He could feel it covering him, a somber rain, those leaden moments. . . . One moment he might be a normal man, someone with hopes and desires like anyone else, and the next he wanted to curl into a ball. To lie down and let his body seep into the ground. A moment of rest" (39). For the novel, the depression and guilt that take Antonio out of the present and into his memories for hours on end posit alternative temporalities that go unrecognized, the reasons for Antonio's personal and Guatemala's national traumas.[12]

As a homeless, undocumented immigrant and a traumatized civil war survivor who has challenging mental disabilities, Antonio is unlikely to become "documented" through political asylum because of U.S. support of the Guatemalan dictatorship during the 1980s.[13] However, Antonio feels that his inability to let go of his past, as manifested by his deep guilt over his family's murders, prevents his assimilation into mainstream American society. Assimilation into an American identity, Tobar posits, requires Antonio not only to "get over" the murders of his family, but also to forget the U.S.-sanctioned violence of the Guatemalan government that supported and trained such killers as Guillermo. The discourses of American innocence through forgetting are only possible through the inordinate sacrifices of these immigrant families and their own personal welfare. For Los Angeles Crisis survivor Fidel Lopez, he and his family daily struggle with the emotional, physical, and financial costs of Lopez's disabilities from his assault. Antonio's repeated longing for Elena both as a friend and political mentor raises the specter of justice that haunts Antonio, qualifying the ostensibly uplifting end of the novel.[14]

Tobar emphasizes this imperative to forget one's life before coming to the United States as having psychic consequences for those immigrants who are casualties of the cold war. Guatemala emerges as the space of this liminality. The legacy of the cold war is distinctive for its potent mixture of cultural persuasion alongside the military dominance that has characterized modern European empires since the fifteenth century. Tobar's novel explores the cold war effects on vulnerable populations in both the United States and Guatemala. Tobar's journalism, fiction, and nonfiction essays provide a crucial background to a critical understanding of the legacy of the cold war that begins with recognition of the misnomer itself. The United States has long held a complacent view of the cold war in how "distant" the violence was and how "the eternal round of diplomacy, arms talks and rhetorical exchanges" merely signaled the "frostiness of superpower relations" rather than the "hundred wars through the Third World" and 20 million dead (Hammond, 1). During the Guatemalan civil war, the Guatemalan people suffered two hundred thousand casualties as part of the U.S. cold war agenda, and the nation often topped lists for human rights abuses throughout the 1980s. Through its extensive influence on and intervention in governments south of the border, as John Stockwell, a former CIA officer, has claimed, the United States used the cold war as its unacknowledged Third World War.

In *The Tattooed Soldier,* both the winners and the losers in the Guatemalan "hot" war meet in Los Angeles. While this chance meeting is also fictionalized from an article Tobar wrote for the *LA Times,* their reunion, made possible by Antonio's exile and Guillermo's immigration, is not wholly a coincidence given migration flows within the Americas and ethnic enclave formations in Southern California. In an echo of Stuart Hall's trenchant quip of postcolonial migration and imperial histories in the British context, "We are here because you were there," Antonio and Guillermo arrive in the same part of the same park on the same day because of the confluence of these international and domestic forces of containment and displacement—genocide and de facto segregation. If Los Angeles is, as journalist David Rieff deems it, the "capital of the Third World," the conditions of this designation—significant immigrant populations, urban concentrations of people from similar regions in Central America, vast inequalities between rich and poor—are effected largely through the legacy of cultural and military imperialisms and U.S. intervention in other nations such as Guatemala.

The Crisis as Revenge

The plot of *The Tattooed Soldier* relies upon the disorder of the L.A. Crisis to create the ideal conditions in which Antonio can avenge his family but end the cycle of vengeance. There will be no witnesses to Antonio's revenge, and Guillermo's death will be unremarkable among the dozens of casualties and hundreds wounded counted in the aftermath of the violence. Antonio takes it upon himself to murder and disappear Guillermo as punishment for Guillermo's commissioned mass killings and assassinations. Revenge depends on a perception of balance, a symmetry of sorts in which the punishment fits the crime, most memorably stated as an "eye for an eye" in the Hammurabi Codex.[15] Tobar's choice of a historical setting, the Los Angeles Crisis, emerges as a crucial catalyst for the plot itself.

By juxtaposing this bloody history of Guatemala with Antonio's and Guillermo's lives on the margins of U.S. society, Tobar starkly connects the surprisingly similar strategies of racist governmentality in the United States and Guatemala.[16] Tobar refers to the crisis as the *quemazones,* in his translation, "the great burnings" (*Translation Nation,* 27). These burnings signify the destruction of buildings and dwellings in Los Angeles as well as echo the obliteration of people and villages in rural Guatemala that Guillermo perpetrated and witnessed during his time in the Guatemalan military. The open signifier of the *quemazones* leads Tobar to claim the 1992 Crisis as part of a Latin American diasporic history. Tobar reads this event as class warfare that has transnational roots in peasant protests: "It was the first Latin American–style class uprising in United States history, the same kind of visceral expression of rage that over the centuries had led peons to burn down the *hacendado's* home, or villagers to turn up the cobblestones of their streets and throw them at marching soldiers" (27). Violence is perceived as signaling the internal instability of a society and state, but, in contrast, state violence is a strategy of state-building and maintaining power. As I discuss later, this strategy of state-building is explicitly spatial, one that classifies neighborhoods and residents as violent or self-destructive in order to justify their displacement or forced removal.

The ease with which the 1992 violence was repeatedly interpreted as revenge necessitates a discussion of how it functions in Tobar's multiple works about the crisis.[17] His award-winning news articles, novels, and essays have helped to coalesce the study of Guatemalan and Salvadoran immigrants, those to whom scholars Michael Jones-Correa, José Luis Falconi, and José Antonio Mazzotti have referred as part of the "other Latinos" and literary critic Arturo Arias as the "Central American-Americans." Jones-Correa notes that 11 percent of Latinas/os self-identified as Dominican, Central American, and South American in 2000 (23) and Dominican and Salvadoran populations had grown to almost the same number of Cuban Americans in the U.S. by 2010 (Ennis et al.). Given the dearth of research on Guatemalan Americans and other Central Americans, a fast-growing segment of the Latina/o population in Los Angeles and the United States since the 1980s, Tobar's writings, most often *The Tattooed Soldier,* have served as the fictional representation of fact in scholarship on Central Americans in Los Angeles and the United States.[18]

Tobar explores the psychic and material costs of peace without justice as it affects Latinas/os, undocumented immigrants, and the homeless. Antonio, recently homeless and searching for work, witnesses the early moments of the violence in the Pico-Union and Westlake areas of the city as people break storefront windows and run away with merchandise. Antonio's best friend, José Juan, asks him for matches and then leaves to demand unpaid wages from a previous employer, hinting that he might set fire to the man's offices. Astonished, Antonio ponders his friend's uncharacteristic behavior, extrapolating the reasons behind it to others' participation in the civil disorder: "*What does he think he's doing?* Getting even. Someone had declared this the municipal day of settling accounts, a day for all vendettas, private and public" (*The Tattooed Soldier,* 283; original emphasis). Antonio recognizes that José Juan—and many others now on the streets of Los Angeles—has long ignored but never forgotten scores to settle and grievances to resolve.

Antonio provocatively refers to the 1992 Crisis as "days of revenge." From his perspective, the violence is retribution for the daily humiliations of un(der)employment, of want in America, the country once believed by immigrants like himself to be the land of plenty: "It was a day without submissiveness, a day without coffee to pour or strangers' babies to feed or the whir of sewing machines in a factory. It was a day to liberate toolboxes and diapers from their glass cages. A day when all the pretty objects in the store windows would mock them no longer" (283). Antonio's description of the "days of revenge" resembles M. M. Bakhtin's notion of the carnivalesque, a period during which political and religious elites encourage and sanction blasphemous or uncivil behaviors. These upended class hierarchies identify the affective dimensions of daily immigrant life for Latinas/os. They reflect, as Mike Davis and others have argued, the largely economic causes of the crisis, more bread riot than criminal mayhem, more economic protest than anarchy. These interpretations of the violence consider the economic privations of communities hit hardest by the 1991 recession, ten years of supply-side economics, the dismantling of the welfare state, the depression of real wages since the 1970s, and increasing anti-immigrant sentiment.

This description of the "riots" as revenge challenges one dominant construction of the 1992 violence, first of all as wanton, purposeless acts. Revenge, whatever its negative valence, is, by definition, deliberate and purposeful. In this way, Tobar's identification of the crisis as a series of acts of revenge provocatively redefines the event itself. Tobar posits revenge-taking as an alternative justice system, a recourse for overlooked victims and unaddressed crimes. Thus, Tobar explicitly refutes a prominent discourse about the L.A. Crisis that maligns racial minorities as perpetrators of senseless destruction. Such a discourse builds on particularly pervasive stereotypes of the underclass in an increasingly stratified U.S. society; these socioeconomic classes and racialized communities have traditionally been impugned as congenitally lacking respect for authority and basic notions of civility in their propensity for violence.

José Juan's experience of wage theft in *The Tattooed Soldier* has added force as a story based on actual events that Tobar covered as a journalist for the *Los Angeles Times* in February 1990. Fidel Chicas, a Salvadoran day laborer in his sixties, protested the dangerous work conditions at a construction site and was summarily fired without pay after three weeks of work. Tobar reported on Chicas's story two years after Chicas had begun regularly picketing the contractor's business, and after Tobar's news article appeared in the *LA Times,* Chicas finally received partial pay. A fictionalized version of Chicas's story appears in *The Tattooed Soldier* in the character and circumstances of Antonio's former coworker and best friend, José Juan, who has been carrying around a garbage bag with the court documents that ordered his former boss to pay back wages. Despite their homelessness, José Juan treats this sack as vitally important as their basic necessities. Similar to Chicas's inability to pay $450 to impound his former employer's car, José Juan could not receive his court-awarded settlement because he was unable to pay a $50 fee for the sheriffs to collect his wages from his employer. In the novel, the employer's wage theft causes José Juan and Antonio's homelessness since they are evicted for being unable to pay their rent. Chicas has to forgo searching for work to protest. Although the claims of both men, real and fictional, are legally vindicated, the ruling means nothing without the money to pay the sheriffs: justice must be paid for and neither man can buy it.

Tobar revisits Chicas's struggles in his fiction and memoirs, telling the story in three different genres over fifteen years.[19] Commenting on both these earlier versions of this story of wage theft in the first chapter of *Translation Nation,* Tobar speculates that the favorable feedback from readers who were impressed with Chicas's persistence was because of what Chicas represented and what these readers hoped all immigrants believed: "My American-born readers liked that story because it suggested that all exotic, Spanish-speaking people living among them really were believers in 'the system,' that they wanted to be good 'citizens,' in the less literal sense of the word" (26). As deserving immigrants, much like the "deserving poor" of U.S. public policy who are promoted as the only justifiable recipients of governmental assistance and public sympathy, Tobar suggests that his English-speaking citizen readers view those immigrants like Chicas as aspirational citizens who deserve uplift through naturalization or economic inclusion. Earlier, the first chapter on the documentary film *Sa-I-Gu* discusses this deliberate construction deployed for Korean Americans who suffered injuries and losses during the crisis in order to make their claims for redress more visible and viable. The second chapter discusses how such a narrow criterion thereby facilitates the strategy to cast the poor or working poor as undeserving. Tobar's news article quotes a representative for an immigrant rights coalition in Los Angeles: "You have to admire Fidel for his persistence. . . . He's trying to follow the system; he's trying to be an American." Chicas and his protests represent immigrants making the system work for them—acting American in their aspirations to be considered Americans or, eventually, citizens. They do so even though this very system works against their claims on America. Immigrant stories like Chicas's reaffirm the legal and moral principles that lay the foundation for the good life in America—justice, however much delayed or incomplete, always prevails because perseverance is rewarded. However, Tobar's analysis of why this story resonates with his readership suggests Chicas's victory was hardly adequate: the time-consuming, years-long protests at his employer's workplace that garnered Tobar's attention for the *LA Times* article and that eventually led to his partial paycheck were never compensated, nor did the employer ever fully pay for the work Chicas had done. Chicas and immigrants like him, such as Fidel Lopez, who struggles daily with permanent injuries from his beating, must instead disproportionately absorb most of the cost of justice.

In *Translation Nation,* Tobar uses Chicas's story to preface his brief description of violence as vengeance and explains how and why he revised the story for *The Tattooed Soldier:* "In the book, the worker who's cheated never gets his money back: that is, after all, what usually happened in real life. Instead, he takes his revenge during the anarchy of the 1992 L.A. riots, the municipal day of settling accounts, a day to settle all vendettas, private and public" (26). In having the character "take his revenge" during the crisis, José Juan's undocumented status makes him more vulnerable to maltreatment through both his exploitation as disposable, surplus labor and the justice system that cannot help him. Justice, Tobar implies, is for the well-off and well-connected: for those who can afford to pay for enforcing judgments or who have the social capital and regular access to the media for public pressure. In his opening essay to the volume, Tobar refers to the 1992 violence as "the other face to Fidel's patient wait for justice, the same frustration channeled outside the system" (26). For his characters, Tobar posits the L.A. Crisis as not solely protests and violence, but also as a more fundamental challenge to the state, an alternative justice available for the inadequate, long-fought victories like Chicas's and for other injustices that remain neither prosecuted nor redressed.

The negative associations that vengeance elicits disproportionately fall on people of color and, in discussions of revenge and the L.A. Crisis, the racialized underclass of Blacks and Latinas/os in particular. But as historians, cultural critics, and legal scholars note, revenge is the foundation of the criminal justice system itself, a cornerstone of civility and law. Because revenge usurps the authority of the state in its mandate to punish, it is condemned as extralegal tribalism that is antithetical to civilization. Vengeful acts are perceived to violate the rules of civilization, and avenging agents are seen as harbingers of the end of civilization, of anarchy and a return to the state of nature: "Conventional wisdom conceives of vengeance cultures as barely cultured at all, as all id and no superego: big dumb hot-tempered brutes looking for excuses to kill" (Miller, *Eye for an Eye*, 96). Legal historian William Ian Miller argues against this construction of revenge as a primitive form of justice, instead identifying vengeance as a tool of juridical power deployed by the state: by reserving revenge-taking for itself, the state wields vengeance as a means of consolidating power ("Clint Eastwood," 161–65). The governed allow the state to deploy revenge on their behalf and this consent largely renders the state civilized— not the presence or absence of revenge. Ceding vengeance, couched as one's civic duty, continually reifies the juridical apparatus of the state. Each transfer of redress for private injury to public punishment reasserts the power of the state. Along with the ability to use violence, the state possessively guards these prerogatives of punishment.

The state solidifies its power through punishment and its concomitant check on individual or group revenge. It continually establishes and redraws the limits of civility not only in punishments for criminal violations of legal codes but also in punishments for violations of civility. Thus, civil transgressions naturalize criminal penalties. The close relationship between revenge and civility explains how quickly narratives of revenge appear as explanations or justifications for punishment. Recent critics of theories of punishment have analyzed how punishment may incorporate vengeful motivations. Political philosopher William Connolly contends that the "call to revenge forms the least discussed and most pervasive force in the desire to punish" (42). Discerning the desire for revenge under the desire to punish, Connolly explains how violations of civility, alongside those of legality, justify retribution "against those who rob upright citizens of goods, time, health, dignity, or life itself [and] revenge against racially marked urban constituencies whose conditions of existence disturb the practices of fairness, neutrality, impartiality, and responsibility said to govern everyone" (ibid.). This indignation and outrage over legal, yet uncivil, behavior and practices conflate them with illegal ones. Furthermore, if suburban citizens feel robbed of their beliefs and resources, then they might support punitive policies against these "racially marked urban constituencies." Conflicts over lifestyle choices and commitments such as religious beliefs or national pride create a powerful drive toward masking revenge as just punishment. In this interpretation of revenge, and in the name of citizens and aspiring ones, the powerful can take action against people who are thought to be unlike them in order to exclude them from civil society. At the very least, it is possible to marshal public opinion, voting preferences, and the media to restrict the imagined community of "upright citizens" and like-minded neighbors. Revenge is coded into identity formation and practiced against groups of people who are racially and spatially identified as inferior and undeserving.

If, as Miller argues, the state appropriation of revenge consolidates its power, then more killings as punishment signify more power. Within this framework Denise Ferreira da Silva posits that a greater loss of life is likely an intentional result of state revenge. Analyzing the deaths of Brazilian residents in a Rio de Janeiro *favela,* or urban slum during confrontations with the police, Silva identifies how the state, under the aegis of self-preservation, justifies the killing of populations demarcated by race and territory. Carried out in the name of the state and its self-preservation, "such killings do not unleash an ethical crisis because these persons' bodies and the territories they inhabit always-already signify violence" (Silva, 213). Because their bodies "always-already signify violence," the state can defend these acts of violence not as revenge but as a reassertion of a *racial equilibrium,* what I discuss at the end of this chapter, on the part of the police and the state: meeting symbolic violence with physical violence. Although many of the *favela* residents are not perpetrators of violence, the state can easily explain the deaths of these innocent residents: if not mourned as collateral damage, their very location in the *favela* criminalizes and pushes them outside the bounds of civility. As such, they have no claims to retribution that other citizens and the state would need to recognize. Configured as the aggressors in the oppositional spaces their bodies inhabit and determined by the state through law and custom as deserving lesser protections and services, the state targets these bodies for abuse, neglect, discrimination, and annihilation.

In Silva's formulation of "no-bodies," belonging to a territory such as the *favela* makes its residents into bare life.[20] Their racialized bodies identify them as belonging to the *favela,* a territory inimical to the state, thereby classifying them too as agents inimical to the state. Civility is apportioned in terms of merit mapped onto neighborhoods and territories and parallels policy decisions regarding who deserves to live and die. The territorialization of violence and incivility likewise determines belonging and bodies in Guatemala and the United States. Antonio's experiences in the United States, especially the violent logics of the L.A. Crisis, echo the violent, exterminatory strategies of Guatemala's repressive government, if not in kind, then in differences of human suffering and scale. Through the experiences of the three protagonist-narrators, Tobar posits different practices of state-building: Guillermo's tortures and murders under the state narratives of revenge and destruction; Antonio's joblessness, homelessness, and undocumented status, which push him outside civil society; and Elena's witnessing the state's creation of a disposable, diseased population through the government's refusals to do anything about the nearby slum's tainted water and the deaths of its residents.

Guillermo has killed for ideals of prosperity, order, and purity that are inspired, if not crafted, by U.S. foreign policies and corporate interests, but he begins to realize that not even Americans could achieve, much less sustain, these ideals for themselves: "Longoria had expected Los Angeles to be like that beautiful military base at Fort Bragg, a city of tidy houses and well-behaved people. He had carried his cigarette lighter into the mountain villages so that Guatemala could start all over again, from scratch. The new Guatemala would be a place like Fort Bragg, like the United States. Instead the infection had followed him to Los Angeles" (292). Guillermo, like Antonio, seems to blame himself for the civil disorder, for the violence and crime he witnesses, albeit to a much lesser extent. Ironically, whether or not Guillermo and Antonio blame themselves, their presence and that of other Latinas/os will be blamed for the violence in Los Angeles and, more broadly, the decline in American fortunes.

The escalating violence during the first hours of the crisis unpleasantly reminds Guillermo of his past, carrying out state-sanctioned murder and destruction; he perceives this involuntary remorse as a sign of weakness. He is emboldened not only by his convictions of right and wrong, but also by the memory of a particularly gruesome and troubling mass killing that wiped out the village of Nueva Concepción in rural Guatemala. Guillermo and his fellow soldiers began to realize that their respected leader was so ruthless that he would annihilate even professed supporters—the adults, children, and priest who had come to welcome the troops to their village in appreciation of their protection from the guerrillas. Guillermo admiringly remembers how Lieutenant Villagrán steeled the shaken resolve of his soldiers by reframing the grisly mass killing as avenging punishment:

> "I lost six men right here, right at this village, because the guerrillas surprised us. . . . When all these people are gone we won't have any more problems," the lieutenant continued, "because there won't be anyone left to give the guerrillas anything to eat. We're going to go through this place and level it, do you understand? The guerrillas will go away and we won't have to fight them anymore." (249)

The lieutenant's simplistic narrative and half truths reassure the shaken soldiers, who would rather accept his specious explanation than acknowledge the innocent blood on their hands. Villagrán's promise of a perfect world without the need for fighting puts the onus of guilt on the guerrillas, and this shifting of blame coincides with Guillermo's guiding principle and his justification for the grimmest form of social engineering and governmentality the state can exercise on its peoples. In fact, Guillermo perceives Los Angeles as ripe for genocide, viewing it as a specific form of state-building that he has perpetrated and witnessed firsthand. Having encouraged such strategies in its cold war agenda, the U.S. deploys similar strategies of containment and restriction on its own internal populations.

The novel organizes memories of Guatemala through Antonio's navigation of the neighborhoods and streets of Los Angeles. There are multiple, crucial juxtapositions: of Antonio's and Guillermo's narratives, of the United States and Guatemala, the past and the present. After being evicted, Antonio and José Juan roam downtown Los Angeles, anxiously looking for a place to sleep under the freeway. They find shelter and, eventually, community in a homeless encampment, but discover that the tents and shacks in the mud cover "the ruins of a lost community, a forgotten neighborhood built with brick and cement" (15). Reading this space through his memories of loss, Antonio grieves for the families who once lived in this demolished neighborhood. The streets are given the names of precious gems, reflecting the name of the neighborhood, Crown Hill. This ghostly place foreshadows the novel's later description of the slum in San Cristóbal, Guatemala, which was ironically named La Joya, "the jewel." The extended flashback of the second part of the novel details Antonio and Elena's escape to San Cristóbal from Guatemala City because they feared persecution for their leftist activism. However, this slum and its diseased and dying residents propel the central tragedy of the novel; Antonio's wife, Elena, writes letters protesting the slum's lack of clean water due to its location downstream from the town dump, acts that will set off a chain of events that result in Elena's and their son's murders and Antonio's permanent exile in Los Angeles.

While foregrounding Elena's narrative in the middle of the novel, this initial flashback crucially connects the United States with Guatemala for the first time, foreshadowing Antonio's losses on both sides of the border. After their first night homeless, José Juan attempts to cheer up Antonio by encouraging him to imagine a house rising from its foundation: "'Over here was the bedroom. And see this? These bricks? This had to be the fireplace. See? A fireplace to sit by when it's cold, like it is now. A nice hot fire to keep warm. Can you see it? Can you?'" (15). Antonio instead imagines that he can hear the happy voices of family life together, and the absence of the former residents, their single-family dwellings, and their neighborhood remind him painfully of other disappearances he has survived and witnessed. In Guatemala, the military pursued scorched-earth policies designed to obliterate political opposition for generations. In Los Angeles, gentrification, urban renewal, and "poor people removal" reflected the prerogatives and profit of city planners and private developers.[21] While these Crown Hill neighborhood families were not brutally murdered by death squads, as Elena and Carlos had been, nor were their villages razed as punishment and warning to antigovernment guerrilla forces, as Nueva Concepción had been, Tobar connects the spatial strategies of displacement between the gentrification projects of urban cities in the U.S. and Mayan Indian villages in Guatemala in terms of containment and control of uncivil populations. José Juan's persistent optimism contrasts with Antonio's pessimistic vision of a disappeared people inhabiting the same ruins: "On the hill, and on the flat plain that extended from its base, he could see a grid of city streets, blocks of land cut in rectangles and bordered with sidewalks, asphalt avenues with iron manhole covers for the sewers. Dozens and dozens of concrete stairs led from the streets to what used to be front lawns. In all, Antonio counted more than forty demolished lots, a whole section of the city leveled to an expanse of wild grasses" (15). Rather than a comforting reminder of the past as it is for José Juan, the leveled neighborhood bespeaks the obliteration of a people for Antonio, who feels haunted by the disappearance of a historic community, a likely forced removal, and the erasure of their social bonds. This kind of business development alludes to the waves of urban renewal and gentrification that displaced long-established communities of color. Antonio conspicuously notes the faded sign announcing the Crown Hill Hotel and Finance Park development, but also the long-standing ruin and neglect that has supplanted the neighborhood of single-family homes the developers have demolished and failed to rebuild.

Deeply moved despite his unfamiliarity with the place and its former residents, Antonio imagines the families: "He could feel the souls of the children who once lived in this place, their after-school games and innocent wanderings. What sins did their parents commit, he wondered, to bring such destruction upon themselves?" (15). According to cultural critic Norman Klein, the answer in the context of Los Angeles is likely the threat of the "Imaginary Chicano City," in which the "fear of a Mexican horde" resulted in neighborhoods being "erased by urban planning in and around downtown" throughout the twentieth century (132). Klein notes that while these neighborhoods were largely multiracial with Mexican Americans comprising less than a third of the population, they were nonetheless "erased" due to "anti-Mexican hysteria" (132). The 1943 White serviceman's riots (the "Zoot Suit Riots") during World War II further inflamed the racial hysteria that often targeted young Latinos in zoot suits; historian Mauricio Mazón identifies "the psychology of symbolic annihilation" that has attempted to both symbolically and physically eradicate Latina/o populations from the Los Angeles area. Designations of "out-of-place" correlate to the built environment of Los Angeles as a growing city with increasing populations and racial tensions, with territories that city planners and policymakers reimagined and repurposed for predominantly White residents and workers (see Cresswell, "Weeds"). Historian Eric Avila notes that city planners designated multiracial neighborhoods as urban blight, the first step toward green-lighting development projects proposed through such euphemisms as urban renewal, gentrification, or private–public partnerships: the Bunker Hill financial district, which uprooted Little Manila; Dodger Stadium, which evicted a largely Mexican American population in Chavez Ravine; and the five-freeway interchange in East Los Angeles that multiply bisected the thriving multiracial community of Boyle Heights.

City planners decided to run freeways and interchanges through vibrant neighborhoods of East Los Angeles and Venice near the coast, pushing out the residents who lived there, destroying property values, and physically separating communities. Former residents' stories of spatial remapping in the face of exclusion and displacement allude to people's attempts to resist and renarrate a long history of vanished residents, buildings, and communities that characterize Los Angeles, what Klein has called its "history of forgetting." Tobar links this forgetting of Los Angeles urban history with the *desaparecidos* of Guatemala's civil war. Such forgetting is the affective and political outcome of U.S. exceptionalism, in which the necessary violence for cold war strategies of containment was waged outside U.S. borders in places such as Guatemala.

Interracial Territories of Incivility

Tobar returns to the displaced and disappeared as a theme in *The Tattooed Soldier,* juxtaposing the Guatemalan disappeared alongside the American displaced, the murdered villagers of Nueva Concepción and Guillermo's other victims alongside the homeless people of Los Angeles, and the vanished Crown Hill neighborhood residents. In this section, I discuss the state's interest in revenge and its zealous guarding of its prerogative by projecting the appropriation of vengeance onto its subjects. The state thus casts revenge in all its connotations as uncivil. The reputations of the neighborhoods of East Los Angeles, Koreatown, Pico-Union, Westlake, and South Central Los Angeles play an important role in how the violence, its perpetrators, and its victims are perceived. It becomes easy to malign people and places and devalue their claims and injuries based on their belonging to these vilified spaces. The justification for revenge usually depends on the perceived worth of the victims of vengeance and their kinship or community ties. Tobar insists on the homeless and immigrant populations as internally displaced peoples and places them within a human rights context.

Such a genealogy of theories of state power through its adjudication of revenge allows the reader to contextualize the tropes that Tobar uses to bring the most compelling features of the novel together. In *The Tattooed Soldier,* Tobar discusses civility primarily in two interconnected ways: the state-sponsored vanishing of a people either by displacement or extermination. Tobar juxtaposes the urban history of Los Angeles with the genocidal violence and repression of Guatemala.

In what Michel de Certeau would distinguish as the difference between spatial strategies and spatial tactics, institutional and governmental appropriations and use of space versus individuals' "acting-out" space, respectively, the newly homeless immigrant characters negotiate the urban terrain that testifies to the transfer of wealth from homeowners to developers through gentrification and city planning.

Here I examine the various justifications for the exclusion and expulsion of people marked as uncivil. The spatializing of revenge and the territorializing of civility are processes most evident in areas subject to policing, containment, and management during the violence. The L.A. Crisis firmly reinscribed the mapping of interracial conflict onto South Central Los Angeles, Koreatown, and Pico-Union. This mapping had legal ramifications, as police arrested those who broke curfew in the "riot" hotspots or in neighborhoods close to the intersection of Florence and Normandie avenues—which journalists and the police referred to as "ground zero"—not those in outlying areas, despite the state-of-emergency declaration and curfew applied to all of Los Angeles County.[22] Already the inner city, like most nonwhite inner cities in major metropolitan areas across the United States, had been mapped as a site of Black crime and violence, most widely disseminated not only via crime statistics but also through gangsta rap and the wave of coming-of-age films set in South Central Los Angeles or Spike Lee's Brooklyn in the 1980s and 1990s. Such dominant perceptions of these cultural artifacts relating to violence overshadowed awareness of the gang truce negotiated almost immediately after the violence and encouraged unsubstantiated claims of gangs as an organized force fighting against the police, federal troops, and National Guard (see Davis, "Uprising"). Because of the focus on African Americans in South Central Los Angeles and people's memories of the 1965 Watts Rebellion and other instances of inner-city unrest in the 1960s, violence in areas of the city and county known for their Asian and Latina/o populations, such as Pico-Union and Long Beach, could be more easily overlooked.

Nonetheless, researchers and journalists often cite demographics that identify Los Angeles as home to the largest number of people of Mexican descent living outside Mexico. Américo Paredes has famously termed this diasporic population "*México de afuera.*" Nora Hamilton and Norma Stoltz Chinchilla note that by the 2000s, "many areas of South Central that had been predominantly black two decades before became predominantly Latino; schools that had been 80 or 90 percent black were now 80 or 90 percent Mexican and Central American" (43).[23] The border crossings and immigrant populations remap the boundaries between the United States and Latin America as borderland spaces characterized by cultural *mestizaje* and mixed-status families of both citizens and immigrants, both documented and undocumented (see Pérez-Torres). Less visibly, but no less importantly, in the mid-1980s populations of Central Americans, especially from Guatemala and El Salvador, began to concentrate in the Pico-Union and Westlake neighborhoods of Los Angeles. Hamilton and Chinchilla report that Los Angeles "has the largest Mexican, Central American, Asian, and Middle Eastern populations in the United States" and, in addition to being the "largest Mexican metropolis outside of Mexico," it is also "the largest Salvadoran metropolis outside of El Salvador" (41). Such diasporic identifications of these Latina/o populations usefully contest U.S. exceptionalism by making visible other forms of cross-border belongings.

In regard to the 1992 Crisis, other interpretations receive less notice, but fall under the heading of revenge. The most prominent and explosive charge castigates deliberate inaction and passivity on the part of the police department; the lesser one condemns a lack of preparedness and accurate assessment of the situation in contingency planning for protests after the verdict of King's police assailants. Law-and-order proponents, previously among his biggest supporters, loudly criticized Daryl Gates, who still continued to serve as LAPD Chief of Police despite his resignation in the wake of Rodney King's beating, and claimed that he failed to adequately prepare his forces and apprise local and state governments of the potentially explosive trial verdict as his personal payback for the public pressure that forced him to announce his resignation in 1991 (Van den Haag, 1658). Obviously, incompetence in the development and execution of plans to contain violence also supplies plausible explanations for the LAPD's inadequate response to the crisis. The areas hardest hit by assaults and property destruction lacked police presence and intervention.

Tobar's novel opens with an escalating argument between Korean and Latino immigrants that conspicuously foregrounds interracial conflict and a precipitating event of the L.A. Crisis as interracial incivility over ownership and private property. In this scene, Tobar effectively rewrites the iconic interracial conflict between Soon Ja Du and Latasha Harlins; in *The Tattooed Soldier,* two adult men of color, both immigrants, both with difficulty communicating in English, struggle. The apartment manager Mr. Hwang evicts Antonio and José Juan for their inability to pay rent, and Antonio tries fruitlessly to convince Mr. Hwang to give them more time to find employment and the money they owe. Tobar portrays each man with complexity: Antonio carefully uses Mr. Hwang's actual last name, trying to acknowledge the other man's Korean identity rather than the disparaging and inaccurate monikers "*el chino*" or "Chang" used by the other Spanish-speaking tenants (6); as Mr. Hwang attempts to evict Antonio and José Juan, the narrator details that the apartment manager initially does so with "a note of regret" (5). But Mr. Hwang hardens his tone during the ensuing exchange, which plays out in "night-school phrases" (3), and each man frustratingly asking the other to repeat his questions and answers or admitting he does not understand what the other has said. However, Mr. Hwang is able to say in "perfect English" (5) that he will call the marshals if they don't leave. The irony is that José Juan's inability to call the marshals, pay for their services, and thereby receive redress for his wage theft is largely the cause of their impoverishment and eviction. The language of the state in its protection of private property and economic exchange ultimately trumps the more measured language of the pair's initial negotiation. In other words, the hierarchies of power engaged in the protection of private property, which are signaled by perfect English rather than the hesitant yet earnest attempts at communication, foreclose the possibility of Mr. Hwang's relenting on Antonio and José Juan's eviction and thwart the human connection and *civility* between Mr. Hwang and Antonio.

The territorialization of civility thus relies on the privatization of space and its protection. Legal scholar Jeremy Waldron redefines homelessness in terms of property rights and freedom, two basic tenets of civil society. He defines the homeless individual as lacking a "place governed by a private property rule where he *[sic]* is allowed to be" (299). Therefore, if most land is owned privately, then there are very few places for someone without their own private property—a home, whether rented or owned—to be. Such limitations on places create limitations on freedoms. Waldron points out the nature of freedom in relation to private property: "Someone who is allowed to be in a place is, in a fairly straightforward sense, free to be there. A person who is not allowed to be in a place is unfree to be there" (302). Waldron draws an important distinction in implicit understandings of freedom, which "usually applies to actions rather than locations: one is free or unfree to do X or to do Y" (ibid.), but importantly notes how one's location allows or prohibits certain actions. Everyday behaviors such as cooking and urinating, which are perfectly acceptable in the kitchen or bathroom, respectively, are unacceptable in most outdoor public places. Those who must perform these tasks in public places, or other places in which they are "unfree" to be, are vilified and criminalized for their out-of-place behaviors and largely deemed pathological failures who are undeserving of further help or consideration.

Physical homelessness connects to other forms of psychic homelessness of the immigrant, especially the undocumented immigrant and political exile. Antonio imagines the circumstances that led to the destruction before him and explains it through his own past—his and his wife's activism that led to his family's murder. Antonio's migration northward into the United States tracks his exclusion from the nation-making of Guatemala and his violent expulsion from its imagined community. Unable to return to Guatemala because of his likely persecution and lack of money, Antonio feels a debilitating psychological homelessness in his new life in Los Angeles. He is also excluded from the U.S. national imaginary despite his residence and cheap labor within its borders. Antonio's physical homelessness in Los Angeles alludes to his psychological homelessness after the murders of his family and his forced exile. By opening the novel with Antonio's and José Juan's eviction, Tobar collapses the physical and the psychic homelessness of undocumented immigrants. Tobar's depiction of Antonio's and José Juan's incorporation into the homeless community in downtown Los Angeles reinforces his class critique of the United States' own production of marginalized surplus labor and persons.

Tobar depicts both Antonio and Guillermo as feeling oddly responsible for the contradictions between their immigrant experiences and these "glimmering" and "orderly" American dreams. This analysis propels Antonio's feelings of his own culpability for the homeless people he encounters. Among L.A.'s homeless, Antonio is surprised to find himself as part of a community, experiencing a profound, intuitive kinship among people like Darryl, a White alcoholic, who have been traumatized by addiction, loss, and violence:

> Alcoholics, the suicidal, battered wives, the perpetually lonely, witnesses to catastrophe, survivors of war: they all came into sharper focus. Antonio could almost spot them across a crowded room. They were like brothers or

long-lost friends. They were different from the other people, the unscarred, those who had never seen or lived the randomness Darryl and Antonio knew too well. These other people walked about the city like well-fed children, bathed in a glow of innocence, the happy haze of unknowing. (236)

Antonio revises his earlier naive dream of Los Angeles that inverts the carefully guarded innocence of the financially prosperous and emotionally unscathed Americans as immature and ignorant of the suffering around them. These shared experiences of trauma are grounds for a collective identity formation that cuts across race, gender, class, nationality, and immigration status. In the United States, Antonio feels a closer bond to these psychically scarred and defeated people than he does with other *guatemaltecos* and even José Juan. Antonio begins to recognize new kinds of division and connection along different lines based on economic experiences and personal struggles. This intersectional affinity symbolizes a geopolitical criticism of the United States in general, the comfort of innocence and prosperity untouched by not only a profound national trauma but also a responsibility for the intentional and collateral damage left in the wake of U.S. foreign policy.[24]

Rather than using the term "homeless," Antonio reclassifies himself and the squatters in human rights terms: "Refugees. That was the term for people who lived like this, in makeshift tents, on barren ground. This was something new. He did not know that gringos could be refugees. *These gringos don't deserve this*" (41; original emphasis). These people are most obviously economic refugees, the people least responsible for their economic exploitation; less obviously, they are internally displaced people whose predicaments and numbers are harder to track since they move within rather than across national borders. Their numbers are the acceptable collateral damage of the hierarchies of capitalism. Antonio is indirectly claiming that he, like them, does not deserve this predicament either. On the level of plot, this is indeed true; Antonio has been actively trying to find work. If José Juan had been fairly compensated, both he and Antonio would not have been evicted. This plot development symbolizes what else has been stolen from those who have been the most vulnerable to these economic abuses of wage theft and exploitation. At the same time, Antonio is reclaiming their dignity from the national language of personal failure in using the international discourse of human rights. He wonders if these seemingly defeated and abandoned people somehow share in his disgrace and misfortune for being unable to find jobs and their place in society:

> Antonio began to imagine that he was somehow responsible for their plight. If his own mind were not clouded with so much pain, they would not exist. *They are what I feel.* Somehow he had tainted the prosperous Americanos with his condition. The pathos of these men was his own creation, an extension of his tortured past, the curse of a man with a dead wife and son. He wanted to apologize to these gringos, to say, "I'm sorry. It's all in my head. My head is full of all this trash, you see." He hadn't meant to put them in this horrible predicament. It was his fault, and they could go home now, back to the lives they had before, to their beaches and ice chests. As soon as Antonio went away, they would slip back into their fit American bodies. (41; original emphasis)

This is a complex moment that reveals the unresolvable contradictions of Antonio's self-perception and his perception of those around him. Antonio desires to be one of the "Americanos," both the homeless and the prosperous, while he also distances himself from them. Helpless in his homelessness and grief, Antonio asserts control over his world by offering himself and his tragic past as an explanation for their own suffering and difficult lives. He inserts himself into their narrative. The homeless are the "natural" outcasts of capitalism who cannot function in the daily lives and life trajectories demanded of the proletariat. Antonio confuses the symptom for the causes that he is unable to identify. He sees this kind of misery around him, and his comments also reveal his growing feelings of kinship with these people and his nascent understanding of the structures that produce his economic devaluation and social worthlessness. Of course, just as Guillermo does, Antonio misplaces the guilt and the blame; however, unlike Guillermo, who blames his victims, Antonio blames himself for the other homeless persons. He inserts himself into their tragic life stories as the willing scapegoat and fellow survivor.

Guillermo's vision of America is one of cleanliness and orderliness; Antonio's is one of community and belonging. These are two juxtaposed images that show the overlapping of the cultural and political imagination. Cultural representations of American life encourage those who are distinctly not one of these consumers—"handsome, fit young people, all with a bounce in their step" (41)—to fail to imagine themselves as a part of it. Both immigrants feel betrayed by their expectations and the sense that their bodies of color seem to have contaminated the perfect American Dream they treasured. As a homeless, undocumented immigrant, Antonio will indeed be blamed for the failing of the American Dream by those who believe themselves entitled to it by virtue of nativity, merit, and racial, gender, and class identities. Guillermo, in his more simplistic world, does not understand that his nonwhite immigrant presence mars his own long-cherished dream of American purity and that his race—not his class, behavior, or military background—primarily excludes him from access to his pure, White, orderly idyll. Believing that his "almost, but not quite" mimicry of U.S. military practices will have earned him a place in this world of tidiness and order, Guillermo is blind to how racial politics will never allow him to truly belong to U.S. society. Guillermo is largely lacking self-awareness—he has always been on the active side, the perpetrator, the observer, never the watched or the observed. He is incapable of this kind of self-understanding, what Hannah Arendt calls "thoughtlessness" in her 1963 treatise on the "banality of evil" inspired by the trial of Nazi bureaucrat Adolf Eichmann. Like Eichmann and other Nazi administrators, Guillermo is eager to please his commanding officers and maintains an intensely blind loyalty to their genocidal vision of a new Guatemala. If Guillermo were capable of this kind of self-reflexive perception, Tobar seems to imply, he might be affected by his actions as much as Antonio is.

Racial Equilibrium and the Post–Civil Rights Context of Racial Revenge

The 1992 Los Angeles Crisis activates political discourses of revenge that are more popularly referenced as retrenchment, backlash, revanchism, and reclamation. Revenge has been marshaled to rewrite the legal concept of racial balance into what I term *racial equilibrium*. As a foremost concern in a 1970s civil rights agenda, racial balance is an assessment for integration and desegregation and a precursor to the more vague goal of "racial diversity" in classrooms and employment in the 1980s and 1990s. Racial balance is the often-stated goal of integration efforts in civil rights struggles, and controversially manifests itself in hotly contested legal rulings in percentage representations and quotas. To counteract the specific remedies of racial balance—affirmative action programs, for example—a discourse of racial equilibrium emerges to counter or minimize such efforts. The state interest in achieving racial balance is often criticized for disrupting an existing or "natural" equilibrium, one established by free market forces and the outcomes of individual choices and freedoms. Instead of racial balance trying to create demographic diversity and parity in classrooms, schools, and employment, racial conservatives disparage measures such as busing and quotas for their interference with the "natural" conditions and individual preferences of where one lives and with whom one associates. This seeming "social engineering" ultimately disturbs the ostensibly right, natural, or *true* equilibrium of racial inequalities. In the discourse of racial equilibrium, any redistributive transfer interferes with the status quo; racial conservatives criticize rectifying past discriminatory outcomes by giving resources to those who have been harmed or who are the descendants of those injured in the past, claiming this redistribution gives an undeserved preference or advantage to the unworthy.

Racial equilibrium, reframed as revenge, facilely solves the problem of racial balance as one group wins and another loses, each seeming to take its turn. In the post–civil rights era, racial conservatives perceive nonwhite groups as having won for long enough, implied by such terms as "reverse racism" or preferences. Racial equilibrium naturalizes certain kinds of violence as inevitable, as racial groups are interpreted as being in the social Darwinian struggle for opportunities and resources. If Whites are perceived as having lost opportunities or resources that they should have deserved based on objective criteria of merit, then nonwhites should now lose those opportunities or resources, even more so because these were never deserved or merited; they were *bestowed*. In the civil rights discourse following the 1992 Crisis, racial balance can now be reimagined as racial revenge.[25] The L.A. Crisis crucially cemented this change: the belief in racial balance was superseded by racial equilibrium and then racial revenge. What was once a state interest in having "balanced" populations through affirmative action is revised as racial equilibrium, and the connotations of equilibrium, of forces in tension, held in conflict; of action, reaction and symmetry, revenge.

This racial balance cum equilibrium is especially evident in media representations and the objectivity in which two divergent sides are presented. This is most apparent in the iconic imagery and stories that dominate representations of the violence: Rodney King is beaten by White police officers alongside a highway and four officers are charged with assault under color of authority, Reginald Denny is beaten by Black men at a city intersection and four are charged with assault. One of the reasons these two events were so memorable was because their contrasting juxtaposition exemplifies this notion of a racial equilibrium: the Black and White victims, the White and Black perpetrators, respectively. The scenario's racial contrasts imply the notion of racial revenge: Black men assault a White man for another Black man's beating by White police officers. The 1992 Crisis intersects with multiple narratives that determine who and what is considered deserving or praiseworthy, part of the interracial family of feeling and part of the civil in-group, as discussed in chapters 1 and 2, respectively. These competing acts of revenge, by individuals, institutions, groups, and the state, collectively determine the 1992 Los Angeles Crisis as the exemplar of retributory violence. In order to carry out such state-sanctioned violence, the state marks bodies and spaces as violent, uncivil, and inhuman, territorializing civility.

This chapter on Héctor Tobar's novel *The Tattooed Soldier* maps the shift in racial thinking from ideas of racial balance rooted in civil rights ideals to those of racial equilibrium, which aims to give reparations to Whites for unfair advantages putatively distributed to people of color. Under the logic of racial equilibrium, these reparations take the form of revenge—that these unfair advantages or preferences should be given back to Whites who have been, in the logic of this discourse, unjustly victimized, rather than unjustly privileged—and the 1992 L.A. Crisis manifests dominant narratives marshaled to legitimize racial revenge exacted on people of color by Whites. Revenge, as a tacit category imagined to belong to the state in the form of legal punishment and justice, is seen as an uncivilized practice and moral failing of people of color. Revenge is further spatialized and territorialized by marking nonwhite bodies. By focusing on the perspectives of the homeless, undocumented immigrants, and refugees, and their memories and perceptions of reality, this chapter also goes beyond the nation-state as the arbiter of justice and revenge, toward the transnational and global world made through U.S. militarism.

Revenge motivates both individual and state actors. It naturalizes the rightness of vengeance against specific kinds of racialized people and communities; civility is territorialized as both a strategy and an outcome. Understanding how revenge is racialized also demonstrates the discourses and ideologies in neoliberalism—most specifically through a state of emergency as the Los Angeles Crisis—that reify and naturalize the violence against poor people, people of color, and undocumented immigrants, the city's most vulnerable and demonized populations. Although much of the discourse, whether critical or journalistic, about the crisis is ultimately about revenge, little, if any, critical scholarship addresses the nuances and ramifications of such allegations. Tobar's writings explicitly identify the violence as "days of revenge" and trace the motivations behind such a naming through the Latina/o community, more specifically, Central Americans in Los Angeles. Tobar posits the spatialization of revenge and the territorialization of civility to organize the themes, plot, characterization, and structure of his debut novel about the lives of Latina/o immigrants at the moment of the 1992 Los Angeles Crisis.

Part II: Counterdiscourse of Civility

4 AT THE END OF TRAGEDY

How did I look without seeing, hear without listening?

—Adrienne Rich, "Notes Toward a Politics of Location"

I don't understand what goes on some times, right, cuz here we
are in this theater, we gettin along just fine. We go outside and
the shit change.

—Richard Pryor

THE 1992 LOS ANGELES "riots" have been deemed tragic by many,
from witnesses interviewed on the city streets to President George
H. W. Bush in his televised White House address to the American
people two days into the civil unrest. Such widespread devastation
elicited months of national and international public media scrutiny of
the causes of the most costly and destructive urban unrest in U.S. history. The crisis and the resulting inquiries into the violent failure of
the American dream exposed long-unresolved contexts of interracial
conflict, immigration, unemployment, poverty, deteriorating urban infrastructure, and deindustrialization. The register of these narratives
has often been tragic. The numerous instances of "tragic" appearing
in media and political narratives about the crisis capture and define
the scope of the destruction and the depth of the emotion beyond
the sense of material and financial loss. These narratives deploy popular connotations of tragedy as a sudden, disastrous reversal: from
general peace to widespread upheaval, from everyday rituals of life
to the unexpected encounters with death. Yet such repeated references to tragedy also elicit some of the foundational debates in the
genre: the distinction between real life and Art, the "death of tragedy"

in today's lack or surfeit of sufficiently tragic worldviews, and the role of tragedy in the cultivation of a citizenry. Moreover, reading the Los Angeles Crisis as tragedy means that we must recognize the selfless heroes, innocent victims, and catastrophic losses, alongside debates over whether the circumstances of poverty and urban decay merited the spectacular notice of and sympathetic claims on national and international audiences. These discussions manifest the vexed relationship between drama and politics, art and the state.

What happened in Los Angeles beginning on April 29, 1992, was too complex to be told by one person, one viewpoint, or even one group of people—whether they were politicians or reporters, police or civilians, city dweller or suburbanite, Black or White, Asian or Latina/o. In the tense atmosphere of heightened racial fear and distrust, a historic one-woman play staged a wide spectrum of conflicting perspectives on the civil unrest. First performed in Los Angeles in 1993, *Twilight: Los Angeles, 1992,* by Anna Deavere Smith, African American actor and playwright, was widely celebrated and noted for its unique artistic methodology of interviewing hundreds of people, recording their reactions to a highly contentious issue, and performing excerpts from their conversations onstage, sometimes in front of the very people who had been interviewed. Smith had perfected her distinctive approach to documentary theater through years of interviews and monologues, generating widespread acclaim for her Off-Broadway, Pulitzer Prize–nominated *Fires in the Mirror* (1992), a play about the 1991 Black–Jewish violence that erupted after the accidental death of a Guyanese American child in the Crown Heights section of Brooklyn. In their structure, methodology, and performance, Smith intends her plays to do the kind of cultural and political work needed to foster more democratic political participation and comprehensive public policies that address the causes of the violence and its aftermath. After studying at the American Conservatory Theatre in the 1970s, Smith launched her series of plays titled *On the Road: In Search of American Character.* While Smith's performances early in her career were well received, *Fires in the Mirror* launched her national recognition as an inimitable actor and innovative playwright at the forefront of documentary drama or testimony theater. After *Twilight* premiered in 1993 and was performed in theaters across the nation, Smith examined the U.S. presidency in the 2000 play *House Arrest* and considered the intersection of the human body, health, and the medical profession in the 2008 play *Let Me Down Easy.* She published her memoirs, *Talk to Me: Listening between the Lines* (2000), which discussed the genesis of her unique artistic method, acting abilities, and theoretical contributions to dialogues and community building and *Letters to a Young Artist* (2006), a guide to success in the arts. She developed the Institute for Arts and Civic Dialogue at Harvard University and has taught at Stanford University and New York University School of Law. Her distinctive plays and performances have garnered praise from such eclectic sources as the Tony and Obie award committees, Supreme Court justices, and the MacArthur Foundation's prestigious "genius grant" judges, who praised her for having "created a new form of theater—a blend of theatrical art, social commentary, journalism and intimate reverie" ("Anna Deavere Smith").[1]

The discussions spurred by her controversial dramas prove enmeshed in many of the literary debates over the definition and function of tragedy. I analyze *Twilight* as a tragedy, albeit an unconventional one. Its focus on the aftermath of the 1992 Los Angeles Crisis and its catastrophic narratives, both personal and collective, largely encourage such a reading, and my study of *Twilight*'s innovative structure reveals its significance to the genre of tragedy in contemporary life and drama. The play's unusual construction and distinctive dramatic elements point toward a neglected component of tragedy in the narratives of the Los Angeles Crisis and *Twilight*'s place in the genre of tragic drama in general, signaling a perpetual condition of unredressed injuries and unrelieved human suffering. Smith, I argue, revises the traditional generic emphasis of tragedy by focusing not on the main plot reversal, which generally defines a text as tragic, but rather on the often overlooked responses of grief and mourning, pity and fear, which typify the cathartic end of the tragic plot. Although *Twilight* remains the most well-known play about the crisis, the monologues from which Smith crafts her dramatic art and the performances themselves conspicuously exclude dramatizations of the protests, looting, arson, and assaults that characterized the historical and media accounts of the violence.[2]

Twilight redirects its audiences' focus from the sensational violence to its potential causes and lingering effects. Smith focuses on the tragedies of survivors and witnesses who lay the foundation for the future state by telling of the grievances and injuries they and their communities suffer and will continue to suffer. I posit that Smith's play should be read within a *tragic framework* in which crucial elements and constitutive parts of traditional tragedy are implied, undermined, or excised altogether. Smith's tragic framework highlights the interrelationship between drama and the state, especially in regard to interpersonal violence. Moreover, in eliciting its uneven effects on the citizenry, Smith deliberately cultivates the uncertainty and incompleteness of these memories of violence through her focus on the misspoken and unspoken communication of the interview subjects—their "articulate silences," elisions, illogic, malapropisms, factual errors, slang, or nonstandard Englishes.[3] *Twilight*, read through the lens of the tragic genre, mediates once more the relationship between politics and race at the end of the twentieth century and foregrounds the twenty-first.

In a more conventional play, audiences might expect these events to be performed as the prologue, first act, or even climax. Instead, *Twilight* is exclusively comprised of the testimonies of the witnesses and survivors of the violence, based on interviews Smith conducted in the weeks and months following the crisis, and the play has incorporated in its various performance runs only the iconic video footage and images of Rodney King's beating, Latasha Harlins's shooting, Reginald Denny's beating, looted stores, and burning buildings.[4] Smith's monologues have much in common with the final scene of tragedy, in which the chorus or the secondary characters eulogize and mourn the foreshortened lives of, say, Antigone or Hamlet. In traditional drama, the tragic actions of suicide and murder would normally prompt the catharsis for their survivors and audiences: the famed, final speeches of *Antigone*'s chorus and Horatio's leading of audiences to their own cathartic purgation and purification of pity and fear, in accordance with Plato's classical definition of the workings of tragedy. In *Twilight*, however, catharsis through the act of telling becomes the peripeteia or the sudden tragic reversal of the drama.

Whether one accepts or dismisses the narratives of the L.A. Crisis as tragedies, the resulting debates in public policy are struggles over competing interpretations of the participants' worth as tragic protagonists in terms of their motivations, circumstances, and virtues. Smith's play is best understood through the generic conventions of tragedy, most notably in the context of the denouements of the final scenes after the deaths have been performed onstage and the witnesses and survivors begin to explain how these losses should be grieved and mourned. Furthermore, most of the people interviewed derived their knowledge of the events almost entirely from print and visual media sources rather than firsthand accounts, and, despite their physical distance and relative safety, they each feel their lives and the very notion of America to have been in jeopardy.

Incorporating a wide array of perspectives and people, Smith intends her dramatic methodology to be not only inclusive but also transformative. Her performances critically expose how the news media and public opinion influence audience assumptions in relation to polarizing issues such as those raised by the L.A. Crisis: interracial relations, civic participation, and democratic principles. In doing so, Smith deploys a range of feminist methodologies: standpoint epistemology, intersectionality, hybridity, world-traveling, and differential consciousness.[5] Antiracist feminists have identified the crisis as an interracial tragedy that signals both the failure of and the need for intersectional alliances and coalitions; Smith's artistic methodology and performance art are, I argue, the theatricalization and innovation of feminist practices of relation that make these alliances and coalitions possible. *Twilight* reveals the very interracial conflict that Smith attempts to bridge in her ethical commitment to transracial relations: transformative reappraisals and realignments of groups and individuals marked by racial difference. Echoing feminist calls for transracial coalition-building (Carrillo-Rowe), Smith also builds on these exhortations for the recognition of different experiences and politics by listening to the voices of marginalized subjects not just including or integrating them into her drama.[6] I posit that Smith's unique drama demonstrates that these formations, moreover, should not be based on reductive assertions of a universal humanity shared by all or a simplistic (often visual) celebration of difference and diversity—both common praises for Smith's play.

In her essays and the introductions to her plays, Smith returns repeatedly to how listening—auditory comprehension and responsiveness to another—is a starting point for one's own self-construction. But listening, I contend, is just one of the many processes of comprehension and recognition that Smith's work incorporates and promotes. While Smith stresses listening to one another, she is most interested in the gaps between words, the pauses and hesitations that mark both the inadequacy of language and the possible emergence of new, more comprehensive forms of communication. Smith attempts to widen our range of sensory responses and broaden our understanding of the many forms of communication. Smith engages in what I call *performances of proximity*, performances that are complexly structured around multiple forms of recognition that are beyond the visual and auditory—of shared experience, feeling, and memory, of our perceived relationships to other subjects and their dynamic relationships to us. Thus, Smith's paradigmatic listener is much more like that of a witness, whose importance is defined by not only her experiential testimony but also her very presence as spectator, survivor, and audience to the event. I examine three monologues in which these speakers' misspeakings and negotiations with the interviewer teach Smith and her audiences how to engage with the presence of the other, recognize and perform this proximity, and thus facilitate and witness this continuous movement between interviewer and interviewee, self and other. Smith is thereby expanding the tragic notion of catharsis and its concomitant experience of pity and fear through her focus on listening and proximity.

Twilight's Tragic Framework

Tragedy is the narrative art of human suffering. From this simple yet undeniably broad claim, the competing definitions of tragedy can be more or less disaggregated into contested clusters of meaning: destiny, catastrophic reversal, sympathetic victim-heroes, fatal flaws, catharsis, and epochal or world-ending events have been some of the most popularly cited elements of tragedy. Indeed, scholars of tragedy often choose one or more of these elements in combination to test the limits of the genre and to model appropriate applications of tragedy to their specific texts. The genre of tragedy provokes assessments of the kind of characters, nature of their struggles, inadequacies of reconciliation, and effects on audiences. Tragic dramas have spurred profound inquiries into the human condition and heated debates over its expression. Audiences, citizens, and bodies politic must engage with what are, in essence, competing moral registers: divine or human law, individual striving or the greater good. Given such diffuse interpretations and functions, the *tragic framework* encompasses the wide-ranging interpretations possible for the genre, style, mode, and ideology of tragedy (Gledhill, 7).[7] Tragedy is intimately connected to the state, whether through the affective terms by which Plato famously banishes tragic poets from his ideal republic, thus acknowledging the subversive power of tragedy to sway the populace, or Aristotle's cultivation of the proper civic responses to fictions of human suffering or the dramatization of attitudes toward crime and punishment that reaffirms or counters the legitimacy of rule. In tragedy, our very human vulnerability to our own governance and to forces beyond human control is painfully, uncomfortably, laid bare.

Under these terms, *Twilight* is both a response to tragedy and a work of tragedy itself. To address the former, I first examine the media and political narratives that shaped the tragic nature of the historical event. The question of whether the L.A. Crisis could be fully accepted as a tragedy would emerge in national politics, reverberating throughout the presidential election later that year and into the decades that have followed. In the aftermath of the crisis, the debates over these narratives were unofficially waged in terms that track very closely to some of the major elements of tragedy: Were the catastrophic reversals and losses based on misfortune or destiny? Were victims sympathetic or criminal? Were media viewers responding with pity or fear? If so, toward what and whom? In their attempts to assess blame and causality, journalists and policymakers evaluated whether the violence and destruction was alterable or avoidable. Was it the victims' terrible misfortune to be in the paths of the fires, to be more likely the victims of random assaults and stray bullets, given the assumed routine violence of their neighborhoods? Or was it their destiny as racialized subjects living in ghettos that fostered gang activities, looting, and arson to experience such losses?

This notion of destiny evokes the so-called culture of poverty that has dominated national discussions of race and inequality and described inner-city neighborhoods as locked into generational cycles of violence and self-destruction.[8] Ascribing to this view, some observers interpret the losses sustained as the just deserts for residents arrested by police, burned out of their homes, or forced to live in neighborhoods with shuttered or burned-out businesses that could no longer provide necessary local services. While scholars would analyze the fact and fiction of answers to these questions, these debates clearly demonstrate how policymakers and pundits were implicitly assessing the events within a tragic framework.

In order to document widely conflicting perspectives on the 1992 Crisis, Smith's work both mirrors and counters the mainstream political and media narratives of Rodney King's beating, filtered by the singular perspectives of the newscasters and reporters for the major news networks. Smith's interviewees join those critics who have condemned the news media during the crisis for its biased coverage of the events, overt racism, and lack of historical perspective. Independent journalists and media critics lambasted mainstream news commentary for reinscribing social hierarchies and stereotypes.[9] In contrast to their later coverage of the crisis, most mainstream media networks covered Rodney King's beating and subsequent trial of his police assailants by calling upon all Angelenos to embrace antiracism efforts. By Thursday evening, April 30, 1992, however, the steady stream of "raw footage" from the "riots" had prompted unscripted and unsubstantiated, often racially derogatory, anti-Black commentaries from the newscasters that described the various participants as "thugs," "hooligans," or "gang-bangers" (Chang and Diaz-Veizades, 60). Moreover, the TV news coverage indicted African Americans for much of the looting and violence, often contradicting the images used as background to the voice-over reporting that showed Latinas/os, Whites, or Asian Americans who were also looting (Gaskins, 123).

Accepting or rejecting the 1992 Crisis as tragedy says much about the popular understanding of the genre: the predestined defeat of the sympathetic hero and the futility of individual strivings against a hostile world portend the failure of remedies. These tragic views of either flawed individuals or intransigent circumstances can make interracial conflict seem inevitable. If the circumstances are tragic, the main protagonists—the store owners defending their businesses, passersby preventing assaults on others, or demonstrators protesting the verdict—as sympathetic or heroic, might make claims on the state. Differently interpreted by U.S. neoconservative and liberal agendas, the ostensible intransigence of interracial conflict shows the futility of well-intentioned policies that the state must now reject or continue. Under such conditions of persistent futility, the recurrence of interracial violence makes it possible to argue, as some historians and social commentators have, that racial exploitation and subordination are inevitable tragedies of the U.S. democratic experiment. Race in America is, thus, conceived as a long-running, self-perpetuating series of racial tragedies, of which the L.A. Crisis is a prominent example. Moreover, the spectacles of violence and suffering during the crisis eclipsed the other tragic narratives of police brutality represented by the beating of Rodney King and of racial and class conflict between neighborhood merchants and their customers, Korean and Black, represented by the shooting death of Black teenager Latasha Harlins by Korean store owner Soon Ja Du and Du's later trial in November 1991.

Twilight's Methods

Tragic reversals often stand in for the whole of the tragedy; the characters' injuries, deaths, and suicides identify tragic plots. Popular and literary references to tragedy often isolate the central tragic action, ignoring all else that comes before or after. To some extent, the larger tragedy is less important than the reversal itself. However, Smith's play portrays the aftermath of the personal and collective tragic reversals suffered during the 1992 violence from multiple perspectives. By choosing to perform the witnesses' testimony to their lives and experiences, Smith's play is both an epilogue to the past and a prologue to the future.[10] Smith also does not provide what most audiences might expect, the speakers' eyewitness accounts of the violence; rather, she attempts to get at the essence of tragedy through the testimony of its survivors, spectators, and participants. Analogously, Smith gets at the essence of contemporary discussions about race and interracial violence not from official news sources, published historical accounts, or commonly held definitions, but from the experiences and narratives of the people she interviews.

While some of the monologues address an aspect of the 1992 violence, many more are only tangentially related to the crisis, if at all. For example, some of the characters Smith performed were those famously involved in the "riots" and publicly praised or reviled for their actions: Reginald Denny, the White truck driver beaten in South Central; Henry "Keith" Watson, one of the four African American men accused and later acquitted for the attacks on Denny; and Daryl Gates, the controversial former chief of the Los Angeles Police Department.[11] However, Smith juxtaposes these speakers with lesser-known ones, such as Rudy Salas Sr., a Chicano sculptor; Mrs. Young Soon Han, a Korean immigrant who lost her store during the crisis; and Elaine Young, a White realtor and Hollywood socialite. In crucial ways, Smith's play, in its use of marginalized or ignored speakers and its inclusion of ostensibly irrelevant anecdotes, seems to circle around the issues raised by the L.A. Crisis. However, Smith uses these details to reveal the character and motivations of each of her interview subjects. Smith's attention to lesser-known figures encourages her audiences to encounter and imagine the "voices of the unheard"—those ignored and forgotten.[12] These voices connect the 1992 violence to past racial injuries and traumas. Some speakers in *Twilight* identify these manifestations and legacies of White settler colonialism and global capitalism: the European invasion of the Americas, the African slave trade, the U.S. takeover of northern Mexico, anti-Mexican persecution during World War II, and Jim Crow segregation.[13] *Twilight*, then, as the composite of these monologues and these legacies, encompasses more than the tragedy of the L.A. Crisis; the play delves further back than even King's beating or Harlins's death, both of which have been often cited as its precipitating events.

But far from asserting a kind of collective truth and knowledge about the crisis, Smith's play points to how the meaning of these interviews is highly subjective and depends on their contexts and form. First, these monologues in *Twilight* exist in multiple forms: two published collections of edited interviews (1994 and 2003), the live performances (1994–95), the documentary film (2000), and performances by other actors and theater troupes since the play's 1993 premiere in Los Angeles. Second, individual performances can differ from night to night and venue to venue as Smith chooses a varying cast of characters for the twenty-odd monologues or changes their order in the performance. Third, Smith also deviates from her interviews and scripts as presented in the 1994 and 2003 published versions of *Twilight* in important ways: she omits large portions of the text, performs monologues of different people spliced together, and rearranges words and sentences within a monologue. In taking such liberties with the original interviews and script, Smith challenges the audience's expectations of an accurate portrayal of the interviewed subject, countering the desire for truth or authenticity to be found in her performances. This eclectic performance history and the many changing interpretations of *Twilight* lay the foundation for the fluidity of racial and cultural productions, the changing terrain of racial discourse, and the uncertainty and variegation of tragic memories.

Smith's creative method emphasizes the labor involved in crafting the performances: namely, Smith's own preparatory research of hundreds of interviews conducted in the field, much like a journalist, historian, or ethnographer. Smith then listens to these recordings in order to match her performance closely with her interview subject's speech mannerisms. Enthusiastic reviewers promote Smith's accuracy in her transcription and interpretation of the interviews by likening her performances to a video camera or tape recorder (Wald, n.p.). Another reviewer describes Smith as a documentary filmmaker "who has simply decided to dispense with the camera. Instead of capturing her subjects on film, she interviews them, then, using their own comments and a few of their mannerisms, portrays them on the stage" (Richards, 5). These metaphors, although complimentary, actually trivialize Smith's artistry, creative agency, and editorial choices. These reviewers deliberately construct Smith's performance as an objective lens that ostensibly provides her audience with unlimited access to these individuals through their own words and the play.

Interestingly, Smith describes her artistic process as a form of replication that critics often applaud; however, she also emphasizes how she alters and rearranges the interviews, a fact that fewer critics address. In the 1994 introduction to *Twilight*, Smith insists that the play "is first and foremost a document of what an *actress heard* in Los Angeles" (xxiv; original emphasis). She is responding to critics' and audiences' expectations of a solution to the conflicts that the L.A. Crisis violently revealed: "The performance is a reiteration of that. When I did my research in Los Angeles, I was listening with an ear that was trained to hear stories for the specific purpose of repeating them with the elements of character intact" (xxiv). Smith's character development, dramatic structure, and performance method have been compared to Bertolt Brecht's notion of *personal gestus,* a foundational concept of his epic theater that he describes in his 1938 essay, "The Street Scene."[14] Brecht explains that a personal gestus is "an eyewitness demonstrating to a collection of people how a traffic accident took place" (52). The witness describes the scene in enough detail that "the bystanders are able to form an opinion about the accident" (ibid.). In addressing the development of characters she will perform, Smith describes a specific vision for the kind of conversations she hopes her interviews will elicit: "I wanted to get people to say those few essential things. And I knew if I talked to somebody an hour, they would only say a few of these things which I would call essential things. In other words: repeatable things, things which are quite distinct, nobody could have said it like they said it" (quoted in Weber, 61).

The "essential things" for both Smith and Brecht might be more aptly imagined as a heterogeneous headnote or sketch for dramatic characters. Smith describes her selection of the monologues as comprised of these "essential things." While Smith does perform the "actual words" of her interview subjects, the slight deviations between the 1994 and 2003 texts, as well as the 2000 PBS *Stage on Screen* documentary, also show that Smith does significantly edit and reorganize the words of her characters. Smith uses the extended metaphor of costuming to explain her use of language and to contextualize her decision to edit the words of her speakers: "And it is that real or essential expression I'm trying for, cutting away the rest of the scraps in there to get that. Even though somebody may have said something which is a much more eloquent narrative and would help me tell my story more quickly, it won't be of use. What's of more use are the bits and pieces of disconnected language with a peculiar syntax which seems to have nothing to do with the rest of the interview" (quoted in Weber, 61–62). Smith explains that she has to work against her interview subjects' wanting to "cloak their narrative with a longer explanation" and thus "it takes questions which really bring back to them either very pleasurable or traumatic experiences to get them to leave the cloak of language and come to the real expression" (quoted in Weber, 61). As philosophers of language since Plato have disdained "ornament" and "sophistry" in human communication, Smith encourages her interview subjects to face the limits of their ability to communicate, the rawer edge of their uncalculated and inchoate responses.

Fine-tuning her artistic methodology since graduating from the American Conservatory Theatre in the 1970s, Smith depends on the act of listening to the words of another, the foundation of her performances. In the preface to her first major play, *Fires in the Mirror* (1993), Smith emphasizes the repetition of another's words as the primary means of portraying or embodying this other person: "If we were to inhabit the speech pattern of another, and walk in the speech of another, we could find the individuality of the other and experience that individuality viscerally" (xxvii). The other person's words thereby become the key to understanding another's distinctive thoughts, perspectives, and opinions. As if metaphorically donning a second skin or costume, the performer inhabits and walks in the "speech pattern of another." Smith points to a speaker's body that is discursively constructed; once she has adopted the speaker's language, she can then draw attention to these discourses, which construct a distinctive individuality and viewpoint. Smith also firmly rejects any notion that she is capable of wholly portraying the interview subject: "To tell you the truth, I was trying to make an accurate document, which is impossible. And I didn't want to impersonate, that would be me, adding things. I was trying to make an accurate document. So, in a way, what you see is as much as I could remember, as much as I could do in the time. I think of it as very unfinished, what I'm doing. The people are only in half their clothes, I never finished making their dresses" (quoted in Weber, 52). Significantly, Smith alludes to the multiple layering and indeterminacy of communication: the speaker's "cloaked" language, Smith's editing or metaphorically cutting away the scraps, and her half-finished performance or half-costumed characters. Such inaccuracy and half-accomplished performance invites the audience to be self-conscious of how they themselves will attempt to complete the costume with what is an admittedly partial representation. Importantly, Smith does not intend for the audience to attempt to finish the costume, but rather for the audience to recognize the unspoken and misspoken in her emphasis on the ungrammatical, the imprecision of spoken language, the physical exchange and gestures that stand in for language and also communicate nonverbally.

By crossing racial and gendered identities, Smith's performances thwart expectations of typecasting, or corresponding racial and gender markers between character and actor. In the 2003 Dramatists Play Service edition of *Twilight*, Smith explicitly ties her cross-racial and cross-gender performances with costuming: "This play is about race relations and the degree to which we make assumptions about others based on the first visual impression they make. Costumes should be seen as an extension of that, with a mind to the fact that poor race relations begin with an inability to see the specific details of any person in front of you" (5). In the context of Smith's repeated metaphors of costuming and communication, she addresses the importance of language in portraying the multiple identities of the speaker: "The actor is performing the specifics of race and identity and working towards those specifics by paying attention to accuracy of language. Ethnicity, age, gender, class identity are all meant to be variables that the audiences sees [sic] shifting" (7).

While Smith disrupts physical markers of race and gender in assessing character, she draws attention to the few costumes or props she does use and the distinctive gestures that set apart each character—on one hand, her performances undermine the primacy of the visual in determining racial or gendered identity; on the other, Smith is also underscoring the speech patterns, gestures, facial expressions, and behaviors that categorize different bodies. Though Smith stresses the importance of listening to one another—among speakers and audiences—she is most interested in the gaps between words, the pauses and hesitations that mark both the inadequacy of language and the possible emergence of a new one for each speaker. Smith points to the inadequacy of preexisting language about race and envisions a new one from these misspeakings. She attempts to widen our range of sensory responses and broaden our understanding of the many forms of communication.

In addition, Smith's decision to perform only one side of the conversation—that of the interviewee—places the audience in the role of the interviewer. Her performance of one side ultimately moves the audience into the silenced role of interviewer and listener simultaneously, identities that she also inhabits and performs onstage. Smith maneuvers *Twilight*'s audience members into this position of unwitting interviewer in order to encourage them to adapt to each interview performed. In this way, audience members are interviewing the speaker onstage as Smith performs the character looking to the audience as the partner in conversation, the interviewer. She reveals the process of her previous interviewing experiences through her performances of the speakers' responses to the absent interviewer's questions or comments. For example, Katie Miller, who lived close to the areas marked by the most devastating destruction of both the 1965 and 1992 civil unrests in Los Angeles, states offhandedly that she didn't loot this most recent time. Miller apparently reacts to the interviewer's—Smith's—disbelief as Miller protests, "Get that out" (130) and swats her hand at the audience as if batting away such thoughts from the interviewer. In the absence of the interviewer's verbal and physical responses, the audience members reconstruct Smith's side of the conversation in retrospect, becoming listeners in the re-performed interviews. Such a positioning reminds her audiences that they indeed once were or could have been the media viewers of the "riots." Smith's prominent featuring of these secondhand witnesses or media spectators in *Twilight* further connects the speakers to the audience members since the latter too might have stories that could later be performed onstage.[15]

Tragic Misspeakings

In her 2001 collection of essays, *Talk to Me: Listening between the Lines,* Smith addresses the importance of listening as central to her theatrical art. Smith privileges not only the words of people, but more important, what is misspoken: "To me, the most important doorway into the soul of a person is her or his words, or any other external communication device. I am a student of words. . . . Life would give me other kinds of characters, nestled in the speakings and misspeakings of the people I met in all walks of life" (*Talk to Me*, 12). The experience of listening is enabled by Smith's performance of what she has previously heard from the interview subjects and the audience's own auditory practice. But by "misspeakings," Smith denotes the imprecision of language or verbal communication that reveals more than the facts conveyed.

In *Talk to Me*, Smith centers these lapses in her creative methodology: "I think we can learn a lot about a person in the very moment that language fails them. In the very moment that they have to be more creative than they would have imagined in order to communicate. It's the very moment that they have to dig deeper than the surface to find words, and at the same time, it's a moment when they want to communicate very badly" (53). Smith tries to record the fiction of people's "everyday discourse"—what they might believe is successful communication—but more important, when their language fails, when the fiction of selfhood falters. Smith's theater productively recovers and reinterprets this moment of failure where these silences frame the possible discomfort and awkwardness between two people in conversation.

The diversity of representations, the "speakings and misspeakings" in the monologues, is made visible by the constancy of Smith's relatively unchanging presence from speaker to speaker; Smith uses very little makeup, no prosthetics, and minimal costuming to mark the distinction among the characters she portrays in succession. Laudatory reviewers often misinterpreted this constancy as manifesting interracial harmony through the recognition of "sameness." However, this interpretation overlooks Smith's primary emphasis on what is not audible or present onstage in her play and in each speaker's unintentional elisions in the monologues performed. Exemplifying the interplay between misspeaking and unspoken, Smith portrays New Jersey Senator Bill Bradley hesitantly beginning his recounting of a Black friend's experience with police harassment decades ago: "I mean, you know, it's still . . . / there are people who are, uh, / who the law treats in different ways" (214). Even a skilled politician like Bradley struggles with precisely communicating the LAPD's racist treatment of his friend; he partially obscures his meaning in his interjections and pauses, and he hesitates even as he connects these aggregate experiences to the 1992 Crisis as if these linkages are difficult to name, it is painful to admit they exist, and he is forced to acknowledge the differently racialized treatment under the laws he creates and upholds as an elected representative. Smith continually points toward that which is missing, toward the listener's incomplete and unfinished accounting. This tragedy of miscommunication or missed communication is productive, the origin of her dramatic art.

Smith shows the range of experiences—what she heard—that have shaped her own self-construction and those she represents onstage and off. In *Twilight,* Smith's acting strategy is simultaneously an attempt to approximate documentary realism through a kind of dramatic verisimilitude and an attempt to portray its failure. This failure is provocative and productive; Smith shows the irreconcilable differences expressed in often-incompatible viewpoints that cannot be smoothed over in a celebratory pluralism or universal humanism. Smith deliberately performs her speakers by privileging the misspoken and exposing the limitations of her art: in a provocative twist on Brecht's alienation effect, instead of trying to disrupt the audience's facile identification with the character onstage, Smith tries to disconnect a presumed political agenda from the subject's racialized or stereotyped identity. By editing down the original interviews, Smith, then, performs the speakers out of context—out of the context of their own words that came before and after the edited monologue and in sound bites deliberately reminiscent of news broadcasts. Smith appropriates this media technique in order to expose the limited power of technologized communications, as well as her own dramatic method, to represent subjects in their complexity. She hopes to teach her audiences to listen as she has listened in the original interview, attending to the spoken and misspoken in the speaker's language represented in her own portrayal.

Some of the most controversial monologues reveal how a single personal history is complexly layered by historical racial injustices. Rudy Salas Sr. was not an eyewitness to the 1992 violence, but his story and family lore intersect with nineteenth-century U.S.–Mexican border conflicts and twentieth-century anti-Mexican discrimination and violence—histories that were largely ignored in media accounts of the L.A. Crisis and its long-standing interracial tensions. Significantly, in both the 1994 text and film versions, Smith chooses Salas's monologue to begin the play in which he testifies to his own beating by the police when he was young and to the racial profiling and police abuse his family has experienced since then, never mentioning the specifics of the crisis itself. As the only speaker for the 1994 prologue, his monologue serves as the historical introduction that is crucial to the thematic structure of *Twilight* and foregrounds Smith's explicit purpose in hearing people's reactions to the violence.

As one of the "zoot-suiters" brutalized by police during World War II, Salas narrates how he lost his hearing in both ears after being repeatedly kicked in the head by four police officers.[16] Salas's traumatic interactions with the police resonate with the beating of Rodney King and with the altercation between police and residents that incited the 1965 Watts Rebellion. Through Salas's monologue, Smith establishes the centuries-long pattern of racism and police brutality waged against communities of color in Los Angeles, of which King's beating was only one of countless others that have gone unrecognized and unredressed. In her interpretation of Rudy Salas's story of his past encounters with the police, Smith documents the violence historically present in the criminal justice system, the illegal and immoral police actions that victimize people of Mexican descent such as Salas. In this way, tragedy reflects a flaw in the social fabric rather than in an individual subject.

In the film version of *Twilight*, Smith performs Salas's passionate speech against the backdrop of a fifteen-foot Mexican flag hanging on a bare soundstage. In the 1994 published version of his monologue, Salas explains how he had to take down the Mexican flag on his van because of the "rednecks and peckerwoods" (4) who had moved into his neighborhood, implying that displaying the flag might become the excuse for verbal harassment or even physical violence. In this case, what remains unspoken is how the flag symbolizes the reassertion of Salas's nationality cum cultural and racialized identity, which has been censored and derided throughout his family's history that he retells. But the flag also serves as a marker for the questions of citizenship that have riven California politics since its acquisition and statehood through anti-immigration campaigns and racial discrimination against Latina/o and Chicana/o communities.

Salas is unable to express his frustration and anger at specific moments in his monologue largely because these past incidents of police brutality are beyond redress—perpetrated, even sanctioned, by the criminal justice system itself. Speaking forcefully in Smith's portrayal, Salas refers to "this madness" (2), "the insanity" (2), and "an insane hatred" (3) that he has felt since childhood, when his Mexican heritage was ridiculed or silenced in school and in his neighborhood, and later when he was brutally beaten by the police as a teenager. He can hardly describe the rage he feels in recounting these incidents during the monologue, instead gesturing, trailing off, or interjecting "Man!" for emphasis:

> They didn't tell me right away,
> because it would make me sick,
> it would make me sick,
> and, uh,
> my oldest son, Rudy.
> Didn't they,
> Margaret,
> Insult him one time and they pulled you over . . .
> The Alhambra cop, they pulled you over
> And, aww, man . . .
> My enemy. (6–7)

The unsatisfactory repetitions highlight the confluence of the unspoken with the misspoken—Salas cannot fully explain or communicate his thoughts despite his partial, misspoken attempts and, thus, the accuracy and entirety of what he attempts to communicate remains unspoken. Psychoanalytic critic Anne Cheng notes that "for Salas, however, it is much easier to name racist acts than to process racism psychically. Salas's narrative begins to veer into a curiously abstract and self-pathologizing language when it tries to describe the emotional repercussions of those confrontations" (171).[17] The easily defined antagonists and perpetrators of racism—the English-only White teachers, the police officers who beat Salas as a young man and harassed his wife and son—incite Salas's frustrated language and gestures that cannot fully express the enormity of his memories and responses. In Smith's performance, Salas pauses and becomes more measured in his storytelling as he remembers the police violence that permanently deafened him and that threatens his wife and son forty years later. More than the fact of the continuity of institutional racism, manifested in the policing of Chicanas/os and Latinas/os, significantly, Salas's unspoken and misspoken words are clustered around his inability to perform a racialized masculinity premised on the safety and integrity of the heterosexual family. He interrupts his interview to yell offstage to his wife, demanding her to confirm his story. His family is trying to protect him by not telling him about being stopped by the Alhambra police because they know how angry he gets with police brutality. His son is home from Stanford and despite this elite educational achievement, he is still harassed by the police. In these gendered-sexualized logics of racial formation, Salas's racialized identity is largely recognizable through the heterosexual father's inability to effectively protect—provide safety and security for—his nuclear family.[18]

Salas's movement from naming his antagonists to his own self-directed frustration, from grievance to grief, as Cheng notes, should also be interpreted within the tragic framework as the denouement at the end of tragedy. Salas is not just unable to psychically process the racist acts that have disabled him and terrorized his wife and son, but he is also unable to counter the repeated manifestations of racism and its invisibility as a criminal act. In Salas's monologue, Smith alludes to the multiple racial tragedies in his family's history. This monologue, with its network of grievances, marks the beginning of *Twilight*, and this play, as an aggregate of these monologues, is wholly the extended denouement of the tragic framework.[19] The conventional endpoint of tragedy thus comprises the entirety of *Twilight*. Smith provides monologues with their constellations of grievances and inarticulable grief ignored or denied as the fraught legacy of these racial tragedies. Smith's play is about both the many conflicting perspectives on the interracial violence in Los Angeles and the proliferating tragedies these speakers reveal.

Performances of Proximity

The repetition of this theme is consistent with Smith's desire to foster better communication between people, and it has larger theoretical implications. Smith often cites her grandfather's maxim, "If you say a word often enough, it becomes you" (*Fires*, xxiii), as the fundamental inspiration for her artistic methodology. She tells of the confusion over her grandfather's exact words as a parable for differentiating her acting methodology from those of others, notably the psychological realism of Method acting. She initially believes him to have said that the words become your own, but a relative later corrects her memory: that with enough repetition, the words become *you*. Theater scholar Debby Thompson notes Smith's "post-structuralist acting practices" in this paradigmatic story: "If words become your own, there is a 'you' pre-existing the words; but if words become 'you,' then your 'you-ness,' your very selfhood is made up of your interaction with words" (133). Rather than a preexisting self that can own or possess the distinctive language of another, for Smith these words come from the monologues of those she has interviewed and performed, expanding the self-constructions of her own identity and her audiences through their encounters with the other.

Echoing Continental philosophers such as Walter Benjamin and Emmanuel Lévinas, Smith's work can be characterized by her fundamental ethical orientation toward the subjects she interviews and her artistic methodology, in which the self begins with the other. Smith's transracial works that center on personal reactions to the Crown Heights and Los Angeles civil disturbances can be read within contemporary human rights discourses that address human suffering and mass violence. Lévinas's philosophy is compelling in its attempts to foreclose the possibility of future Holocausts through a fundamental concern for the other: "his thesis that ethics is first philosophy, where ethics is understood as a relation of infinite responsibility to the other person" (Critchley, 6). Political scientist Robert Meister spatializes this infinite responsibility to the other in terms of an "ethics of the neighbor." He identifies Lévinas's interest in the proximity of time and place, and Meister thus argues for the spatialization of ethics:[20] "Lévinas's point is that in ethics, unlike politics, we do not ask who came first and what we have already done to (or for) each other. The distinctively ethical question is rather one of proximity—we are already here and so is the other, cheek-by-jowl with us in the same place. The neighbor is the figure of the other toward whom our *only* relationship is that of proximity" (Meister, sec. 5; original emphasis).

Like Lévinas and Meister, Smith is fundamentally interested in proximity and the influence such contiguity might have on constructions of the self. Smith's notion of proximity, in both her methodology and art, opens up a discussion of a feminist politics of relation: how one's identity is shaped by the relations in which one engages. This set of relations is manifested through the practice of intersectionality, the analysis of identity along multiple axes simultaneously. The separate, yet intersecting, axes of race, class, gender, sexuality, and ability have often obscured the depth of historical inequalities faced among different social groups. In order to provide a critique of feminism's unacknowledged racism, critic Aimee Carrillo-Rowe posits this politics as *the means* by which to effect a coalitional subjectivity:

> The meaning of self is never individual, but a shifting set of relations that we move in and out of, often without reflection. . . . It gestures toward deep reflection about the selves we are creating as a function of where we place our bodies, and with whom we build our affective ties. I call this placing a "politics of relation." It moves theories of locating the subject to a relational notion of the subject. It moves a politics of location from the individual to a coalitional notion of the subject. (16)

Once recognizing this often overlooked contingent "set of relations," a subject can then recognize its primary construction as coalition; this "politics of relation" thus leads to a coalitional notion of subjectivity.

Arguing for an auditory proximity, Smith criticizes her audience's reliance on physical and ideological proximities instead of auditory ones and for refusing to acknowledge the "set of relations" that connect even the dissimilar, the other. Each of Smith's plays thus becomes a performance of proximity: her juxtaposition throughout her texts of her hundreds, if not thousands, of interviews. Through the structure of her performances, Smith hopes to move her audiences into the role of the listener, sensitive to the language—the racial language—of another. Using the concept of proximity, Smith responds to her critics who have pressured her to find a single representative perspective to somehow unify the fragmented citizenry of post-1992 Los Angeles:

> I think there is an expectation that in this diverse city, and in this diverse nation, a unifying voice would bring increased understanding and put us on the road to solutions. This expectation surprises me. There is little in culture or education that encourages the development of a unifying voice. In order to have real unity, all voices would have to first be heard or at least represented. Many of us who work in race relations do so from the point of view of our own ethnicity. This very fact inhibits our ability to hear more voices than those that are closest to us in proximity. Few people speak a language about race that is not their own. If more of us could actually speak from another point of view, like speaking another language, we could accelerate the flow of ideas. (Smith, *Twilight*, xxiv–xxv)

Smith's performing body becomes a spatiotemporal palimpsest as she performs her subject and herself as both former listener and interviewer. By privileging the aggregate of the many characters she performs, rather than emphasizing how her own performance incorporates the perspectives of her interviews, the critics' expectations largely obscure Smith's own identity onstage and the changes she performs herself undergoing over the course of the work. Smith is performing a speaker more like herself with each new character, but further from a person that has been marked by a static racial identity in the way these critics assign her.[21]

Smith undermines her audiences' understanding of her speakers' personal tragedies of uncertainty and inauthenticity through not only her performance but also the information her speakers convey. Smith encourages her audiences to question her performance, her speakers' words, and our very understanding of the monologues and the tragedies they relate. We are misinterpreting the words of the speakers because their accurate meaning is lost in translation: telling stories to different audiences, conveying feeling and thought in language, and tailoring one's expression to the audience. It is a deeper tragedy not only of human suffering but also of the inability to communicate accurately and translate these sufferings to others. Smith tries to reclaim the unspoken and misspoken—what would be dismissed as miscommunication and failure, especially for this unprecedented interracial conflict as the L.A. Crisis among people of color. Just as African Americans are criminalized, Latina/o and Asian communities were also portrayed as linked to illegality and illegitimacy; they experienced an oppressive visibility in the media through the wholesale constructions of all Latinas/os and Chicanas/os as illegal immigrants and of Korean immigrant storeowners as opportunists exploiting nonimmigrant (African) American communities for profit.

As discussed in chapter 1, mainstream media sources and policymakers frequently cited the contentious relationship between Korean Americans and African Americans as an important factor that precipitated the violent events of the crisis. The various New York City boycotts of Korean American grocers by Black residents in 1990–91 and the murder of Latasha Harlins, an African American teenager, by a Korean storeowner in Los Angeles entrenched a new media paradigm in discussions of racial tensions: the "Black–Korean conflict" in the inner cities. In national media coverage, African Americans claimed that Korean American store owners exploited customers from surrounding communities by charging higher prices than other businesses farther away and usurping opportunities for Black ownership and economic mobility. Moreover, African American residents also complained that alcohol sales contributed to the social and moral decay of neighboring communities. Korean Americans responded by explaining how they faced anti-Asian discrimination and their own lack of resources—financial means to buy businesses in more expensive neighborhoods, social networks, English-language facility—that would allow these entrepreneurs to operate stores in other areas. Two major communities of color voiced very different histories and experiences of discrimination in the United States.[22]

Cultural critic Elaine Kim has explicitly identified the "tragic legacy" of the Korean diaspora: the brutality of Japanese colonialism, the Korean War, and repressive, U.S.-backed regimes during the cold war. Kim extends this "tragic legacy" of the diaspora to the racial injuries of the U.S. nation-state: "Perhaps the legacy is not one carried across oceans and continents but one assumed immediately upon arrival, not the curse of being Korean but the initiation into becoming American, which requires that Korean Americans take on this country's legacy of five centuries of racial violence and inequality, of divide and rule, of privilege for the rich and oppression of the poor. Within this legacy, they have been assigned a place on the front lines" (220). Immigrants come into the United States in the midst of this American tragedy of race, forced to accept the benefits and drawbacks of a racial hierarchy and the aftermath of racial suffering.

Much like Salas, who passionately identifies his "enemies"—the police who assaulted him and caused his deafness, the "nice white teachers" who demeaned Chicana/o culture and the Spanish language—Mrs. Young Soon Han names her antagonists: African Americans, the government, and the looters and arsonists who destroyed her store and livelihood during the 1992 violence.[23] In her monologue, she assails African Americans for their government aid as well as the government for failing to provide emergency benefits and aid. Her frustration is directed primarily at African Americans, a frustration compounded by their celebration after the federal trial of the four LAPD officers, which Han expresses through the awkward word choice "hilarious." But as her monologue unfolds, she reveals her ambivalence toward the African Americans portrayed in the television news coverage she watched, her antagonists becoming less clear and more complicated. Mrs. Han moves between incompatible emotions and thoughts: being "happy" for African Americans because "at leasteh *[sic]* they got

something back" (248). She also alludes to the historical costs of the
Black freedom struggles:

> Because of their effort and sacrificing,
> other minorities, like Hispanic
> or Asians,
> maybe we have to suffer more
> by mainstream. (248)

Despite her frustration and anger directed at African Americans and
the people who destroyed her store, Mrs. Han's words suggest a tenta-
tive understanding of racial suffering shared among people of color
under long-standing conditions of institutional racism.

Here the audience listens to Han's "misspeakings" in her struggle
to find the right English words during her interview. Smith performs
Han in halting, broken English, and Han's deliberate, careful word
choices and syntax remind the audience of what is potentially lost in
Han's translation of her thoughts into English and in Smith's translation of Han's physical presence to *Twilight*'s audience. In the film
version of *Twilight*, Smith portrays Han by supporting her upper
body with her arms on the low coffee table; Smith is curved over and
somewhat supported by the surface of the table that fills the bottom
half of the screen. The shiny, coffinlike table mirrors the elegiac quality of Han's words as she mourns her painful struggles and the unful-
filled promises of life in the United States. Her arms bent in front of
her both entreat the audience to understand her frustration and losses
and protect her from the interviewer, Smith, and the translators on the
other side. The table also separates Han from the absent interviewer
and Smith's audience, reinforcing Han's physical and social isolation.
Throughout her monologue, Han is indignant that the government
failed to provide economic relief to the middle-class Korean Americans who were hardest hit by the violence. Smith first performs Han's
anger over the destruction of her store at the hands of the arsonists
and looters and then over the lack of response from the police and the
U.S. government during and after the 1992 Crisis:

> Why do we have to be left out?
> *(She is hitting her hand on the coffee table)*
> We are not qualified to have medical treatment.
> We are not qualified to get, uh,
> food stamp

(She hits the table once),
not GR [governmental relief]
(Hits the table once),
no welfare
(Hits the table once).
Anything. (245)

As Han struggles with communicating her feelings and conveying her thoughts in her nonnative language, these gestures and sounds conveyed by the parenthetical stage directions articulate that which cannot be expressed in either English or Korean. Han's poignant question that asks why Korean Americans are "left out" points to their socially marginalized position as nonnative, non-English-speaking, nonwhite immigrants who have been refused real incorporation into the American body politic. Han argues that Korean Americans, whether citizens or immigrants, deserve the aid and consideration owed to tax-paying U.S. residents, which was sorely lacking in the confused aftermath of the violence.

After this part of the monologue, Han expresses resentment toward unemployed African Americans affected by the L.A. Crisis, who previously "never" had to work yet receive some welfare or emergency assistance unavailable to Korean American small business owners like herself. But after this contentious statement, Han immediately switches to narrate her reaction to the guilty verdict in the second federal court trial of Rodney King's attackers. Han offsets the resulting celebration she saw portrayed on the television news by reemphasizing the continuing injustice for the Korean American victims who were again left out in their belief that justice did not prevail for them or their injuries. This exclusion parallels the portrayal of Han's own isolation in the minimal stage setting of her house, which is darkened by lowered blinds and furnished in muted beiges and grays in the film version. Toward the end of her monologue, Smith portrays Han as becoming more pensive and less agitated; her hands then rest on the table. Han describes how she felt distanced from the celebration, "watching them"— the African Americans who were celebrating on television. Because of the continual victimization of Korean Americans by U.S. society and governmental institutions, Han expresses pessimism for transracial understanding:

I wish I could
live together

> with eh *[sic]* Blacks,
> but after the riots
> there were too much differences.
> The fire is still there—
> how do you call it?—
> igni . . .
> igniting fire.
> *(She says a Korean phrase phonetically: "Dashi yun gi ga nuh")*
> It's still dere *[sic]*.
> It canuh *[sic]*
> burst out anytime. (249; original emphasis)[24]

During this part of the monologue in the film version of *Twilight*, the verbal break represents Han's struggles with the English word for "igniting." She then silently asks for a translation with a hand outstretched to an unknown audience to her left, the unseen Korean American translators who Smith will later identify as her "partners" in these interviews with Asian Americans, especially Korean Americans, in Smith's 2002 essay for the *Los Angeles Times* on the ten-year anniversary of the violence ("Insights," 6). Although unable to find the word to convey her feeling, Han successfully communicates her belief in future uprisings, verbally triumphant at the precise moment that she forewarns her interviewers of the dire possibility of later violence. In the film performance, Han is briefly jubilant in her ability to express herself through language to the interviewer, Smith, and, at the moment of the performance, this triumph implies her successful communication with the audience as well. Han's repeated attempts to pronounce "igniting" emphasize the word and establish a more assured cadence for the final lines of the monologue.

In Smith's portrayal, Han appears to acquiesce to the translation of "igniting" offered by the translators, but then provides her own words in Korean for what she wants to say, *"Dashi yun gi ga nuh."* Another possible translation of the phrase that the translators do not provide is "smoke starts again."[25] In this quick exchange, Han revises her initial thoughts for a more accurate meaning; perhaps the translators allowed a misinterpretation of her phrase to stand given Han's cue of "igni . . ." In either case, the accuracy of the translation matters less than the range of meanings made possible by the "misspoken." For example, "smoke starts again" emphasizes the effect of the conflagration; smoke is the effect or warning of fire, not the process of creating or igniting it, and implies a physical distance from the fire itself, reinforcing the isolation Han feels so acutely. In her Korean phrase, Han stresses the possible recurrence of the smoke and alludes to the persistence of the factors that create the fire that causes it. As the effect and not the cause, the smoke also distances the viewer from the fire's ignition, just as Han expresses frustration with her inability to change circumstances for Korean Americans who sustained such tremendous losses in the crisis and their continuing exclusion from justice afterward. This exclusion forces Korean Americans into the role of isolated, passive viewers instead of active participants and stakeholders in the U.S. body politic. Han's untranslated, misspoken words are about the fire that is lying in wait, obscured or signaled by the smoke. Ultimately, these unspoken causes that Han identifies could remain unaddressed without the audience's attention to the "misspeakings" of her monologue.

Han's monologue, titled "Swallowing the Bitterness," is represented at length in both the PBS documentary first aired in 1999 and the two collections of monologues Smith published in 1994 and 2003. Han's narrative is so compelling because it is richly contradictory in crucial ways. Han's affiliation toward African Americans against Whiteness and her affiliation toward Whites against Blackness shift. But Han also blames African Americans for government failures of justice. She is conflicted between her empathy for other victims of racism and her indignation that the state redressed some of the wrongs against African Americans but not against Korean Americans. Han is further frustrated that the media's recognition of anti-Black racism superseded that of anti-Korean racism.

Similarly, Salas's monologue, provocatively titled "My Enemy," exemplifies the confluence of melodrama and tragedy operating in *Twilight*.[26] The central story of his permanent deafness from police brutality has the easily identifiable villains of melodrama—the police officers who beat him as a teenager, his "nice, white teachers" who disparaged Mexican culture and identity—but his discussion of the larger history of race in terms of U.S.–Mexico relations has the complex moral entanglements of tragedy. In an examination of tragedy and the European intellectual traditions that produce the "colonial enlightenment," David Scott defines the tragic narrative in terms of competing values and irreconcilable choices: "For tragedy, the fact of the plurality of values and ends does not present an occasion to affirm a rational calculus on the basis of which to choose the best way to proceed. What interests the tragedians are those instances in which the plurality of values is such that it is impossible to choose satisfactorily—to choose without remainder—between rival goods. . . . In such circumstances one may be obliged to choose a value that is false to other just as deeply held values, an end that damages or diminishes other important ends. In such circumstances choice is tragic" (182–83). For audiences to respond sympathetically to the confessions of human suffering in *Twilight*, they must hold often-contradictory affective and political allegiances: for example, those who support law-and-order politics, which in the 1990s were heavily criticized for coded racism in its ostensibly colorblind goals of personal safety and crime-deterrence that nonetheless centered upon more violent policing and invasive surveillance of Black and Brown neighborhoods. In *Twilight,* the monologues of the defendant in the beating of Rodney King, LAPD officer Theodore Briseno; Chief Daryl Gates; and Mrs. Han allude to these politics. But Smith confronts audience members who might support the latent racism of law-and-order platforms with those who might be identified as their "enemy": critics of the LAPD like Salas, community activist Paul Parker, gang member Twilight Bey, and defendant in the beating of Reginald Denny, Henry "Keith" Watson, who explicitly identify the police and the criminal justice system as *their* antagonists.

Insofar as tragedy is not only about victimization, but also about crime and punishment, the tragic reversal comes in the form of the outsized punishment to the crime committed, often unwittingly or unwillingly. If tragedy merely causes a defeatist and fatalist interpretation that enervates readers and viewers—Bertolt Brecht's view—and leaves audiences to despair, mourn, and grieve in isolation, then why were the tragic narratives of the L.A. Crisis so forcefully contested in the political discourses in 1992 and beyond?

Twilight's Tragedy of the State

While some influential definitions of tragedy require the end of the fictive world through catastrophic reversal, the Trojan War continues on, after the tragic events of the *Iliad.* Hector's death and his final funeral rites at the end are a mere respite from violence. The magnitude of the "fall of the City," one of George Steiner's tragic elements, appears to demand so much of its critics that they too end or limit their studies to the fall of the City and the death of the hero. Others note the necessity of an uplifting end for many tragedies across historical periods, essentially the blueprint for what is to come: Creon, the lawgiver chastened by the deaths in his immediate and extended family, will be wiser; Horatio, the loyal truth-teller, will tell all that he knows to Prince Fortinbras, in essence to smooth the transition from King Claudius to the new ruler. Tragedy includes the anxious, violent transition from one state to another, from one imagined community to another.

Moreover, the end of tragedy is the blueprint for regime change. The horrific violence or mass deaths that mark the tragic sequence of events represent the emphatic end of the old regimes. As such, the genre of tragedy indicates not only literary debates but also the political legitimacy upon which the emerging state is founded.[27] These claims for tragedy foreground the possibility that Smith's work will allude to, if not negotiate, a new social contract that incorporates the claims to injury and suffering brought to the surface by the monologues. On one hand, the crisis marked a change in U.S. politics, from the cold war to its aftermath. On the other, the L.A. Crisis further entrenched the disavowal of the tragic nature of its violence, one of ready discourses that would be available to temper the outpouring of public sympathy and the extent of governmental aid suggested by policymakers.

In her preface to the 1994 collection of monologues, the first published version of *Twilight*, Smith posits the political importance of her text: "I played *Twilight* in Los Angeles as a call to the community. I performed it at a time when the community had not yet resolved the problems. I wanted to be a part of their examination of the problems" (xxiv). Smith's text encourages the audience to reconsider the ostensible objectivity of reported information, especially during the 1992 Crisis. In her 2002 *L.A. Times* essay, Smith reflects on her experiences during the research, writing, and performing of *Twilight* and explains her political conception of the artist in relation to the playwright's vision and actor's preparation: "Do we dare ask the public to trust us to communicate to them about the issues that are serious in their lives? . . . In this ever-fractious world, artists have a bigger role to play, as those who not only mirror societies, but those who also bring things together in a different way" ("Insights," 6). Elaborating on this point in her casting and production notes for the 2003 Dramatists Play Service version of *Twilight,* Smith identifies actors who are tasked with this "bigger role" as "cultural workers," who are "meant to help society work on its problem with tribalism in a time that it prevails all over the world" (7). Smith explains that actors should "suspend judgment and stereotype at all times" (ibid.) and "reach towards that which is 'other' than themselves, to reach towards that which is different from themselves" (6).

The essence of tragedy is not the tragic action of catastrophic reversal or the irremediable disaster, but how the characters react to these dire events or, more accurately, their flawed perception of these events. What Smith's political project contends is that the essence of a character is not what they know about a particular event, no matter how devastating it might be. Instead, *Twilight*'s consideration of the 1992 Crisis marks this shift in tragic emphasis. The tragedy can only be known or legible through its aftermath, its effect on its survivors, who are always living in the aftermath of tragedy or unwittingly preparing for the next one. Paradoxically, such an essence of tragedy is, for Smith's plays, about multiple, interrelated tragedies about social and economic injustices and the uncomfortable realization that they have lingered without justice, without remedy.

In *Twilight*, the tragedies her speakers suffer and the consequences they face range from the horrifyingly life-threatening to what appears on the surface to be the trivial. I consider Elaine Young, whose portrayal has caused some of Smith's feminist critics, most notably, Tania Modleski, some irritation. In light of this criticism, Smith's acting choices might be interpreted as a weakness of her approach: that in focusing on gesture and speech, Smith might also tend toward caricature for the characters she portrays. Young is a minor celebrity through her marriage to actor Gig Young, which ended in a scandalous divorce, and Young's activism against silicone injections once routinely used in plastic surgery resulted in her appearances on national television and before Congress. In the film version of *Twilight*, Young discusses her minor celebrity status for a minute or so, partially alluding to why Smith might have initially become interested in interviewing her. Smith performs affected mannerisms in her portrayal of Young: a high nasal voice, pursed lips, and a facial tic that is possibly the result of nerve damage from ruptured silicone implants and the seventeen reconstructive surgeries she mentions during her monologue. In this second, brief opening monologue of the film, Smith represents Young as initially restless with fidgety movements—applying lipstick, fussing with her purse, putting sugar in her coffee, and looking everywhere but directly at the camera, the audience, and, likely Smith, the interviewer. At first glance, there seem to be few compelling reasons for Young's inclusion except for her reaction to the violence, apparently typical of her social class, financial resources, and elite circles: her decision to congregate in the packed Beverly Hills Hotel, where she and many others stayed in the Polo Lounge until the early morning believing there was "safety in numbers" (*Twilight,* 161). The Polo Lounge and the hotel are long-standing symbols of exclusive wealth and power in Los Angeles and are not considered the first refuge for most other residents in the city.

Because Smith's performance of Young generated some of the few criticisms of *Twilight,* it is important to examine the contribution of Young's monologue to the live performance, written text, and the film in terms other than comic relief. Young represents a view of the media in which one's words and intentions are taken out of context and misinterpreted. However, after a few minutes of unbroken speech, Young abruptly looks at the camera, perhaps in response to the interviewer's (and, likely, the audience's) lack of patience with her succession of trivial personal details. Subduing all fidgety gestures—she no longer performs such absent-minded rituals as putting on lipstick or taking off the lid of her coffee—Young says directly to the camera and audience, "But maybe I should back up and explain why I was so frightened" (*Stage on Screen*). Nodding as if to agree with her interviewer, Young then focuses on her experiences during the L.A. Crisis, ostensibly narrating her thoughts and reactions to what was happening during that time. This abrupt consideration of the audience, so different from Young's previous self-involvement, is awkward but noteworthy; the audience is forced to reconsider her previous chatter in light of her newly focused, watchful gaze. Quite possibly, her volubility can be explained in retrospect as an indication of her nervousness about the topic of the crisis and some strongly worded, anonymous criticism of her reactions to the violence that she will eventually recall from memory for the audience.

In addition, Young's fear is somewhat unfounded given her relative physical distance from the violence itself—the sprawling geography of Los Angeles separates Pico-Union and South Central Los Angeles from suburbs a few miles away in the outer rings of the city. However, her desire to flee to the familiar is not unlike other speakers in *Twilight,* who drove back to their neighborhoods, panicked, or otherwise isolated themselves and their families at home. Young's narrative provides more critical possibilities than merely opportunities to caricature the White, upper-class self-involvement that she might represent. At the moment Young changes her focus and her mannerisms, where and what she does during the crisis becomes less important than what the audience's responses will be to her story and persona as performed. Smith encourages the emphasis less on what Young says and more on how she communicates her own perspective and when words fail her. As with Salas and Han, Smith's portrayal prompts her audiences to listen to the misspoken in Young's words.

In the film, for example, Young is the first monologue that explicitly discusses the idea of context and how meaning is misinterpreted when communicated out of context. She tells of how she once received a letter calling her a "dumb shit bimbo" in response to a television interview in which she offhandedly mentioned her flight to the Beverly Hills Hotel during the L.A. Crisis. In the interview for *Twilight,* Young seems compelled to explain herself to this anonymous critic among others, suggesting that she has been victimized by the unforgiving media sound bite and insisting that her tone has been wrongly perceived as flippant in regard to the crisis. She yearns to provide context to the anonymous letter-writer and explain that her flight to the hotel was not about pleasure but rather fear. This refuge was the norm within her circle of friends, not unlike those who huddled in suburbs, around their television sets, in expensive hotels, or other safe houses of one's custom and class. Young feels unfairly targeted since her flight is akin to those who lived and worked in neighborhoods largely unaffected by the crisis violence.

Young's primary grievance in her monologue elicits a consideration of context and how it is only when Young's words and actions are taken out of their context that she begins to see where the misunderstandings arise. Tania Modleski argues that Young's peculiar version of elitism and what might be considered affectation in her primping gestures undercuts her words to the point that her manner invalidates her experiences and reactions to the crisis relative to other monologues. However, this judgment results primarily from the audience's possible irritation with Young's self-presentation—the "fiction" of her "everyday discourse"—and we would thereby fail to note the brief moment, the pause, when language has failed for her and when Young looks directly into the camera and seems to consider her audience for the first time. Another critical possibility becomes apparent at the end of Young's monologue in the film version, when Smith rips off her glasses, blazer, and earrings and unexpectedly jumps through the picture window of Young's office. Landing on the soundstage littered with debris outside the office window, Smith begins to speak as Henry "Keith" Watson, one of Reginald Denny's alleged assailants.

In her performances and documentary film, Smith's sudden transition from character to character, from setting to setting, emphasizes the disparity between the two worlds, as the camera follows her movement from the background setting of Young's well-lit, orderly, warm-pinkish and gold-toned office to the atticlike debris littered on an otherwise barren soundstage, the wreckage especially stark against the black walls and floor. In the medium of the film, the littered soundstage is an appropriate juxtaposition to Young's office, which allows Smith to provide a different context not only for Young's self-involvement in the narrative but also for the audience's own preoccupation for what was inside Young's office. When Smith surprisingly jumps through the window to reveal the disorder outside, her audience has also failed to look beyond what was presented onstage. The set outside Young's window was not an unused, offstage backdrop, but is actually another set entirely, the background for the next speaker. The audience has experienced a privileged vantage point just as Young herself has. More important, Smith implies that, just as Young was unable to understand why her White privilege might be subject to attack, the audience must recognize its own blind spot: its failure to see beyond what was represented. This method of interpretation can then be applied to the other monologues—to consider their words, but, more important, what they have misspoken or failed to communicate accurately. During Smith's performance of Young's monologue, the audience must listen despite reactions to Young's self-presentation and be attentive to Smith's often-clever manipulation of *contexts*.

At the End of Tragedy

By emphasizing the "misspeakings" and "unspoken" of Smith's interview subjects such as Rudy Salas Sr., Mrs. Young Soon Han, and Elaine Young, *Twilight* encourages its audiences to recognize that, just like their misspoken words or unspoken thoughts, our understanding of their lives and personalities is incomplete. The overarching tragedy of *Twilight* is the irreconcilability of the one and the many injustices that are also almost impossible to fully communicate. All three feel that they have been arbitrarily and undeservedly punished for the "crime" of their identities and experiences. I posit that Smith's insistence on the active, continual interchange between speaker and listener counters possible passive responses to tragedy. Literary critic Rita Felski notes that "the fortunes of tragedy suffered a precipitous decline with the rise of political criticism in the 1980s and '90s" as a "Brechtian account of tragedy" (4) reigned in which audiences respond to tragedy with political inaction, not mobilization; this Brechtian account contends that tragic audiences feel pushed to accept unjust fates or outsized punishment for crimes. In the aftermath of such natural disasters as Hurricane Katrina or the tsunamis in the Indian Ocean and northern Japan, and human catastrophes such as 9/11, the global financial crisis, and police brutality, the political investments in tragedy most strongly appear in how fiercely its critics attempt to undermine or promote these narratives as tragedy. These debates are as much about cultural values as they are about naturalizing policy decisions. They expose how much audiences might want to refuse tragic sympathy by rejecting tragedy as the experience for some people—these survivors and their stories are neither tragic heroes nor circumstances. In *Principles of Tragedy* (1968), Geoffrey Brereton surveys the use of tragedy to value some circumstances or people who suffer over others: "'Tragic' has the advantage of conferring a certain nobility upon whatever it qualifies and by the same process it removes us a step or two from the contemplation of harsh physical reality. It is used here as a statusword. One does not look down on people described as 'tragic'" (8). Terry Eagleton has quipped that one person's tragedy is often not another's. Such a flexible identification of tragedy reveals the central incommensurability that, while we might call events tragic, only some of those people's experiences are tragic.

Who are these people who suffer and yet for whom their personal tragedies have been denied? Smith's work highlights the radical individualism of tragedy in *Twilight*'s sequence of monologues. Tragedy bespeaks the failure to avoid human suffering. And of these failures, many of the personal tragedies were caused by interracial conflicts among communities of color. Antiracism scholars, of whom many were feminists, were frustrated by the interracial antagonisms made manifest in the 1992 violence, notably among Blacks, Koreans, and

Latinas/os, and how such spectacles became political fodder as prime examples of the undeserving, criminalized, and impoverished. The L.A. Crisis underscored the deep human cost of material inequities and racial hierarchies, inspiring antiracist feminists to more self-reflexively question the adequacy of existing paradigms to foment transracial coalition-building that might not only deter future outbreaks of violence, but also forge broader political alliances that could effectively address the persistent issues of inequality and injustice experienced by communities of color. Literary critic Susan Stanford Friedman exhorts U.S. feminists to consider what the crisis in Los Angeles—a crisis of binary thinking about race—might engender in terms of "creative possibilities for feminists to think about, talk about, and act upon this difficult dimension of race in a more fruitful way" (4).

Smith's artistic methodology and documentary theater, exemplified by *Twilight*'s various performance and prose versions, respond to these calls to theorize in multiple dimensions as a contribution to antiracist feminist traditions. Without their differentiated bodies and performed on the sameness of Smith's own, the speakers' identities are created in the contexts of their monologues and the words of other speakers, or how they are heard and listened to, and not primarily by visible markers of race, class, gender, sexuality, and ability—those physical characteristics and behaviors that are distinguished in order to construct differences and justify material inequalities.[28] Her powerful performances are intersectional analyses of their "interlocking and mutually constitutive" (Hong, ix–x) identity formations as Smith reveals points of commonality through the juxtaposition of so many different people. These potential connections are provisional moments of intersectional identity formation. In the documentary film of her performance, Smith's virtuosic transformation from character to character, often changing significant parts of her costume or props in the midst of speaking, shows the *intermeshed* processes of an individual's identity formation, what María Lugones finds is a more apt descriptor than *interlocking* (459). Recognizing these intermeshed identities, we can better articulate the privileges and oppressions within and among what we once thought of as fixed or homogeneous, as Jennifer Nash has exhorted intersectionality scholars to do (13). By encouraging her audiences to think of other connections beyond racial identity among her speakers, Smith echoes in her artistic methodology an analytic process akin to what Leslie McCall has identified as intercategorical complexity in its provisional characterization, contradictory and conflicting expressions, and emerging similarities and differences among speakers during each speaker's monologue. In her documentary dramas, Smith not only provides the material for these analyses in her uninterrupted series of monologues, but she also exemplifies the analytic process for her audiences to then implement on their own.

Because Smith performs her interviewees, she models a relationality that recent feminists of color, such as Aimee Carrillo-Rowe and Grace Kyungwon Hong, have marked within intersectional analysis as a means of envisioning a coalitional subject formation. As mentioned earlier, Smith, a Black woman, portrays a variety of speakers with controversial perspectives: Daryl Gates, who has been criticized for targeting Black and immigrant communities for surveillance and harassment;[29] Rudy Salas Sr., a victim of police brutality, who derides the anti-Mexican police; and Young Soon Han, who alternately expresses resentment and support for African American participants and victims of the uprisings. With the very range of Smith's monologues and her various juxtapositions of conflicting perspectives, her audiences themselves are engaged in this intersectional analysis as they witness the play. Thus, Smith explicitly develops a structure of coalitional subjectivity through her performance and exemplifies the *practice* of such a subject formation that her audiences can then put into practice themselves inside and outside the theater.

Smith's aesthetics engage with contemporary feminist debates over the convergence of identity and coalition formation. These two formations might appear antithetical to each other, but only if a single identity is perceived as being owned or "possessed" by the individual. Instead, prominent feminist theorists such as Kimberlé Crenshaw consider the possibility of the coalitional subject, one that expresses both identity and coalition formations, the many in one. Indeed, Crenshaw emphasizes the inevitable multiplicity within identity, that "the organized identity groups to which we find ourselves are in fact coalitions, or at least potential coalitions waiting to be formed" (1299). Smith's play and artistic methodology lay the foundation for this nascent coalitional identity. Her speakers, of various racial and class backgrounds, men and women, reveal unexpected alliances with one another, even as they air their grievances against and distrust of other racialized communities. Rather than focusing on how one unified identity emerges from the ruins of Los Angeles, Smith is primarily interested in how coalitional identities are forged through the panoply of voices she performs in her play.

This structure of a coalitional subjectivity is developed through the psychological tension between self and other that Smith uses productively in her art. I recognize Smith's imperative to begin with the other in the context of recent discussions of relationality developing within women of color feminism. My analysis of *Twilight* identifies a telling gap in criticism about the political ramifications of Smith's aesthetic practices: critics, while praising Smith's performance of others, fail to recognize the moments in which she uses the words of others to redefine the self, a recursive and continual movement between other and self. By looking at Smith's own memoirs and reflections on her art, I contend that short-circuiting her recursive process undermines the radical potential in her work. Because Smith performs all the speakers in succession, her body becomes hypervisible as the intersection of the speakers' various and contradictory identities; most important, she constructs her identity out of theirs. The largely unacknowledged discussion of Smith as a woman of color interviewer, actor, and artist and how her identity is comprised of her interview subjects parallels a subdued, albeit growing, recognition of a politics of relation in feminist debates.

Smith's work reveals the importance of recognizing a politics of relation as essential to building transracial coalitions. She performs her characters with little visual verisimilitude; this dissonance disrupts entrenched patterns of identity formations. This slippage between expectation and actuality, the Brechtian "alienation effect,"[30] gestures toward that which defies representation: the recursive process of moving between the other and the self. Although often overlooked in critical discussions of Smith's theater, this back-and-forth process exemplifies the process of a coalitional subject formation crucial to the political possibilities enabled by her art and supported by the auditory proximity of listening, her fundamental aesthetic and political practice.

While ostensibly attempting to perform the process of embodying and witnessing the other, Smith performs the spoken and the misspoken, demanding her audiences' own performances of proximity. Instead of seeing differences trivialized into a universal humanism, *Twilight*'s audiences must themselves undergo a complex process of coalitional identity formation. Smith attempts to transmit her vision of an ethics of transracial formations by placing the audience members into the interviewer's role and conditioning them to listen for the audible and inaudible, the spoken and misspoken. This process of listening, of proximity, connects the different monologues and visual elements and emphasizes a racializing process that is provisional and always changing. Illustrating the fluidity of a transracial coalition built through listening—the technique that she continually cites as the foundation of her artistic methodology—Smith's methodology countermands the increasing refusal in American politics and society to acknowledge the uneven material effects and experiences that undergird complex and collective racial identity formations beyond static classifications of race and racism. Smith points to the performance, proximity, and presence that is available in communication in order to emphasize the way in which language changes self-constructions. The value of Smith's *Twilight* is in the audience's persistent practice of coalitional identity formations as a continual process of negotiation and engagement, one that her audience must witness and perform.

Recent literary and philosophical debates perceive contemporary society as holding too little of a tragic worldview, or too much. Perhaps we refuse to see or acknowledge the tragic in the millions, if not billions, of representations of those and their suffering that our immediate, real time, digital technologies bring uncomfortably close. Whether or not we live in a tragic time, the term's persistent popular use and the contested interpretation of historical events such as the L.A. Crisis as "tragedies" have political consequences, naturalizing policy outcomes or propelling us to develop the theories and methodologies to imagine ourselves in relation to one another. The workings of genre produce the terms of the debate as the arbiters of the debate produce the workings of the genre. In this entanglement between culture and politics, drama and the state, the battle over tragedy influences our political life and these debates impact the transracial proximities that are represented and imagined within the literary genre and feminist theory.

5 THE MEDIA SPECTACLE OF RACIAL DISASTER

This is the America where reading is only good for reading signs
and price tags. There is no story, no myth, no history, no art.
Only TV. And now that the U.S. Marines and the army have had
a taste of treating American streets like Panama and Grenada,
I wonder if they can go home again.

—Frank Chin, "Pidgin Context along I-5"

As noted by many others, climatic change in L.A. was different
from other places. It had less perhaps to do with weather and
more to do with disaster. For example, when the city rioted or
when the city was on fire or when the city shook, the program
was particularly apt, controversial, hair-raising, horrific, intense—
apocalyptic, if you will.

—Karen Tei Yamashita, *Tropic of Orange*

THIS CHAPTER ADDRESSES a recurring meme that the 1992 Los
Angeles Crisis augured a coming racial apocalypse. This racial disaster,
for opponents of nonwhite immigration and the extension of full rights
and privileges of citizenship, would result from an overly permissive
U.S. democratic experiment and foolhardy quest for racial equality.
This cataclysmic pessimism coincides neatly with the region's propensity for costly and destructive natural disasters—the earthquakes, mud-
slides, flooding, and wildfires that routinely plague Los Angeles and
its environs.[1] The 1992 Crisis provided a media spectacle within this
epic apocalyptic tradition. After the Persian Gulf War and its round-
the-clock cable broadcasts conditioned viewers to expect minute-by-
minute coverage of conflicts and catastrophes, whether next-door or
around the world, national and global audiences closely monitored the

unfolding events. The unprecedented violence in the spring of 1992 occurred in a city infamous worldwide not only for its self-consciously mediatized existence and perpetual entertainment spectacles, but also for its increasing nonwhite and immigrant populations in the city and its suburbs. Given these rapidly changing demographics and their attendant media coverage, media spectacle often implied racial disaster, in which certain interracial hostilities are believed to trigger the downward spiral of U.S. society. Represented by reports of crime and police brutality, the violence of gangsta films and rap, postindustrial urban blight, or interracial conflict in multiracial neighborhoods and spaces such as the corner store and street, these antagonisms galvanized deep anxieties of U.S. decline. Los Angeles has been dually characterized as a multiracial paradise or inferno, and, given these fluctuating depictions, the L.A. Crisis was perceived not just as an isolated interracial conflict but also as a racial disaster, perhaps the opening salvo of the coming race war or even the beginning of the end times. While various critics disagree over how to describe the 1992 violence and how to identify its root causes, cultural anxieties about interracial conflict revolve around racial disaster and the apocalytic narratives it engenders and confirms.

Reading the L.A. Crisis as both a racial disaster and media spectacle in this chapter, I look at how the convergence of these two frameworks shapes concepts of media citizenship and political activism in the wake of the 1992 violence. Karen Tei Yamashita's 1997 novel, *Tropic of Orange,* explores this interconnection between media spectacle and racial disaster and its impact on subjectivity and social life. Following the interconnected lives of seven characters for one week in Los Angeles, the plot culminates in a military massacre of the local homeless population and an epic wrestling match between two allegorical figures: El Gran Mojado, the self-proclaimed "Great Wetback," and SUPERNAFTA, symbolic of U.S. economic and military imperialism. While largely influenced by the traditions of magical realism and speculative fiction, the novel engages with the features of contemporary life that pundits have hailed as harbingers of our revolutionary future: a postnational world without borders and the global media communications that get us there. As a fictional response to the pressures of civil society and state violence, the novel imaginatively takes up the question of what it means to exist under conditions that are wholly mediatized and acutely unequal and how each has exacerbated the other. In a world defined and remade through the media, analyzing the L.A. Crisis as a media spectacle is crucial to understanding how race connotes disaster.

Yamashita's novel provides the naturalized flow and segmentation of mediatized environments such as television, radio, and the Internet, showing how these environments shape her protagonists' subjectivities—and, thus, the textual narrative and the novel form itself. In addition to Yamashita's intensely detailed focus on the lives of seven memorable characters and their interactions with one another, the novel's structure, like a week of television programming, narrates the complex interplay of globalized media capital and its material effects on those forced outside the U.S. body politic (the nonwhite and non-citizen) and those perceived outside the economy (the nonworker). For these invisible denizens of Los Angeles, Yamashita identifies the way they live their lives in consonance and counterpoint to the rhythms of media and the transnational demands of its corporate forms. Yet unlike these mainstream media offerings, the programs we watch in the chapters we read follow the intertwined narratives of the seven protagonists—Asian, Black, Chicana/o, Latina/o—around the multiracial neighborhoods of Los Angeles and back and forth across the U.S.–Mexico border. The novel self-reflexively gestures toward the mediatized in its structure and themes as it permeates the everyday experiences of those at the margins of mainstream media discourse. In addition to the multifaceted perspectives this narrative strategy provides, Yamashita also creates characters that appropriate different media forms, styles, and genres, positing that, in order to understand the perspective of others, one must adopt their media ideologies and media technologies that they use to tell their stories. Yamashita interrogates how our patterns of media consumption and appropriation shape identities among racial groups and socioeconomic classes.

I read the novel as an indictment of the media culture and spectacle that creates the continual threat and highlights the perpetual eruptions of racial disaster in ways that result in very restrictive notions of race.[2] In *Tropic of Orange,* the racial disasters are the homeless massacre, the mutual annihilation of El Gran Mojado and SUPERNAFTA, and the convergence of Southern California and Latin America. A few decades or so into the future, a tiny, withered orange falls off a tree planted right on the Tropic of Cancer, just before the summer equinox. Carried northward by a five-hundred-year-old performance artist known as Arcangel, a man who has fantastically lived since the time of Columbus's first voyage to the Americas, the orange, strung on the Northern tropic, pulls the entire southern half of the continent across the U.S.–Mexico border and into Los Angeles. *Tropic of Orange* ends with the splitting of this orange and the border it carried, leaving its readers to wonder if the future will be chaos or, perhaps, a utopic world without borders. This particular story revels in the stuff of disbelief—of myth, of legend—as the migrating orange distorts the time and space upon which nation-states depend for their global circuits of capital and imagined communities of belonging. In towing an entire continent northward, the orange's journey is a powerful allegory for the legacies of U.S. imperialism such as cold war foreign policy and NAFTA that have pulled immigrants and global capital into the United States.

Racial Disasters and Media Spectacles

The threat of racial disaster marks some people—those routinely categorized as anti-American, illegal, and criminal, such as Asians and Latinas/os, or criminals, such as Blacks—outside civility and a threat to already-established norms. I situate my analysis of the novel within a broader study of the role of media in facilitating a civic discourse that challenges and replaces these troubling, yet conventional, ways of portraying and perceiving people of color. With its seven protagonists of various racial, economic, and social backgrounds, Yamashita's novel explores the cross-racial alliances that are crucial to strengthening civil society. But unlike most of the civility scholars directing national discourse in the mid to late 1990s, Yamashita goes beyond such commonly touted pro-social concepts of friendship, mutual respect, reciprocity, and trust—the traditional foundations of social relations that have been promoted as building social capital and civility. Instead, Yamashita ties each character to a distinctive means of consumption and critique of the media, and in the final days of the novel, some characters pass on their own mediatized perceptions to other characters. In this narrative recycling of character traits, Yamashita theorizes intersectionality in fiction through her characterization and plot, positing the formation of identity around one's media consumption and encouraging her readers to self-consciously examine the ways in which media scripts our reality and limits our imaginations. Yamashita's novel offers a conceptual framework for her readers to become aware of the shifts in our knowledge and practices resulting from our media consumption. *Tropic of Orange* earnestly considers the people who must negotiate these old and new parameters of mediatization and inequality that all too often have meant the difference between life and death, success and failure, legality and illegality, citizen and alien.

In this chapter, I argue that Yamashita's novel posits a negotiation of racial difference that is transformative, exposing the internal incoherence of the binaries and divisions affirmed by the interracial or even the multiracial and into the *trans*racial, inspiring egalitarian transnational alliances.[3] The novel's unusual organization, characterization, and plot trajectory function, I argue, as an allegory for intersectional reading practices that go beyond mainstream multiculturalism and the promotion of interracial unity. Yamashita's seven protagonists function as transformative figures, the tricksters of this intersectional origin story, who use media technologies for their representational strategies, logics, and even ideologies in innovatively oppositional ways. In order to outline the major concern of *Tropic of Orange*—how the media both facilitates and thwarts the revolutionary imagination— Yamashita articulates a transracial vision that is predicated on an intersectional approach to character.

Tropic of Orange highlights the interplay of different media—the novel, print and online journalism, performance art, radio, television, and the Internet. Because the media structures the experience of the reader, *Tropic of Orange* provides a reading strategy for the novel that approximates a technique of viewing media, explicitly translating and parodying a reading of the written into an interpretation of the visual, what Jay David Bolter and Richard Grusin have termed "remediation," or the theory of media in which older forms incorporate the styles and structures of newer media *and* newer forms integrate the older.[4] The novel encourages its readers to think of other, perhaps hybrid, ways of viewing that might lead to more committed democratic civic engagement and political activism, if not even a revolutionary imagination. Yamashita engages with the historical shortcomings of media communication: bias toward White establishment figures and institutions, little representation of the everyday lives and concerns of nonwhite communities, few journalists of color or others familiar with these communities, and the overrepresentation of nonwhite criminality.

Through a fictive state of emergency that lasts one week, Yamashita parodies governmental and media responses to past emergencies that have made Southern California the disaster capital of the nation. Using the city's international notoriety for interracial conflicts and natural disasters as a backdrop, Yamashita anchors the novel's fictional media events in terms of the specific and wide-ranging social and economic issues raised by the L.A. Crisis: immigration anxieties, unemployment, deteriorating cities, crime rates, declining social mores, a contracting economy. Through allusions and direct references to this internationally televised violence, the media coverage of the 1992 Crisis emerges as a template for how the novel's fictional media events—namely, the military massacre of the homeless and an epic wrestling match—will be interpreted for television audiences and shape public policy. For generations of viewers and voters, the L.A. Crisis solidified various discourses that had been simmering in terms of how race was represented in the United States as a disaster. How disasters are experienced, managed, and interpreted explains how citizens are interpellated in relation to the state and determines who receives the rights, privileges, and protections from it.

In her contributions to speculative fiction and abiding fascination in utopian futures, Yamashita is one of the visionaries of Asian American literature. This critically acclaimed, award-winning poet, playwright, and novelist was born and grew up in Los Angeles. After receiving a fellowship to travel to Brazil, she stayed there for ten years. Many of her works consider the Japanese diaspora and Japanese Brazilians in particular. Her first published novel, *Through the Arc of the Rainforest* (1989), considered the destruction of the Brazilian rainforest and the multiple narrators whose lives intersected with transnational migrations, globalization, and U.S. imperialism. Her second book, *Brazil-Maru* (1993), details the utopian Christian community of Japanese descent in Brazil. The *Circle K Cycles* (2001) is a mixed-media text documenting the hybrid experiences of Japanese Brazilians who have returned to Japan as guest workers. A winner of the California Book Award and a finalist for the National Book Award, her 2010 novel *I Hotel* documents numerous perspectives on the interracial activism and protest movements that converged in the communal space of the International Hotel, lodgings that provided affordable housing for elderly Chinese and Filipino laborers; attempts to stop its demolition and the eviction of its residents galvanized the Asian American political movement in the 1960s and 1970s. *Anime Wong:*

Fictions of Self-Performance (2014) collects Yamashita's plays written over the past three decades.

Since the publication of her first novel in 1989, her oeuvre has become central to the transnational contexts of Asian American and American literature at the turn of the twenty-first century.[5] Yamashita's imaginative worlds conspicuously incorporate the entirety of the Americas rather than focusing on the United States and Canada, which is more common among Asian North American writers. As literary critics Kandice Chuh and Jinqi Ling have argued, Yamashita's writings reorient her readers along a north–south axis and necessitate hemispheric studies as well as a broader constitution of American literature. Yamashita's texts provide a critique of Asian American and American cultural studies that have followed the east–west orientation of global capitalism and exploitation, a troubled legacy of U.S. Western expansion, and historical routes forged by U.S. and European imperialism. Yamashita's transracial ensemble casts of protagonists envision new kinds of social relations and community formation based on different constructions of personhood and citizenship. In *Tropic of Orange,* the U.S.–Mexico border is just one line the characters repeatedly cross, but these journeys portend the metafictional crossings throughout the text: among genres, races, and subjectivities. The novel's multiple investments organize research agendas for the cultural legacy of the U.S. imperial project since its inception.

Tragedy has long been the mode for the history of race in America. Indeed, the incalculable human suffering caused by genocide, chattel slavery, lynching, and terror in the wake of the European invasions of the Americas demands this form of telling as well as its less-acknowledged politics of redress and reparations. In chapter 4, Anna Deavere Smith's play *Twilight* considered the aftermath of tragedy, and this chapter analyzes, through the novel *Tropic of Orange,* how the repetition of future racial disasters, the perception of suffering as media spectacle, characterizes the post–civil rights era. The expectation of repeated racial disaster and media spectacle paradoxically coincides with the post–civil rights shift in racial discourse, insisting that America's racial history of oppression should no longer be viewed as an ongoing tragedy, but rather as a triumph, an ignoble chapter of U.S. history that has been thankfully closed by the success of the modern civil rights movement in Equal Protection jurisprudence and more racially tolerant public attitudes. Thus, with the wrongs of injustice righted by a more robust enforcement of equal protection in the courts and legislation as well as public vigilance, any further racial grievances are baseless. At this juncture the causes of racial disaster are not historical inequalities but are the fault of populations once deemed vulnerable and now are resistant to betterment. This reading that places interracial conflict in the past incorporates the belief that race's equivalence to tragedy is inexorable: while such outcomes as wealth and income disparities, diminished qualities of life, or second-class citizenship are tragic, they are inevitable and intractable to remedy. As the previous chapters have identified, racism is disaggregated into a collection of isolated events or spectacles rather than an integral structuring principle of social, political, and economic life. Michael Omi and Howard Winant posit the U.S. government as "the racial state" because "major institutions and social relationships of U.S. society— law, political organization, economic relationships, religion, cultural life, residential patterns, etc.—have been structured from the beginning by the racial order" (79).[6] I choose the term "racial disaster" because disaster connotes, on one hand, natural catastrophes, a causation distinct from human agency. These calamities are thereby perceived as inevitable.[7] As a *racial* disaster, there is no individual's malicious or involuntary intention and there should not be moral or legal expectations of human resolution, remorse, or guilt.[8] If racial conflict is inevitable and lacks human intention and will, then society needs no active remedy.

On the other hand, the narrative of racial disaster functions also as a threat of coming anarchy or state of emergency against which citizens must remain vigilant. The so-called culture wars were memorably waged in national electoral politics with national and international attention focused on the 1992 presidential election between George H. W. Bush and Bill Clinton. These national debates focused on cultural mores and values that had religious and racial dimensions in addition to political and public-policy ramifications. As one of the most closely watched national events after the L.A. Crisis, the 1992 presidential race, in its series of competing narratives and policy proposals, provided a blueprint for how a nation should remember the violence. One way was to use the crisis, its causes, participants, motivations, and effects, to take one's stand in the so-called culture wars. At the height of these debates, the L.A. Crisis marked a turning point in attitudes toward social welfare, immigration, and people of color. For self-styled culture warriors, Americans must avert racial disaster, and stories of the 1992 Crisis are visceral reminders of this racialized fear, however far away people were from bodily harm and destruction. The discourse of racial disaster uses the language of emergency to distinguish this predicament from other conflicts, this media spectacle from other spectacles.[9] Yamashita's novel posits racial crisis as structural rather than an unpreventable disaster and thus requiring human intervention.

In a post–cold war era that refigured the United States as the last superpower standing, Pat Buchanan, former primary challenger to the incumbent president George H. W. Bush, delivered a speech that illustrated this need to remain vigilant against racial disasters, which had ramifications well beyond the 1992 presidential election. In one of the most electrifying nominating speeches of that election year, and enduringly famous for delineating the stakes of the so-called culture war, Pat Buchanan identified the presidential election as a "struggle for the soul of America." This speech ended with poignant stories about the Los Angeles Crisis. Buchanan notes that his campaign has taken him from one end of the United States to another and alludes to the many people he had met while on the campaign trail, commending the "brave people of Koreatown," who "still live the family values we treasure, and who still believe deeply in the American dream." He then recounts meeting young soldiers who, their commanding officer says, had been protecting an elderly convalescent home from a looting and fire-starting mob. Buchanan's final salvo juxtaposes these soldiers' heroic acts in the face of mortal danger with an exhortation for his audience's future courage in the face of moral peril: "And as they took back the streets of LA, block by block, so we must take back our cities, and take back our culture, and take back our country."[10] Of course, at the Republican National Convention, Buchanan's rhetoric is deliberately martial in galvanizing the troops of volunteers for winning the coming election. He heightens the exigency of his call to action beyond the election by constructing the streets of L.A. as a war zone. Just as Buchanan names the "enemy," he rewrites such partisan struggles as an epic battle over "what we believe" and "what we stand for as Americans." The L.A. violence was indeed one of the major battles, if not the opening salvo, in this war over belief and values. In his extended metaphor, Buchanan implies that America is occupied territory, stolen from its rightful occupants and owners, who must "take" our nation back from its enemies. The implicit enemies are the criminals, racialized as Black and Latina/o, and immigrants, racialized as Asian and Latina/o, whose values and practices are antithetical to U.S. law and custom, the American way of life. Until then, Buchanan implies, we are living under the tyranny of the mob, in a moral state of emergency, in the chaos of racial disaster.

In response to the intense xenophobia and racism at the height of the culture war, Yamashita imagines other kinds of racial disasters. In settings from Mazatlán to Los Angeles, seven main characters clamor for the reader's attention. Four—Bobby, Rafaela, Emi, and Gabriel— hold livelihoods and interests tied to forms of capitalism. As petty capitalists Bobby and Rafaela own and operate a janitorial service and, though married, become separated by the U.S.–Mexico border throughout the novel. As an engine of corporate media profits, Emi produces local television news shows and inventively links product marketing to news segments, frequently adjusting the news to sell products more effectively. As the author of media content, Gabriel writes for the *Los Angeles Times*, often about the city's underrepresented populations, but aspires to cover a groundbreaking story about the urban underworld worthy of the Pulitzer Prize. The other three characters, with their peripatetic, wandering lifestyles, are the more unconventional and memorable of the seven: Buzzworm is a seven-foot-tall Black Vietnam veteran who wears multiple wristwatches as he walks around downtown Los Angeles dispensing information about social services to his inner-city neighbors; Manzanar is a homeless former Japanese American surgeon who conducts symphonies of sounds made by passing cars and trucks from downtown freeway overpasses; and Arcangel is a five-hundred-year-old performance artist of uncertain racial and ethnic heritage who can tow trucks singlehandedly with ropes looped through lobes on his back.

Intersectional Character Formation

I posit the character formation in *Tropic of Orange* as an allegory for a new model of citizenship through a counterdiscourse of civility; Yamashita asks what kind of media citizenship is needed for a radically democratic future. In addition to such widely varying experiences based on differences in age, gender, class, occupation, immigration history, and citizenship status, these characters come from racialized populations often forgotten in media representations of Los Angeles because of their marginalization from the economic mainstream: the poor, the homeless, the working class, and the immigrant. Her critique of the media asks which stories and representations usually, if not always, exceed the frame, the lens, the recording. Yamashita's characterizations also open up political possibilities for conceptualizing identity formations. Politically incisive, her characterizations innovatively negotiate practices of intersectionality or the analysis of identity along multiple axes simultaneously. Having its genesis in women of color feminism, the intersection of race, class, gender, and sexuality that has often obscured such historical inequalities among categories of identity can become visible. Critical race theorist Kimberlé Crenshaw, who gives this phenomenon a name, locates this idea of intersectionality as a strategy of coalition building—to find points of commonality among different groups. Yamashita's characterization is closely tied to the fictionalization or translation of such an approach into fictional form.

Given the alchemy of identity formations such as race, gender, class, sexuality, and immigration status, Yamashita's unusual characterization allegorizes intersectional identity formation. I argue that Yamashita's characterization over the course of the novel closely parallels what sociologist Leslie McCall identifies as an emerging research area in "intercategorical complexity," in which the categories one uses to begin comparing and contrasting identities are provisional and are likely to be revised to reflect the dynamism of the now more permeable or expansive understanding of the original categories (McCall, 1773). Yamashita highlights the characters' similarities based on their media consumption strategies. But while these characters have distinctive life histories, Yamashita relies on their idiosyncrasies to represent the intersectional nodes between identities, perhaps most imaginatively characterized by Arcangel's many lives, Buzzworm's many neighbors, and Bobby's many identities. My discussion of the many identities read onto characters such as Arcangel and Bobby, spaces such as Buzzworm's neighborhood and the range of his acquaintances, would coincide with an agenda of pluralist multiculturalism, or what critics have variously dismissed as "mainstream," "corporate," or "world-beat" multiculturalism.[11] Yamashita's wide-ranging characterization could conceivably be reduced to a platitudinous multiculturalism, diversity that is primarily interested in representations of static identity formations, no matter how dynamic and complex these formations might be.

However, Yamashita shapes the reading practices of her audience through self-conscious methods of mediatized reading and an organization that initially appears rigidly structured and equally divided but gives way to the "intercategorical complexities" of intersectional identity formation. I posit that this intentionally deceptive arrangement at the beginning exposes the limitations of the "additive" approach to diversity that pluralist multiculturalism promotes (Hancock). Through two unusual tables of contents that ostensibly organize the novel, Yamashita distinguishes her characters and their narratives through a rigidly segmented structure of forty-nine "chapters" in both tables: each protagonist narrates one segment of her or his own story once a day for a week—seven segments for the seven characters. Each table is divided into the seven days of the week, and each day is organized into seven chapters. At first glance, the first one appears to be a traditional table of contents with a linear schedule of the days of the week and seven subheadings per day; Yamashita numerically orders the chapters and their titles and divides them evenly under the days of the week. But, unlike convention, the page numbers are actually first on each line. While a minor difference, this inversion of page number and chapter title alludes to the time, channel, and program order of the week's daily television program schedule that used to be printed in Sunday newspapers—a form of remediation of television culture in novelistic practices. Thus, the novel's daily list of page, chapter, and chapter title corresponds to the television schedule's daily lineup of time, channel, and program, respectively, and the characters parallel the different channels. Mimicking the flow and segmentation of a television schedule, the structure of the novel shapes our reading practices and perception, which must accommodate such a mediatized experience of time.

The second table of contents even more conspicuously refers to remediation in narrative with its title "HyperContexts," inspired by the leading spreadsheet software of the 1990s, *Lotus 1–2–3*. The chapters are organized along a vertical axis with the names of the seven characters and a horizontal axis with the seven days of the week. In this table, the numbers of the chapters are subordinated to the chapter titles, character names, and days; the page numbers are missing entirely. The numerical order is reorganized spatially under the main narrator of each chapter. The grid format of the "HyperContexts" evokes the simultaneous video feed of a news editing room with its many monitors, news segments, and rival news networks playing on multiple screens. As it would take a sophisticated viewer to make sense of these competing media narratives, so too will it take a well-versed reader to make sense of the juxtaposed narratives and the information grid. This remediation of news editing into print and of digital outputs into novelistic convention emphasizes how the narrative structure of the novel provides the main critique of static characterization and identity formation.

These multiple narrators, intermingled stories, and contrasting narrative styles are crucial to achieving the flexible character formation and hybrid racial identities in *Tropic of Orange*. Significantly, the novel's organizational precision is deliberately misleading. For example, the characters' individual stories appear in different orders for each daily cycle. Although a reader could follow one character's cycle of stories or read the episodes of the different characters consecutively through the grid of chapter titles, Yamashita both encourages and frustrates such a systematic reading strategy: the characters' narratives that initially appear idiosyncratically differentiated become increasingly permeated with each other's narrative styles and quirky personal traits. The permeable narratives, and indeed identities, of characters parallel the increasing geographical distortions in the strict boundaries that divide the city from its suburbs, the United States from Mexico. The boundaries of self-identity are not as distinct as the divisions make them seem. The "HyperContexts" table is less representative of individual perspectives than of political communities forged around specific forms of media.

Yamashita provides the fictional equivalent of intersectional identity formations. But rather than using race, class, or even gender as primary axes of identity and identification for analyses, Yamashita instead relies upon her characters' attitudes toward and use of the media. Thus, media consumption becomes its own axis. This form of identity construction undergirds all the others. The media often replaces and, at the very least, shapes personal interactions, relations made even more difficult and unlikely across and among different identities because of de facto segregation in residential neighborhoods and communities.[12] Ultimately, Yamashita argues that there is not enough that media representation can do, whether it reaches a broader, more

inclusive audience or provides broader, more inclusive representations of people of color; it cannot galvanize media viewers and transform them from spectators into participants, bystanders into citizens.
Yamashita exhorts her readers to recognize themselves as media citizens and vice versa.

Activists, Artists, Visionaries

The novel's multiple protagonists originally appear grouped by their
social connections to one another either through their upwardly mobile
class aspirations or conspicuous lack thereof. These groupings, however, are merely provisional, since the final events of the novel, the
homeless massacre and the fatal wrestling match, drastically reshuffle
these affiliations: some main characters who die or who are otherwise
silenced at the end of the novel pass their idiosyncratic perspectives
to the ones still living, transforming them. Yamashita initially establishes geographical, social, and class disparities among these protagonists in order to emphasize how they later transgress these divides.
In the next section I will focus on Arcangel, Manzanar, and Buzzworm, three of the most unconventional and allegorical characters in
Tropic of Orange. Analyzed together, they provide a trenchant critique
of media representations of race, class, and urban violence.[13] Their
aesthetic practices are closely tied to their concerns for their media
reception, audience, and mediatized dissemination. These characters
exemplify Yamashita's impressive fictive imagination that portrays
the richness and multiplicity of the often-ignored or unacknowledged
communities of color. But most of her characters are forced to give up
their distinctive aesthetic practices, and their eventual fates—separation from family and even death—complicate such facile interpretations of this diversity. Even these remarkable, perhaps even magical,
characters are forced to confront the limitations of their already-
expansive and inclusive artistic and political practices of media consumption. Arcangel, for example, posits the ethical dilemma of art and
audience in the very functionality of his own performances: he needs
an audience to recognize his art, but the resulting spectacle is so mes-
merizing that it fosters passivity in his audience members. If people
are watching him perform his miraculous feats, then they are not joining him in the collective goals and social movements he hopes to inspire.
As a recycler of sounds, Manzanar imagines his body is a recording

device, bearing witness to the events that are happening within ear-shot from his overpass podium; however, he remains apart from the actions, stands aloof from the human suffering he often hears, and emerges as a creature of media spectacle, too much the passive audience himself, however inclusive his art may be considered. Going beyond Arcangel's and Manzanar's metaphysical and allegorical roles, Buzzworm actively seeks out intercultural exchanges through his interracial friendships among residents of his neighborhood. Although Buzzworm tries to connect with others he meets by listening to their favorite radio stations in languages he doesn't understand and, during the homeless occupation of the downtown L.A. freeway, hosts an impromptu television talk show with his homeless friends as his guests, even he comes to realize that his reliance on such media is an inferior stand-in for transracial alliances.

The provocative actions of these visionary characters in *Tropic of Orange* form an instructive allegory for the practices of civility. By identifying their aesthetic-political practices around media as well as its creation, consumption, and critique, the characters and their interactions with others represent alternative strategies for civility—in effect, *media* strategies—that often undergird the concepts of friendship, trust, mutual respect, and reciprocity and have regularly been prescribed for a flourishing civil society. Buzzworm most obviously models this civil behavior in building community: as the self-named Angel of Mercy, he walks around the neighborhood informing his neighbors of the social services available to them. Manzanar's aesthetic principles reclaim and include the overlooked and evanescent sensory experiences in the urban soundscape, drawing his audience's attention anew to their communities and environments they move through and affect.

I discuss Arcangel first of these three not only because he is the main plot catalyst for both of the final climactic events of the novel, but he is also the character who provides the most comprehensive and relentless critique of media citizenship. In terms of civility, Arcangel represents an engaged citizenry, one of the multitudes who will sacrifice his own self-interest and his very life for his fellow citizens without hesitation.[14] Inspired by Gabriel García Márquez's short story "The Old Man with Wings" and Guillermo Gómez-Peña's performance art (Quintana), Arcangel has fantastically lived too many lives and survived too many oppressive regimes across the entire American

continent; his audiences have enthusiastically applauded his performances or brutally tortured him since the late fifteenth-century invasion of the Americas by Columbus. Arcangel speaks a language rooted
in many regional idioms and historical experiences across the Americas, "a jumble of unknown dialects, guttural and whining, Latin mixed
with every aboriginal, colonial, slave, or immigrant tongue" (47). Arcangel's narratives prominently invoke elements of magical realism and
performance poetry, portraying a world in which the willpower of one
wizened old man can pull a one-ton truck out of the mud, just as the
dried-up, off-season orange he carries can somehow pull an entire
continent northward, eradicating national borders, physical and symbolic, by uprooting an entire land mass and its peoples and delivering
them into Los Angeles.

In Arcangel's cycle of stories, Yamashita advances her criticism of
what Guy Debord has called "the society of spectacle." According to
Debord, spectacle is not just something we watch or create: it "is not
a collection of images, but a social relation among people, mediated
by images" (12). Arcangel's audience members are particularly resistant to recognizing their place in the dynamic relations between his
performance and themselves, instead captivated by the spectacle and
stripped to their inert selves. On the second day of the novel, Arcangel
encounters a truck broken down on the side of the road and offers
to pull it for the disbelieving driver and passersby who soon gather
around him. As Arcangel attaches steel hooks to skin flaps on either
side of his torso and pulls the truck as "securely as an ox to its plough"
(74), the scene is narrated as a poem:

> *Those who witnessed this performance*
> *felt themselves the excruciating weight*
> *of the machine and its fruit*
> *tearing at their bodies. . . .*
> *Why should they allow him to do such a thing?*
> *What were they thinking?*
> *They should push the truck themselves!*
> *Fools!*
> *But they all strained themselves*
> *with watching and yearning in hushed awe*
> *that the feat should be achieved* (74; original italics)

The spectacle of Arcangel's skin drawn taut with the weight and his
astonishing ability to move the truck mesmerize the bystanders. In the

narrative's paratactic succession of questions, "*Why should they allow him to do such a thing? / What were they thinking?*," the speaker berates Arcangel's audience as they fail to recognize the possibility of collectivity in action as they bear witness to his miraculous feats. Yamashita emphasizes how this superhuman feat blinds the spectators from envisioning what they would have been able to accomplish together if they had all helped push the truck. Echoing Debord, in which the spectacle "is by definition immune from human activity, inaccessible to any projected review or correction" (17), Yamashita, through the speaker, indicts the passivity of the audience in the presence of spectacle, those who "in submissively consuming spectacles one is estranged from actively producing one's life" (Kellner, 3).

Of all the characters, Arcangel provides the most extensive and polemical critique of this passivity. Arcangel's commentary criticizes the audience's passivity, which renders them mutely awestruck and immobile as they watch his performance instead of adding their strength to his and each other's, instead of experiencing their collective strength rather than their individual fascination. Yamashita heightens the irony by juxtaposing their transfixed fascination to Arcangel's terrible physical strain as his audience ironically "*strained themselves / with watching and yearning . . .*" (74; original emphasis). Arcangel's feat symbolizes the imaginative potential possible for those who act and for those who act collectively. His very actions shame those on the sidelines who are fully capable of helping yet remain passive spectators of the event. Because of their collective inaction, the crowd waits for a miraculous performance such as Arcangel's to solve problems. Yamashita presents a provocative paradox: the passivity of the audience that creates the occasion for Arcangel's art. By their collective inaction, Arcangel accomplishes this epic feat, but if they had participated, they would not have been able to witness, and be inspired by, Arcangel's heroism and superhuman abilities. Preceding Arcangel's migration to Los Angeles and the massacre of the homeless at the conclusion of the novel, this story evolves into a resonant parable for these climactic events in which spectacle precludes collective action. The speaker's commentary on Arcangel critiques the passive bystanders' refusal to distribute work more equally and according to each person's capability. In a parallel sense, the reader, the audience, and the citizenry wait too long and rely too often on spectacle.[15] Arcangel's narrative provides a critique of the idea of a vanguard or charismatic leader as necessary for a movement. The narrator also indicts the reader as a fool, like the fictional audience.

In a work that is already narratively complex with seven protagonists, Arcangel's cycle of stories has a distinctive style that mixes third-person limited omniscient with stanzas of italicized free verse. Instead of dialogue set off by quotation marks, this feature of Arcangel's passages is evocative of speech, thought, and memory as well as between first- and third-person narrators. Akin to indirect discourse, Arcangel's prose narrative occasionally echoes the tone and subject matter of the poetic lines, but the prose narrator and the poetic speaker are not identical. The tone of the poetic stanzas, rife with exclamatory sentences and rhetorical questions, is polemical, disgusted, indignant. Situated in this delimited space between prose and poetry, these free verse sections function akin to ancient Greek choruses that provide commentary on the plot and represent the voice of the people. Giving Arcangel this collective voice, Yamashita uses the interaction between the narrator and speaker to emphasize how the people have lost their voice as they voluntarily become speechless bystanders.

Yamashita repeats this episode, in which Arcangel again single-handedly pulls another broken-down truck, but this time his miraculous feat is broadcast on live television. Oddly, television audiences, unlike the mesmerized crowds, are unable to recognize the extraordinary achievement for what it was. Arcangel's response evaluates the limited potential of media transmission to accurately represent his performance:

> If there were a dozen local and national stations, there were a dozen eyes, translating to a dozen times a dozen times a dozen like the repetitious vision of a common housefly. Arcangel strained for this vision even though live television had no way of accommodating actual feats of superhuman strength. The virtually real could not accommodate the magical. Digital memory failed to translate imaginary memory. Meanwhile, the watching population surfed the channels for the real, the live, the familiar. But it could not be recognized on a tube, no matter how big or how highly defined. There were not enough dots in the universe. In other words, to see it, you had to be there yourself. (198)

Yamashita makes a provocative claim about the difference between the virtually real-digital memory and magical-imaginary memory, positing the live in terms of the virtually real against the magical, which, in this novel, is the actually real. The viewers can only see what is familiar and expected, accepting what is live with what is real within the framework of their limited viewing experience through the television. So surprised they can't even comprehend what happened, the onlookers overlook Arcangel's magical exploit, and it remains the unreal, the unfamiliar, and, finally, the unwatched. From Arcangel's perspective, although newsworthy events are usually considered out of the ordinary, ironically, the truly extraordinary event of the collective effort, not the individual one of his magical feat, is what exceeds representation and memory. A digital recording cannot match "imaginary memory" because it is representational, not transformational, which is Arcangel's main objective.

For Arcangel, as for Yamashita, this collective imagination and memory is the ultimate goal. Yamashita uses the magical as an epistemological challenge to the world that media can represent and control. Arcangel's magical achievements are rendered invisible to the watching population that chooses virtual representations of their own reality rather than the imaginary possibilities Arcangel offers: a collective endeavor of helping him push the truck rather than individual spectators marveling at what he could do by himself. Yamashita demonstrates how a digital recording cannot match the "imaginary memory" or the communities imagined by Arcangel and the other characters. The difference between the digital and the magical is akin to the difference between a technical recording and memory. The magical for Yamashita incorporates much of the idea of the imagination and memory: that we take the past and incorporate it into our vision for the future. Arcangel wants the ability to see from multiple perspectives not just for an aggregate panoramic vision or even a detailed perception, but a more expansive one unavailable to technology: what exceeds the frame, the constellation of what else can be imagined or remembered.

The audience is unable to recognize and act upon the truly magical because they are deadened by the "usual," or formulaic, responses to crises and the issues they raise. Media events must be precisely managed and scripted despite being ostensibly unscheduled. Television news coverage responds in predictable narratives to a wide array of unexpected news events, such as traffic accidents, natural disasters, and even international conflicts.

As the semis went up in flames, there were the *usual* questions of traffic safety, whether trucks should be confined to operation during the hours between midnight and dawn or to truck-only corridors. As the homeless flocked onto the freeway, there were also the *usual* questions of shelter and jobs, drug rehabilitation, and the closing of mental health facilities. And as car owners watched on TV sets or from the edges of the freeway canyon, there were the *usual* questions of police protection, insurance coverage, and acts of God. The average citizen viewed these events and felt overwhelmed with the problems, felt sympathy, or anger and impotence. (122; emphasis added)

Repetition of "there were the usual questions" to the televisual presentation of the past is what television critic John Thornton Caldwell has named "historification"—the style of television that constructs a visual history from image and video archives. Television provides a viewing experience that is "on the scene" because it already has stock photos, images, and video to illustrate the news report. In order to represent events, the past is selectively mined to support present-day, contemporary narratives. For Benjamin, it is time and memory that forgets events and "crystallizes" others; for Caldwell, the cataloguing vagaries of the archive are responsible: that which is not appropriately categorized, labeled, and cross-referenced is quietly lost to media history. Representations of current media events are pastiche: series of images plucked from file footage, sequences of ready-made mediatized memories. The novel's readers are in a continual present that reimagines and rewrites the recent past through the novel's rearrangement of these mediatized memories. In the preface, Yamashita mimics the logic of the presentness of television as well as the televisual practice of on-the-spot historification by insisting that "we were all there," together, watching the events that will soon unfold in the novel. And the spontaneity and unpredictable nature of the live is heightened by the extreme spontaneity and unpredictability of a civil disturbance of the magnitude as that of the Los Angeles Crisis. Caldwell uses the events of the 1992 Crisis to exemplify his delineation of historification in terms of the "crisis televisuality": the immediacy and unplanned nature of crisis results in overly simplified narratives as news teams scramble to provide enough dramatic content and information for round-the-clock reporting. The subsequent coverage of the 1992 violence was unable to incorporate complexities of both race and class, and what "did not fit television's historicized and binary racial model, then, was simply ignored" (317).

Of course, the presence of nonwhite, noncitizens, and nonworkers is generally perceived to be a crisis in and of itself.[16] If the poor and people of color are perceived as a perpetual crisis in the United States, then their everyday lives are part of this crisis. This is the essence of the live, privileged over the virtually real: it is collectively felt and experienced—so unpredictable and unexpected that there are no typical narratives that could adequately communicate the occurrence. However, despite the repetition of "the usual," that all occurrences are eminently predictable, the narrator identifies the "imminent collective sense of immediate live real-time action" (120), the potential of collective action to be achieved through live media representation.

Applying this idea of media consumption to theories of hegemony, my reading highlights the possibility that what is the usual and the ordinary are the "official" transcripts in negotiations of power; Yamashita wants to get at the heart of what is hidden, off the record, and privately imagined. The characters' self-expression and sense of invisibility or hypervisibility, unacknowledged or recognized only in terms of stereotypical behaviors, is key. In uncovering the "arts of resistance," James C. Scott identifies cultural practices that, in Yamashita's work, translate into practices of media consumption—whether it's how corporations encourage viewers to buy products advertised or how oppositional media practices might counter such passive reception. Scott distinguishes between the official and unofficial, or "hidden," transcripts, the cultural narratives that record acts of resistance or oppositional sentiment that are unrecognized or overlooked by the powerful. These narratives are manifested through such cultural forms and practices as "tales of revenge, use of carnival symbolism, gossip, rumor" or the "development of dissident subcultures," evident in "folk religion, myths of social banditry and class heroes, world-upside-down imagery or myths of 'good' rulers and leaders from previous eras" (Scott, 198). These cultural forms are perpetuated through performance in the face of domination. For Scott, a complete, public record includes "nonspeech acts such as gestures and expressions" (2 n. 1). This comprehensive record operates for Yamashita much like Scott's "arts of resistance," or the attempts to unveil hidden transcripts and cultural narratives that record acts of resistance that the dominant culture attempts to place out of view. The commodification of resistant performances—their absorption into the mainstream and assimilation into dominant culture—manifests the ways in which power responds

and adapts to these hidden transcripts in the form of cultural stereotypes, justification for economic and social dependence, laws, and
physical force.[17]

Yamashita reenvisions the novel form as a mediatized record of
collective, imaginary memory. Although Arcangel understands the dis-
appointing limitations of the media coverage of his work or any other
event, he still "strains" for a multiple vision, likened to the housefly's
multifaceted sight, in order for these many alternative news narratives to trigger the political imaginations of his television audiences.
In her portrayal of Arcangel, Yamashita posits this performance artist
as the ideal deliberative citizen who works so hard to imagine the
multiple perspectives ideally fostered in a democracy. But Yamashita
argues that virtual representations cannot replace or equal the magical; the digital record of Arcangel's feats and very existence cannot
record the imaginative scope of what he actually accomplished in the
collective possibilities he opens up and the audiences he might inspire.
Arcangel rejects each media report's attempt to serve as the official
truth, the official transcript; he strains for a multiple vision that would
counteract a reductive media representation with multiple perspectives and interpretations to, in essence, have the hidden and the official
transcript of his performance coincide. Yamashita posits Arcangel's
media practices as a model form of democratic media citizenship and
a crucial foundation of civility.

Manzanar and Buzzworm: The Cartographers

While Arcangel's five centuries of experiences across the Americas
reverberate in the free verse poetry that interrupts or responds to his
narrative, the character Manzanar Murakami believes that his body
records the sounds of the city, as he finds music from what others
overlook and makes musicians and instruments out of unwitting commuters and urban life. Manzanar believes he is conducting and recording the "greatest orchestra on Earth" (37), the complex and random
patterns of sounds he hears from a downtown Los Angeles freeway
overpass. In the visual rhythm of a conductor's baton keeping time for
the musicians to create a musical whole, Manzanar conducts as events
unfold, begging the question of who is leading and who is following—
the conductor or his music. Manzanar attempts to create patterns of
what is assumed to be patternless and happenstance in order to make

music, art, and aesthetic appreciation out of the discarded, overlooked, and unappreciated. He makes music from what is accidental and after the fact, apparently armed with an artistic methodology that is also exhibited in the work of composers such as Philip Glass or John Cage.[18] Manzanar imagines his musical scores from his understanding of various maps and grids, from the "very geology of the land" of artesian rivers and tectonic fault lines to the "man-made grid of utilities" of water, electricity, and sewage, as if they were the staves of multiple instruments and vocals on a conductor's score: "For each of the maps was a layer of music, a clef, an instrument, a musical instruction, a change of measure, a coda" (57). Attuned to his natural and urban environment, Manzanar comprehends the broad historical and geographical complexity in ways that other "ordinary persons never bother to notice"—that these "thousand natural and man-made divisions, variations both dynamic and stagnant, patterns and connections by every conceivable definition from the distribution of wealth to race, from patterns of climate to the curious blueprint of the skies" (57) are one great symphony of expected and chance outcomes.

Manzanar's penchant for maps is significant in that the structures, geographical markers, and patterns detailed on them make certain actions, and for Manzanar, their resulting sounds, more likely and predictable: Manzanar tells time by the downtown traffic patterns of a workday and the season by the unclogging of freeway arteries based on school holidays. His provocative claims of conducting connote the activities of keeping time and cueing instrument parts' beginning and end; however, his performance is a *response* to, rather than an anticipation or expectation of, the sounds he hears. Manzanar's inverted approach to conducting represents the future anterior time of endless anticipation and expectation, of applying "methods of retrospection to the future" (121) as Alain Lipietz has identified.[19] The perspective of the future anterior is the process that uses the future outcome as a means to evaluate the actions of the present. Lipietz exhorts us to "apply the methods of retrospection to the future," which he defines as "knowing the theoretical presuppositions of the future mode, to search for the historical conditions in the present" (121). Such a search, Lipietz argues, will "illuminate the future" in which "a prediction of the future anterior ('the present will have prepared the future')" (ibid.). Thus, the future anterior, as an action that will be completed or a condition that will be achieved in the future, applies to the preface because the reference point in the future is the act of our reading or acknowledgment. Which sounds happen to be available create the different movements of the symphonies that Manzanar imagines. An orchestra conductor keeps time and signals when certain instruments or sections begin or end their parts in order to produce a unified rhythm and accurate interpretation of the score itself. For Manzanar the process is inverted: the sounds occur and he conducts in response to them. This proleptic inversion of the conductor's relationship to the musical score and orchestra reveals the scattershot process of making patterns and meaning out of that which is random and disordered and exposes the selective, and often arbitrary, processes of deductive reasoning and knowledge production. The future anterior time demands us to ask ourselves, in order to achieve the future that we imagine, what would need to happen now, in the present? Manzanar's proleptic vision is a pedagogical strategy that is imperative to conversations about urban policy, interracial conflict, and material inequalities that haunt the aftermath of the L.A. Crisis.

Despite Manzanar's inclusive art and proleptic aesthetics, he is a persistent figure of exclusion. He attempts to incorporate all the sounds that he hears, and, by extension, he hopes to document all the acts that have created them. This is analogous to how we, the novel's readers, like the unsuspecting freeway commuters, have been part of a performance we may not recognize, and this lack of acknowledgment is a failure to include Manzanar and his artistic vision in our imagined community.

> Those in vehicles who hurried past under Manzanar's concrete podium most likely never noticed him. . . . And perhaps they thought themselves disconnected from a sooty homeless man on an overpass. Perhaps and perhaps not.
> And yet, standing there, he bore and raised each note, joined them, united families, created a community, a great society, an entire civilization of sound. (35)

While Arcangel's larger political project may not be understood, his abilities are inordinately useful and celebrated, and while Buzzworm's advice may be ignored, he is still welcomed within his neighborhood. Unacknowledged and even disdained by his "musicians," or the people going about their daily lives in downtown Los Angeles, Manzanar's art is, as he himself is, ignored and marginalized. Manzanar is the other side of exclusion; all of his audiences except, notably, Buzzworm refuse to incorporate him into their landscapes of the city, of normalcy. Significantly, Manzanar's exclusion is long-standing; as a World War II Japanese American concentration camp survivor who bears the name of one, he was once stripped of his citizenship, its rights and protections, and segregated in the hinterlands of California because of his ethnicity and race.[20]

Manzanar self-consciously imagines his body as an instrument and site of resistance through his performative practices. By incorporating the sounds of pain and death into his musical compositions, Manzanar tries to "record" the violence and suffering resulting from the spectacles he witnesses. His concept of recording is more akin to acts of recognizing and registering the aftereffects of action. He conducts "everything" throughout, "fearlessly" recording "every horrible, terrifying thing—in music" (53) until the colliding vehicles have come to a stop and customary traffic patterns have been restored. The collision of a sports car with a propane truck creates a colossal traffic jam on the freeway and initiates one of the major subplots of the novel— the homeless encampment in the abandoned cars and the military massacre of these freeway squatters that ends the novel. The third-person narrator details "the metallic crash and crunch of the unfortunate . . . , the snap of delicate necks, the squish of flesh and blood" (55). Yamashita emphasizes the horror of the multiple, simultaneous accidents in the phrase's harsh alliteration: the cacophonous "c" and "t" sounds in the ripping metal and flesh and the fricative consonant blend "sh" in the oozing oil and blood. The violent sounds of this episode are drowned out by the quietude of the final image of Manzanar, who "innocently hummed the recurrent melody of the adagio" (57). Yamashita emphasizes the disparity between the spectacular violence on the freeway and Manzanar's ostensible equanimity on the overpass.

Manzanar continues to conduct despite and because of the accident and the firestorm that engulfs many of the homeless shantytowns hidden alongside the freeways. In his theory of musical maps, he dwells in abstraction, feeling courageous for his ability to conduct, to witness, despite the horror Yamashita captures in her language. His physical distance symbolizes his emotional and artistic distance, a separation between other lives and his own in his art. Manzanar only acknowledges the violence and suffering he has witnessed by his incorporation of those sounds of pain and death into the music he conducts as surprising, however disturbing, additions to the daily rhythms. But Manzanar can only imagine these maps from high above the events as they occur, himself physically and emotionally distanced from the action—far from the actual clashes and conflicts that cause the sounds he conducts for his street symphonies. Manzanar's perch atop the freeway overpass replicates the distanced perspective of the media, the disconnection between viewer and events, reminiscent of the "helicopter journalism" evident during the L.A. Crisis (Chang and Diaz-Veizades, 61). Manzanar fails to intervene or help in ways that might be effective. He is never moved beyond the completion of the piece and remains isolated on his perch. He is so focused on making himself into a recording machine, rather than living and enabling life.

Akin to Arcangel's nomadic lifestyle and awestruck, ineffectual audiences, Manzanar's homelessness resonates with his passive spectatorship, however active he believes his conducting to be. Guy Debord's concept of alienation in relation to spectatorship is particularly appropriate to Manzanar's refuge in conducting:

> The alienation of the spectator to the profit of the contemplated object (which is the result of his own unconscious activity) is expressed in the following way: the more he contemplates the less he lives; the more he accepts recognizing himself in the dominant images of need, the less he understands his own existence and his own desires. The externality of the spectacle in relation to the active man appears in the fact that his own gestures are no longer his but those of another who represents them to him. This is why the spectator feels at home nowhere, because the spectacle is everywhere. (29)

Yamashita literalizes Debord's metaphor of metaphysical homelessness in Manzanar's rejection of his family, home, profession, and even his makeshift encampment alongside the freeway. On the last day of the novel, horrified by the initial assault on the homeless encampment on the freeway, Manzanar finally reacts to the events around him. As he watches and conducts while the freeway becomes a massacre and a graveyard, he notes: "The motley community of homeless and helpless and well-intentioned ran in terror, surrendered, vomited, cradled the dying. Manzanar recorded every scream and cry and shudder with dumb incomprehension" (240). Manzanar hears but has been unable to register the human suffering in his maps and in his music. Previously, he was able to identify the sounds, but failed to consider what they meant, the human cost of the bumper-to-bumper traffic, the emergency sirens, the crash and crunch of bodies. In reaction to what he is now witnessing "dumbly," Manzanar gradually remembers his own history and the family he has forgotten. His memory triggers the loss of his ability to hear the sounds and to see the patterns of music and the collectivity forged through this artistry.

The odd yet resonant figure of Manzanar also provides allegorical practices for civility. For Yamashita, Manzanar is the consummate listener. However, Manzanar is trying to avoid emotion and must deny his own responses to what he sees or, more accurately, what he hears. But unlike Buzzworm, who is addicted to listening to his radio in any language and uses what he hears but doesn't understand to start conversations with Asian and Latina/o neighbors, and Arcangel, whose straining to hear the media responses to his performance allegorizes the back-and-forth of conversation and democratic deliberation, Manzanar's relentless hearing is a model for listening that is necessary to an informed citizenship and encouraged by proponents of civility.[21] Manzanar is too far on one side of the spectrum: his active listening to all that is forgotten or overlooked is revealed to be passive and inadequate in the wake of the homeless massacre and his granddaughter's death. Manzanar only witnesses the sounds, the decontextualized markers and signs of life in the city. Much like Arcangel's passersby, Manzanar discerns music from the diversity and unexpectedness of the sounds themselves, but he ultimately fails to register their importance and to alleviate the violence and suffering they indicate.

These two prominent character pairings show how transracial alliances are enacted in *Tropic of Orange* and that Yamashita features prominently in the novel: the friendship between Manzanar and Buzzworm and the more unexpected connection between two strangers, Arcangel and Bobby. Yamashita uses these characters to represent the depth and range of life in Los Angeles, within the common markers of identity, race, and neighborhood. Her characters pass on their own distinctive idiosyncrasies to each other or to the other main characters on the last day of the novel. Manzanar and Buzzworm, the first pair I consider, are self-styled recyclers, as Yamashita recycles the idiosyncratic traits of these characters. Manzanar ordains himself the consummate recycler of sounds as he conducts and records the daily noise of the city—not only surprising in its traffic accidents or other emergencies, but also surprising in its regular daily and seasonal rhythm. Buzzworm attempts to connect the homeless and other residents of his South Los Angeles neighborhood to local social services as he walks around the city. Through the pairing of Manzanar and Buzzworm, Yamashita optimistically suggests that we are not as distinct and contentious as racial divisions and segregated communities would imply.

Manzanar views the destruction of downtown and hears only silence; he can no longer hear the entire symphonies of urban sounds he once conducted. But his loss is Buzzworm's gain: Buzzworm appears to have assumed the most definitive characteristics of Manzanar's talent. He now hears the music that Manzanar once conducted: "Unplugged and timeless, thinking like this was scary, Buzzworm gritted his teeth. Took a breath. Manzanar's symphony swelled against his diaphragm, reverberated through his veteran bones. Solar-powered, he could not run out of time" (265). No longer dependent on media channels, however eclectic or ethnic, Buzzworm integrates Manzanar's artistic approach into his own urban environment. Unlike before, Buzzworm no longer needs any accessories, such as his watches and trademark Walkman, to connect him to the different voices, sights, and sounds of the communities he tries to help. Although Manzanar is silenced and no longer conducting, in the final narratives of the other protagonists, each notes that they see people on the street, on overpasses, in auditoriums, who are spontaneously conducting their own symphonies of sounds. Manzanar's loss is recycled and reused as Buzzworm takes up Manzanar's artistic perspective. Most important, unlike Manzanar's rejection of his past and his family, including his granddaughter, Emi, Buzzworm does not abandon his previous life, nor does he have to reject his own history or present calling as the self-proclaimed Angel of Mercy in order to hear the music of the city.

Arcangel and Bobby: *Los Héroes de la Lucha*

The other prominently paired characters, Arcangel and Bobby Ngu, conclude the novel in Bobby's Sunday installment, the final day's segment. Significantly, Arcangel passes on his visionary understanding to a character whose middle-class aspirations, narrow-minded focus on individual economic success, and deep pride in his exploited labor and that of his immigrant wife contradict Arcangel's own political vision. Bobby is defined by his consumption and labor and this economic identity is most memorably explained by Emi, a local television producer, who ironically quips, "'if you are making a product you can actually touch *and*,' she emphasized *and*, 'making a comfortable living at it, you are either an Asian or a machine'" (23; original emphasis). Prosperity or comfort in productive labor and its commodities is reserved for Asians or technology; this equivalence constructs Asians as machines or highly skilled technicians, but denies them their humanity, citizenship, or belonging to a nation instead of a factory. Thus, as the willingly passive instruments of capital accumulation, the Asian American characters, such as Emi and Bobby, are most marked by consumption: Emi sells advertisements, consummately matching product to program. Bobby runs a nighttime janitorial service that enables him to purchase a house in Koreatown, two cars, and expensive household appliances for his wife, Rafaela, and son, Sol. The chapter headings of his narratives in "HyperContexts," the novel's second table of contents, highlight economic transactions involving his labor ("Benefits," "Social Security"), middle-class wealth ("Second Mortgage," "Life Insurance"), and conspicuous consumption ("Car Payment Due," "Visa Card," "American Express"). Moreover, his narratives are filled with the specificity of trademark slogans, brand names, and model numbers that distinguish the quality of his conspicuous consumption and middle-class aspirations.[22] But these symbols of success, the fruits of his labor, are also built on the alienated labor of others like him.

Arcangel's narrative derides this paltry exchange of consumer goods and enviable socioeconomic status for alienation and oppression: "*The myth of the first world is that / development is wealth and technology progress. / It is all rubbish. / It means that you are no longer human beings but only labor*" (258–59; original emphasis). The hegemony of the so-called developed, First World is reasserted by Bobby's blind consumption and production. Bobby's fervent dream to become a petty capitalist responsible only for the survival of his family unit contrasts with and thwarts Arcangel's work among the people in political movements across the Americas. Although Arcangel dies in a spectacular media event, Bobby is transformed into Arcangel's successor, and he must symbolically let go of the deeply entrenched, yet unnatural and inhumane, divisions that function to keep Rafaela and Sol across the border and his model minority status intact.

With their notable flexible identities, both he and Arcangel share polyglot and tricksterlike abilities. As a Spanish-speaking Asian immigrant from Singapore who is mistaken for a Vietnamese refugee and lives in Koreatown, Bobby exploits his multiple identities and turns himself into the quintessential self-made man. His last name, Ngu, a homonym for "new," emphasizes his ability to adapt in order to capitalize on each new opportunity, first, by pretending to be a Vietnamese refugee so that he might immigrate to the United States, and later developing a reputation as El Chino Loco or "The Crazy Chinese" while in school with "the Mexicans and the centroamericanos," where he gets a "latinoamericano education" (203). As an immigrant of ambiguous racial and cultural affiliations, Bobby, initially the embodiment of capitalist energies, paradoxically emerges as the champion of the immigrant working class, documented and undocumented, when he takes over Arcangel's place in the novel. In some ways, Bobby's diverse background defies stereotypes in his many flexible identities;[23] however, these flexible identities that enable his success are also in the service of capitalism and for the benefit of racism, patriarchy, and U.S. imperialism.

In using his potentially transgressive identity and talents, Bobby is a mishmash of a number of stereotypes about Asian Americans. Much like Emi and Gabriel, he is also deeply connected to capitalism and similarly takes quiet pride in his model minority status.[24] Gabriel, Emi, and Bobby reinforce categories of identities. Even though there are few other Chicana/o news reporters, Japanese American women in television news productions, or successful, self-made Asian immigrant individuals claiming such a background as Bobby, none of these characters begins the week questioning the circumstances of their success, their categories of self-definition, or their upwardly mobile perspectives that depend on the exploitation of others through affective ties or the self-exploitation of their own labor. Throughout the novel, Bobby hopes to win back his wife, Rafaela, a Mexican immigrant, and to bring home his son, Sol. Bobby's separation from his wife symbolizes the separation of the Asian American model minority from other communities of color and more recent immigrant groups. In his inability to see beyond the task at hand and his own narrow aspirations, he conforms to a prominent stereotype of Asians as robots, the fiction that has launched a thousand speculative fictions: he is the other Asian American character most overtly connected to capitalism and, like Emi, is upwardly mobile despite being "not quite" White and "not quite" American.[25]

Although Bobby professes love for his family, he treats Rafaela and his son as possessions that he not only protects but also owns. His patriarchal, neoliberal privilege is supported by the "culture war" platform:

the family values and antifeminism of social conservatives. Bobby is exasperated by the political ideas a college education has given to his brother and his wife: "Like the kid brother, got consciousness about what's it to be a minority. Required course: cultural politics. Gabriel . . . [was p]utting ideas into Rafaela's head" (161). His enterprising wife leaves precisely because Bobby refuses to recognize her developing political consciousness and belief in collective organizing through labor unions, namely, the Justice for Janitors campaign. Not only is Rafaela learning about cultural politics and thinking more expansively about her work as an employee of Bobby's janitorial business, but she is also stepping beyond her gendered roles as wife and mother. In trying to reunite with his family, he begins to understand his wife's increasing unhappiness with his patriarchal materialism and political myopia.

An idealized model minority subject, Bobby is particularly signifi- cant as the putative head of the only nuclear family in the novel. More- over, the interracial family is the site of future civility in a novel of im- migrant narratives where the men leave their female relatives behind, whether they be mothers, sisters, wives, or daughters. Bobby's son, Sol, like the orange, is carried northward. Bobby, Rafaela, and Sol are, ironically, representative of the "people of Koreatown" to whom Pat Buchanan ambiguously referred in his culture-war speech. Bobby's happiness, his American dream, is the apotheosis of the classical liberal individual, as the male head of the household. The offensive under- current in his delight in his self-reliant nuclear family is the exploita- tion of his wife and his own unacknowledged self-exploitation. Bobby believes in hard work, self-sacrifice, and his and his family's own self- sufficiency. When, merely a teenager, Bobby was single-parenting his younger brother, this desire to care for his brother, his wife, and his child motivates him to work harder and sacrifice as much as he can:

> Never been so happy as when he got married to that woman. Can't explain.
> Happier he is, harder he works. Can't stop. Gotta make money. Provide
> for his family. Gotta buy his wife nice clothes. Gotta buy his kid the best.
> Bobby's kid's gonna know the good life. (17)

Rafaela leaves because she refuses to see her husband drive himself too hard in order to buy things for her and their child, but her leaving is also a critique of Bobby's treatment of her and their son as objects, as his property. While Bobby appears to be the gendered and racial- ized ideal of the husband-provider, his beliefs and actions reestablish the classical liberal relationship between individual and household in which wives, children, and slaves were property in addition to that which was nonhuman—the livestock, the land, the tools. In the third-person limited omniscient narrative, Bobby's narratives are characterized by short, choppy fragments and imperative sentences that often lack subjects. Yamashita creates a fast-paced narrative style that efficiently and relentlessly moves onward beyond the self in its content and syntax: "He don't have time to tell stories. Too busy. Never stops. . . . Always working. Hustling. Moving" (16). Driven and determined, Bobby reveals the demands and expectations that he continually places on himself through these imperative sentence structures. His narrative, through its distinctive indirect discourse, appears not to have even enough time for the subjects of sentences. Bobby is so fiercely independent that he doesn't seem to even need the first-person pronoun, "I," but this grammatical thrift and independence also has the effect of erasing his subjectivity.

But the lack of subjects in the sentences of his narrative also manifests Bobby's disconnection from his family and his community in his single-minded determination to succeed as the breadwinner. [26] The indirect discourse blurs the line between not only Bobby's demands on himself but also the societal pressure on him to prove his worth and upward mobility. In Bobby's consumption and attitudes toward work, he appears to be the epitome of the neoliberal man. However, his self-sacrifice, ostensibly so altruistic toward his family and so valued by a capitalist economy, causes Bobby to use his family to maintain his neoliberal lifestyle and politics. He feels the loss of his family in affective terms and also in terms that he cannot identify: in the political economy of the family, the fundamental unit of liberal individualism, as Wendy Brown and other feminist citizenship scholars have proposed, he, the patriarch, has lost standing in the public sphere. His small business is also jeopardized as an extension of the private domain. As an Asian immigrant, Bobby doesn't quite live in the public sphere. Moreover, because he refuses to make his labor and politics visible, his entire family also disappears from view. Bobby overlooks how his life, his very identity, depends on familial labor and exploits his wife and child as well as himself. Bobby symbolizes the larger linchpin in capitalism, an unwitting cog in the capitalist machine as another machinic body in the service of the products produced and the elites that profit.

Arcangel is one of the many overt biblical allusions in the novel; the characters Gabriel and Rafaela allude to two archangels in Abrahamic religions, and Arcangel could thus be Michael, the protector and leader of God's armies against evil. His spectacular death intimates the apocalyptic possibilities beyond the cataclysmic homeless massacre and the symbolic, larger-than-life death match between El Gran Mojado and SUPERNAFTA. The seven days of Yamashita's novel allude to the seven days of creation in Genesis. The novel ends on a Sunday, the final day where God rested in Judeo-Christian religions, with the subtitle "Pacific Rim." Arcangel has been the one who has recognized the orange's function and importance in order to carry it northward. He recognizes the metaphors and ironies of the land and sees the entire history of the discovery of the Americas and the political borders drawn in terms of apocalyptic time. On this final day of stories, the reader witnesses the death of Arcangel by SUPERNAFTA; however, in the concluding lines, Yamashita quickly sustains hopes of another challenger's return and possible success as the rhythms of work, profit, and leisure are reasserted. Redemption appears imminent through Bobby. It is not enough, however, for Bobby to identify with El Gran Mojado, the Arcangel, or to understand his performances. Bobby's transformation connotes his sudden realization that his individual decisions and ambitions structurally reinforce the impassable borders between him and his family.

Arcangel dies so that others can take up the cause and begin their own forms of media and political resistance. As El Gran Mojado, Arcangel ceremoniously throws Bobby the orange before dying. Given this unusual gift, Bobby's final action before being reunited with his son emphasizes his Christ-like figuration: "Just Bobby grabbing the two sides. Making the connection. Pretty soon he's sweating it. Lines ripping through the palms. How long can he hold on? Dude's skinny, but he's an Atlas. Hold on 'til his body gets split in two. Hold on 'til he dies, famous-like" (267). Here, Bobby appears to hold the burden of the world in his hands. The U.S. economy is symbolically dependent on his personal investment in capitalism (alongside hundreds of millions of others) as well as the international and intranational boundaries and rigid identities created to enforce a stable workforce and polity. Until this point in the novel, Bobby's identity and his economic, social, and political aspirations are antithetical to El Gran Mojado's (Arcangel's) existence—Bobby is one of the many who SUPERNAFTA represents and it is for his petty capitalism that SUPERNAFTA vanquishes his enemy, El Gran Mojado.

However, Bobby suddenly realizes that, by holding onto these lines and these borders, he is preventing the symbolic and physical reunification of his family. Although he is seeking to connect them to U.S. middle-class consumer culture by his hard work and belief in the possessive individualism of American enterprise, Bobby is forced to reject his beliefs, reuniting his family, ironically, by letting go: "What's he gonna do? Tied fast to these lines. Family out there. Still stuck on the other side. He's gritting his teeth and crying like a fool. What are these goddamn lines anyway? What do they connect? What do they divide? What's he holding on to? What's he holding on to?" (268). When Bobby can no longer find a compelling answer to these questions, he can no longer narrow-mindedly value limited upward mobility in exchange for the continual exploitation of himself and his wife. In releasing the lines that hold his family and the two hemispheres apart, Bobby is also obviating the necessity of the cataclysmic fight between El Gran Mojado and SUPERNAFTA. The wrestling ring is no longer the focus of attention, but, rather, there is no longer a division between the participants in the fight to the death and the onlookers.

Transracial Alliances

I have read *Tropic of Orange* as an allegory for interpreting the Los Angeles Crisis as both a media spectacle and racial disaster, thus shaping the conversation about race, class, and gender in the final decade of the twentieth century. In this conclusion, I propose another strategy of reading *Tropic of Orange* in terms of the novel's depiction of interracial relations and transracial alliances in order to posit Yamashita's concept of collective subjectivity. The L.A. Crisis, as a racial disaster, demanded a new model of informed media citizenship. The three visionary characters, Arcangel, Manzanar, and Buzzworm, each constructively focus on the kinds and methods of political communication fundamental to building civility. And most important, in Arcangel's death and Manzanar's silence, Yamashita not only depicts the passing of one character's distinctive trait—or unique style of media consumption and critique—to another, but also emphasizes how a more inclusive, more collective vision is manifested in their heirs. Even her most visionary characters are not above scrutiny or critique.

In conclusion, I return to the novel's beginning. The narrator's conspiratorial address with the reader-viewer retrospectively interrogates our inaction and shows that, while we are inattentive or passive, representations are being written or produced in our name and our pasts are overwritten. We have somehow overlooked a revolution that has already been waged, lost, or won in our names. The novel functions as both a counterhistory and a countermemory precisely because the events are occurring, the narrator insists in the preface, as the reader imagines them: "Gentle reader, what follows may not be about the future, but is perhaps about the recent past; a past that, even as you imagine it, happens" (n.p.). In a clichéd sense, this second-person address could be an exhortation that we are making history as we live our lives. However, the quotidian lives of Yamashita's characters are far from mainstream narratives of history. Yamashita is exhorting her readers not only to think differently at this Benjaminian moment of danger, but also to think differently about the lives of her characters as a means of transforming our past from the conformism of the status quo.[27]

Yamashita's prefatory address to the reader and collective audience is revealing. The narrator thwarts the attempt to identify the exact date of events in the novel and instead insists on a recent past that is written or occurring even as the reader imagines it. The narrator insists that "we," the readers, have collectively witnessed the media events portrayed in the novel and that "our fascination" has scripted what the readers have all seen together. We have thus *allowed* events to happen by our very individual and collective passivity. Yamashita indicts her readers for not taking responsibility for such events and the narrator disavows the existence of a single author or "single imagination" in favor of the "collective mindlessness" of the viewing audience. The television media event manifests a collective memory, what "we all saw," and the narrator implies that all viewers are complicit in the novel's plot as witnesses of the events in the narrative. The viewer's very passivity supplants agency as the "collective mindlessness that propels our fascination forward." The reader's linear reading of the novel itself parallels this ostensible inattention that drives the narrative to its end. Given this idleness without intention on the part of the audience, media interests dictate and engender events. I believe Yamashita's larger condemnation is that, with this collective mindlessness, we enact the worst kind of passivity, as the chained prisoners in Plato's cave, hoodwinked by the shadows on the wall.

With her visionary characters, the novel posits the primary habits of media consumption and rejection (the defining traits of her protagonists) as crucial to the construction of their identities, and the adoption of another's habits and media practices undergirds the possibility of interracial relations that extends beyond the fictive world of the novel. In the end, *Tropic of Orange* cautions against the failure of imagination and memory to consider what can be accomplished collectively and how capitalism, globalization, and patriarchy have restricted the resistant and revolutionary imagination.

EPILOGUE

Lives That Matter

You're just not walking right.

—Rubén Martínez

ALTHOUGH THE SPECIFIC DETAILS of the 1992 Los Angeles Crisis recede from our collective memory, the same clusters of meaning and analyses emerge again and again. We are still fighting the civility wars. We continue to have public conversations over right and wrong behaviors: how walking in the middle of the street or walking around middle-class neighborhoods late at night with the hood of a sweatshirt up makes some of us into criminals and justifies some of our deaths. Or how being undocumented, mentally disabled, intoxicated, or just plain unlucky might also justify the lethal force used against some of us.

The right to equal protection from the police hinges on civility. Presumed incivility thus justifies the denial of civil, political, and human rights. These frameworks of rights and protections are often withheld from people of color and people who might also be multiply identified as transgender, queer, poor, homeless, immigrant, and disabled. In the courts, in the media, and on the streets, we are told that this denial is due to our own deficiencies, the lack of civility in our behaviors. This excuse of our bad choices masks what I call earlier in Paul Beatty's novel *The White Boy Shuffle* the *biologization of civility* or civility as an inheritable trait, which is largely impossible in our very racialized existence. We cannot but be uncivil.

Race shaming, much like "slut shaming," blames the victim. It not only puts the survivors or victims on trial for their behaviors, but it ridicules those who would protest the violence of the crimes themselves by publicly humiliating the survivor-victims and their supporters. This form of incivility attempts to keep people from asserting their rights, to hound them into silence, to diminish their claims on the state. The moral outrage that counters the moral outrage is a competing discourse of who belongs to the political community as a legitimate voice. Such an example of race shaming can be seen in relation to the stories and narratives constructed after the murder of Michael Brown in Ferguson, Missouri, on August 9, 2014.

One of the many moments that sparked the anger and frustrations of Ferguson residents and national audiences was how Brown's body was left for four hours on a hot summer street. Residents of the Missouri suburb speculated that his body was left as a warning to this largely Black neighborhood and community, the hundreds who saw and photographed his decomposing body, and the millions who viewed the pictures through news and social media. The *St. Louis Post-Dispatch* explained the delays and mistiming on the part of the police, the investigative unit, and the coroner in moving Brown's body out of public view, but an African American county official voiced the racial indignation felt about the treatment of his body: "You'll never make anyone black believe that a white kid would have laid in the street for four hours" (Hunn and Bell). Critics interpret the treatment of Brown's body as both the devaluation of Black lives and a violation of human rights. *Esquire*'s Charles Pierce argues that this kind of public display of bodies that have been tortured, mutilated, and killed occurs in countries with dictators and warlords. That this horrible spectacle occurred in the United States holds a mirror up to a country that perceives itself as the beacon of democracy in which its citizens enjoy freedom from fear.

While the grand jury deliberated whether to indict Brown's killer in November 2014, Michael Brown's parents, Lesley McSpadden and Michael Brown Sr., traveled to Geneva, Switzerland, to testify before the United Nations Committee against Torture, presenting a report written by legal experts that identified patterns of excessive police use of lethal force against Black men and women in the United States. In response to their UN testimony, Brown's parents faced a barrage of criticism from the U.S. press and social media outlets. I look at two instances of race shaming in this slew of criticism and how tacit assessments of civility justified a variety of incivilities. The first instance appeared as a largely unverified news story, "UN Dismisses Michael

Brown Case: 'We Will Not Be Intervening in the Matter,'" in the online newspaper *National Report*. Circulating virally and erroneously
believed accurate by thousands of social media commenters, it was
subsequently re-blogged and linked in numerous comments responding to other online news stories and opinion pieces on Michael Brown's
death and the protests in Ferguson.

This report claimed to cover the reactions of UN officials to
McSpadden and Brown Sr.'s testimony and quoted a UN "chair member" who assailed the "sense of entitlement these people displayed,"
referring to Michael Brown's parents, and implied that their concerns
did not merit a human rights inquiry: "We deal with legitimate and
widespread instances of human rights violations, and frankly the issues
presented to us here are not even a blip on our radar" (quoted in Agni).
This alleged spokesperson explains the committee's blanket exoneration of Officer Darren Wilson: "after reviewing all the evidence that
the officer in question committed absolutely no wrong doing. . . . My
colleagues and I went over the surveillance footage, as well as other
evidence documented in the case, and we believe that Michael Brown
is indeed guilty of the acts of which he is being charged" (quoted in
Agni). Online fact-checking sites debunk the claims made in the ostensible news article and question the credentials of the UN spokesperson, but this parodic approximation of the UN's assessment and
procedures is written in a authoritative style noticeably different from
the carefully worded press releases of the UN Special Rapporteurs, who
"voiced deep concern" and "urge[d]" the U.S. government to examine
the violent deaths of Black men and women at the hands of the local
police ("Legitimate Concerns"). The unverified UN spokesperson disciplined Brown's parents for their allegedly illegitimate actions and
behaviors and, most disconcertingly, thousands eagerly linked these
sentiments as factual support.

A brief opinion piece for the conservative journal *National Review*
that appeared later the same month echoes similar sentiments as the
unverified sources in the *National Report*. In it, conservative columnist Ian Tuttle mocks Brown's parents for their collaboration with
activist organizations and for going outside the U.S. judicial system to
the United Nations. The columnist complains that, despite being "the
involuntary targets of the myriad influence-peddlers exploiting events
in Ferguson," McSpadden and Brown Sr. are not currying "any favors
with this latest ploy" (Tuttle). The article further criticizes what Tuttle

perceives as their rejection of the U.S. criminal justice system: "that the Brown family would turn away from the American judicial system—which, for its many flaws, is as fair as any there has ever been." The word choice is revealing: "favors" implies that neither Brown's parents, nor their dead son, are equally rights-bearing subjects, but those in an extralegal economy that hierarchizes and judges their civil behaviors in order to accord value to their claim of the murder of their son. Both articles criticize the deep skepticism held by many communities of color that U.S. law can protect their rights and are offended by McSpadden and Brown Sr.'s internationally publicized attack on U.S. exceptionalism that these critics feel the UN testimony of Brown's parents represents. Human rights violations, they imply, cannot exist in a nation with as fair and sophisticated a justice system as the United States.

The UN testimony of Brown's parents and these two articles expose a divided nation, not along Black–White lines or the two racially divided Americas of the 1968 Kerner Commission report after the urban unrest of the 1960s, but between those who believe the U.S. system is "as fair as any there has ever been" and those who believe otherwise. For the latter their life experiences and collective histories testify to the debilitating injustice of the system's "many flaws" that have harmed entire communities. This division transcends Black–White conflicts. This trust or distrust of the state is manifested in assessments of Michael Brown's civility that justify or refute the reasons for his death: Which criminal behaviors and terrorizing actions are attributed to which bodies, civilian or police officer, Black or White? When Brown turned toward the police car after the altercation, did he mean to surrender to or threaten Wilson? Supporters of excessive use of force thought Brown's hands were up; his detractors argued that he was lunging toward Wilson. Who receives the benefit of the doubt?

Both pieces reveal uneasiness with international scrutiny and the comparison of U.S. human rights violations to those in other countries such as Brazil and North Korea. Even in the unverified news report, Brown's legitimacy as a human rights subject is denied because U.S. violations are "not as bad" as past and present totalitarian regimes. Largely ignoring the range of concerns that Brown's parents presented to the UN—from alleviating the disproportionate harassment and incarceration of Black and Brown people to establishing a national database of cases of police brutality—the alleged UN spokesperson in the *National* article shames them for airing their concerns about anti-Black patterns of police brutality. By extension, both articles shame people of color and other vulnerable speakers for talking about issues that affect themselves and those who share the brutality they experience as racialized subjects. Ironically, this logic of U.S. exceptionalism that these supporters and their fans demand—minimizing the impact and number of U.S. human rights violations—is denied to Michael Brown and his transgressions: there are worse offenses than walking in the middle of the residential street, obstructing traffic, that do not merit immediate death; there are other, less lethal forms of force than the multiple gunshots that wounded and killed Brown.

Like any other complainant, Brown's parents are allowed to file a complaint and testify in front of a world organization. For the authors of these articles and their myriad supporters, the claim for justice for Brown's death is diminished by his parents' behaviors, which allegedly reveal their lesser intellects, character, and morality: they are unthinking puppets serving the interests of "myriad influence-peddlers" (Tuttle) and outside agitators. These specific criticisms that have delegitimized the protests in Ferguson are also those that have patronizingly denied Black political autonomy since the beginning of Black freedom struggles. These criticisms furthermore suggest that not only is Brown's parents' definition of justice self-serving, but that their actions subvert U.S. sovereignty and undermine its global reputation for the fairness of its legal system by appealing to an inferior extranational governing body. They and their uncivil behaviors—their illegitimate claims and for bypassing the U.S. legal system—do not belong.

Coalition, Solidarity, Alliance

Just as accusations of incivility met Brown's memorials and protests against state violence, so too do these accusations discredit activists by framing their behaviors as uncivil. And in this case, subverting what the protesters are saying with an emphasis on how they say it has been a powerfully effective strategy to diminish their claims. In this logic uncivil behaviors do not deserve consideration; uncivil bodies do not merit protection. Moreover, one or one's group must be deemed civil to earn racial equality or antiracist efforts. The question of civility has caused tension among allies. New coalitions are forming around combating anti-Black violence and police brutality that include new activist allies such as Christian college students and political conservatives concerned about police surveillance and violations of civil liberties. But these broad-based networks have activated new manifestations of racial privilege, White supremacy, and anti-Black sentiment even among allies. The behind-the-scenes controversy over the use and purpose of the #BlackLivesMatter Movement brings together the arguments of this book, organized under the counterdiscourse of civility.

The #BlackLivesMatter Movement arose in protest of the 2012 killing of Trayvon Martin and the exoneration of his killer a year later. It has continued to coordinate activism around police brutality and murders of Black people through organizing protests in Ferguson, keeping anti-Black violence a national issue and serving as a source of information. The success of this influential online activist movement has generated numerous spin-off organizations and slogans, touting interests and often goals that have countered the movement's mission. Because this appropriation is occurring with such regularity, the founders of #BlackLivesMatter have felt the need to remind supporters and detractors alike of the movement's continuing goals and of their expectations for groups claiming their solidarity and alliances with the movement. In her online essay "A Herstory of the #Black LivesMatter Movement," one of its founders, Alicia Garza, demands recognition for the Black feminist and queer origins of this powerful organizing slogan and solidarity, not appropriation, from the many groups that want to ally themselves with the movement. Garza describes how these groups might seemingly support #BlackLivesMatter through their riffs on the name, the most contentious and widespread having been "All Lives Matter." However, in their unattributed appropriation and exploitation of Black queer women's and people of color's antiracist innovations and work, the self-professed good intentions of these groups have proved misguided at best, and racist, sexist, and queerphobic at their worst: "When you drop 'Black' from the equation of whose lives matter, and then fail to acknowledge it came from somewhere, you further a legacy of erasing Black lives and Black contributions from our movement legacy. And consider whether or not when dropping the Black you are, intentionally or unintentionally, erasing Black folks from the conversation or homogenizing very different experiences" (Garza). Garza reminds her readers that intersectionality is not intersectionality if one uses the multiple axes of this analytic tool not as opportunities for coalition but for lines of flight from Blackness. The erasure of Black lives and experiences in the United States is a human rights concern.

The movement's founders demand recognition of Blackness at the center of calls for justice and the singular focus of energies and resources of their members, and they point to the many ways in which their ostensible allies and supporters shift themselves to the center and crowd out the mission of supporting and sustaining Black lives: "It is appropriate and necessary to have strategy and action centered around Blackness without other non-Black communities of color, or White folks for that matter, needing to find a place and a way to center themselves within it" (Garza). The movement argues for a heavily qualified inclusion that has been loudly criticized by self-professed aspiring allies. To refuse inclusivity is to risk accusations of incivility. However, the founders counter that to risk inclusivity is to risk appropriation and even the reinstantiation of anti-Black agendas that marginalize Black issues once again. The founders have to fend off accusations of multidiscrimination because of their unwavering focus on Black lives instead of everyone's. While "All Lives Matter" becomes a way to incorporate distinctly non-Black experiences, this ostensible inclusion weakens already thin resources specifically supporting Black lives and can even promote goals and agendas that can and have embodied anti-Black racism. Such abstractions that purport to encompass all of humanity have historically codified the most pernicious discriminations against women and people of color in "we the people," and while some laws have changed, the same patterns of White supremacy and heteropatriarchy continue: the media attention on White suffering, the celebration of middle-class norms, and the devaluation of Black experiences. The external demands for inclusion and recognition operate in what I identify as a characteristic of the post–civil rights era in Héctor Tobar's novel *The Tattooed Soldier,* the logic of *racial equilibrium* or the belief that the same action or behavior is interpreted the same regardless of who is the agent. Thus, because African Americans have faced exclusion and segregation in the past, they are expected to be inclusive and integrationist in all aspects of their lives. This kind of reciprocity is believed to be a form of civility; denying reciprocity is couched as incivility, rather than as a necessary political strategy for a movement with limited resources and whose members are under imminent physical threat.

The founders exhort their readers and supporters to recognize the political and affective ties that bind them to centering Black lives and concerns. To this end, the founders of #BlackLivesMatter invoke the family, "our family": "When Black people cry out in defense of our lives, which are uniquely, systematically, and savagely targeted by the state, we are asking you, our family, to stand with us in affirming Black lives. Not just all lives. Black lives. Please do not change the conversation by talking about how your life matters, too. It does, but we need less watered down unity and a more active solidarities *[sic]* with us, Black people, unwaveringly, in defense of our humanity. Our collective futures depend on it" (Garza). Much like Dai Sil Kim-Gibson's documentary *Sa-I-Gu*, the founders exhort their supporters to create a transracial *family of feeling* not based in the sentimental heterosexual nuclear family but instead on activist ties combating anti-Black racism. The founders assert Michael Brown's death, among many others, as a "legitimate human rights violation" against a wide swath of the U.S. body politic that condemns his life and behaviors before his death as well as his parents' efforts to claim his death worthy of redress and justice. Rejecting his parents' claims by marking Brown an undeserving victim, he then cannot represent the universality and immanence of international human rights discourse. This logic inversely parallels how #BlackLivesMatter is in danger of being appropriated for non-Black exclusivity under the guise of an expansive and "universal" humanism.

Interracial solidarity recognizes the racist hierarchy in which others are treated as if they were Black, stripped of their civility and humanity. Expressions of solidarity are what I refer to in my discussions of Anna Deavere Smith's play *Twilight* as *performances of proximity*, and Smith's ethical demands support the call for Black Lives Matter no matter one's positionality. Smith exhorts her audiences to begin with the other to return to the self, but a self that is changed through walking "in the speech of another" (*Fires,* xxvii). We should not deploy identity as if it were fixed, but instead engage in the continual recursive cycle of other-directed engagement and self-interrogation. The ethics of comparative racialization necessitates these changes and exchanges between and among these racial identities. We cannot continue to pretend that identities are stable and fixed so as to refuse to acknowledge the value of other identities in shaping our own: that our privileges and oppressions are related to those of others.

We live this racial disaster daily, whether or not we acknowledge it, whether or not we think it affects others who look, think, and behave like us. In our times of interracial crisis, we must find new ways to counter the continual denial of the civil, political, and human rights of others since it is ultimately a denial of our own. We rehearse old ways of racist knowing and must struggle for an antiracist becoming. These struggles that begin with uncivil bodies and behaviors and demand justice must motivate any appeal for civility.

ACKNOWLEDGMENTS

I have had the pleasure of talking with different audiences across the nation, some whose encounter with what I call the Los Angeles Crisis was a brief snippet on international news to people who lived in the most affected neighborhoods. I have come to find that readers engage with my work and the narratives of the violence with vastly different expectations and memories when they read analyses of the L.A. Crisis; the violence is a Rorschach inkblot with overdetermined interpretations. These interlocutors, colleagues, students, friends, family, and audience members have contributed their experiences and knowledge, generously sharing their reactions and thoughts about the 1992 violence and the continuing state violence across the nation.

This book began with my training under my senior thesis adviser Jonathan Fortescue, without whom I might never have known what good scholarly writing was or that I might be capable of it, and Wendy Motooka, who first introduced me to the critical possibilities in Asian American literature. Thanks to Merry "Corky" White and Mary E. Vogel for their mentorship before I even had a career. George S. Wang, Jedidiah Yueh, Sue Sweet, Dori Takata-Aspuru, and Kelly and Gen Tanabe helped me through college with lifelong memories. Debra Bronstein, Jennifer L. Chang, June Chung, Melanie Ho, Meredith Neuman, Terry Smith, and Jim Gatewood got me through most of grad school and life's obstacles carrying me on their backs. I also thank some excellent teachers who started me on a lifetime of learning and passed on to me a love of teaching: Mrs. Caroline Angus, Mrs. Marge Stouffer, Mr. Joe Kelly, Mr. Rod Flagler, and Mr. Jim Ryono. I am grateful to my dear friends from way back with our big dreams: Scarlet

Kim, Jenny Lynn, and Joanna Demers. And to my son's Grandma Gail O'Brien and Grandpa Tony LaVopa, much love.

Thanks to the authors who talked to me about race and writing, Héctor Tobar, Gary Phillips, and Karen Tei Yamashita. Don Nakanishi, Jinqi Ling, Kyeyoung Park, David Wong Louie, Rachel Lee, and Shu-Mei Shih are teachers and mentors who set me on the right path in Asian American studies at UCLA, and I return daily to many of their questions and wise words. I appreciate Karen Brodkin, Richard Yarborough, and Jim Lee, whose guidance and advice helped launch this project. Jerry Kang, Devon Carbado, and Eric Sundquist helped shepherd its early form and inspired me with their brilliance. I thank the audiences at the Asian American Studies Program at the University of Minnesota; the Literature and Research Colloquium at the University of Montana; the Japanese American National Museum in Los Angeles; the UCLA Americanist Research Colloquium; the Asian American studies workshop led by Eric Hayot and Tina Chen at Penn State; American studies at Northumbria University directed by Brian Ward; and the Asian American Studies Program, Comparative Studies Department, Diversity and Identity Studies Collective (DISCO), and Institute for Korean Studies at The Ohio State University, which have all provided generous opportunities for feedback on parts of this book. This research was made possible from grants and fellowships from the Historical Society of Southern California, the UCLA Department of English, the University of Montana College of Arts and Sciences, and the Ohio State University College of Arts and Sciences and Departments of English and Women's, Gender, and Sexuality Studies.

From the 2006 NEH Summer Institute on African American Civil Rights Struggles in the Twentieth Century at the W. E. B. Du Bois Research Institute at Harvard, I thank Henry Louis Gates Jr., Waldo Martin, and Pat Sullivan for their leadership, as well as Ed Blum, Thomas Bynum, Alison Dorsey, Jennifer Frost, Hasan Jeffries, Randal Jelks, Lolita Paiewonsky, Lisa Szefel, and Annie Valk. I thank Angel Lawson for her close friendship and laughter during our initial tenure-track journey as "two old women" together. My friends in Missoula have been so dear to me and my family: Clint Carroll, Casey Charles, Debra Magpie Earling, Katie Kane, Max and Russ Kubisiak, Prageeta Sharma, Dale Sherrard, Robert Stubblefield, David Moore, Kate Shanley, and Caleb.

I am deeply grateful to all those members of the onsite and online writing groups who made sure that I wrote each day, every day: Jian Chen, Eunjung Kim, Tasleem Padamsee, Sylvia Mendez-Morse, Sophia Isako Wong, Fabienne Doucet-Gibson, Anne Marie Garth, Anna Agbe-Davis, June Chung, Gumiko Monobe, Zelideth Maria Rivas, Monica Guerra, and Diane Bassham. I also appreciate Krupal Amin, Kimberly McKee, Ricky Haberstroh, Larin McLaughlin, Mitch Lerner, Chan Park-Miller, Cheryl Naruse, Steven Jin, Kristin Mercer, Joel and Inés Wainwright, Judith and Jorge Coelho, Ike Newsum, Katra Byram, and especially Simone Drake for providing a much-needed writing retreat at a critical juncture. For the OSU Asian American Studies Program, Annabelle Estera, Jian Chen, Namiko Kunimoto, Joe Ponce, and Judy Wu continue to provide essential intellectual and practical support.

I thank my WGSS colleagues for their enthusiasm and good care: Cindy Burack, Guisela Latorre, Treva Lindsey, Katherine Marino, Cathy Rakowski, Corinne Reczek, Wendy Smooth, Mytheli Sreenivas, Jenny Suchland, Mary Thomas, Lexie Beer, Andy Cavins, Lynaya Elliott, and Tess Pugsley. Linda Mizejewski, Cricket Keating, Juno Parreñas, Rebecca Wanzo, and Shannon Winnubst provided helpful critiques of various ideas and drafts. My English colleagues also deserve special mention for their help and encouragement throughout: Frederick Aldama, Richard Dutton, Pranav Jani, Molly Farrell, Ruth Friedman, Ryan Friedman, Jill Galvan, Maura Heaphy, Wendy Hesford, Nan Johnson, Leslie Lockett, Koritha Mitchell, Debra Moddelmog, Beverly Moss, Sean O'Sullivan, Amy Shuman, Robyn Warhol, Andreá Williams, Wayne Lovely, Jerod Young, Tiffany Quattlebaum, and Nicole Cochran. For invaluable research assistance, I thank Jennifer Otter, Galen Amy, Emily Joy, Vivien Tam, Juwon Lee, Varsha Chitnis, Krista Benson, Katelyn Hancock, and Haley Swenson. Molly Reinhoudt's careful editing and David Martinez's detailed interrogation of everything have made it so much better.

Thanks to Randall Williams, Grey Osterud, Leslie Bow, and Josephine Lee for reading early drafts of the manuscript and asking tough questions. My endless gratitude to Susan Hwang for organizing the most amazing dissertation writing group, and Tammy Ho and Julia H. Lee for their patient and rigorous scrutiny. I also thank June Chung, Theresa Delgadillo, Cindy Franklin, Linda Greenberg, Joanne Tong,

Ariana Vigil, Leslie Wingard, and David Witzling for reading parts of the manuscript. I deeply appreciate Daniel Kim and Cathy Schlund-Vials for their critiques that moved the book forward and pushed me to do better; Daniel deserves extra thanks for naming the "counterdiscourse of civility." I am grateful to Richard Morrison, who initially supported the project, and deeply appreciative to Danielle Kasprzak, Anne Carter, and Cherene Holland, who made sure the book was the best it could be.

I especially thank Jill Bystydzienski, Valerie Lee, Debra Moddelmog, Judy Wu, and Joe Ponce for bringing me to OSU, looking out for me, providing endless support in all things, and continuing to be my inspirations in the personal and professional. I am profoundly grateful to King-Kok Cheung, whose generosity and love for her students is an inspiration, and Rafael Pérez-Torres, who made sure I survived graduate school and my first years on the tenure track with his thoughtful advice and encouragement at many critical moments. I am humbled by the generosity of incomparable interlocutors Jeehyun Lim and Jinah Kim, who interrogated every word and more of this manuscript. Jennifer Gully has provided so much daily and hourly encouragement and instant editing for years now, *vielen Dank*.

My love to the Hamaokas and Itagakis in Hawai'i. My late grandparents, Shigeru and Yuriko Itagaki, Tomoye and Robert Takumi Hamaoka, made sure that the privilege of higher education was in all our futures. I have always wanted to make them proud. I thank the Texas Fergus family, Will, Debbie, Bella, and Diego, and the New Jersey one, Troy, Sonia, Little Troy, and Tori, for their support and care over the years. I am grateful to Mr. Willie Fergus Sr. and the late Mrs. Jane Field Fergus, whom I never met but who both clearly shaped their son in ways I can only hope to shape mine. I thank my parents, Brian and Gale Itagaki; Lori, Lisa Itagaki-Louie, Greg Chau-Louie, nephews Greyson and Grady Louie, those roly-poly cuties.

Devin Fergus deserves more than words can say, making all things possible and inspiring me daily with his brilliance and care. Devin Hiro Fergus, our Ziggy, shows me that there is no joy or hope that holds more endless wonder and gratitude. But if Ziggy gets the first word, Devin gets the best at last.

NOTES

Preface

1. Pem Davidson Buck discusses the "violence of the status quo" in relation to police brutality.

2. Zimmerman's mother is a Peruvian immigrant and his father is White American. The national media often referred to Zimmerman as "white," "white Hispanic," or "white Latino," rather than biracial, likely due to the official U.S. census that classifies Hispanic or Latino as an ethnicity and not as a distinct racial group (P. Taylor et al.). The 2010 Census Briefs found that 53 percent of respondents self-identifying as Hispanic or Latino chose "White" on the 2010 census, while 37 percent chose "some other race," 6 percent chose two or more racial identity boxes, and only 3 percent chose "Black" (Humes, Jones, and Ramirez, 6).

3. As one example of this rhetoric blaming Ferguson and New York City protests for the shooting of two NYPD police officers, the *Wall Street Journal* article headline read "Killings of New York Police Officers Spark Backlash to Protests" (Haddon).

4. Chandan Reddy's concept of "freedom with violence" explains the state's monopoly on legitimate forms of violence that criminalize other forms of "violence" or direct action (even when those other forms of unrest are not physically violent): "Queer of color cultural expressions and movements are in this moment crucial forces that reveal the specifically racial limits of egalitarianism and state reform; they reveal that every inhabiting of legitimate violence for more egalitarian ends will, in the absence of thinking and living with race, continue the racial cruelty that is inextricable from the nation's material conditions of possibility and the state of institutions that reproduce the state form" (46).

5. The 2014 report *Beyond Broke*, by the Center for Global Policy Solutions, shows that more than half a decade after the 2007–8 global recession and despite national indicators showing economic recovery, Black households have increased one cent to owning seven cents of wealth for every dollar held by White households (Tippett et al., 4).

6. Army specialist Charles "Chuck" Graner Jr. and Staff Sergeant Ivan "Chip" Frederick served the longest sentences for the abuse of Iraqi prisoners in the Abu Ghraib prison outside Baghdad, made public in thousands of photographs and inciting a global scandal in 2004. As civilians in the Army Reserves before their tours in Iraq, both worked as corrections officers in Pennsylvania and Virginia prisons, respectively (Finkel and Davenport; Leung).

7. Although this militarization of police forces took place well before the "drawdown" in Afghanistan and Iraq and civil disturbances across the nation, the American Civil Liberties Union 2014 report *War Comes Home: The Excessive Militarization of American Policing* identifies the "amount of military equipment being used by local and state police agencies has increased dramatically—the value of property transferred though the program went from $1 million in 1990 to $324 million in 1995 and to nearly $450 million in 2013" (23).

8. For an overview of implicit bias research, see Banaji and Greenwald; for research on microaggressions, see Sue, Bucceri, et al., and Sue, Capodilupo, et al.

9. See Jackson; Armour; and Stewart and Coleman for a critique of statistical and taste-based discrimination.

10. See Bonilla-Silva, *Racism without Racists*.

11. My initial thinking in this vein was inspired by critical race scholar Eric Yamamoto's *Interracial Justice: Conflict and Reconciliation in Post–Civil Rights America* (1999) and his legal research on these events, which connected grassroots efforts for resolving local conflicts with national movements toward truth and reconciliation commissions.

Introduction

1. My sequence of questions echoes those of Chilean writer Ariel Dorfman in his essay describing the origins of his play *Death and the Maiden* in the state violence of Pinochet's dictatorship in Chile: "How can those who tortured and those who were tortured co-exist in the same land? How to heal a country that has been traumatized by repression if the fear to speak out is still omnipresent everywhere? How do we keep the past alive without becoming its prisoner? How do we forget it without risking its repetition in the future? Is it legitimate to sacrifice the truth to ensure peace? And what are the consequences of suppressing that past and the truth it is whispering or howling to us? . . . And given these circumstances, can violence be avoided? And perhaps the most urgent dilemma of them all: how to confront these issues without destroying the national consensus which creates democratic stability?" (Dorfman, 188). I thank Randall Williams for this source.

2. Of those who were arrested during the crisis, 1,044 were undocumented immigrants who were then turned over to the Immigration and Naturalization Services (Bailey).

3. As Darnell Hunt points out, the television news media repeated and cemented the idea that the trial outcome was a direct cause of the ensuing crisis.

The international coverage of King's drowning death in June 2012 shows how iconic King was to global audiences' understanding and memories of the violence.

4. In his book-length discussion of the literary and filmic texts of the crisis, Min Hyoung Song uses a similar argument to explain his use of the word "riots": "Certainly, the term *riots* suggests multiplicity, fragmentation, competing points of view. It gestures toward an absence that has to stand in for what could not be captured as a whole" (13). I contend that the term "riots" is too overwhelmingly pejorative in ascribing incivility and inhumanity to the less powerful in their responses to oppressive structural conditions. See Schneider for her research on the demographics of those participating in violence during more recent civil disturbances in New York and Paris.

5. See Thomas Sugrue's discussion of "the origins of the urban crisis" in his case study of twentieth-century Detroit and Scott Kurashige's critique of Sugrue's Black–White framework. Kurashige argues for a more interracial approach in order to identify how in post–World War II Los Angeles, African Americans became negatively tied to "urban crisis," while Japanese Americans became positively linked to the notion of the metropolis as a "world city" (7).

6. In *The Souls of Black Folk*, W. E. B. Du Bois foregrounds the myriad terms by which policymakers should understand the "urban crisis" by parodying the persistent question of the "Negro problem" as a White concern over the equal incorporation of African Americans into U.S. society by asking a question eliciting the perspective of African Americans themselves: "How does it feel to be a problem?" There are multiple perspectives rather than one answer to both these questions, the former largely privileging White prerogatives. "Crisis" also alludes to Du Bois's later choice to title the official journal of the NAACP *The Crisis* in 1910, stating that "the editors believe that this is a critical time in history of the advancement of men *[sic]*" (*The Crisis Magazine*).

7. Communication studies scholar Ronald Jacobs has defined the 1992 violence in Los Angeles as a "crisis of civil society": "Crisis develops when a particular event gets narratively linked to a central cleavage in society and demands the attention of citizens as well as political elites" (Jacobs, 9). Media scholar John T. Caldwell echoes this notion of crisis by positing the 1992 L.A. violence as a foremost example of "crisis televisuality": the style of televised programming and its sociopolitical impact that both enables audience's media or televisual literacy and the industry's self-conscious critique (5–8).

8. In sociologist Darnell Hunt's study of reactions to media representations of the violence, he ironizes the term "riots" with scare quotes, to identify simultaneously dominant discourse and to question it. In the run-up to the Democratic primaries and on the fifteenth anniversary of the violence, then-Senator Barack Obama used the oxymoron "quiet riots" in a well-publicized and controversial speech that addresses both the most popular connotations of disorder, chaos, and mayhem and how the term "riots" drowns out the long-standing deterioration of the region and alludes to a 1988 study of the same name. See Harris; Willens.

9. *La Opinión,* the highest-circulation Spanish-language newspaper in Southern California, referred to the 1992 violence as the Rodney King riots.

10. Linda Williams acknowledges the multiracial constituency but overwrites its importance: "Although this particular riot was also multiracial, with Hispanic rioters joining African Americans and with Asian store owners often as targets, its flashpoint was nevertheless the traditional black/white antinomy of previous American riots" (357 n. 6).

11. This tendency to focus on Black–White conflict obscures other interracial conflicts in U.S. history, for example, the 1943 White servicemen's "Zoot Suit" riots in Los Angeles and the nineteenth-century massacres of Chinese immigrants in the American West. Unfortunately, Hunt's *Screening the Los Angeles "Riots,"* despite its important attention to Latinas/os, discusses White, African American, and Latina/o reactions to a news segment on the crisis but fails to consider Asian American viewpoints.

12. Historian Nell Painter argues that the term "riots" has become negatively synonymous with African American protest since the 1960s and refers to the violence as the "war of '92" (84). In his 1992 Republican National Convention speech, former presidential primary candidate Pat Buchanan used the National Guard's presence in Los Angeles as a primary example in the religious and cultural war "for the soul of America" (Buchanan). But some scholars find such words as "rebellion," "uprising," and "insurrection" inapplicable because they imply the "planning and organization o[f] what was still a spontaneous reaction" (Williams, 357 n. 6). These terms can even "glamorize what was in fact deadly and symptomatic of deeply underlying problems in our society" (Song, 15). Explaining his use of the term "riots" and its pejorative connotations, Min Hyoung Song uses the framework of the modern civil rights movement to assess the post–civil rights era, which overlooks the grassroots basis of the initial protests against police brutality in the beating of Rodney King and against the criminal justice system after the light sentencing of Soon Ja Du in the shooting death of Latasha Harlins. Song argues against the use of rebellion or revolution to describe the violence: "There was no discernible tradition of established oppositional political organization at work, no fully expressible leadership rooted in the needs of the multitudes, and no thought-out way for channeling the rage at an unjust judicial and economic system toward productive social protest" (15).

13. Novelist and Pulitzer Prize–winning *Los Angeles Times* journalist Héctor Tobar refers to the violence as the *quemazones,* or the great burnings, echoing the seasonal wildfires that annually threaten the L.A. suburbs. Local attorney Angela Oh, a second-generation Korean American who became a spokesperson for the Korean American community in Los Angeles on national broadcasts and later served on the advisory board for President Clinton's presidential initiative on race, "One America in the 21st Century," prefers the expressions "civil unrest" and "civil disturbance" to riots or rebellion, which she considers more politically charged terms.

14. These strong civic bonds created through "networks of civic engagement" are analyzed in Robert Putnam's continuing work on social capital. He defines social capital as the "features of social organization such as networks, norms, and social trust that facilitate coordination and cooperation for mutual benefit" (Putnam, "Bowling Alone: America's Declining Social Capital," 67). Putnam finds social capital analogous to "notions of physical capital and human capital—tools and training that enhance individual productivity" (67). In his widely celebrated book-length study on the topic, *Bowling Alone* (2001), Putnam's criteria for social capital laud cities with the highest rates of civic volunteerism; however, Putnam himself notes the limitations of his earlier analysis, finding in later research that the cities with the highest social capital also "rank low on interracial trust," which was characterized by the racially homogeneous memberships in these groups (quoted in Allen, xv). Thus, measurements of social capital cannot be the only criteria for a broad-based civil society, since these networks and norms are generated under de facto segregated conditions and indicate the absence of social capital in the form of trust.

15. In conceptualizing the gendered and sexualized dynamics of comparative racialization as well as the stakes of this inquiry, see Hong and Ferguson. These scholars have importantly identified the analytics of women of color feminism and queer of color critique that have constituted the field and provided foundational methodologies for comparative racialization. Acknowledging "scholarship that simply parallels instances of historical similarity across racial groups in the United States," Hong and Ferguson urge future studies that also try "imagining alternative modes of coalition beyond prior models of racial or ethnic solidarity based on a notion of homogeneity or similarity" (1). Literary critic Leslie Bow, inspired by postcolonial theorist Homi Bhabha's notion of the "interstitial," analyzes this unhierarchized cultural hybridity as a dual form of "disorientation" and reorientation of "established perspectives and definitions": "The racially interstitial can represent the physical manifestation of the law's instability, its epistemological limit, the point of interpellation's excess. Yet it may also be the site of cultural reinscription, the place where difference is made to conform to social norms" (4). Bow's notion of interstitiality captures the contradictory and bivalent, even multivalent, forces in the operation of comparative racialization within radical and reactionary racial politics. These scholars have been deeply influential in my own analysis and understanding of comparative racialization and its methods.

16. For recent work on racial discrimination in the northern and western United States, see Sugrue, *Sweet Land*; Q. Taylor; Kurashige; Almaguer; and Ancheta.

17. Legal scholar and activist john powell provides an overview in his essay "An Agenda for Post–Civil Rights," in which the goals of the past civil rights movement are still in question, as are the successes and failures of the movement in achieving its goals. Cultural critics Avery Gordon and Christopher Newfield define post–civil rights America by examining how such a term exposes the limitations of the achievement of civil rights: "The genuine progress represented by civil rights has not been enough to withstand embedded institutional and psychological

resistances like the white backlash against affirmative action programs or unabating white anxiety about the presence of social and political actors who insist on the continuing significance of racism" ("White Philosophy," 739).

18. Providing a range of perspectives on evaluating racism in the law, john powell points to the various constituencies that fracture the agenda of civil rights activism and usher in the dissension within the post–civil rights era: "There is broad consensus that the civil rights movement was designed to attack and repeal the more explicitly racist laws, but what about the other laws, those that were racial but that appeared to be 'neutral' and 'symmetrical?' Here, the consensus begins to disintegrate. Some argue that as long as laws are logically neutral, racial classification per se is not problematic. Others argue that it is the effect of the law, examined contextually and historically, that determines its permissiveness, and that any ostensibly neutral law that has a discriminatory effect is problematic. Some argue that the civil rights movement only fought against formal inequality and governmental acts. Others argue that the civil rights movement focused not only on eradicating explicitly racist state laws, but also on private acts of discrimination against racial minorities" (powell, 880–91).

19. In the racial dictatorship of the United States, as discussed by Michael Omi and Howard Winant, White governing elites could grudgingly concede the possibility of political equality and ensure its failure through the lack of economic and social equality. Jim Crow segregation was the apotheosis of such exclusionary reasoning and psychic comfort by White elites. The majority opinion of *Plessy v. Ferguson* (1896) smugly argued that Blacks only bore the *social* stigma of separation that they themselves put upon such separate but ostensibly equal accommodations.

20. See Sugrue for a more detailed discussion of the much earlier origins of deindustrialization and how government at all levels embraced "free market" remedies based on beliefs in technological determinism rather than the larger trends of globalization (*The Origins*, 164). See Dubey for an examination of how deindustrialization created the cultural milieu for postmodern Black literature, and see James Kyung-jin Lee for an analysis of how, in response to the profound consequences of deindustrialization, cultural and political elites crafted discourses of multiculturalism in the 1980s to mask the sharply growing inequalities along racial lines.

21. The logic of these justifications is not new: the notion of waiting was often deployed against the demands of the modern civil rights movement, most famously rebutted by Martin Luther King Jr.'s "Letter from a Birmingham Jail." Another prominent argument against the modern civil rights movement was the concept of *earning* one's rights: intersecting with notions of merit and that those deemed unequal should *prove* their abilities before becoming fully equal participants in politics, economy, and society.

22. This kind of treason, at worst, and lack of patriotism, at best, marked these people as anti-American. According to Ruth Wilson Gilmore, the beating of Rodney King is a moment of nation-building through the violent disciplining of the anti-American body. Even more provocatively, it is a moment of nation-building through the racial and gender subordination represented in the disciplining of

both Black male and White female bodies. California Highway Patrol officer Melanie Singer is told to step aside by LAPD Sergeant Stacey Koon in King's arrest: "Here, the protection of womanhood is actually the reassertion of race/gender in the national hierarchy: to keep Singer from being accused (in austere times of having a man's job; of trying to do a man's work without succeeding), King must stand in for both Willie Horton and for Melanie Singer. He must become the accused, in service of the rehabilitation of the nation" (29).

23. Present-day essentials of police procedures such as the Special Weapons and Tactical (SWAT) unit and helicopter surveillance were developed in response to the Watts Rebellion of 1965 and originated in military maneuvers used in the Vietnam War. Three decades later, the military strategies used in the Los Angeles Crisis were part of an emerging concept of military operations in urban terrain, or MOUTs. The military maneuvers used during the L.A. Crisis were the only domestic conflict included in the conference on MOUTs and the subsequent publication of the conference proceedings in 2000 (see Desch). James L. Delk, major general and commander of the California National Guard, has documented such maneuvers in presentations and writings, such as his contribution to the conference and his 1994 book, *Fires & Furies: The L.A. Riots—What Really Happened.*

24. In his memoir of the beating and the trial, *Presumed Guilty: The Tragedy of the Rodney King Affair* (1992), the supervising officer, Stacey Koon, refers to what he believed was the precipitating cause for the officers' brutal assault on Rodney King: "[King] grabbed his butt with both hands and began to shake and gyrate his fanny in a sexually suggestive fashion. As King sexually gyrated, a mixture of fear and offense overcame Melanie. The fear was of a Mandingo sexual encounter" (Koon and Deitz, 145). Koon unabashedly reads the violence of slavery and King's threatening Black male sexuality into his account of King's behaviors. In the context of Koon's description of King as a sexual and physical threat to Melanie Singer, the White female CHP officer, as well as to his other police officers, Koon repeatedly alludes to a controversial, sexually explicit 1975 film about the illicit sexual relationship between a Black slave and his White owner's wife. Koon says that he took charge of King's arrest, breaking protocol in which the suspect's apprehension is the jurisdiction of the first officers on the scene or Singer and her partner, who was also Singer's husband. The subpoenaed radio conversation between officers on the scene and central dispatch referred to King as a "gorilla."

25. This logic appears in Jasbir Puar's insightful reading of the figure of the Muslim terrorist in *Terrorist Assemblages*. This figure's foreign (and religious) threat reasserts White Americanness in its very antagonistic relations and "coheres the attacker as a patriotic vigilante" in such a way that it "obscures the reading of the attacker's violence in favor of locating the attackee's probable always about to occur violence" (Puar, 183–84). Such a logic of preemption enacted on these marked bodies reduces them to their bare life, stripped of the rights and protections of the state.

26. Historian Gordon S. Wood cites sixty-nine constitutions that were written in the past two decades, from "post-communist Central and Eastern Europe, to

South Africa, to Afghanistan and Iraq" and even extending to the European Union (44).

27. See Todorova for the way in which the Balkan Peninsula has been imagined. "Balkanization" has referred to the instability of the Balkan Peninsula for a century; it had revived global currency in the early 1990s as some of the various states once grouped together under the Socialist Federal Republic of Yugoslavia declared their independence at the end of the cold war. Just a few weeks before the 1992 L.A. Crisis, the Bosnian War began with its devastating strategies of ethnic cleansing. See Schlesinger for the concern that ethnic identities will "disunite" a presumably "united" America; see Duster and Sears et al. for refutations of "ethnic balkanization."

28. See Karst and Harris for a further discussion of how such a division echoes distinctions between substantive and formal *equality:* formal equality relies on the race-neutral language of the law and substantive equality has often been defined through parity in outcomes.

29. Building on his previous work with Italian subnational governments, Putnam turns his inquiry and expectation to the United States in his evaluation of U.S. society's social capital. He begins his landmark essay, "Bowling Alone: America's Declining Social Capital," in the *Journal of Democracy* by juxtaposing "advanced Western democracies" with the new nation-states of the communist bloc and "developing" world in the aftermath of the cold war: "Many students of the new democracies that have emerged over the past decade and a half have emphasized the importance of a strong and active civil society to the consolidation of democracy. Especially with regard to the postcommunist countries, scholars and democratic activists alike have lamented the absence or obliteration of traditions of independent civic engagement and a widespread tendency toward passive reliance on the state. To those concerned with the weakness of civil societies in the developing or postcommunist world, the advanced Western democracies and above all the United States have typically been taken as models to be emulated. There is striking evidence, however, that the vibrancy of American civil society has notably declined over the past several decades" (65). One of Putnam's most prolific critics, Michael Schudson, argues for the monitorial citizen, a citizen who picks and chooses her battles. Schudson illustrates this concept through the hypothetical example of parents who carefully monitor their children in the swimming pool and spring into action at the moment of a perceived crisis. I believe the benefit and limitation of this allegory can be perceived in citizen participation and television and Internet viewing patterns: (1) citizens who now join groups organized around a single issue or restricted agenda rather than joining an organization with various issues on the agenda, and (2) viewers are more passionate about what they watch and websites they read, but they tend to watch the same fare of channels and websites for their information (Powers). In analyzing urban protests of the poor and working class in Brazil, James Holston posits the notion of an "insurgent citizenship" that counters widespread formation of "a citizenship that manages social differences by legalizing them in ways that legitimate and reproduce inequality" (4).

30. In a contradictory fashion echoed by many civility advocates, Stephen Carter notes both the perennial and unique condition of civility's demise in the United States: "In short, although we Americans have always thought civility is collapsing, I think, this time, we may be right" (*Civility*, xi). Each new decade has proven yet another general uptick in incivility; each new discussion of civility argues that this moment is the worst and the most alarming.

31. Historian Daryl Michael Scott discusses a "racial neoconservative" perspective that criticized liberals for being "too apologetic for what they viewed as the riotous behavior of urban blacks, and emphasized the need for law and order. More important here, they also tended to have serious reservations about preferential programs such as affirmative action and efforts to promote integration such as school busing. They reasserted the traditional liberal call for a color-blind state, which would protect only the civil rights of individuals" (xiv).

32. See Jamieson.

33. Although civility is informal in the sense that it is not explicitly legislated or mandated by the state, it does not mean that civility does not have statist benefits. As Norbert Elias argues in *The Civilizing Process*, one of the foundational historical surveys of civility, governing elites or the nobility needed to encourage and promote self-regulation of those governed in response to increasingly complex and bureaucratic societies. Gary S. Becker posits taste-based discrimination in *The Economics of Discrimination* (1957), touted as one of the first economic theories of discrimination. Contrary to beliefs that racism is an irrational behavior, employers rationally decide to discriminate and believe that there are economic incentives to do so.

34. Classifying incivility based on the type of parties in conflict, Jonathan Schonsheck attempts to provide a typology for incivility by isolating more substantive definitions in terms of "rudeness, rasp, and repudiation" that correlate to incivilities between individuals, individual and group, and groups, respectively: "Very generally, *rudeness* is essentially impoliteness. *Rasp* is the friction of jostling political, moral, religious, and ethnic groups that is inevitable in any multicultural 'liberal democracy'—a system, or theory, or philosophy of government that cherishes the values of toleration and mutual respect. Not everyone, however, subscribes to toleration and mutual respect; the *repudiation* of these values generates the third, and most serious, category of incivility" (169; original emphasis).

35. Such incivilities comprise one of the ostensible bases for the Black–Korean conflict, a deceptively persuasive narrative of Asian immigrants ignorant of U.S. social customs or disdainful of their non-Asian customers. Jennifer Lee describes how "civility in the city" is maintained through merchants who studiously and carefully strategize their daily behaviors to diminish or defuse potential interpersonal conflicts with their customers: "An important untold story is the mostly quotidian nature of commercial life in neighborhoods like New York's Harlem and West Philadelphia. The everyday interactions between Jewish, Korean, and African American merchants are not antagonistic, but rather positive, civil, and routine. The ordinariness of these merchant-customer relations is perplexing because

it contradicts both media accounts and the past scholarly research that highlight intergroup conflict in urban communities" (5–6).

36. In determinations of civility, bodies in public became divided in terms of spatial planning of neighborhoods and municipal areas. One way in which oppression and discrimination function is by ascribing uncivil bodies as too easily susceptible to hypersexuality or nonheteronormative sexualities and capable of moral and pathogenic contamination (see Shah).

37. Boyd mentions the lack of research that conclusively connects small acts of formal civility to big feelings of substantive civility that promote such crucial democratic principles as "civic equality" (865).

38. Boyd uses the 2005 civil unrest in France as an instructive example of incivility and its destructive ends (874). Michael Katz asks a provocative question from the other end of the civility spectrum: Why don't American cities burn? Or why don't they burn very often? He notes that many of the conditions identified by the 1968 Kerner Commission persist, often worsening socioeconomic conditions, yet there are no widespread protests (80).

39. In detailing the benefits of civility, Boyd importantly exposes some assumptions: "civility presupposes an active and affirmative moral relationship between persons. Being civil is a way of generating moral respect and democratic equality. Regardless of its functional role in maintaining the peace and order of society, civility is a moral obligation borne out of an appreciation of human equality" (875).

40. This logic makes incivility synonymous with savagery or stunted civilization. Norbert Elias argues that as civilization becomes more sophisticated, the distinction between adult and child widens. This distinction of maturity also divides and hierarchizes peoples and civilizations: separating the more advanced from the more backward, distinguishing the more modern from the more primitive. For nonwhite racial groups, for example, Black adult men and women were regularly addressed and referred to as "boys" or "girls" in the Jim Crow era and to portray the aspirations of U.S. empire at the turn of the nineteenth century, political cartoons commonly depicted invaded and annexed nations such as the Philippines, Hawai'i, Cuba, and Puerto Rico as squalling, unruly babies or children. See Ignacio et al.

41. That these nonwhites, noncitizens, and nonhumans can suffer and feel pain serves as a means of asserting their humanity and being recognized as human, but this interpellation also presupposes their original condition as being "almost the same, *but not quite*" human, to borrow Homi Bhabha's resonant phrase of the partial and incomplete presence of the colonial subject in contrast to the whole European citizen (319). No one who was considered as having a legitimate *a priori* claim *to* her humanity would have to *prove* it. To do so, Blacks and other nonwhites need to suffer so that Whites can feel sympathy for their plight or, within the meritocracy, to be perceived as worthy and prove themselves to be equal with Whites rather than being considered as inalienably equal. I take up this sentimental logic in chapter 1 and this paradox of meritocracy in chapter 2.

42. Asian Americans and Latinas/os routinely face stereotypes and perceptions of foreignness and, with it, illegality and criminality as immigrants are perceived to usurp the economic rights of citizens or dominate the jobs, wealth, and profits of the U.S. economy. These groups are perceived as perpetual foreigners, always alien to American politics and society and thus needing to prove their loyalty explicitly in order to demonstrate their desire for citizenship or naturalization in ways not expected for White European immigrants and their descendants. Proving one's civility also figures strongly in the continued struggles for civil rights. Through civil rights legislation, the state largely protects, even under the strict scrutiny test, immutable circumstances and characteristics: ability, gender, race, age, to name a few. Kenji Yoshino argues that the last battle of civil rights struggles is among those discriminated actions identified as "mutable behaviors," or the choice of the individual and group in terms of hairstyles, dress, public gestures, and linguistic ability and preference. Such behaviors are those prohibited in privatized spaces or workplaces, such as Disneyland, that restrict gay and lesbian couples from holding hands in public, require women to wear makeup on their job, prohibit Black flight attendants from wearing cornrows, and mandate bilingual employees speak only English in their workplace when not communicating with Spanish-speaking customers. These mutable behaviors are considered changeable without an undue or discriminatory burden placed on the parties involved and an emphasis on their ability to choose or inhabit other spaces where such behaviors would be tolerated. Homosexual couples can decide not to go to Disneyland or they may hold hands in other places, women can find another job without such a makeup requirement or where wearing makeup is of trifling consequence, Black flight attendants can wear a "natural" or other approved hairstyle instead, and bilingual employees can still communicate among themselves just as effectively in English.

43. I deliberately reference the exact language of the Declaration of Independence rather than revise this iconic phrase to include women or imply that women are also indexed in the universalist use of "men." In *States of Injury,* Wendy Brown argues that the family is the fundamental unit of traditional liberalisms and, within this unit, female and nonwhite citizens have always been conspicuous in the public sphere that was conceptualized to be the exclusive domain of White propertied men: their bodies and actions in public are hypervisible and uncivil, and rarely are they unseen and civil.

44. Thus it is crucial for democratic societies to account for the most unfree of individuals in determinations that affect the abstract citizen.

45. Contrary to U.S.-based civilitarian discourses, Étienne Balibar claims that "'Civility' is certainly an ambiguous term, but I think that its connotations are preferable to others, such as civilization, socialization, police and policing, politeness, and the like. In particular, 'civility' does not necessarily involve the idea of a suppression of 'conflicts' and 'antagonisms' in society, as if they were always the harbingers of violence and not the opposite" (15).

46. As sociologist Mary Jackman has noted in her analysis of paternalism, *The Velvet Glove: Paternalism and Conflict in Gender, Class, and Race Relations,* such gifts as love, friendship, and affection are used as rewards for successfully embodying the "idealized traits that have been assigned to her group" (78). By reframing such unequal power relations between groups into ones of "charming complementarity and mutual obligation," the dominant group defines "what the subordinates' needs are," which "permits them to cast their own role as magnanimously providing" for them (79). In *Scenes of Subjection: Terror, Slavery, and Self-Making in Nineteenth-Century America,* Saidiya Hartman identifies such feelings as charity and generosity in discourses of uplift that were developed around "fashioning obligation" for Blacks to Whites. Hartman is focused on the twinning of "consent and coercion, feeling and submission, intimacy and domination, and violence and reciprocity constitute what I term the discourse of seduction in slave law. . . . Seduction makes recourse to the idea of reciprocal and collusive relations" (81).

47. For Bonilla-Silva, "storylines" that deny guilt and displace responsibility are signaled by such memes as "The past is the past," "I didn't own slaves," "My (friend or relative) didn't get a (job or promotion) because a black (usually man) got it," "If (ethnic groups such as Jews, Italians, Irish, or Chinese) made it, how come blacks have not?" (12).

48. Feminist theorist Aimee Carrillo-Rowe exhorts us to engage in "transracial coalition building" and defines "transracial" to allude to "the transformative potential of such alliances in reconfiguring lines of difference, as well as the transnational component of such ties" (41 n. 4). I posit the transracial through Carrillo-Rowe's genealogy and connotations while importantly acknowledging the term's application and contested history in adoption studies that defines transracial "as *the adoption of a child that is of a different race than the adoptive parents.* The term most often refers to children of color adopted by white families in the Global North, and has been extensively examined and documented for more than 50 years by academics and members of the adoption triad: adoptees, birthparents, and adoptive parents" (McKee et al.; original emphasis). While Carrillo-Rowe primarily focuses on the term's liberatory possibilities, transracial adoption studies richly provide the troubled stakes of positing the "transracial" in its emphasis on family formation beyond blood and biology, naturalized kinship ties, inherent hierarchies in this family of feeling, racial conflicts among parents and children. See Simon and Alstein; McKee; Patton; Trenka et al.

49. Crystal Parikh's "ethics of betrayal" organizes these feelings and attitudes through the nuances of the traitorous minority subject: "In another significant variant, we might say that the nation betrays the minority subject by failing to uphold the promise of equal protection and treatment of all its citizens. In this instance, betrayal can only be described as unwittingly ethical, insofar as we must read for otherness *against* the foreclosure that the state attempts to accomplish" (16; original emphasis). Parikh's ethics of betrayal, which must necessarily be violations of trust and inclusion, are the ethical underpinnings of paradigms and relationships of racial triangulation and racial pyramidization.

1. Model Family Values and Sentimentalizing the Crisis

1. An immigrant from North Korea, Kim-Gibson is a filmmaker, painter, and memoirist. In collaboration with award-winning filmmaker Christine Choy and Asian American studies professor Elaine H. Kim, Kim-Gibson wrote, narrated, and directed the documentary that would collect the interviews of Korean immigrant women in Los Angeles three months after the crisis. Ten years later she would direct a reexamination of the violence, interviewing some of the same Korean Americans alongside Black, Latina/o, and White interviewees living and working in L.A. Kim-Gibson has also been a prominent advocate for reparations for the sexual slavery of Korean women during World War II and in 1998 directed *Silence Broken: Korean Comfort Women,* detailing their struggles, and in 1999 published a collection of these women's oral histories. Her films have been screened internationally and are often included in retrospectives of the 1992 violence and film festivals celebrating Asian American and Korean American communities.

2. Abelmann and Lie note that in 1990, two hundred thousand of the eight hundred thousand total Korean American population in the United States resided in Southern California.

3. Elaine Kim writes of how Korean Americans felt abandoned by the state and were devastated by the apparent travesty of American ideals: "When the Korean Americans in South Central and Koreatown dialed 911, nothing happened. When their stores and homes were being looted and burned to the ground, they were left completely alone for three horrifying days. How betrayed they must have felt by what they had believed was a democratic system that protects its people from violence. Those who trusted the government to protect them lost everything; those who took up arms after waiting for help for two days were able to defend themselves. It was as simple as that. What they had to learn was that, as in South Korea, protection in the United States is by and large for the rich and powerful. If there were a choice between Westwood and Koreatown, it was clear that Koreatown would have to be sacrificed. The familiar concept of privilege for the rich and powerful would have been easy for the Korean immigrant to grasp if only those exhortations about democracy and equality had not obfuscated the picture" (219).

4. See Gotanda; Stevenson, "Latasha Harlins" and *The Contested Murder of Latasha Harlins.*

5. As I discuss later, I build on the frameworks and discussions of Sumi Cho, Neil Gotanda, and especially Claire Jean Kim.

6. For a more thorough discussion of the media and its representation of the Korean American community, see Elaine H. Kim; Zia.

7. In an interview, Elaine Kim discusses a woman in a demonstration at the Los Angeles City Hall who was excited to talk to a PBS reporter through her daughter, who translated. But the interview was never broadcast in translation, only the image of the woman with ink on her face (Song, 241 n. 2).

8. Brenda Stevenson provides a detailed succession of events for the entire tape: "Harlins approached the store's counter. She had a backpack in her hands.

She and Du exchanged words. Du tried to grab Harlins's backpack. Du grabbed Harlins by her sweater and pulled her across the counter. Harlins struck Du in the face four times. Du fell back. She got up and pulled again at the backpack. Du got the backpack and tossed it behind the counter. She picked up a stool and threw it at Harlins, who moved out of the way. Du bent down behind the counter. She stood up with a holstered gun. Harlins bent down, picked up the bottle which had fallen from the backpack to the floor. As she started to place it on the counter, Du struggled to get the gun out of the holster. Du swatted the bottle off of the counter. Harlins turned to walk away from the counter. Du pointed the gun at Harlins. The gun went off. Harlins fell face down to the floor. Soon Ja Du crawled up on the checkout counter and looked down at Harlins's body" ("Latasha Harlins," 158–59).

9. The controversy over Harlins's death, Du's trial, and Karlin's reduced sentencing would sink efforts to achieve conciliation between Blacks and Koreans through organizations such as the Black-Korean Alliance, one of the first interracial institutions established to mediate between these communities (Zia, 174–81).

10. The odd phrasing of Karlin's colloquy in this quotation, that Du would not be "beginning a life of crime," is a telling phrase when juxtaposed to Karlin's claims that Harlins, had she survived, might have been charged with assault. Given Du was fifty-four years old at the time of the shooting and Harlins's youth, the notion of "beginning a life" or career seems more applicable to Harlins than to Du. Karlins is implicitly arguing that Harlins's life is even more worthless given she was beginning her life as a future career criminal.

11. Before sentencing, Harlins's grandmother made a plea for justice for her granddaughter's tragic death. But Du's light sentence and Karlin's reasoning might have depended on how much Karlin blamed Harlins's multigenerational and extended family, her mother's violent death, and her father's desertion. These factors beyond Harlins's control likely impacted the judge's decision that Harlins was not a victim. In terms of what constitutes a normative middle-class family, Karlin would privilege Du's nuclear family over Harlins's multigenerational, extended one. Rather than seeing Harlins as a young girl subject to her difficult circumstances, Karlin instead recognized Du's difficult circumstances within the context of her family dynamics as more sympathetic and deserving in her colloquy.

12. Harlins's life and family circumstances were prominently featured in the appeal: "The probation report also reveals that Latasha had suffered many painful experiences during her life, including the violent death of her mother. Latasha lived with her extended family (her grandmother, younger brother and sister, aunt, uncle and niece) in what the probation officer described as 'a clean, attractively furnished three-bedroom apartment' in South Central Los Angeles. Latasha had been an honor student at Bret Harte Junior High School, from which she had graduated the previous spring. Although she was making only average grades in high school, she had promised that she would bring her grades up to her former standard. Latasha was involved in activities at a youth center as an assistant cheerleader, member of the drill team and a summer junior camp counselor. She was a good athlete and an active church member" (quoted in Gotanda, 242).

13. Du would testify that she thought Harlins was a gang member after her son had told her how to identify dangerous customers. Du herself was working on March 16, 1991, in place of her son, who had been threatened by the Crips because of his promise to testify against two gang members (Stevenson, "Latasha Harlins," 158).

14. Given Judith Halberstam's concept of "queer temporalities" in direct opposition to "repro-time" of the traditional family, I take up the queer and crisis dimensions of state-building discourse of the heteropatriarchal, nuclear family in more detail elsewhere; see Itagaki.

15. I cite Collins's work, although I acknowledge a long tradition in anthropological and sociological research on the family, especially in terms of innovations in family structure and affective ties across different cultures and historical periods. For the purposes of this chapter, I am most interested in the repeated return to the heteropatriarchal nuclear family and how one's identity, privileges, and rights are assessed from one's deviation or cleavage to this putative norm.

16. Immediately after the L.A. Crisis, then Vice President Dan Quayle delivered what has become known as the "Murphy Brown" speech in May 1992 in which he argued that "the lawless social anarchy which we saw is directly related to the breakdown of family structure. [*sic*] personal responsibility and social order in too many areas of our society" (Quayle).

17. Here I allude to Samuel Huntington's influential and often-cited work on foreign policy, *The Clash of Civilizations and the Remaking of World Order*.

18. For a recitation of these socioeconomic successes, see Bell; McGurn. A central position for Asian American studies since its inception has been to challenge and debunk the model minority thesis; for a foundational refutation, see Osajima.

19. Attempting to appeal to Asian Americans in terms of small government and free market principles, this article exhorts Asian Americans to join with Whites to create "a bona-fide American language of civil rights," rejecting a language that McGurn accuses of only benefiting Blacks. In his focus on Asian immigrant communities and their assumed shorter history in the United States, "their adoptive land," McGurn defines this "one language" as having excluded Asian Americans, rather than acknowledging how civil rights initiatives have been used to support Asian Americans' upward mobility.

20. In her short essay "The Afro-Asian Analogy," Lye provides an important critique of Kim's racial triangulation. Lye posits that Kim's psychological and political justifications for her influential relational schema do not fully explain the uneven racialization of African Americans and Asian Americans: "If the black struggle for advancement has historically rested on appeals to racial equality," Kim writes, "the Asian American struggle has at times rested on appeals to be considered white (and to be granted the myriad privileges bundled with whiteness)" (47). This characterization of the assimilationist tendency of Asian American politics is undermotivated by the theory of racial triangulation, since it is not clear why the subjects of exclusion should be more likely than the subjects of inferiority to substitute a desire for whiteness for their real desires. We might observe, though, that the reification of whiteness Kim attributes to a mistaken Asian American

politics inheres in her account of the original agency of Asian American racialization, which is an inherited white supremacy constituted in relation to black slavery" (Lye, 1733). Lye importantly provides a corrective for Asian American studies and intellectual desires to elaborate a "nonderivative nature of Asian racialization" (ibid.). I would also add to Lye's critique that both these Asian American studies scholars, as well as those positing the anchoring "antiblackness" of comparative race studies (see Sexton), often do not fully contend with the colonial indigenous object of antiblackness that a work such as Denise Ferriera da Silva's *Global Idea of Race* traces through the intellectual history of liberal humanist philosophy. In this sense indigeneity is the obfuscated analytic or vertex in my schema of racial pyramidization.

21. Karlin clearly wanted to reward or, at the very least, take into account her reading of Du as a good mother and part of a good family in Du's decision to take her son's place in tending the store.

22. Not until after the 1992 Crisis, and after significant community pressure, was a Korean American reporter appointed to the editorial board of the *Los Angeles Times* for the first time. Korean Americans were especially infuriated by one national network's coverage: "Ted Koppel of ABC News dedicated two weeks of *Nightline*'s programs to on-site coverage in Los Angeles, visiting with African American gang members and discussing black-Korean tensions. But Koppel didn't speak to Korean Americans. Finally, after complaints of bias by Asian Americans in Los Angeles, attorney Angela Oh was brought on *Nightline* for a few minutes as a lone Korean voice" (Zia, 183). Academic studies of the L.A. Crisis have also reflected an absence of Korean or Asian American perspectives. For example, Darnell Hunt's important study on Black, Latina/o, and White focus-group responses to news footage of the crisis leaves out a comparable Asian American group of viewers.

23. Although Kim-Gibson alludes to works such as Anna Deavere Smith's documentary drama *Twilight* in *Wet Sand*'s interracial mix of community activists, authors, experts, and people she encounters (for example, a White employee of a craft store, a Black grandmother on her front porch), the 2004 documentary follows the stories of two Korean American families, interviewing each of the family members and showing their places of worship and work: the Lees and another couple who bought a café in a Whiter, more upscale neighborhood after losing their business in the 1992 Crisis. While other racial perspectives are included, I posit that clearly the affective heart of *Wet Sand* mirrors that of *Sa-I-Gu:* the financial and familial losses of Korean Americans from the L.A. Crisis.

24. In U.S. sentimental discourse, Little Eva's death is the archetype, "the epitome of Victorian sentimentalism," in Harriet Beecher Stowe's *Uncle Tom's Cabin* (1852), "the *summa theologica* of nineteenth-century America's religion of domesticity, a brilliant redaction of the culture's favorite story about itself—the story of salvation through motherly love" (Tompkins, 269).

25. Sociologist Edward Chang has written extensively on how "the riots raised the important question of what it means to be 'Korean American'" and how the 1992 Crisis forged a Korean America ("America's First Multiethnic 'Riots,'" 113).

26. And the kind of misrepresentation in the media are for reasons akin to the repeated coverage of Reginald Denny's beating to the point in which Denny becomes just as famous a household name, if not more, than Rodney King, news reporters ignoring the dozens of beatings and assaults taking place at that intersection afterward. The media expected its audiences to identify with Denny, the unwitting interloper into a full-scale civil unrest, just as we, the media viewers, might have believed ourselves to be such hapless captive audiences.

27. Journalists and scholars have already likened the response to anti-Korean violence in the L.A. Crisis—the development in Korean American identity—to other group and national identities forged in such events as the Nazi Holocaust and U.S. imperialist interventions abroad (see Prashad).

28. Elaine Kim, in "Home Is Where the *Han* Is," discusses how U.S. news coverage of a protest against the Korean government failed to interview any of the protesters or leaders, but the story that immediately followed covered protests in Poland in which reporters interviewed and translated the answers of some Polish citizens, including President Lech Walesa. Kim also notes the furious responses to her *Newsweek* essay that often insulted her U.S. loyalty and patriotism, cast doubt on her U.S. citizenship, told her to go "back to Korea," and accused her of being ungrateful for the U.S. blood and treasure expended for democracy in Asian countries.

29. Sylvia Wynter exposes the invisibility and dehumanization of these subjects in her essay "No Humans Involved," taking the slang of the criminal justice system for sex workers and young Black and Latino men to show their lack of access to the legal claims of full citizenship (13).

2. In/Civility, with Colorblindness and Equal Treatment for All

1. For a genealogy of the "badman" in African American folk heroic creation, see Roberts. The badman is an outlaw folk hero that is a combination of "conjurer and trickster" after emancipation: "The badman emerged as an outlaw folk hero whose characteristic actions offered a model of behavior for dealing with the power of whites under the law that created conditions threatening to the values of the black community from both within and without" (215).

2. Over the nineteenth century, the property requirement was first lifted for White men and the post–Civil War constitutional amendments extended citizenship and the franchise to former male slaves. Of course, Jim Crow voting laws after Reconstruction would drastically reduce this latter franchise for Black and poor White voters, given their literacy or good character qualifications—in essence, their *merit* was assessed in any manner that local, county, and state voter registrars saw fit; the Voting Rights Act of 1965 outlawed such arbitrary tests.

3. I reference here the famous article "Broken Windows," which dominated restrictive law-and-order policies well into the 2000s; see J. Wilson and Kelling. The argument's most controversial and famous implementation was to deter crime in New York City under Mayor Rudy Giuliani; see Neil Smith. In this logic,

broken windows, graffiti, and other small crimes and misdemeanors should garner an outsized response. This show of force and punishment, Wilson and Kelling posit, deters crimes of escalating number and magnitude as well as dissuades others from such behavior. It is a familiar logic of excessive reactions for minority individuals and communities in U.S. history, given, for example, the often brutal repression sanctioned by "racial etiquette" under Jim Crow in which entire Black communities were terrorized, burned out, and members lynched in order to punish Black citizens for their perceived encroachment onto Whites' interests through successful businesses, voting rights, or interracial relationships (see Mitchell).

4. Even such a flexible concept of putatively limited descriptive value as Benedict Anderson's notion of nationalism as an imagined community relies upon exclusion. In the case of the U.S. body politic, there is a disjunction between actual political citizenship and the imagined community of those who merit its privileges, rights, and protections.

5. See James C. Scott.

6. See Ferguson; D. M. Scott; Tolentino; and Lasch-Quinn.

7. Ellis clearly distinguishes the NBA's revisionism of Black freedom struggles from that of Black conservatives such as Thomas Sowell and Stanley Crouch: "Nationalist pride continues to be one of the strongest forces in the black community and the New Black Aesthetic stems straight from that tradition. It is not an apolitical, art-for-art's-sake fantasy. We realize that despite this current buppie artist boom, most black Americans have seldom had it worse" (Ellis, "New Black Aesthetic," 239). Ellis, moreover, identifies how state and state-sanctioned anti-Black violence continues to forge a collective racial consciousness across class lines: "The culturally mulatto *Cosby* girls are equally as black as a black teenage welfare mother. Neither side of the tracks should forget that. Edmund Perry, bouncing from Harlem to Exeter and on his way to Stanford, might have been shot by that white police officer because the old world, both black and white, was too narrow to embrace a black prep from Harlem" (235).

8. Insofar as injury and suffering generate the claims for protest, Beatty's aims would largely coincide with James Baldwin's famed critique of the protest novel: "The 'protest' novel, so far from being disturbing, is an accepted and comforting aspect of the American scene, ramifying that framework we believe to be so necessary. Whatever unsettling questions are raised are evanescent, titillating; remote, for this has nothing to do with us, it is safely ensconced in the social arena, where, indeed, it has nothing to do with anyone, so that finally we receive a very definite thrill of virtue from the fact that we are reading such a book at all" (19). Baldwin lambasts the self-congratulatory sentimentality with which readers understand protest novels, and I posit that Beatty's novel is a protest of "everybody's protest novel," which disrupts and makes self-conscious such "thrills of virtue" on the part of readers.

9. I use this term in the ironic, multilayered way in which Stephen L. Carter deployed this term in his 1992 memoirs, *Reflections of an Affirmative Action Baby*.

10. I allude to both the trauma of chattel slavery in Toni Morrison's 1987 novel *Beloved* and the "unspeakable things unspoken" as Morrison memorably describes

trauma's absent aftermath in American literature and culture in her Tanner Lectures on Human Values given at the University of Michigan in 1988.

11. I am referring to the discussion of "rational discrimination" in legal jurisprudence in legal critic Jody K. Armour's study *Negrophobia and Reasonable Racism*. In outlining "reasonable racism," Armour identifies how White fear of Black violence has been used successfully in self-defense and disability legal arguments: since Blacks are disproportionately convicted of violent crimes, a "reasonable man" could conclude that all Blacks are violent and intending to harm (3).

12. In his classic work centering Whiteness studies, *Wages of Whiteness: Race and the Making of the American Working Class* (1991), David Roediger traces how White elites actively cultivated an anti-Black, White working-class identity to usurp possible transracial class alliances between White and Black laborers. In this conflict, Beatty alludes to the late twentieth-century manifestation of such de facto segregation and interracial hostilities: on the one hand, the truck driver's negrophobia, and on the other, Gunnar and Nick's frustration with the middle-class values, rules, and aspirations that regulate their lives.

13. In the introduction, I discuss these two primary "meanings clusters" of civility as outlined in Virginia Sapiro's framework.

14. See C. Harris, "Constitution."

15. The vexing question of how to increase diversity in higher and postgraduate education is increasingly contested in university admissions processes. In terms of Equal Protection jurisprudence, the Supreme Court transformed the attempt to provide equal opportunities in education into the emphasis on creating the circumstances for equal competition in college and graduate admissions. *The Regents of the University of California v. Bakke* (1978) provided the legal architecture for political colorblindness, setting the precedent for later cases that eroded at affirmative action in hiring and allocation of government contracts. Colorblindness comprises a constellation of practices and ideals: racial neutrality, equal treatment, and individual merit that are delineated in Justice Lewis Powell's opinion.

16. In the lead-up to his signature "workfare" in the Welfare Reform Act of 1996, President Bill Clinton gave a speech in 1993 at the same church as Reverend Martin Luther King Jr.'s final sermon before his assassination in 1968. In terms that overlap with former Vice President Quayle's, Clinton exhorts his immediate and national audience to personally ensure their own communities' safety and upward mobility in a public-private partnership, or, more uncharitably, to compensate for what the state refuses to ameliorate: "But unless we deal with the ravages of crime and drugs and violence and unless we recognize that it's due to the breakdown of the family, the community, and the disappearance of jobs, and unless we say some of this cannot be done by Government, because we have to reach deep inside to the values, the spirit, the soul, and the truth of human nature, none of the other things we seek to do will ever take us where we need to go" (Clinton).

17. Quayle's speech reprises the myth of upward mobility that promises the working poor prosperity for themselves or, at least, their children: "And in America

we have always had poor people. But in this dynamic, prosperous nation, poverty has traditionally been a stage through which people pass on their way to joining the great middle class. And if one generation didn't get very far up the ladder—their ambitious, better-educated children would" (Quayle). Such well-entrenched beliefs of expanding opportunities and genealogical uplift deploy a constellation of troubling assumptions. First of all, in genealogical uplift, one might never see the recognition of one's personal ambitions or enjoy access to better education, but one's children are promised such opportunities. Such a deferred dream is promoted as an equivalent exchange for one's own diminished life opportunities and material rewards—an equality achieved only across the generations. In these terms, poverty is merely a temporary socioeconomic way station for the deserving. Those with the meritorious qualities of ambition and perseverance would undoubtedly push their future generations up the ladder of success—despite how rare such movement actually is for those at the bottom. Even more astounding is the implicit corollary to this statement: that those in disadvantaged circumstances today are actually the products of past generations of failure, vice, and immorality; therefore, impoverished children *justly* bear the sins of their unsuccessful ancestors in the form of diminished life chances and opportunities.

18. The family's embrace of such unsavory accounts is even more heightened by the likelihood that these ancestral exploits are, in fact, made up.

19. In analyzing how *The White Boy Shuffle* "rejects the trajectory of native sons and masculine privilege for a postmodern option of dismantling gender hierarchies and binaries" (99), L. H. Stallings provides a complex reading of what appears to be a recitation on an exclusively patriarchal lineage that is furthermore exalted by Gunnar's mother, who has adopted this ancestry as her own. Gunnar's male ancestors and these generations of White assimilationist role models belie Myrdal's and Moynihan's arguments about the pathology of the Black family through its matriarchal structure: "Beatty revises that determination to the father, as, according to Myrdal, access to the father's name and law would mean a functional heteronormative family resembling the white family. However, Beatty reveals the fictions of sociological assessments of the black family and black men in his revision" (105).

20. Young anticipates that this elite, based on such a limited notion of talent and ability, would deincentivize the cultivation and recognition of talents that do not directly benefit industry and technology driven by the cold war, even though these abilities might be just as important to society. Such a meritocracy has its critics who resent or find limiting this unbalanced workforce. The maintenance of a meritocracy requires tools of exclusion and limited valuations of people and their abilities, a form of social engineering in a putatively free market of labor. Young satirizes the future of British society in which, after the implementation of a meritocratic structure, the meritorious elite emerges through people's abilities to make scientific and technological advances.

21. Young cautions that the traditionally wealthy and powerful can now justify their unequal resources as earned, since they are putative outcomes of a meritocracy.

This defense creates an awkward tautology of merit and its rewards: "Virtue leads to success, success makes a person virtuous, success indicates virtue, or apparent success is not real success unless one is also virtuous" (Hochschild, 23). The transformative potential of success alludes to the paradox that Beatty parodies in Gunnar's ancestral lineage: even iniquity can be transformed into virtue.

As McNamee and Miller point out in their overview of the "meritocracy myth," the deeper the inequality, the stronger the ideology. They note the difficulty in measuring how much of an impact the traits of "innate talent, hard work, proper attitude, and moral virtue" have on "getting ahead" (16). So much so that the *ideal* ideology is one that cannot be disproved: for example, one's reward in the afterlife or next life in a caste society and the divine right of kings in a monarchy (McNamee and Miller, 3–4). Thus, the belief in the meritocracy is shaped by the idea that the "right attitude and moral character" (16) directly leads to merit and its rewards, and precisely because this cause-and-effect is so difficult to prove, empirically and quantitatively, this direct correspondence between the "right stuff" and success is so tenacious a truism (25).

22. Specifically, the enduring material legacy of slavery, the failure of Reconstruction in the systemic anti-Black terror and violence of what historian Rayford Logan terms "the nadir," and the infamous Counter-Intelligence Program (COIN-TELPRO) of the Federal Bureau of Investigation that hounded and undermined post–World War II Black and Third World radical activism.

23. Feminist geographer Mary Thomas notes a similar pattern in a Los Angeles school, where the teachers and students espoused what Jodi Melamed has defined as neoliberal multiculturalism while still showing racist and xenophobic behaviors.

24. In a charitable interpretation, this nonsensical saying represents the teacher's attempt to encourage the students to realize their own self-worth and potential whatever their racial identities and serve perhaps as an inspiration for them to treat others in a race-neutral way. However, the slogan's awkward personification of the sun, and its placement above the blackboard in a symbolic governance of and inspiration for the class, alludes to the largely discredited proposition that race is linked to differential moral or intellectual capacities, which dominated scientific studies to the mid-twentieth century and continue to persist in influential research studies. The widely discussed synthesis of studies, *The Bell Curve,* attests in its collation of data to show a racial hierarchy of intelligence quotients for Asians, Blacks, and Whites; see Herrnstein and Murray.

25. There is perhaps another, more sinister reading possible of his teacher's shirt slogan and its graphic, given the mass death Gunnar will later promote in the novel's conclusion.

26. The warring elephants of black and white that become a harmonious gray mimic the genetic concept of incomplete dominance in which experiments of cross-fertilizing white and red flowering snapdragon or four o'clock plants produce pink flowers. However, the complex genetic and phenotypic expressions of

animals cannot always be simplified into the mixing of shades and colors in art—white and red make pink, white and black make gray.

27. This intermarried, multiracial future is manifested in what Donna Haraway terms a "SimEve," the simulated visual image of a woman, an "ideal racial synthesis," created through an "odd computerized updating of typological categories of the nineteenth and early twentieth centuries" (259). In the fall of 1993, *Time* magazine's special issue on immigration ran the computer-generated face of a light-skinned woman with slightly wavy dark hair on the cover, dubbing her the "remarkable preview" of "The New Face of America: How Immigrants Are Shaping the World's First Multicultural Society." Haraway further comments that the development of computer morphing programs "has proved irresistible in the United States for 1990s mass cultural racialized kinship discourse on human unity and diversity. Never has there been a better toy for playing out sexualized racial fantasies, anxieties, and dreams" (261). And unlike the mid-1990s of Haraway's essay, which required computer programmers and cutting-edge technology, today such morphing possibilities are the everyday function of smart-phone apps and handheld gaming consoles.

28. Of course, there is also further gendered limitation to this metaphor: the level playing field is the single-sex province of male *or* female competitors, not both. Similarly, in Equal Protection jurisprudence stemming from affirmative-action test cases, the Supreme Court fails to address both the racial *and* gender identities of the applicant, and how arguments against affirmative action, such as those deployed in support of California's Proposition 209, for example, generally ignored the explicit affirmative action benefits to White women, one of the target populations.

3. The Territorialization of Civility, the Spatialization of Revenge

1. In his essay "The 'Underclass' as Myth and Symbol," Adolph Reed identifies the condemnation of individual behaviors of non-middle-class, female, and young nonwhites (Black and Latina/o) that is especially evident at the intersection of these identity formations in terms of how the opposition to teenage pregnancy and sexuality derides a most vulnerable population. Nonwhite, poor, or working-class teenage girls are vilified; their "living and reproductive practices" are condemned as "the transmission belt that drives the cycle" of poverty (191). He criticizes the circular logic that motivates this condemnation of individual behaviors: "If the one woman's decision expresses pathology because she makes it in poverty, then we have fallen into a nonsensical tautology: she is poor because she is pathological and pathological because she is poor" (184).

2. Antonio emerges covered in mud and Guillermo's blood from the sewer tunnel; he is symbolically reborn into the United States, apparently ready to embrace the life his friend José Juan has miraculously found for both of them: a home and jobs. Providing Antonio with figurative salvation after the violence and his personal vengeance, José Juan fulfills the roles to which both his names allude,

the father Joseph and cousin John the Baptist of Jesus, male nurturers and protectors of Christ.

3. While both immigrants and citizens are identity formations of the liberal state, the facility with which documented immigrants are made illegal and racialized citizens are made into (illegal) immigrants is important here. Aside from the shifting borders of U.S. territorial expansion that have affected Caribbean, Mexican, Central American, and Pacific Islander populations, to name a few, the lived histories of U.S. citizens without papers persist on the margins of U.S. discourses of inclusion. The criminalization of immigration—what was once a civil tort—has become a criminal offense framing an entire political identity; see Ngai.

4. Antonio has been unable to reconcile his life in Los Angeles with his past life in Guatemala City and then San Cristóbal. Significantly, Guillermo is made vulnerable by finally recognizing the blurring of the past and present, a past identity and life that he has deliberately forgotten. However, such a psychic blurring sutures memories and actions in Guatemala with those in the United States, showing how domestic policies are shaped by international ones. Later in this chapter, I will discuss how Tobar thematically links U.S. domestic policies of racial containment with human rights violations occurring in Guatemala.

5. Tobar refers to his main characters as Antonio and Longoria. I refer to these characters by their first names not only for parallelism but also because the thematic arc of the text, as evidenced in the references to Guillermo in the section titles, from "the Sergeant" to "Guillermo," shows the stripping of the character's brutal identities and genocidal desires and a return to the joyful innocence of his younger self before his military conscription. At the end of the novel, Tobar depicts Guillermo's dying vision of planting seeds with his mother in the time before his conscription and crimes against humanity.

6. It is less clear why Guillermo might have immigrated from Guatemala, although Tobar implies that he was impressed with the cleanliness and orderliness of the U.S. military bases during his counterinsurgency training in North Carolina.

7. Begun with the 1994 Oslo Accord, the Accord for a Fair and Lasting Peace in 1996 finalized the truce between the Guatemalan government and the opposition army, the Guatemalan Revolutionary National Unity (URNG).

8. The overturning of former President Ríos Montt's conviction in 2013 led observers to question the efficacy of the Guatemalan legal process in the indictments and trials of future defendants. Guatemalan President Otto Pérez Molina himself is accused of personally supervising the mass killings of the Mayan Ixil under the orders of then-General Ríos Montt.

9. Critics argued that the CEH was the weakest of the truth commissions being conducted at the time (R. Wilson, 20), since it had no civil society representatives, no mandate for legally enforceable outcomes, no naming of perpetrators and victims, and an implausibly short time frame of six months to a year to investigate thirty-six years of civil war; eventually the commission would operate for two years. Furthermore, its scope was limited to abuses linked to "armed conflict," excluding "journalists, researchers and US citizens" and did not have the legal powers of

"search, seizure and subpoena" like South Africa's Truth and Reconciliation Commission (ibid.). Moreover, the government and military could argue that their brutal scorched-earth policies were a necessary evil of armed aggression. However, the findings of the CEH helped Spanish courts to indict former President Ríos Montt along with several other high-ranking officials in 2003 and issue warrants for their arrest, a decade before Guatemalan courts convicted Ríos Montt.

10. However, even REMHI, despite its more comprehensive findings and identification of perpetrators and victims, faced criticism that it might encourage Christian forgiveness rather than legal punishments and reparations (R. Wilson, 20).

11. See Huggins, Haritos-Fatouros, and Zimbardo.

12. I have argued elsewhere about "crisis temporalities" in relation to human rights and how the conception of time shapes the urgency and remedy of the issue. See Itagaki.

13. The Guatemalan government and military were supported by the Reagan administration and this support was a factor in the extraordinarily low numbers of applicants who were approved for asylum. The State Department refused to grant political asylum to almost all Salvadorans and Guatemalans fleeing the genocide—only 328 of 3,373 Salvadorans and 3 of 761 Guatemalans—in 1984 because these refugees were labeled economic migrants instead of political refugees. As a point of comparison, Hamilton and Chinchilla note the much higher percentages of successful applicants from such countries as Afghanistan, China, and Poland and whose asylum was a cold war prerogative (Hamilton and Chinchilla, 135).

14. Assimilation paradoxically requires such forgetting or even a kind of necessary disloyalty to one's past and present obligations. The two men are ostensibly lifted out of homelessness because José Juan is able to create a new life in the United States with a new girlfriend in Los Angeles, who provides him and Antonio with a home and jobs. Her generosity will allow both some kind of fresh start despite José Juan's wife and family across the border and Antonio's dead wife and son. The naming of Antonio's friend and benefactor alludes to a famed human rights activist in Guatemala, Bishop Juan José Gerardi Conedera, the motivating force behind the REMHI report. Two days after its publication, Bishop Gerardi was assassinated and three military officers were convicted in his murder; a fellow priest was sentenced for conspiracy.

15. The difference between the colloquial meaning and historical purpose is instructive. The Hammurabi Codex is one of the earliest examples of a state constitution. The most famous of its wide-ranging set of laws is its punishment in kind, "an eye for an eye." In contemporary use, the phrase connotes vengeance; however, the codex was established precisely in order to reserve punishment for the state, taking private acts of revenge and punishment out of the hands of individuals or groups in conflict; see Miller, *Eye for an Eye*.

16. I posit that Tobar's methodology is not necessarily comparing the scale of human suffering between the United States and Guatemala in terms of which populations suffered more terror or victimization—more specifically, between displaced

peoples such as the homeless people or evicted residents of Los Angeles and the thousands dead or disappeared during the Guatemalan civil wars. I instead claim that Tobar is deliberately juxtaposing two governmental strategies for making some populations disposable by pointing to very similar juridical rationales given for inflicting human suffering or property losses, although with different outcomes.

17. Tobar was one of four dramaturges that playwright Anna Deavere Smith consulted in developing *Twilight: Los Angeles, 1992,* which premiered at the Mark Taper Forum in Los Angeles in 1993.

18. For an example of how scholars have used Tobar's fiction and journalism to discuss Central American history, identity, and community in the United States, see Hamilton and Chinchilla, 206–7.

19. On the author's personal website, he links the original *Los Angeles Times* news articles he wrote on Chicas's battle (www.hectortobar.com).

20. According to Giorgio Agamben, the first steps in the annihilation of a people are containment, such as in the Warsaw ghetto, and a sequential stripping of the legal, political, civil, and, finally, human identity to render bare life, an anonymous, unsacrificial, and thus unpunishable death. This logic of escalating nonpersonhood justifies the state's actions in relation to its constituency.

21. I thank Lilia Fernandez for the last phrase.

22. A 1993 report, *Civil Liberties in Crisis: Los Angeles during the Emergency,* published by the American Civil Liberties Union (ACLU), aggregated the numerous incidents that occurred that supported such claims of state vengeance exacted against residents of Los Angeles whose daily routines were rendered criminal or illegal. These were the homeless and nightshift employees who lived in or near the crisis's "hot spots" and who unwittingly violated a *voluntary* curfew under Mayor Tom Bradley's state of emergency; yet they were arrested, jailed, and then encouraged not to contest their charges. Suburban residents of L.A. County were not similarly apprehended and punished, despite being under the same emergency orders. The ACLU report details how the criminal justice system used the thousands arrested and overloaded courts to suspend the right to a speedy trial and threaten the people arrested with a wait of up to thirty days in jail before being arraigned if they didn't plead out to a misdemeanor, whether guilty or innocent. The ACLU noted that this threat disproportionately disadvantaged those without bail money who were pressured to take an unfavorable plea bargain rather than risk losing their wages for thirty days and, quite possibly, their jobs.

23. Hamilton and Chinchilla note that despite the large number of Latinas/os in Koreatown and South Central Los Angeles, media and political discourse rarely characterized these areas as Latina/o, instead identifying Black residents as the representative population.

24. I allude to the deep resistance to national conversations about slavery and U.S. foreign policy from the cold war through the War on Terror.

25. Like a balance scale with weights added or taken away from one side and then the other, one action can cancel out the other, but there is no consideration whether the scale was unfairly balanced beforehand, and this balance is largely

imagined as between two racial groups rather than among multiple constituencies. With racial balance reframed as racial equilibrium, we should not try to rectify the past but, rather, we should be more fair and balanced from this day forward, secure in our newly enlightened racial consciousness. This is an awkward contradiction to punishment in terms of reparation and atonement. It is ludicrous for the justice system to operate as if no injury can be repaired, so it is more revelatory that it is this area in which reparations are so unpopular. Of course, most losses are those for which there can never be adequate remedy; however, the question remains why there is no attempt by the public and private sector even to consider reparations.

4. At the End of Tragedy

1. Smith credits Supreme Court Justices Ruth Bader Ginsberg and Stephen G. Breyer as a "major impetus" for filming *Twilight* after they told her that the play should be seen by all high school students (Weinraub, C15).

2. Smith's performances of *Twilight* in the mid-1990s largely relied on her audiences' heightened consciousness of the media coverage of the L.A. Crisis. The 1993 audiences for *Twilight* at the Mark Taper Forum in Los Angeles were perhaps particularly well informed regarding the crisis. An overwhelming majority (77 percent) of Los Angeles households watched part of the continual news coverage of the violence on May 1, 1992 (Hunt, 1). Audiences around the nation and the world followed the events in Los Angeles through print and visual media networks. Because audiences present at Smith's performance are likely to have seen some of the local or national news coverage of the crisis, there is the inclusive possibility that anyone could have been interviewed and that anyone could have been included in Smith's performance as bystanders.

3. I allude here to literary critic King-Kok Cheung's study of silence as a strategy in Asian American women's writing.

4. The play's earliest form as previews at the Mark Taper Forum did not have video footage shown onstage, but her later shows across the nation did. The 2003 Dramatists Play Service version of *Twilight* geared toward performance recommends that the play should be staged with these video images or footage with the option of re-creating the scenes onstage (Smith, 4).

5. Here I allude to the pathbreaking theorizations by Sandra Harding, Patricia Hill Collins and Kimberlé Crenshaw, Gloria Anzaldúa, María Lugones, and Chela Sandoval, respectively.

6. Feminist theorist Aimee Carrillo-Rowe defines her use of "transracial" in the following way: "I use the term transracial in lieu of the term 'multiracial' to signal the transformative potential of such alliances in reconfiguring lines of difference, as well as the transnational component of such ties" (41 n. 4).

7. I allude to Christina Gledhill's comprehensive overview of what she identifies as "the melodramatic field" in film, intentionally choosing "field" rather than a definition because of the challenges of classifying melodrama in any one way:

"genre? style? mode? ideology?" (7). I posit that the similarly sprawling nature of tragedy demands a comparable recognition of its challenges to definition and function but prefer "framework" as an organizational metaphor.

8. Some landmark policy and polemical texts in this vein are Oscar Handlin's classic 1961 study, *The Uprooted;* the legendary 1965 Moynihan Report, officially titled *The Negro Family: The Case for National Action;* and Charles Murray's controversial 1981 neoconservative polemic, *Losing Ground.*

9. For more of these op-eds, features, and essays culled from independent and alternative print sources, see Hazen.

10. I also hesitate to reference an aftermath to tragedy because such phrasing would imply that tragedy is equivalent to the tragic action.

11. Given that events and participants in the L.A. Crisis are gendered in male terms, where are the women in retelling narratives of it? And in noting this absence as just one starting point, the political investments of the dominant narratives emerge. The actors most memorably involved in the crisis represent patriarchy, governmental authority, and militarism: King, Denny, King's police attackers and Denny's assailants, LAPD Chief Daryl Gates, Mayor Tom Bradley, the National Guard and federal troops, Governor Pete Wilson, and President George H. W. Bush. Violence and action, just like the seemingly ungendered term "youths," are used as descriptors of the crisis. White-on-Black/Black-on-White violence is read as masculine, an epic struggle between Black and White men over property, a category that includes women and children in addition to material resources. In fact, there were numerous women who played a significant role in the events leading up to the crisis and who were elided or forced out of the events: California Highway Patrol officer Melanie Singer, the first officer to arrive on the scene of King's arrest, who was then pushed aside by male LAPD officers; one of these men would later describe such a breach of protocol as protecting Singer from King's sexual advances. The only nonwhites on the jury were two women of color, one Filipina and one Latina; the latter would later reveal the enormous pressure she felt from the other jurists to acquit the officers of their charges. See Reinhold.

12. Smith transcribed a speech given by 35th District Congressional Representative Maxine Waters and titled the monologue in the 1994 published version of *Twilight,* "The Unheard," to foreshadow Waters's closing words that the "riot" was the "voice of the unheard." Waters refers to Martin Luther King Jr.'s famous response to the civil unrest in the urban centers of Newark and Detroit in a summer 1967 speech, which asserted that a "riot is at bottom the language of the unheard."

13. These unresolved traumas have been embodied in highbrow and popular culture in the forms of the Vanishing Indian and Tragic Mulatta/o, two tragic figures at the center of a self-consciously American literature fashioned in the nineteenth century. Both figures and their common plots rendered the diminished existences, precarious futures, and deaths of racialized others inevitable. Their tragic fates naturalized beliefs in racial segregation and White supremacy, as well as the collective violence necessary to maintain these racial states. For the genealogy of

the Vanishing Indian in popular culture, see Berkhofer; for that of the Tragic Mulatta/o, see Sollors.

14. In a 1995 interview with Smith, Carl Weber, Brechtian scholar and director, likens Brecht's famous notion of a personal gestus to Smith's notion of character.

15. One such audience member who contacted Smith after seeing a performance of *Twilight* was Maria, a postal worker and jury member of the federal trial of King's police assailants. Her monologue is prominently featured in the film version of the play.

16. According to recent histories of these events, White servicemen on leave and the police were responsible for instigating much of the violence against Latino, Black, and Filipino men who were wearing these zoot suits. For their discussions of the print media, military, and general citizenry who encouraged the often-unprovoked attacks on the "zoot-suiters," see Sánchez; Mazón.

17. Anne Cheng and Min Song have noted the failure of individual and private grief to be fully translated into effective claims of redress and reparations. Cheng argues that Smith's body accumulates the residues of grief from each character even as she embodies new characters: "By the end of Smith's performance, key words that are meant to address grief—words such as 'justice' and 'reparation'—begin to take on peculiar and unstable meanings: a crisis not of no meaning but of too much meaning" (173). Where there was absence before, a lack of acknowledgment, Cheng argues that the multiple racial tragedies are too excessive to be legally legible. For Cheng, the tragedy of the Los Angeles Crisis is one of "racial retribution" in which racialized individuals and communities wreak vengeance upon each other, a racial revenge I examine in chapter 3.

18. I explore this concept elsewhere. See Itagaki.

19. The movement from grievance to grief in the monologue is the shift to the denouement of the plot. The denouement, or the "untying," in the tragic plot would expose the stark situation to the characters and possibly to the audience. Coming after the main actions, the denouement I posit is a repeated recognition of trauma experienced by the speaker, in this case, Salas, whose permanent disability and memories propel him to relive these tragic narratives again and again.

20. The full quotation reads, "It is useful to think of the ethics of the neighbor as a *spatializing* discourse within ethics, as distinct from a 'temporalizing' discourse that subordinates ethics to political rhetorics associated with memory and identity" (quoted in Meister, sec. 6; original emphasis). Meister's consideration of the ethics of the neighbor is a useful category, especially within Los Angeles, where neighbors reacted violently toward one other, neighbor rising up against neighbor.

21. Feminist critic Tania Modleski argues that Smith's "departure from that role" of "the black woman [who] has traditionally occupied the most fixed place in this country's representational practices" is her true achievement in her plays (58). Theater scholar Cherise Smith notes that Smith's flexibility as a performer in portraying so many identities might actually result in further circumscribing boundaries and differences: "Yet, with its emphasis on the individual transformation of the artist, it also portends a deeply private, individualistic, and maybe even

self-referential worldview and discourse wherein the very identity-boundaries she seeks to trespass are stabilized rather than destabilized. To say it differently, the prominence of Smith's own identity mobility threatens to undermine the humanist utopia that *Twilight: Los Angeles,* 1992 imagines" (135–36).

22. Missing from this designation of a Black–Korean conflict are the negotiations of less visible power elites in mediating this discourse. In Korean immigrant Soon Ja Du's fatal shooting of her Black customer, Latasha Harlins, legal scholar Neil Gotanda has pointed out Los Angeles Superior Court Judge Joyce Karlin's reliance on stereotypes of the Asian model minority in handing down a controversially light sentence with time already served to Du in 1991; see Gotanda. In a similar vein, inner-city communities have suffered from a history of "redlining" by insurance companies, a practice that inhibits the protection of property and the aggregation of wealth for communities of color consistent with White communities. In the L.A. Crisis, for example, this historically documented discrimination translated into the complete loss of uninsured goods and property that disproportionately affected businesses in red-lined, inner-city neighborhoods.

23. When identifying the speakers and their occupations, I use Smith's exact wording from her prefaces to their monologues.

24. Smith's performances of Korean Americans and the use of untranslated Korean in her monologues have received mixed reviews. Critics responded negatively to one of her performances in which the opening monologue was performed entirely in Korean with subtitles.

25. I thank Junehee Chung and Juwon Lee for providing this alternate translation. In the 2003 Dramatists Play Service version of the play, Smith oddly omits this transliteration and instead includes stage directions for the Korean words for "igniting fire," which, given the losses of meaning in translation, may be provocatively represented onstage as another synonymous Korean phrase, a translation of a translation.

26. In Gledhill's review of the common distinctions between melodrama and tragedy in literary history, she cites Raymond Williams's argument for "melodrama's bourgeois inheritance": "Many dramatic histories locate the inception of melodrama in the degeneration of bourgeois tragedy. Raymond Williams's study, *Modern Tragedy* (1966), by historicizing the *category* of tragedy as well as its form, opens up the implications of this perception, suggesting how bourgeois appropriation altered the aesthetics of tragedy in ways that both contributed to melodrama and eventually led to its critical repudiation" (16; original emphasis). Film critic Linda Williams argues against this devaluation of melodrama: "Melodrama can be viewed, then, not as genre, an excess, or an aberration, but as what most typifies popular American narrative in literature, stage, film, and television when it seeks to engage with moral questions. It is the best example of American culture's (often hypocritical) attempt to construct itself as the locus of innocence and virtue" (17). I posit that the narrative drive of the melodramatic form creates the desire for resolution and an ordering of a moral world. But the thwarting of such a resolution is the makings of a tragic framework.

27. One context is the contradictory tensions of Plato's provocative, yet rather baffling, claim in *Laws* that constitutional legislators are tragedians and the constitutions they produce are tragedies, the "finest and best" that will represent the "finest and noblest life."

28. As a point of reference, Michael Omi and Howard Winant define race as "a concept which signifies and symbolizes social conflicts and interests by referring to different types of human bodies" in order to delineate their concept of racial formations: a "sociohistorical process by which racial categories are created, inhabited, transformed, and destroyed" (55).

29. See Davis, "Uprising" and *City of Quartz*.

30. The Brechtian "alienation effect" as a "representation that alienates is one which allows us to recognize its subject, but at the same time makes it seem unfamiliar. . . . The new alienations are only designed to free socially-conditioned phenomena from the stamp of familiarity which protects them against our grasp today" (quoted in Thompson, 130).

5. The Media Spectacle of Racial Disaster

1. Cultural critic Mike Davis has, in a book-length study, *The Ecology of Fear*, examined the various cultural manifestations of Los Angeles's long-standing connection to disaster. My aim here is not to provide a genealogy of disaster in relationship to Los Angeles's particular and universal lessons, but instead to consider how disaster reveals certain anxieties of race war that have haunted the nation's origins since the founding of European colonies in the Americas (Faludi). In his book-length analysis of the "aesthetic experiments" about the 1992 Los Angeles Crisis, Min Song explains the pessimism manifesting itself through discourses of national decline: "All of these works, by introducing us to particular aspects of the riots as they pertain to the pervasive sense that recent history has robbed the United States of its national momentum, allows us to explore the pessimism that seems to have hijacked the imagination of our collective future" (26).

2. Media scholar Douglas Kellner follows Guy Debord's analysis of media spectacle as a "'permanent opium war' (ibid., Section 44), which stupefies social subjects and distracts them from the most urgent task of real life—recovering the full range of their human powers through creative practice. The concept of the spectacle is integrally connected to the concept of separation and passivity, for in submissively consuming spectacles one is estranged from actively producing one's life. Capitalist society separates workers from the products of their labor, art from life, and consumption from human needs and self-directing activity, as individuals inertly observe the spectacles of social life from within the privacy of their homes (ibid., Sections 25 and 26)" (Kellner, 3).

3. Transracial describes a relationship among racial identities in a way that multiracial, meaning identities or communities of many races, does not. Feminist theorist Aimee Carrillo-Rowe defines her use of "transracial": "I use the term transracial in lieu of the term 'multiracial' to signal the transformative potential of such

alliances in reconfiguring lines of difference, as well as the transnational component of such ties" (Carrillo-Rowe, 41 n. 4).

4. As examples of this cross-referential interaction, films and television programs might introduce their shows' storylines with the turning pages of a book to simulate reading practices while their audiences are viewing the moving images; web versions of print newspapers will mirror the column format and perhaps even include the words "fold" or "jump" to separate the front-page lead from the rest of the article. Remediation is thus an interplay of media, or *"the mediation of mediations,"* in which every "act of mediation depends on other acts of mediation. Media are continually commenting on, reproducing, and replacing each other, and this process is integral to media. Media need each other in order to function as media at all" (Bolter and Grusin, 55).

5. In its range of styles, the novel is unlike other best-selling texts by Asian American authors that focus on the immigrant bildungsroman, intergenerational conflict, the desire for national or public acknowledgment of the history and experience of a particular Asian ethnic community, for example, enduringly popular foundational literary texts such as *The Woman Warrior* (1976) by Maxine Hong Kingston and *Joy Luck Club* (1989) by Amy Tan.

6. "In contrast to this, we suggest that the state *is* inherently racial. Far from *intervening* in racial conflicts, the state is itself increasingly the preeminent site of racial conflict" (Omi and Winant, 82; original emphasis).

7. And like most "natural" disasters, there is a human element that contributes and even escalates the damages and loss of life: overdevelopment in perennial wildfire areas, infrastructure built on top of multiple fault lines, and suburban sprawl sustained by water piped over long distances.

8. Historian Matthew Frye Jacobson posits that the shift from the civil rights framework to the replacement of White supremacy with White primacy depended on the reworking of the origin myth of the founding fathers into one of a nation of immigrants. This emphasis on U.S. society as one of immigrants arriving at the turn of the nineteenth century deliberately overlooks current legacies of a past that historically condoned chattel slavery and failed to restructure society to grant the full and equal benefits of citizenship to people of color.

9. "In advanced capitalist societies *hegemony* is secured by a complex system of compromises, legitimating ideologies (e.g., 'the rule of law'), by adherence to established political rules and bureaucratic regularities, etc. Under all but the most severe conditions (economic collapse, war), this severely limits the range and legitimacy of both dominant and oppositional political initiatives, no matter how heavy the conflicts among contemporary U.S. political institutions and their constituents may appear to be" (Omi and Winant, 84).

10. Buchanan alludes to a new kind of warfare, these military operations in urban terrain (MOUTs) that have become increasingly common since the Vietnam War; see Desch.

11. For "mainstream multiculturalism," see Nancy Fraser; for "corporate multiculturalism," see Avery Gordon; and for "world-beat multiculturalism," see scholar-activist-artist Coco Fusco.

12. See Erna Smith; Entman.

13. Sue-Im Lee, in her study of different types of universalism manifested in the characters of *Tropic of Orange,* identifies Arcangel with "Third World universalism," Buzzworm with "particular universalism," and Manzanar with "romantic universalism." I think Lee is right in identifying how Yamashita provides a critique and corrective of universalism through "a new collective subject positioning that can express the accelerated movement of capital and humans traversing the world" (502). The complexity of Yamashita's vision through her characters often gets lost in praise for her experimental fiction.

14. As some everyday examples of the salvific exchange of the heroic bystander, I think of the popular discourse of public servant or protector, most commonly identified as the police officer, firefighter, or soldier.

15. In this logic, Fraser's arguments against an overwhelming tendency to privilege political recognition over material redistribution parallel the recognition of Arcangel's miraculous feats of strength that fail to incite long-standing systemic changes.

16. The immigration crisis focuses on the people rather than the structural conditions that serve as push-and-pull factors in their countries of origin and destination. In his interracial history of Watts, historian Scott Kurashige has posited that African Americans have become increasingly tied to "urban crisis" in the post–World War II era, while Japanese Americans and, by extension, most other Asian Americans have been tied to the transnational future and globalized economy.

17. Scott notes three different forms of domination and its practices or responses to resistance from the less powerful: (1) "material domination" in the form of "appropriation of grain, taxes, labor, etc."; (2) "status domination," "humiliation, disprivilege, insults, assaults on dignity"; and (3) "ideological domination," "justification by ruling groups for slavery, serfdom, caste, privilege" (198).

18. It is the business of art that makes the music: the avant-garde composer's cultural capital, the publicity and the prestige his person and work garners, the audience who comes to see his latest piece, or the orchestra who agrees to "play" by not playing his work.

19. Jinqi Ling's writings on Yamashita's works introduce Lipietz's discussion of the "future anterior" as an interpretive strategy in her first novel, *Through the Arc of the Rainforest.* Yamashita's interest in time, memory, and space can be traced throughout her oeuvre since this first publication.

20. Manzanar names himself after the Japanese American concentration camp in central California, where he spent his youth during World War II. There is also a moral indictment that he is hiding from the trauma of Japanese American internment during World War II and the responsibilities of family—the future generations represented by his granddaughter Emi. She realizes that he used to sing songs to her and this fragile memory identifies Manzanar as her grandfather for readers. Despite this connection, Manzanar is unable to talk with Emi before her death, suggesting his inability to pass on his history to her. Her violent death, unlike previous fatal traffic accidents and urban disasters he has witnessed, silences his musical talent.

21. Political theorist Benjamin Barber implicitly argues for silence as enabling hearing, a crucial part of democratic deliberation: "One measure of healthy political talk is the amount of *silence* it permits and encourages, for silence is the precious medium in which reflection is nurtured and empathy can grow. Without it, there is only the babble of raucous interests and insistent rights trying for the deaf ears of impatient adversaries" (Barber, 175; original emphasis). As discussed in this chapter and previous ones, the civil virtue of reciprocity that taking turns between listening and speaking requires is often not extended to those not considered worthy of hearing.

22. I thank Susan Hwang for this suggestion.

23. For frameworks for analyzing heterogeneous and flexible identity formations, see Lowe; Ong.

24. The mainstream press celebrated Asian Americans as the "model minority" at the height of the modern civil rights movement. Touted as examples of economic and educational successes during the 1960s, statistics on Asian American educational and economic achievements surpassed those of other racial minorities, such as African Americans. But these favorable generalizations about Asian Americans overlook other statistics: below-average per capita income, uncompensated overtime, underemployment, and poverty among more recent immigrant groups and even across more established Asian American communities. Critics of the model minority thesis have noted that these comparisons mask the underlying structural conditions that perpetuate poverty, un(der)employment within Black, Latina/o, *and* Asian American communities; see Osajima.

25. I allude to postcolonial scholar Homi Bhaba's central discussion in "Of Mimicry and Man," in which colonial hierarchies are maintained through a cultural imperialism; although culture can be mimicked, racial or biological distinctions cannot.

26. Considerations of Asian American masculinity are a vibrant discourse in the field of Asian American studies. Given critical attention is the emasculation or feminization of Asian Americans in mainstream discourse, the legacy of immigration restrictions and wars in Asia. Bobby's "embrace" at the end is a complex moment. What kind of Asian American masculinity is produced through the experience and perspective of this man of color? Bobby is a transnational product of the Vietnam War and the humanitarian crisis of its aftermath. He is trying to be what cultural critic Robyn Wiegman has isolated in the post–cold war era as the "more nuanced masculine interiority, a 'soft body' of emotionality, inward struggle, and familial crisis and confrontation" (175). Wiegman references Susan Jeffords's critique of "hard bodies" in blockbuster films during the Reagan–Bush years that would save Americans from Communism and kick the Vietnam syndrome.

27. Yamashita's ideas about time in the novel coincide with those of Walter Benjamin's "Theses on the Philosophy of History" and the concern for the antiegalitarian uses to which history and memory may be put. In one of his most often-quoted statements, Benjamin defines history in terms of danger and power:

"It means to seize hold of a memory as it flashes up at a moment of danger. . . . The danger affects both the content of the tradition and its receivers. The same threat hangs over both: that of becoming a tool of the ruling classes." Benjamin's discussion reminds his readers about how history and memory can be used to perpetuate subordination or for those who "wrest tradition away from a conformism that is about to overpower it" (Benjamin, 255).

BIBLIOGRAPHY

Abelmann, Nancy, and John Lie. *Blue Dreams: Korean Americans and the Los Angeles Riots.* Cambridge: Harvard University Press, 1995.

Agamben, Giorgio. *Homo Sacer: Sovereign Power and Bare Life.* Translated by Daniel Heller-Roazen. Stanford: Stanford University Press, 1998.

Agni, Jane M. "UN Dismisses Michael Brown Case: 'We Will Not Be Intervening in the Matter.'" *National Report,* November 2014.

Alexander, Elizabeth. "'Can You Be Black and Look at This?': Reading the Rodney King Video(s)." *Public Culture* 7 (1994): 77–94.

Allen, Danielle. *Talking to Strangers: Anxieties of Citizenship since Brown v. Board of Education.* Chicago: University of Chicago Press, 2004.

Almaguer, Tomás. *Racial Fault Lines: The Historical Origins of White Supremacy in California.* Berkeley: University of California Press, 1994.

Ancheta, Angelo. *Race, Rights, and the Asian American Experience.* New Brunswick, N.J.: Rutgers University Press, 1998.

Anderson, Benedict. *Imagined Communities: Reflections on the Origin and Spread of Nationalism.* New York: Verso Books, 2003. Originally published in 1983.

"Anna Deavere Smith on Art and Politics." *PBS NOW,* August 11, 2006.

Appadurai, Arjun, and Carol Breckenridge. "On Moving Targets." *Public Culture* 2, no. 1 (1989): i–iv.

Anzaldúa, Gloria. *Borderlands/La Frontera: The New Mestiza.* San Francisco: Aunt Lute Books, 1987.

Arendt, Hannah. *Eichmann in Jerusalem: A Report on the Banality of Evil.* New York: Penguin Books, 1994.

Arias, Arturo. "Central American-Americans: Invisibility, Power, and Representation in the US Latino World." *Latino Studies* 1 (2003): 168–87.

Armour, Jody D. *Negrophobia and Reasonable Racism: The Hidden Costs of Being Black in America.* New York: New York University Press, 1997.

Avila, Eric. *Popular Culture in the Age of White Flight: Fear and Fantasy in Suburban Los Angeles.* Berkeley: University of California Press, 2004.

Bailey, Eric. "After the Riots: The Search for Answers: Rohrabacher Asks Bush to Expel Seized Illegal Aliens." *Los Angeles Times,* May 7, 1992.

Bakhtin, Mikhail M. *Problems of Dostoevsky's Poetics*. Edited by Caryl Emerson. Minneapolis: University of Minnesota Press, 1984. Originally published in 1929.

Baldassare, Mark, ed. *The Los Angeles Riots: Lessons for the Urban Future*. Boulder, Colo.: Westview Press, 1994.

Baldwin, James. *Notes of a Native Son*. Boston: Beacon Press, 1955.

Balibar, Étienne. "Outlines of a Topography of Cruelty: Citizenship and Civility in the Era of Global Violence." *Constellations* 8, no. 1 (2001): 15–29.

Banaji, Mahzarin R., and Anthony G. Greenwald. *Blindspot: The Hidden Biases of Good People*. New York: Random House, 2013.

Barber, Benjamin. *Strong Democracy: Participatory Politics for a New Age*. Berkeley: University of California Press, 2003. Originally published in 1984.

Barclay, Paris, director. *Don't Be a Menace to South Central While Drinking Your Juice in the Hood*. 1996. Film.

Barkoukis, Leah, and Charles Villa-Vicencio. *Truth Commissions: A Comparative Study*. Washington, D.C., and Cape Town: Conflict Resolution Program, Georgetown University, Washington, D.C., and Institute for Justice and Reconciliation, Cape Town, 2011.

Beatty, Paul. *Big Bank Take Little Bank*. New York: Nuyorican Poets Café, 1991.

———. *Joker, Joker, Deuce*. New York: Penguin, 1994.

———. *The White Boy Shuffle*. New York: Henry Holt and Company, 1996.

———. *Tuff*. New York: Anchor, 2001.

———. "Black Humor." *New York Times,* January 22, 2006.

———, ed. *Hokum: An Anthology of African-American Humor*. New York: Bloomsbury Publishing, 2006.

———. *Slumberland*. New York: Bloomsbury USA, 2011.

———. *The Sellout*. New York: Farrar, Straus and Giroux, 2015.

Becker, Gary S. *The Economics of Discrimination*. Chicago: University of Chicago Press, 1957.

Bell, David A. "The Triumph of Asian-Americans." *The New Republic,* July 1985, 24–31.

Bell, Derrick A., Jr. "*Brown v. Board of Education* and the Interest-Convergence Dilemma." *Harvard Law Review* 93 (1980): 518–33.

———. "Racial Realism." *Connecticut Law Review* 24 (1992): 363–79.

Benjamin, Walter. "Theses on the Philosophy of History." In *Illuminations: Essays and Reflections*. Edited by Hannah Arendt, 253–64. New York: Schocken Books, 1988.

Berenbiem, Glenn, writer. "Honeymoon in L.A.: Part 2." *A Different World,* directed by Debbie Allen. October 1, 1992. Television.

Berkhofer, Robert. *The White Man's Indian: Images of the American Indian from Columbus to the Present*. New York: Alfred A. Knopf, 1978.

Berlant, Lauren. "Slow Death (Sovereignty, Obesity, Lateral Agency)." *Critical Inquiry* 33 (2007): 754–80.

Bernstein, Richard. "Black Poet's First Novel Aims the Jokes Both Ways." *New York Times,* May 31, 1996.

Bhabha, Homi K. "Of Mimicry and Man: The Ambivalence of Colonial Discourse." In *October: The First Decade, 1976–1986*. Edited by Annette Michelson et al., 317–25. Cambridge: MIT Press, 1987.

Blake, John. "The New Threat: 'Racism without Racists.'" *CNN.org*, November 28, 2014.

Bobo, Lawrence D., James Kluegel, and Ryan Smith. "Laissez-Faire Racism: The Crystallization of a Kinder, Gentler, Antiblack Ideology." In *Racial Attitudes in the 1990s*. Edited by Steven A. Tuch and Jack K. Martin, 15–44. Westport, Conn.: Praeger, 1997.

Bolter, Jay David, and Richard Grusin. *Remediation: Understanding New Media*. Cambridge: MIT Press, 1999.

Bonilla-Silva, Eduardo. *White Supremacy and Racism in the Post–Civil Rights Era*. Boulder, Colo.: Lynne Rienner, 2001.

———. *Racism without Racists: Color-Blind Racism and the Persistence of Racial Inequality in the United States*. Lanham, Md.: Rowman and Littlefield, 2003.

"Border Patrol Abuse since 2010." *Southern Border Communities Coalition*. March 19, 2015.

Bow, Leslie. *Partly Colored: Asian Americans and Racial Anomaly in the Segregated South*. New York: New York University Press, 2010.

Boyd, Richard. "The Value of Civility?" *Urban Studies* 43, no. 5/6 (2006): 863–78.

Brecht, Bertolt. *Brecht on Theatre: The Development of an Aesthetic*. Translated by John Willett. New York: Hill and Wang, 1964.

Brereton, Geoffrey. *Principles of Tragedy: A Rational Examination of the Tragic Concept in Life and Literature*. Miami: University of Miami Press, 1968.

Brown, Wendy. *States of Injury: Power and Freedom in Late Modernity*. Princeton: Princeton University Press, 1995.

Buchanan, Patrick J. "1992 Republican National Convention Speech." 1992.

Buck, Pem Davidson. "The Violence of the Status Quo." *Anthropology News*, September 9, 2014.

Bunting, Eve. *Smoky Night*. Illustrated by David Diaz. New York: Voyager Books, 1994.

Caldwell, John Thornton. *Televisuality: Style, Crisis, and Authority in American Television*. New Brunswick, N.J.: Routledge, 1995.

Carrillo-Rowe, Aimee. "Be Longing: Toward a Feminist Politics of Relation." *NWSA Journal* 17, no. 2 (2005): 15–46.

Carter, Stephen L. *Reflections of an Affirmative Action Baby*. New York: Basic Books, 1992.

———. *Civility: Manners, Morals, and the Etiquette of Democracy*. New York: HarperPerennial, 1998.

Certeau, Michel de. *The Practice of Everyday Life*. Translated by Steven F. Rendall. Berkeley: University of California Press, 2011.

Chafe, William H. *Civilities and Civil Rights: Greensboro, North Carolina, and the Black Struggle for Freedom*. Oxford: Oxford University Press, 1981.

Chang, Edward T. "America's First Multiethnic 'Riots.'" In *The State of Asian America: Activism and Resistance in the 1990s*. Edited by Karin Aguilar-San Juan, 101–17. Boston: South End Press, 1994.

———. "'As Los Angeles Burned, Korean America Was Born': Community in the Twenty-First Century." *Amerasia Journal* 30, no. 1 (2004): vii–ix.

Chang, Edward T., and Jeannette Diaz-Veizades. *Ethnic Peace in the American City: Building Community in Los Angeles and Beyond*. New York: New York University Press, 1999.

Cheng, Anne A. *The Melancholy of Race*. Oxford: Oxford University Press, 2001.

Cheng, Wendy. *The Changs Next Door to the Díazes: Remapping Race in Suburban California*. Minneapolis: University of Minnesota Press, 2013.

Cheung, King-Kok. *Articulate Silences: Hisaye Yamamoto, Maxine Hong Kingston, Joy Kogawa*. Ithaca: Cornell University Press, 1993.

Chin, Frank. "Pidgin Contest along I-5." *Bulletproof Buddhists and Other Essays*. Honolulu: University of Hawai'i Press, 1998.

Chuh, Kandice. "Of Hemispheres and Other Spheres: Navigating Karen Tei Yamashita's Literary World." *American Literary History* 18, no. 3 (2006): 618–37.

Civil Liberties in Crisis: Los Angeles During the Emergency. Los Angeles: ACLU Foundation of Southern California, 1992.

Clinton, Bill. "Remarks to the Convocation of the Church of God in Christ in Memphis." Miller Center, University of Virginia, November 13, 1993.

Collins, Patricia Hill. "It's All in the Family: Intersections of Gender, Race, and Nation." *Hypatia: A Journal of Feminist Philosophy* 13, no. 3 (Summer 1998): 62–82.

Combs, Barbara Harris. "Black (and Brown) Bodies out of Place: Towards a Theoretical Understanding of Systematic Voter Suppression in the United States." *Critical Sociology* (2015): 1–15.

———. *Black Feminist Thought: Knowledge, Consciousness, and the Politics of Empowerment*. 2nd ed. New York: Routledge, 2000.

Connolly, William E. *The Ethos of Pluralization*. Minneapolis: University of Minnesota Press, 1995.

Cosby, Bill, creator. *A Different World*. 1987. Television.

Coscarelli, Joe. "Graphic Video Shows St. Louis Police Shoot and Kill Kajieme Powell near Ferguson." *New York Magazine Online*, August 20, 2014.

Crenshaw, Kimberlé. "Mapping the Margins: Intersectionality, Identity Politics, and Violence against Women of Color." *Stanford Law Review* 43 (1991): 1241–99.

Crenshaw, Kimberlé, and Gary Peller. "Reel Time/Real Justice." In *Reading Rodney King/Reading Urban Uprising*. Edited by Robert Gooding-Williams, 56–70. London: Routledge, 1993.

Cresswell, Tim. *In Place/Out of Place: Geography, Ideology and Transgression*. Minneapolis: University of Minnesota Press, 1996.

———. "Weeds, Plagues, and Bodily Secretions: A Geographical Interpretation of Metaphors of Displacement." *Annals of the Association of American Geographers* 87, no. 2 (1997): 330–45.

Critchley, Simon. "Introduction." In *The Cambridge Companion to Levinas*. Edited by Simon Critchley and Robert Bernasconi, 1–32. Cambridge: Cambridge University Press, 2002.

Cundieff, Rusty, director. *Fear of a Black Hat*. 1994. Film.

Davis, Mike. *City of Quartz: Excavating the Future in Los Angeles*. New York: Vintage Books, 1992.

———. "Uprising and Repression in L.A." In *Reading Rodney King/Reading Urban Uprising*. Edited by Robert Gooding-Williams, 142–54. New York: Routledge, 1993.

———. *Ecology of Fear: Los Angeles and the Imagination of Disaster*. New York: Metropolitan Books; Henry Holt and Company, 1998.

Debord, Guy. *The Society of Spectacle*. Translated by Donald Nicholson-Smith. New York: Zone Books, 2008. Originally published in 1994.

Delk, James D. *Fires & Furies: The L.A. Riots—What Really Happened*. Palm Springs, Calif.: ETC Publications, 1994.

Desch, Michael C., ed. *Soldiers in Cities: Military Operations on Urban Terrain*. Carlisle, Pa.: Strategic Studies Institute, U.S. Army War College, 2001.

Dickson-Carr, Darryl. *African American Satire: The Sacredly Profane Novel*. Columbia: University of Missouri Press, 2001.

A Digest of Materials Prepared by the Annenberg Public Policy Center of the University of Pennsylvania for Hershey I and II. Hearings of the Subcommittee on Rules and Organization of the House of Representatives, April 1999.

Dimock, Wai Chee. "After Troy: Homer, Euripides, Total War." In *Rethinking Tragedy*. Edited by Rita Felski, 66–81. Baltimore: Johns Hopkins University Press, 2008.

Dorfman, Ariel. "Final and First Words on *Death and the Maiden*." In *Other Septembers, Many Americas: Selected Provocations, 1980–2004*, 186–89. New York: Seven Stories Press, 2004.

Dubey, Madhu. *Signs and Cities: Black Literary Postmodernism*. Chicago: University of Chicago Press, 2003.

Du Bois, W. E. B. *The Souls of Black Folk*. Library of America. New York: Vintage Books, 1990. Originally published in 1903.

Dudziak, Mary L. *Cold War Civil Rights: Race and the Image of American Democracy*. Princeton: Princeton University Press, 2000.

Duster, Troy. "They're Taking Over! And Other Myths About Race on Campus." *Mother Jones*, September/October 1991, 30–33, 63–64.

Dylan, Bob. Quoted in Robert Shelton, *No Direction Home: The Life and Music of Bob Dylan*. Milwaukee: Backbeat Books, 2010. Originally published in 1986.

Eagleton, Terry. *Sweet Violence: The Idea of the Tragic*. Oxford: Blackwell, 2003.

Elias, Norbert. *The History of Manners*. New York: Pantheon Books, 1982.

Ellis, Trey. "The New Black Aesthetic." *Callaloo* 38 (1989): 233–43.

———. "Response to NBA Critiques." *Callaloo* 38 (1989): 250–51.

Ennis, Sharon R., Merarys Ríos-Vargas, and Nora G. Albert. *The Hispanic Population: 2010*. U.S. Census Briefs. Washington, D.C.: U.S. Census Bureau, May 2011.

Entman, R. M. "Blacks in the News: Television, Modern Racism, and Cultural Change." *Journalism Quarterly* 69 (1992): 341–62.

Fales, Susan, writer. "Honeymoon in L.A.: Part 1." *A Different World,* directed by Debbie Allen. September 24, 1992. Television.

Faludi, Susan. "America's Guardian Myth." *New York Times,* September 7, 2007.

Fanon, Franz. *The Wretched of the Earth.* New York: Grove Press, 2004. Originally published in 1963.

Felski, Rita, ed. *Rethinking Tragedy.* Baltimore: Johns Hopkins University Press, 2008.

Ferguson, Roderick A. *Aberrations in Black: Toward a Queer of Color Critique.* Minneapolis: University of Minnesota Press, 2004.

Finkel, David, and Christian Davenport. "Records Paint Dark Portrait of Guard before Abu Ghraib, Graner Left a Trail of Alleged Violence." *Washington Post,* June 5, 2004.

Fitzpatrick, David. "Officers Face Murder Charges in 2014 Albuquerque Homeless Man's Shooting." *CNN.com,* January 13, 2015.

Ford, Andrea. "Videotape Shows Teen Being Shot After Fight . . ." *Los Angeles Times,* October 1, 1991.

Forni, P. M. *Choosing Civility: The Twenty-Five Rules of Considerate Conduct.* New York: St. Martin's Griffin, 2003.

Fraser, Nancy. *Justice Interruptus: Political Reflections on the "Postsocialist" Condition.* New York: Routledge, 1997.

Friedman, Susan Stanford. "Beyond White and Other: Relationality and Narratives of Race in Feminist Discourse." *Signs* 21, no. 1 (1995): 1–49.

Fukuyama, Francis. *The End of History and the Last Man.* New York: Penguin Books, 1992.

Fusco, Coco. *English Is Broken Here: Notes on Cultural Fusion in the Americas.* New York: New Press, 1995.

Garza, Alicia. "A Herstory of the #BlackLivesMatter Movement." *BlackLivesMatter.org,* December 6, 2014.

Gaskins, Bill. "What's in a Word." In *Inside the L.A. Riots: What Really Happened—and Why It Will Happen Again.* Edited by Don Hazen, 123–24. New York: Institute for Alternative Journalism, 1992.

Gates, Henry Louis, Jr. *Figures in Black: Words, Signs, and the "Racial" Self.* New York: Oxford University Press, 1987.

Gilmore, Ruth Wilson. "Terror Austerity Race Gender Excess Theater." In *Reading Rodney King/Reading Urban Uprising.* Edited by Robert Gooding-Williams, 23–37. New York: Routledge, 1993.

Gledhill, Christine. "The Melodramatic Field: An Investigation." In *Home Is Where the Heart Is: Studies in Melodrama and the Woman's Film.* Edited by Christine Gledhill, 5–39. London: British Film Institute, 1987.

Gordon, Avery. "The Work of Corporate Culture: Diversity Management." *Social Text,* no. 44 (Autumn–Winter 1995): 3–30.

Gordon, Avery F., and Christopher Newfield. "White Philosophy." *Critical Inquiry* 20, no. 4 (1994): 737–57.

————. "Multiculturalism's Unfinished Business." In *Mapping Multiculturalism.* Edited by Avery F. Gordon and Christopher Newfield, 76–115. Minneapolis: University of Minnesota Press, 1996.

Gotanda, Neil. "Multiculturalism and Racial Stratification." In *Mapping Multiculturalism.* Edited by Avery F. Gordon and Christopher Newfield, 238–52. Minneapolis: University of Minnesota Press, 1996.

Gramsci, Antonio. *Selections from the Prison Notebooks.* Edited by Quinton Hoare and Geoffrey Nowell-Smith. New York: International Publishers, 1971.

Gross, Jane. "Body and Dreams Trampled, a Riot Victim Fights On." *Los Angeles Times,* October 22, 1993.

Guatemala: Never Again! The Official Report of the Human Rights Office, Archdiocese of Guatemala. REMHI Recovery of Historical Memory Project. Maryknoll, N.Y.: Orbis Books, 1999.

Haddon, Heather. "Killings of New York Police Officers Spark Backlash to Protests." *Wall Street Journal Online,* December 21, 2014.

Haggis, Paul, director. *Crash.* Lionsgate, 2004. Film.

Halberstam, Judith. *In a Queer Time and Place: Transgender Bodies, Subcultural Lives.* New York: New York University Press, 2005.

Haley, Alex. *Roots: The Saga of an American Family.* Los Angeles: Vanguard Press, 2007. Originally published in 1974.

Hamilton, Nora, and Norma Stoltz Chinchilla. *Seeking Community in a Global City: Guatemalans and Salvadorans in Los Angeles.* Philadelphia: Temple University Press, 2001.

Hammond, Andrew. *Cold War Literature: Writing the Global Conflict.* New York: Routledge, 2006.

Hancock, Ange-Marie. "When Multiplication Doesn't Equal Quick Addition: Examining Intersectionality as a Research Paradigm." *Perspectives on Politics* 5, no. 1 (2007): Originally published in 1974.

Handlin, Oscar. *The Uprooted: From the Old World to the New.* London: Watts, 1951.

Haney López, Ian F. "Is the 'Post' in the Post-Racial the 'Blind' in Colorblind?" *Cardozo Law Review* 32, no. 3 (2011): 807–31.

Haraway, Donna J. *Modest_Witness@Second_Millennium.Femaleman©_Meets_Oncomouse™.* London: Routledge, 1997.

Harding, Sandra. "Rethinking Standpoint Epistemology: What Is 'Strong Objectivity'?" In *Feminist Theory: A Philosophical Anthology,* edited by Ann E. Cudd and Robin O. Andreasen, 218–36. Oxford: Blackwell, 2005.

Harris, Cheryl I. "Whiteness as Property." *Harvard Law Review* 106, no. 8 (1993): 1707–91.

————. "The Constitution of Equal Citizenship for a Good Society: Equal Treatment and the Reproduction of Inequality." *Fordham Law Review* 69 (2001): 1753–83.

Harris, Fred R., and Roger W. Wilkins, eds. *Quiet Riots: Race and Poverty in the United States.* New York: Pantheon Books, 1988.

Hartman, Saidiya. *Scenes of Subjection: Terror, Slavery, and Self-Making in Nineteenth-Century America*. New York: Oxford University Press, 1997.

Hazen, Don, ed. *Inside the L.A. Riots: What Really Happened—and Why It Will Happen Again*. New York: Institute for Alternative Journalism, 1992.

Heilman, Robert Bechtold. *Tragedy and Melodrama: Versions of Experience*. Seattle: University of Washington Press, 1968.

Herrnstein, Richard J., and Charles Murray. *The Bell Curve: Intelligence and Class Structure in American Life*. New York: Free Press, 1994.

Hochschild, Jennifer L. *Facing up to the American Dream: Race, Class, and the Soul of a Nation*. Princeton: Princeton University Press, 1995.

Holder, Eric H., Jr. "Attorney General Eric Holder Delivers Remarks During the Interfaith Service and Community Forum at Ebenezer Baptist Church." Justice News, United States Department of Justice, 2014.

Holloway, Karla F. C. *Codes of Conduct: Race, Ethics, and the Color of Our Character*. New Brunswick, N.J.: Rutgers University Press, 1995.

Holston, James. *Insurgent Citizenship: Disjunctions of Democracy and Modernity in Brazil*. Princeton: Princeton University Press, 2008.

Hong, Grace Kyungwon. *The Ruptures of American Capital: Women of Color Feminism and the Culture of Immigrant Labor*. Minneapolis: University of Minnesota Press, 2006.

Hong, Grace Kyungwon, and Roderick A. Ferguson, eds. *Strange Affinities: The Gender and Sexual Politics of Comparative Racialization*. Durham: Duke University Press, 2011.

Hsu, Hua. "The Civility Wars." *New Yorker*, December 1, 2014.

Huggins, Martha K., Mika Haritos-Fatouros, and Philip G. Zimbardo. *Violence Workers: Torturers and Murderers Reconstruct Brazilian Atrocities*. Berkeley: University of California Press, 2002.

Hughes, Allen, director. *Menace II Society*. 1993. Film.

Humes, Karen R., Nicholas A. Jones, and Roberto R. Ramirez. *Overview of Race and Hispanic Origin: 2010*. Washington, D.C.: U.S. Census Bureau, March 2011.

Hunn, David, and Kim Bell. "Why Was Michael Brown's Body Left There for Hours?" *St. Louis Post-Dispatch*, September 14, 2014.

Hunt, Darnell M. *Screening the Los Angeles "Riots": Race, Seeing, and Resistance*. New York: Cambridge University Press, 1997.

Huntington, Samuel P. *The Clash of Civilizations and the Remaking of World Order*. Chicago: University of Chicago Press, 1996.

Ignacio, Abe, Enrique de la Cruz, Jorge Emmanuel, and Helen Toribio. *The Forbidden Book: The Philippine-American War in Political Cartoons*. San Francisco: T'Boli Publishing, 2004.

Itagaki, Lynn Mie. "Crisis Temporalities: States of Emergency and the Gendered-Sexualized Logics of Asian American Women Abroad." *Feminist Formations* 25, no. 2 (Summer 2013): 195–219.

Jackman, Mary R. *The Velvet Glove: Paternalism and Conflict in Gender, Class, and Race Relations*. Berkeley: University of California Press, 1994.

Jackson, John L. *Racial Paranoia: The Unintended Consequences of Political Correctness*. New York: Basic Books, 2008.

Jacobs, Ronald N. *Race, Media, and the Crisis of Civil Society: From Watts to Rodney King*. Cambridge: Cambridge University Press, 2000.

Jacobson, Matthew Frye. *Roots Too: White Ethnic Revival in Post–Civil Rights America*. Cambridge: Harvard University Press, 2006.

Jamieson, Kathleen Hall. *Civility in the House of Representatives: The 105th Congress*. Washington, D.C.: United States House of Representatives, 1999.

Jayadev, Raj. "How Little Cau Bich Tran's Death Taught Us." *San Jose Inside*, May 28, 2009.

Jefferson, Thomas. "Letter to James Madison, January 30, 1787." In *The Political Writings of Thomas Jefferson: Representative Selections*. Edited by Edward Dumbauld, 67. Indianapolis: Bobbs-Merrill, 1995.

Johnson, James H., Jr., Cloyzelle K. Jones, Walter C. Farrell Jr., and Melvin L. Oliver. "The Los Angeles Rebellion: A Retrospective View." *Economic Development Quarterly* 6, no. 4 (1992): 356–72.

Johnson, Kevin, Meghan Hoyer, and Brad Heath. "Local Police Involved in 400 Killings Per Year." *USA Today*, August 14, 2014.

Jones-Correa, Michael. "Swimming in the Latino Sea: The Other Latinos and Politics." In *The Other Latinos: Central and South Americans in the United States*. Edited by José Luis Falconi and José Antonio Mazzotti, 21–38. Cambridge: David Rockefeller Center for Latin American Studies, Harvard University, 2007.

Karst, Kenneth. *Belonging to America: Equal Citizenship and the Constitution*. New Haven: Yale University Press, 1989.

Kasson, John F. *Rudeness & Civility: Manners in Nineteenth-Century Urban America*. New York: Hill and Wang, 1990.

Katz, Michael. *Why Don't American Cities Burn?* Philadelphia: University of Pennsylvania Press, 2010.

Kelley, Robin D. G. *Freedom Dreams: The Black Radical Imagination*. Boston: Beacon Press, 2002.

Kellner, Douglas. *Media Spectacle*. New York: Routledge, 2003.

Kennedy, Randall. "The Case against 'Civility.'" *American Prospect* 41 (1998): 84–90.

Kim, Claire Jean. "The Racial Triangulation of Asian Americans." *Politics & Society* 27, no. 1 (March 1999): 105–38.

———. *Bitter Fruit: The Politics of Black-Korean Conflict in New York City*. New Haven: Yale University Press, 2000.

Kim, Elaine H. "Home Is Where the *Han* Is: A Korean American Perspective on the Los Angeles Upheavals." In *Reading Rodney King/Reading Urban Uprising*. Edited by Robert Gooding-Williams, 215–35. New York: Routledge, 1993.

Kim, Jodi. *Ends of Empire: Asian American Critique and the Cold War*. Minneapolis: University of Minnesota Press, 2010.

Kim-Gibson, Dai Sil, director. *Sa-I-Gu: From Korean Women's Perspectives.* Edited by Dai Sil Kim-Gibson and Christine Choy. National Asian American Telecommunications Association, San Francisco, 1993. Film.

———, director. *Silence Broken: Korean Comfort Women.* 1998. Film.

———, director. *Wet Sand: Voices from L.A. Ten Years Later.* National Asian American Telecommunications Association, San Francisco, 2004. Film.

Kingston, Maxine Hong. *The Woman Warrior.* New York: Vintage Books, 1989. Originally published in 1975.

Klasfeld, Marc, director. *The L.A. Riot Spectacular.* 2005. Film.

Klein, Norman M. *The History of Forgetting: Los Angeles and the Erasure of Memory.* New York: Verso Books, 1997.

Knight, Charles A. *The Literature of Satire.* Cambridge: Cambridge University Press, 2004.

Kolodny, Annette. *The Land before Her: Fantasy and Experience of the American Frontiers, 1630–1860.* Chapel Hill: University of North Carolina Press, 1984.

Koon, Stacey C., and Robert Deitz. *Presumed Guilty: The Tragedy of the Rodney King Affair.* Washington, D.C.: Regnery Gateway, 1992.

Kurashige, Scott. *The Shifting Grounds of Race: Black and Japanese Americans in the Making of Multiethnic Los Angeles.* Princeton: Princeton University Press, 2010.

Lasch-Quinn, Elisabeth. *Race Experts: How Racial Etiquette, Sensitivity Training, and New Age Therapy Hijacked the Civil Rights Revolution.* Lanham, Md.: Rowman and Littlefield, 2001.

Lee, James Kyung-jin. *Urban Triage: Race and the Fictions of Multiculturalism.* Minneapolis: University of Minnesota Press, 2004.

Lee, Jennifer. *Civility in the City: Jews, Blacks, and Koreans.* Cambridge: Harvard University Press, 2002.

Lee, John H. "Looking at a Ravaged Koreatown . . ." In *Understanding the Riots: Los Angeles before and after the Rodney King Case.* Edited by the *Los Angeles Times*, 157–58, 1993.

Lee, Spike, director. *Do the Right Thing.* 1989. Film.

Lee, Sue-Im. "'We Are Not the World': Global Village, Universalism, and Karen Tei Yamashita's *Tropic of Orange.*" *Modern Fiction Studies* 52, no. 3 (2007): 501–27.

Lee, Ye Hee Lee. "The Viral Claim That a Black Person Is Killed by Police 'every 28 hours.'" *Washington Post,* December 24, 2014.

"'Legitimate Concerns' over Outcome of Michael Brown and Eric Garner Cases— UN Rights Experts." United Nations Human Rights, Office of the High Commissioner for Human Rights, December 5, 2014.

Leung, Rebecca. "Abuse at Abu Ghraib." *CBSNews.com,* May 5, 2004.

Ling, Jinqi. "Toward a North-South Perspective: Nikkei Migration in Karen Tei Yamashita's Transnational Geographies." *Amerasia Journal* 32, no. 3 (2006): 1–22.

"Link Round Up: Feminist Critiques of SlutWalk." *Feminist Frequency,* May 16, 2011.

Linshi, Jack. "Why Ferguson Should Matter to Asian-Americans." *Time*, November 26, 2014.

Lipietz, Alain. "From Althusserianism to 'Regulation Theory.'" In *The Althusserian Legacy*. Edited by E. Ann Kaplan and Michael Sprinker, 99–128. London: Verso Books, 1993.

Lipsitz, George. *The Possessive Investment in Whiteness: How White People Profit from Identity Politics*. Philadelphia: Temple University Press, 1998.

Logan, Rayford Whittingham. *The Negro in American Life and Thought: The Nadir, 1877–1901*. New York, Dial Press, 1954.

Lorde, Audre. "The Uses of Anger." In *Sister Outsider: Essays and Speeches by Audre Lorde*, 124–33. Berkeley: Crossing Press, 1984.

Lowe, Lisa. "Heterogeneity, Hybridity, Multiplicity: Marking Asian American Differences." *Diaspora: A Journal of Transnational Studies* 1, no. 1 (1991): 24–44.

———. *Immigrant Acts: On Asian American Cultural Politics*. Durham: Duke University Press, 1996.

Lowe, Lisa, and David Lloyd, eds. *The Politics of Culture in the Shadow of Capital*. Durham: Duke University Press, 1997.

Lugones, María. "Purity, Impurity, and Separation." *Signs* 19, no. 2 (Winter 1994): 458–79.

Lye, Colleen. "The Afro-Asian Anaology." *PMLA* 123, no. 5 (October 2008): 1732–36.

"Man Heads to Trial in Teen's Death." *Click on Detroit*, November 28, 2011.

May, Elaine Tyler. *Homeward Bound: American Families in the Cold War Era*. New York: Basic Books, 1988.

Mazón, Mauricio. *The Zoot-Suit Riots: The Psychology of Symbolic Annihilation*. Austin: University of Texas Press, 1984.

McAdam, Doug, Sidney Tarrow, and Charles Tilly. *Dynamics of Contention*. Cambridge: Cambridge University Press, 2001.

McCall, Leslie. "The Complexity of Intersectionality." *Signs: Journal of Women in Culture & Society* 30, no. 3 (2005): 1771–800.

McGurn, William. "The Silent Minority." *National Review*, June 24, 1991.

McKee, Kimberly. "Beyond Grateful: The Politics and Performance of Adoption." Unpublished ms.

McKee, Kimberly, et al. "An Open Letter: Why Co-opting 'Transracial' in the Case of Rachel Dolezal Is Problematic." *Medium*, June 16, 2015.

McNamee, Stephen J., and Robert K. Miller Jr. *The Meritocracy Myth*. Lanham, Md.: Rowman and Littlefield, 2009.

Meister, Robert. "'Never Again': The Ethics of the Neighbor and the Logic of Genocide." *Postmodern Culture* 15, no. 2 (2005): sections 1–95.

Melamed, Jodi. *Represent and Destroy: Rationalizing Violence in the New Racial Capitalism*. Minneapolis: University of Minnesota Press, 2011.

Menchú, Rigoberta. *I, Rigoberta Menchú: An Indian Woman in Guatemala*. New York: Verso Books, 1984.

Miller, William Ian. "Clint Eastwood and Equity: Popular Culture's Theory of Revenge." In *Law in the Domains of Culture*. Edited by Austin Sarat and Thomas R. Kearns, 70–89. Ann Arbor: University of Michigan Press, 1998.

———. *Eye for an Eye*. Cambridge: Cambridge University Press, 2006.

Mitchell, Koritha. *Living with Lynching: African American Lynching Plays, Performance, and Citizenship, 1890–1930*. Urbana: University of Illinois Press, 2011.

Modleski, Tania. "Doing Justice to the Subjects: Mimetic Art in a Multicultural Society: The Work of Anna Deavere Smith." In *Female Subjects in Black and White: Race, Psychoanalysis, Feminism*. Edited by Elizabeth Abel, Barbara Christian, and Helene Moglen, 57–76. Berkeley: University of California Press, 1997.

Mohanty, Chandra Talpade. "On Race and Voice: Challenges for Liberal Education in the 1990s." *Cultural Critique* 14 (1989–90): 174–208.

Morrison, Peter A., and Ira S. Lowry. *A Riot of Color: The Demographic Setting of Civil Disturbance in Los Angeles*. Santa Monica: RAND, 1993.

Morrison, Toni. *Beloved: A Novel*. New York: Knopf, 1987.

———. "Unspeakable Things Unspoken: The Afro-American Presence in American Literature." *Michigan Quarterly Review* 28, no. 1 (1989): 1–19.

Moynihan, Daniel Patrick. "The Negro Family: The Case for National Action." 1965. BlackPast.org.

Murray, Charles A. *Losing Ground: American Social Policy, 1950–1980*. New York: Basic Books, 1984.

Nash, Jennifer C. "Re-Thinking Intersectionality." *Feminist Review* 89 (2008): 1–15.

Nelson, Dana D. "Sympathy as Strategy in Sedgwick's *Hope Leslie*." In *The Culture of Sentiment: Race, Gender, and Sentimentality in Nineteenth-Century America*. Edited by Shirley Samuels, 191–202. Oxford: Oxford University Press, 1992.

Ngai, Mae M. *Impossible Subjects: Illegal Aliens and the Making of Modern America*. Princeton: Princeton University Press, 2014.

Ninh, erin Khuê. *Ingratitude: The Debt-Bound Daughter in Asian American Literature*. New York: New York University Press, 2005.

Nopper, Tamara K. "The 1992 Los Angeles Riots and the Asian American Abandonment Narrative as Political Fiction." *New Centennial Review* 6, no. 2 (Fall 2006): 73–110.

Obama, Barack. "Remarks to the Hampton University Annual Ministers' Conference in Hampton, Virginia." Gerhard Peters and John T. Woolley, *The American Presidency Project*, June 5, 2007. http://www.presidency.ucsb.edu/ws/?pid =77002.

The Official Report of the Human Rights Office, Archdiocese of Guatemala Proyecto Interdioceseno De Memoria Historia. 4 vols. 1999.

Omi, Michael. "Rethinking the Language of Race and Racism." *Asian Law Journal* 8 (2001): 161–67.

Omi, Michael, and Howard Winant. *Racial Formation in the United States: From the 1960s to the 1990s*. 2nd ed. London: Routledge, 1994.

Ong, Aihwa. *Flexible Citizenship: The Cultural Logics of Transnationality*. Durham: Duke University Press, 1999.

Osajima, Keith. "Asian Americans as the Model Minority: An Analysis of the Popular Press Image in the 1960s and 1980s." In *Reflections on Shattered Windows: Promises and Prospects for Asian American Studies*. Edited by Gary Y. Okihiro et al., 165–74. Pullman: Washington State University Press, 1988.

Painter, Nell. "The War of '92." In *Inside the L.A. Riots: What Really Happened—and Why It Will Happen Again*. Edited by Don Hazen, 83–84. New York: Institute for Alternative Journalism, 1992.

Palumbo-Liu, David. "Los Angeles, Asians, and Perverse Ventriloquisms: On the Functions of Asian America in the Recent American Imaginary." *Public Culture* 6, no. 2 (Winter 1994): 365–81.

Parikh, Crystal. *An Ethics of Betrayal*. New York: Fordham University Press, 2009.

Patton, Sandra. *Birthmarks: Transracial Adoption in Contemporary America*. New York: New York University Press, 2000.

Payne, Leigh A. *Unsettling Accounts: Neither Truth nor Reconciliation in Confessions of State Violence*. Durham: Duke University Press, 2008.

Pérez-Torres, Rafael. *Mestizaje: Critical Uses of Race in Chicano Culture*. Minneapolis: University of Minnesota Press, 2006.

Pierce, Charles. "The Body in the Street." *Esquire*, August 22, 2014.

powell, john a. "An Agenda for the Post–Civil Rights Era." *University of San Francisco Law Review* 29 (1995): 889–910.

Powers, William. "The Massless Media." *Atlantic Monthly*, February 2005, 122–24, 26.

Prashad, Vijay. *Everybody Was Kung Fu Fighting: Afro-Asian Connections and the Myth of Cultural Purity*. Boston: Beacon Press, 2001.

Puar, Jasbir K. *Terrorist Assemblages: Homonationalism in Queer Times*. Durham: Duke University Press, 2007.

Pulido, Laura. *Black, Brown, Yellow and Left: Radical Activism in Los Angeles*. Berkeley: University of California Press, 2006.

Putnam, Robert D. "Bowling Alone: America's Declining Social Capital." *Journal of Democracy* 6, no. 1 (1995): 65–78.

———. *Bowling Alone: The Collapse and Revival of American Community*. New York: Touchstone Books, 2001.

Quayle, Dan. "Address to the Commonwealth Club of California." May 19, 1992.

Quintana, Alvina E. "Performing Tricksters: Guillermo Gómez-Peña and Karen Tei Yamashita." *Amerasia Journal* 28, no. 2 (2002): 217–25.

Ray, Leslie, and David Steven Simon, writers. "Will Gets Committed." *The Fresh Prince of Bel-Air*, directed by Shelley Jensen. September 21, 1992.

Reagan, Ronald. "Address Before a Joint Session of Congress on the State of the Union." Gerhard Peters and John T. Woolley, *The American Presidency Project*, January 25, 1988. http://www.presidency.ucsb.edu/ws/?pid=36035.

Reddy, Chandan. *Freedom with Violence*. Durham: Duke University Press, 2011.

Reed, Adolph L. *Stirrings in the Jug: Black Politics in the Post-Segregation Era*. Minneapolis: University of Minnesota Press, 1999.

Reed, Ishmael. "Hoodwinked: Paul Beatty's Urban Nihilists." *Village Voice*, April 1, 2000.

Reinhold, Robert. "After the Riots: After Police-Beating Verdict, Another Trial for the Jurors." *New York Times,* May 9, 1992.

Richards, David. "And Now, a Word from Off Broadway." *New York Times,* May 17, 1992.

Rieff, David. *Los Angeles: Capital of the Third World.* New York: Touchstone Books, 1992.

Rivas, Jorge. "'Sa-I-Gu' Documentary Explores How Korean Women Remember the L.A. Riots." *ColorLines,* April 29, 2013.

Roberts, John W. *From Trickster to Badman: The Black Folk Hero in Slavery and Freedom.* Philadelphia: University of Pennsylvania Press, 1989.

Roediger, David. *The Wages of Whiteness: Race and the Making of the American Working Class.* New York: Verso Books, 1991.

Roitman, Janet. *Anti-Crisis.* Durham: Duke University Press, 2014.

Ruby, Jay. "Speaking For, Speaking About, Speaking With, or Speaking Alongside: An Anthropological and Documentary Dilemma." *Visual Anthropology Review* 7, no. 2 (Fall 1991): 50–67.

Samuels, Shirley. "Introduction." In *The Culture of Sentiment: Race, Gender, and Sentimentality in Nineteenth-Century America.* Edited by Shirley Samuels, 3–8. Oxford: Oxford University Press, 1992.

Sánchez, George. *Becoming Mexican American: Ethnicity, Culture, and Identity in Chicano Los Angeles, 1900–1945.* New York: Oxford University Press, 1993.

Sapiro, Virginia. "Considering Political Civility Historically: A Case Study of the United States." Paper delivered at the Annual Meeting of the International Society for Political Psychology, Amsterdam, 1999.

Sarat, Austin. "When Memory Speaks: Remembrance and Revenge in Unforgiven." *Indiana Law Journal* 77 (2002): 307–29.

Savalli, Kirsten West. "Black Women Are Killed by Police, Too." *Salon.com,* August 18, 2014.

Schickel, Richard. "How TV Failed to Get the Real Picture." *Time,* May 11, 1992, 29.

Schlesinger, Arthur M., Jr. *The Disuniting of America: Reflections on a Multicultural Society.* Revised and expanded edition. New York: W. W. Norton, 1998.

Schneider, Cathy Lisa. *Police Power and Race Riots: Urban Unrest in Paris and New York.* Philadelphia: University of Pennsylvania Press, 2014.

Schonsheck, Jonathan. "Rudeness, Rasp, and Repudiation." In *Civility and Its Discontents: Essays on Civic Virtue, Toleration, and Cultural Fragmentation.* Edited by C. T. Sistare, 169–85. Lawrence: University Press of Kansas, 2004.

Schudson, Michael. *The Good Citizen: A History of American Civic Life.* Cambridge: Harvard University Press, 1998.

Scott, Daryl Michael. *Contempt and Pity: Social Policy and the Image of the Damaged Black Psyche, 1880–1996.* Chapel Hill: University of North Carolina Press, 1997.

Scott, David. *Conscripts of Modernity: The Tragedy of Colonial Enlightenment.* Durham: Duke University Press, 2004.

Scott, James C. *Domination and the Arts of Resistance: Hidden Transcripts.* New Haven: Yale University Press, 1990.

Sears, David O., Jack Citrin, Sharmaine V. Cheleden, and Colette van Laar. "Cultural Diversity and Multicultural Politics: Is Ethnic Balkanization Psychologically Inevitable?" In *Cultural Divides: Understanding and Overcoming Group Conflict*. Edited by Deborah Prentice and Dale Miller, 35–79. New York: Russell Sage Foundation, 1999.

Sen, Amartya. "Merit and Justice." In *Meritocracy and Economic Inequality*. Edited by Kenneth Arrow, Samuel Bowles, and Steven Durlauf, 5–16. Princeton: Princeton University Press, 1999.

Sexton, Jared. *Amalgamation Schemes: Antiblackness and the Critique of Multiracialism*. Minneapolis: University of Minnesota Press, 2008.

Shah, Nayan. *Contagious Divides: Epidemics and Race in San Francisco's Chinatown*. Berkeley: University of California Press, 2001.

Silva, Denise Ferreira da. *Toward a Global Idea of Race*. Minneapolis: University of Minnesota Press, 2007.

———. "No-Bodies: Law, Raciality and Violence." *Griffith Law Review* 18 (2009): 212–36.

Simon, Rita James, and Howard Altstein. *Adoption Across Borders: Serving the Children in Transracial and Intercountry Adoptions*. New York: Rowman and Littlefield, 2000.

Smith, Anna Deavere. *Fires in the Mirror: Crown Heights, Brooklyn and Other Identities*. Directed by George C. Wolfe. The Public Theater, New York City, May 1, 1992.

———. *Fires in the Mirror: Crown Heights, Brooklyn and Other Identities*. New York: Anchor Books, 1993.

———. *Twilight: Los Angeles*. Directed by Emily Mann. Mark Taper Forum, Los Angeles, June 13, 1993.

———. *Twilight: Los Angeles, 1992*. New York: Anchor Books, 1994.

———. *House Arrest: First Edition*. Directed by Mark Rucker. Arena Stage, Washington, D.C., November 19, 1997.

———. *Talk to Me: Listening between the Lines*. New York: Random House, 2000.

———. "Twilight: Los Angeles." Translated by Anna Deavere Smith. In *Stage on Screen*. Edited by Marc Levin. New York: PBS Home Video, 2000.

———. "Insights from a Perpetual Outsider." *Los Angeles Times*, April 28, 2002.

———. *Twilight: Los Angeles, 1992*. New York: Dramatist's Play Service, 2003.

———. *Letters to a Young Artist: Straight-up Advice on Making a Life in the Arts For Actors, Performers, Writers, and Artists of Every Kind*. New York: Anchor Books, 2006.

———. *Let Me Down Easy*. Directed by Eric Ting. Long Wharf Theater, New Haven, Conn., January 16, 2008.

Smith, Cherise. *Enacting Others: Politics of Identity in Eleanor Antin, Nikki S. Lee, Adrian Piper, and Anna Deavere Smith*. Durham: Duke University Press, 2011.

Smith, Erna. *Transmitting Race: The Los Angeles Riot in Television News*. Cambridge: The Joan Shorenstein Center for Press, Politics, and Public Policy at the Kennedy School of Government at Harvard University, 1994.

Smith, Neil. "Global Social Cleansing: Postliberal Revanchism and the Export of Zero Tolerance." *Social Justice* 28, no. 3 (2001): 69.

Sollors, Werner. *Neither Black nor White yet Both: Thematic Explorations of Inter-racial Literature*. Cambridge: Harvard University Press, 1997.

Song, Min Hyoung. *Strange Future: Pessimism and the 1992 Los Angeles Riots*. Durham: Duke University Press, 2005.

Stallings, L. H. "Punked for Life: Paul Beatty's the *White Boy Shuffle* and Radical Black Masculinities." *African American Review* 43, no. 1 (Spring 2009): 99–116.

Steiner, George. *The Death of Tragedy*. New Haven: Yale University Press, 1996. Originally published in 1961.

Stevenson, Brenda E. "Latasha Harlins, Soon Ja Du, and Joyce Karlin: A Case Study of Multicultural Female Violence on the Urban Frontier." *Journal of African American History* 89 (2004): 152–72.

———. *The Contested Murder of Latasha Harlins: Justice, Gender, and the Origins of the LA Riots*. New York: Oxford University Press, 2013.

Stewart, James B., and Major Coleman. "The Black Political Economy Paradigm and the Dynamics of Racial Economic Inequality." In *African Americans in the U.S. Economy*. Edited by Cecilia A. Conrad et al., 118–32. Lanham, Md.: Rowman and Littlefield, 2005.

Sue, Derald Wing, C. M. Capolidupo, Gina C. Torino, Jennifer M. Bucceri, Aisha MB Holder, Kevin L. Nadal, and Marta Esquilin. "Racial Microaggressions in Everyday Life: Implications for Clinical Practice." *American Psychologist* 62, no. 4 (2007): 271–86.

Sue, Derald Wing, Jennifer Bucceri, Annie I. Lin, Kevin L. Nadal, and Gina C. Torino. "Racial Microaggressions and the Asian American Experience." *Cultural Diversity and Ethnic Minority Psychology* 13, no. 1 (2007): 72–81.

Sugrue, Thomas J. *The Origins of the Urban Crisis: Race and Inequality in Postwar Detroit*. Princeton: Princeton University Press, 1996.

———. *Sweet Land of Liberty: The Forgotten Struggle for Civil Rights in the North*. New York: Random House, 2008.

Tan, Amy. *The Joy Luck Club*. New York: Penguin, 2006. Originally published in 1989.

Taylor, Paul, Mark Hugo Lopez, Jessica Martínez, and Gabriel Velasco. "When Labels Don't Fit: Hispanics and Their Views of Identity." Pew Research Center (online), April 4, 2012.

Taylor, Quintard. *In Search of the Racial Frontier: African Americans in the American West, 1528–1990*. New York: W. W. Norton, 1998.

Tervalon, Jervey. *Geography of Rage: Remembering the Los Angeles Riots of 1992*. New York: Really Great Books, 2002.

Thomas, Mary E. *Multicultural Girlhood: Racism, Sexuality, and the Conflicted Spaces of American Education*. Philadelphia: Temple University Press, 2011.

Thompson, Debby. "'Is Race a Trope?': Anna Deavere Smith and the Question of Racial Performativity." *African American Review* 37, no. 1 (2003): 127–38.

Tippett, Rebecca, Avis Jones-DeWeever, Maya Rockeymoore, Darrick Hamilton, and William Darity Jr. *Beyond Broke: Why Closing the Racial Wealth Gap Is a Priority for National Economic Security*. Washington, D.C.: Center for Global Policy Solutions; Durham: Duke Research Network on Race and Ethnic Inequality, May 2014.

Tobar, Héctor. "Immigrant Day Laborer Fights for His Paycheck." *Los Angeles Times*, February 8, 1990.

————. *The Tattooed Soldier*. New York: Penguin Books, 1998.

————. *Translation Nation: Defining a New American Identity in the Spanish-Speaking United States*. New York: Riverhead Books, 2005.

————. *Barbarian Nurseries*. London: Sceptre, 2011.

————. *Deep Down Dark: The Untold Stories of 33 Men Buried in a Chilean Mine, and the Miracle That Set Them Free*. New York: Macmillan, 2014.

Todorova, Maria Nikolaeva. *Imagining the Balkans*. New York: Oxford University Press, 1997.

Tolentino, Cynthia. *America's Experts: Race and the Fictions of Sociology*. Minneapolis: University of Minnesota Press, 2009.

Tompkins, Jane. *Sensational Designs: The Cultural Work of American Fiction*. New York: Oxford University Press, 1986.

"A Transcript of Remarks by Los Angeles Superior Court Judge Joyce A. Karlin in the Sentencing of Soon Ja Du." *Los Angeles Daily Journal*, November 22, 1991.

Trenka, Jane Jeong, Julia Chinavere Oparah, and Sun Yung Shin, eds. *Outsiders Within: Writing on Transracial Adoption*. Cambridge: South End Press, 2006.

Tuttle, Ian. "Michael Brown's Parents Testify before U.N. Committee against Torture." *National Review*, November 11, 2014.

Van den Haag, Ernest. "Causes, Alleged and Actual, of the L.A. Riots." *Southern California Law Review* 66 (1993): 1657–64.

Vargas, João H. Costa. "The *Los Angeles Times*' Coverage of the 1992 Rebellion: Still Burning Matters of Race and Justice." *Ethnicities* 4, no. 2 (2004): 209–36.

The Verdict and the Violence. Produced by Jonathan Haft and Mari Sunaida. Idiot Savant Records, Los Angeles, 1992.

Wald, Gayle. "Anna Deavere Smith's Voices at Twilight (Review Essay)." *Postmodern Culture* 4, no. 2 (1994).

Waldron, Jeremy. "Homelessness and the Issue of Freedom." *UCLA Law Review* 39 (1991–92): 295–324.

Wanzo, Rebecca. "Proms and Other Racial Ephemera: The Positive Social Construction of African Americans in the 'Post'–Civil Rights Era." *Washington University Journal of Law & Policy* 33 (2010): 75–107.

War Comes Home: The Excessive Militarization of American Policing. New York: American Civil Liberties Union, June 2014.

Warren, Kenneth W. *So Black and Blue: Ralph Ellison and the Occasion of Criticism*. Princeton: Princeton University Press, 2003.

Wayans, Kennan Ivory, creator. *In Living Color*. 1990. Television.

Weber, Carl. "Brecht's 'Street Scene'—on Broadway, of All Places? A Conversation with Anna Deavere Smith." *Brecht Yearbook* 20 (1995): 50–64.

Weinraub, Bernard. "Condensing a Riot's Cacophony into the Voice of One Woman." *New York Times*, June 16, 1993.

West, Cornel. *Race Matters.* New York: Vintage, 1993.

White, Khadijah Costley. "Black and Unarmed: Women and Girls without Weapons Killed by Law Enforcement." *Role Reboot,* August 12, 2014.

Wiegman, Robyn. "Missiles and Melodrama (Masculinity and the Televisual War)." In *Seeing through the Media: The Persian Gulf War.* Edited by Susan Jeffords and Lauren Rabinovitz, 171–88. New Brunswick, N.J.: Rutgers University Press, 1994.

Willens, Michele. "'Twilight' Time: Revisiting the 1992 L.A. Riots on TV." *Los Angeles Times,* April 28, 2001.

Williams, Linda. *Playing the Race Card: Melodramas of Black and White from Uncle Tom to O.J. Simpson.* Princeton: Princeton University Press, 2001.

Williams, Patricia J. *The Alchemy of Race and Rights.* Cambridge: Harvard University Press, 1991.

———. *Seeing a Color-Blind Future: The Paradox of Race.* New York: Noonday Press, 1999.

Wilson, James Q., and George L. Kelling. "Broken Windows." *Atlantic Monthly,* March 1982, 29–38.

Wilson, Richard. "Violent Truths: The Politics of Memory in Guatemala." In *Negotiating Rights: The Guatemala Peace Process.* Edited by Rachel Seider and Richard Wilson, 18–27. London: Conciliation Resources, 1997.

Winston, Brian. "The Tradition of the Victim in Griersonian Documentary." In *Image Ethics: The Moral Rights of Subjects in Photographs, Film, and Television.* Edited by Larry P. Gross, John Stuart Katz, and Jay Ruby, 34–57. New York: Oxford University Press, 1988.

Wood, Gordon S. "Revolutionary Manners (review of Eric Slaughter's *The State as a Work of Art*)." *New Republic,* July 1, 2009.

Wynter, Sylvia. "No Humans Involved: An Open Letter to My Colleagues." *Voices of the African Diaspora: The CAAS Research Review* 8, no. 2 (1992): 13–16.

Yamamoto, Eric. *Interracial Justice: Conflict and Reconciliation in Post–Civil Rights America.* New York: New York University Press, 1999.

Yamashita, Karen Tei. *Through the Arc of the Rainforest.* Minneapolis: Coffee House Press, 1990.

———. *Brazil-Maru.* Minneapolis: Coffee House Press, 1993.

———. *Tropic of Orange.* Minneapolis: Coffee House Press, 1997.

———. *Circle K Cycles.* Minneapolis: Coffee House Press, 2001.

———. *Anime Wong: Fictions of Self-Performance.* Minneapolis: Coffee House Press, 2014.

Yoshino, Kenji. *Covering: The Hidden Assault on Our Civil Rights.* New York: Random House, 2007.

Young, Michael. *The Rise of the Meritocracy.* New Brunswick, N.J.: Transaction Publishers, 1994. Originally published in 1958.

Zia, Helen. *Asian American Dreams: The Emergence of an American People.* New York: Farrar, Straus and Giroux, 2000.

INDEX

Abelmann, Nancy, 2, 5, 37, 56, 59, 243n.2

abstract citizen: homogenizing and universalizing tendencies of, 22, 241n.44

Abu Ghraib, xiii; soldiers serving sentences for abuse of Iraqi prisoners in, 232n.6

ACLU, 232n.7, 255n.22

adoption studies: transracial defined in, 242n.48

aesthetics and politics: relationship between, 72, 74

affirmative action, 14, 66, 67, 75, 91, 100, 136, 137, 236n.17, 239n.31, 249n.15, 252n.28

Afghanistan: militarization of police with equipment from war in, xiii, 232n.7

African American literature: Beatty's first encounter with, 76–77; debates over realism in, 72–74; genre of Black bildungsroman in, 77–78; satirical tradition in, 70–71. *See also White Boy Shuffle, The* (Beatty)

African Americans: "badman" in African American folk heroic creation, 65, 247n.1; breakdown of Black family in inner city, violence of L.A. Crisis blamed on, 44–45; conflicts with Korean American store owners, 39–40, 45, 164–65 (*see also* Black–Korean conflict); contempt and pity as primary clusters of attitudes about, 77–79; as countercitizens, 61, 80; criminalization of, 47, 49, 79, 164; feminization of Asian Americans in relation to, 42; imagined community of, Black body as center bringing together, 61; mapping of interracial conflict onto South Central Los Angeles and focus on, 130; media indictment of, for looting and violence, 150; middle class, growth of, 74, 248n.7; negatively tied to "urban crisis," 233n.5, 262n.16; politicians' attacks on, for brutality in L.A. Crisis, 60; race shaming of, 217–21; racial injustices by state institutions targeting, 91, 251n.22; relative valorization and civic ostracism of, compared to Asian Americans, 7, 46; sociological cliché of dysfunctional African American family, 45, 79, 250n.19; stereotypes of, 80, 91, 95, 100; unemployed, during 1991 recession, 12; wealth held by Black households, compared to White households, xii, 231n.5

"Afro-Asian Analogy, The" (Lye), 245n.20

participants' worth as tragic protagonists, 146; theories of psychological damage used in making and justifying social policy, 78
punishment: state appropriation of revenge as just, 123–26, 129–36, 254n.15, 255n.22
Putnam, Robert D., 15–16, 235n.14, 238n.29
Pynchon, Thomas, 76
pyramidization, racial, 8–9, 104–5, 242n.49, 246n.20

Quayle, Dan, 84, 249n.16–17; Murphy Brown speech, 84, 245n.16
queer of color critique, 231n.4, 235n.15
quemazones ("great burnings"): L.A. Crisis in Tobar's *Tattooed Soldier* as, 107, 118, 234n.13

race: biologization of culture and, 84–85; in civil discourse, alleged illegitimacy of, 25–26; differential moral or intellectual capacities and, persistence of idea of, 251n.24; gender and, in Du–Harlins case, 42–43, 50; historical conflation with class, 81, 249n.12; media conventions and technological innovations shaping issues of, 30–31; Omi and Winant's definition of, 260n.28; physical markers of, disrupted in *Twilight,* 155–56; refusal to recognize racial difference and refusal to include people of color and their experiences, relationship between, 94–95; rights and claims on the state and politics of, 2–3; uncivil recognition of racial difference as conflict, struggle or disruption, 90
race fatigue, 6
race shaming, 217–21; murder of Michael Brown in Ferguson, Missouri, and, 218–21

racial balance: cum equilibrium evident in representations of Crisis violence, 137–38; as goal of integration efforts in civil rights struggles, 136; racial equilibrium discourse to counteract specific remedies of, 136–37, 255n.25
racial burnout, 6–7
racial civility, 24. *See also* civility
racial disaster(s), 181–216, 225; Los Angeles Crisis as media spectacle within epic apocalyptic tradition, 181; media spectacles and, 182, 184–90; threat of, marking people outside civility, 184; use of term, 188. *See also Tropic of Orange* (Yamashita)
racial diversity in education and employment, 136; misguided strategies to achieve, 90–98
racial equilibrium, 136–39, 223; legal concept of racial balance rewritten into, 136–37, 255n.25; reframed as revenge, 136, 137–39; reparations to Whites in form of revenge, 138
racial hegemony, 7
racial identity as biological, genetic, and inheritable: historical conception of, 96
racialization: comparative, ethics of, 31–32, 224; comparative, field of, 7, 235n.15; racialized identity in gendered-sexualized logics of racial formation, 161
racial laundering of social and capitalist hierarchies, 48
racial neoconservative perspective, 239n.31
racial pyramidization, 8–9, 104–5, 242n.49, 246n.20
racial terms: use of, ix
racial triangulation, paradigm of, 7, 8, 60–61; ethical underpinnings of, 242n.49; gender and class

LYNN MIE ITAGAKI is assistant professor of English and women's, gender, and sexuality studies and program coordinator in Asian American studies at The Ohio State University.